T0334665

PERFORMANCE THROUGH DIVERSITY AND INCLUSION

Leveraging Organizational Practices for Equity and Results

This book provides practical guidance for managers, leaders, diversity officers, educators, and students to achieve the benefits of diversity by focusing on creating meaningful, inclusive interactions. Implementing inclusive interaction practices, along with accountability practices, enhances performance outcomes for the organization and improves equity for members of historically underrepresented and marginalized groups.

The book highlights the need to challenge existing approaches that have overemphasized representational—that is, numerical—diversity. For many decades, the focus has been on this important first step of increasing the numbers of underrepresented groups. However, moving beyond representation toward a truly inclusive organizational culture that produces real performance and equity has been elusive. This book moves the focus from achieving numerical diversity to achieving frequent, high-quality, equitable, and productive interactions that enable individuals to leverage their distinctive talents and provides the steps to do so. The benefits of this approach occur at the individual, workgroup, and organizational levels. Real-life examples of good inclusive practices are provided from across the for-profit, nonprofit, and governmental sectors and in various organizational contexts.

The book is ideal not only for those charged with diversity, equity, and inclusion efforts in organizations but also for organizational leaders and managers who can create and/or support the implementing of inclusive organizational practices and also for postgraduate and undergraduate students studying human resource management, organizational behavior, management, or diversity, equity, and inclusion.

Ruth Sessler Bernstein is Assistant Professor of Nonprofit Management at Pepperdine University, USA. Her research, which focuses on diversity, equity, and inclusion and nonprofit governance, has been published in *Nonprofit Management & Leadership*, *Nonprofit & Voluntary Sector Quarterly*, and the *Journal of Business Ethics*.

Paul F. Salipante is Emeritus Professor at the Weatherhead School of Management, Case Western Reserve University, USA, with engineering and business degrees from the Massachusetts Institute of Technology (MIT) and the University of Chicago. His publications cover training for disadvantaged workers, equal employment opportunity (EEO), employment conflict, nonprofit governance, and evidence-informed management.

Judith Y. Weisinger is a scholar, educator, and consultant. She has most recently served as Associate Professor of Management/Business at New Mexico State University and Mills College, USA, and as Visiting Associate Professor of Management at Bucknell University, USA. Her research on diversity, equity, and inclusion and on cultural knowing has been published in *Nonprofit Management & Leadership*, *Nonprofit & Voluntary Sector Quarterly*, the *Journal of Business Ethics*, and the *Journal of Management Inquiry*.

PERFORMANCE THROUGH DIVERSITY AND INCLUSION

Leveraging Organizational Practices for Equity and Results

Ruth Sessler Bernstein, Paul F. Salipante, and Judith Y. Weisinger

Routledge
Taylor & Francis Group

LONDON AND NEW YORK

First published 2022
by Routledge
2 Park Square, Milton Park, Abingdon, Oxon OX14 4RN

and by Routledge
605 Third Avenue, New York, NY 10158

Routledge is an imprint of the Taylor & Francis Group, an informa business

© 2022 Ruth Sessler Bernstein, Paul F. Salipante and Judith Y. Weisinger

The right of Ruth Sessler Bernstein, Paul F. Salipante and Judith Y. Weisinger
to be identified as authors of this work has been asserted by them in accordance
with sections 77 and 78 of the Copyright, Designs and Patents Act 1988.

British Library Cataloguing-in-Publication Data
A catalogue record for this book is available from the British Library

Library of Congress Cataloging-in-Publication Data
A catalog record has been requested for this book

ISBN: 978-0-367-42179-3 (hbk)
ISBN: 978-0-367-42178-6 (pbk)
ISBN: 978-0-367-82248-4 (ebk)

DOI: 10.4324/9780367822484

Typeset in Bembo
by Newgen Publishing UK

We dedicate this book to our spouses and children:
Dr. Jeffrey Bernstein (1954–2018), Dr. Ethan Bernstein,
Prof. Zachary (and Prof. Loretta Torrigno) Bernstein
Anne Salipante (1944–2018), Elizabeth (and Gregory) Carter,
Jeffrey (and Linda King) Salipante
Joseph Weisinger, Landon Weisinger, Maya Weisinger
And to all those striving to foster inclusivity and equity in their organizations

CONTENTS

FIGURES

ACKNOWLEDGMENTS

The authors had the support of many colleagues, friends, and family members in writing this book. We would first like to acknowledge the valuable feedback we received from Dr. Daniel Sessler and Maya Weisinger as advance readers of parts of the manuscript as well as for providing us with constructive feedback. We extend a very special thanks to Robert Salipante, who read many manuscript drafts and provided substantive and insightful detailed suggestions and comments that enabled us to make substantial improvements.

We are especially grateful to the interviewees, whose names remain anonymous, for sharing their experiences and insights with us.

We also owe a huge debt of gratitude to:

- The University of Washington Tacoma for allowing Ruth Sessler Bernstein a research quarter to focus exclusively on researching and writing this book
- Pepperdine University for research support
- The Doctor of Business Administration (formerly known as Doctor of Management) Program at Case Western Reserve University for providing feedback during numerous workshops. In particular, we would like to acknowledge Jennifer Bishop and Jason Brooker, Doctor of Business Administration (DBA) students, for their valuable discussions with the authors
- Faye Cobb for engaging in frequent discussions offering constructive feedback and for providing the opportunity to present our work in her class
- Brian Kovak for numerous discussions and assistance in deciphering several economic studies
- Morgan Bulger for her contributions to our prior work
- Dr. Sarabajaya Kumar, Regina Weichert, and Allison Lucas for listening and providing invaluable support and feedback

- Alexis Antes for her assistance with formatting the manuscript
- Rebecca Marsh and Routledge Publishing for providing us with the opportunity to write this book

A special thanks to Paul Salipante from Ruth Sessler Bernstein and Judy Weisinger for being our mentor and friend, and for engaging with us on this academic journey.

PREFACE

To bolster the outcomes of the currently dominant diversity programs, this book presents a *Framework for Inclusive Interactions*. This evidence-informed, practice-based book explores opportunities for organizations and individuals to benefit realistically from diversity and inclusion. When properly managed, inclusive interactions among diverse members of an organization generate the social connections and deeper understandings needed for higher workgroup performance and greater equity. Informed leadership action is essential as organizations of all types are increasingly diverse or operating internationally across cultures. Society is currently at a "tipping point" of skepticism about whether contemporary approaches labeled as diversity actually enhance social and performance outcomes. This tipping point drives organizations to consider how they can move from diversity as representation—a necessary first step—toward an evidence-based focus on inclusion. The performance impact of diversity without inclusion is complex, with negative effects on performance at least as likely as positive effects. To guide action, the *Framework for Inclusive Interactions* specifies concrete practices shown to improve performance, shape productive relationships and equity, and enhance skills and learning among organizational members.

> The Framework can be thought of as a flow diagram, capturing the dynamics that lead from diversity to inclusion to beneficial outcomes, and, through feedback, to the reduction of anti-inclusive practices and the evolution and vitality of inclusive practices over time.

This book provides practical guidance for managers, diversity officers, educators, researchers, and students to achieve the benefits of diversity by focusing on creating meaningful, inclusive interactions. Achieving inclusion not only enhances perform-ance outcomes but also improves the job outcomes of historically underrepresented and marginalized groups. By engaging in structured, inclusive interactions, organ-izational members are not only given the opportunity to equally contribute in a meaningful way to key tasks and decisions in their workgroup and organiza-tion but also to experience adaptive learning through working with diverse others, and a sense of safety, trust, and justice. Managers can structure practices for inclu-sive interactions to assist in their efforts to be more equitable and to give their organizations a competitive advantage.

In at least a small way, this book is intended to remedy what has been a quite dysfunctional relationship between academics and managers, and among academics themselves, with regard to generating and implementing relevant, practical know-ledge. We are reminded of our missed opportunities by the recent increase in racial, ethnic and gender-based tensions in virtually all aspects of society and by calls to participate in constructive change. The persistence of tensions and inequities is indicative of the limitations and weaknesses of existing strategies, making it more critical that organizations and workgroups find new ways of engaging with diversity, inclusion, and equity. To do better than we have in the past, educators, researchers, and managers can recognize some flaws in our past efforts. As educators, we taught the importance of fair employment practices and diversity training, relying in some cases on theory rather than evidence to propose that these diversity approaches would ensure equitable and effective use of human capital. We now know that these approaches have been inadequate and, in some cases, counterproductive. Furthermore, we researchers pursued our inquiries on diversity by focusing on our own academic discipline's theories and methods, with too little use of research in other disciplines and with a focus on theory development rather than managerial application. Moreover, organizational leaders and managers continued to rely on diversity practices supported by societal institutions, including the judicial system and training providers, rather than being more critical and informed by emerging research evidence. The basic point is that all three groups can do better. Drawing from the experience of evidence-based clinical practice in medicine, we can create partnerships in which success evolves from an interplay of research and practice. This book seeks to contribute to that interplay by synthesizing up-to-date, rigorous research-based evidence across many academic fields and organizational contexts. Based on that evidence, the book provides a new approach to achieving equity and improving organizational performance, simultaneously, through managers struc-turing everyday practices of inclusive interaction among organizational members.

As we gradually expanded our scope, we unexpectedly discovered much empir-ical research and theory that was new to us. Like many academics, we had been oper-ating in narrow fields of study. However, our research took us on a transdisciplinary journey where we discovered that some of the most important work for managing diversity had been published in journals in psychology, organizational studies, soci-ology, and economics. Combining scholarly research from various fields with our own personal research and experiences enabled us to formulate a comprehensive framework that highlights practical opportunities few managers and organizations have exploited.

In writing this book, we draw upon our diverse demographics, our studying of diversity and inclusion in different settings, and our varying emphases in teaching human resources management, organizational behavior, and research courses. In addition, in building the *Framework for Inclusive Interactions*, we brought our various research backgrounds. Dr. Ruth Sessler Bernstein is a researcher in the areas of (1) diversity, intercultural interactions, and inclusion within multicultural communities such as voluntary organizations, universities, and nonprofit boards of directors and (2) nonprofit governance. She serves on various community nonprofit boards and has significant practitioner experience in working with nonprofit organizations. Dr. Paul F. Salipante conducts research in the areas of (1) diversity and pluralism, including practices for bridging ethnic differences; (2) the genesis and constructive handling of workplace conflict; (3) organizing practices of high-level volunteers, including governing boards; and (4) the nature of practitioner-scholarship that bridges the academic and practice communities in management. He has guided several organizations, including Fred Rogers Productions, in using appreciative inquiry (AI) processes in their strategic planning. Dr. Judith Y. Weisinger's research examines (1) diversity, equity, and inclusion in nonprofit organizations, with current interests in the role of organizational structuring for inclusive interactions and (2) the role of social capital in organizational diversity efforts and immigrant-founded enterprises. She has also served as an academic consultant on diversity and inclusion to a number of organizations.

The practices introduced in this book have been demonstrated to achieve substantive changes that enable diverse individuals to engage in meaningful, inclusive interactions. The book moves the focus from achieving diversity in terms of numerical representation to achieving frequent, high-quality, equitable, and productive interactions that enable individuals from differing backgrounds to leverage their distinctive talents. The payoffs are individual and social benefits such as equity, cross-cultural friendships, leadership development, and organizational benefits in performance, reputation, and member commitment. In contrast, failure to be fully inclusive threatens the legitimacy and ability of organizations to fulfill their diversity and inclusion mandates, as seen by their key stakeholders—employees, communities, regulators, customers, and shareholders. In the spirit of inclusion, we welcome managers, researchers, educators, and students from all fields and backgrounds. We encourage you to apply your perspective and knowledge to the ideas we present.

Ruth Sessler Bernstein, Paul F. Salipante, and Judith Y. Weisinger

A READER'S GUIDE TO THE CHAPTERS

This book is divided into three parts. Part I, Leveraging the Framework for Inclusive Interactions to Improve Performance and Equity, provides an overview of the book, its key arguments, and central framework, the Framework for Inclusive Interactions. Part II, Moving from Diversity to Inclusion: Evidence-Based Guidance for Making Diversity and Inclusion Work, presents key theory and research evidence from multiple disciplines that present the Framework's conceptual underpinnings. Part III, Achieving Sustainable Inclusion: Multilevel Outcomes, highlights case examples of the Framework in practice and discusses how organizations can achieve sustainable inclusion using the practices discussed in the book.

Here, we provide a brief overview of each of the chapters.

The Introduction (The Elusive Goal: Diversity and Inclusion for Equity and Performance) makes the case that inequalities for those from underrepresented groups in organizations, including women, have been persistent and intractable despite decades of antidiscrimination legislation, affirmative action programs, and diversity initiatives in organizations. Further, we assert that interactions among those from different groups are frequently tense, with those from underrepresented groups exhausted from being consistently stereotyped and stigmatized, unable to authentically contribute to their organizations, while those from dominant groups walk on eggshells, afraid of offending those holding different cultures, ideas, and beliefs. Diversity training has, by and large, not significantly helped the situation. We suggest that the economic costs, including opportunity costs, of this failure to facilitate inclusive interactions and organizational cultures are significant for both organizations and society. Beyond this, equity and social justice for underrepresented groups continue to be challenging to achieve. As a result, we state that novel approaches are needed to help organizations leverage diversity for performance and equity. We present our novel approach, represented by the "Framework for Inclusive Interactions," which integrates the best transdisciplinary research evidence to show

how organizations can achieve *sustainable inclusion* centered on *structured interaction practices* designed to facilitate diverse organizational members' engaging in positive, ongoing interactions that overcome the otherwise common *anti-inclusive practices* of stereotyping and stigmatizing, self-segregating, interacting anxiously, and making decisions based on implicit bias. We also discuss why a *practice-based* approach is more effective than extant approaches to diversity and inclusion in organizations. Finally, we describe the key elements of an inclusive culture that we use in the book.

Chapter 1 (Doing Better: Achieving Equity and Performance from Diversity) introduces how workgroups, teams, and organizations may achieve performance benefits through developing and maintaining inclusive interactions. The chapter begins by tracing the historical roots of workplace diversity. We begin with the legal imperatives outlined in the Civil Rights Act of 1964 and progress through the adoption of affirmative action and the "business case" for diversity to present-day tensions that demand new approaches. Reviewing this history brings to light the lack of progress that has been made toward inclusion and equity. Second, the chapter outlines the moral and social imperatives for moving from a focus on representational diversity to inclusive interactions and equity. Contemporary views on diversity are shifting, with a greater emphasis on equity, particularly because the commonly applied business case for diversity does not take into account differences in intergroup outcomes. That is, increasing members of underrepresented groups to more effectively develop underserved markets and clients often leads to these employees being pigeonholed in these areas and not having opportunities to advance to higher levels in the organization. Third, the chapter examines the limitations and failures of current approaches to diversity and inclusion. Current strategies to improve diversity, inclusion, and equity often depend on specialized diversity training. Despite a lack of evidentiary support, such diversity training remains a ubiquitous approach for addressing these issues. Other commonly used approaches by diversity specialists are presented and reviewed. Fourth, an overview of the research methodology used in developing our Framework for Inclusive Interactions is discussed. The chapter concludes with a consideration of the organizational conditions that support inclusion, including adopting programs and values that support diversity and inclusion, having representational diversity, and a willingness of leaders to use evidence-informed management techniques such as this book proposes. It also previews key concepts that are developed in later chapters.

Chapter 2 (The Framework: Improving Performance and Equity through Inclusive Interaction Practices) uses the concepts of practice theory and organizational socialization to introduce our Framework, which specifies six practices needed to facilitate meaningful, inclusive interactions that positively impact performance and social outcomes. Each practice—pursuing a shared task-orientation or mission, mixing members frequently and repeatedly, collaborating with member interdependence, handling conflict constructively, exhibiting interpersonal comfort and self-efficacy, and ensuring equal insider status to all members—will be briefly introduced and put into the context of the larger Framework. The Framework places emphasis on how the practices help to counter anti-inclusionary forces that otherwise, by default, inhibit inclusive interactions: stereotyping and stigmatizing, self-segregation, interaction discomfort, and implicit bias. The inclusive practices foster workgroup members' inclusive behaviors such that over time, these interactions will promote adaptive learning, skill development, and high group performance. Through managerial tweaking and customizing, the six evidence-informed practices are applicable in a wide range of situations. Merit and accountability practices, along with the adaptive learning resulting from inclusive interactions, lead to *sustainable inclusion*. The multilevel outcomes of sustainable inclusion comprise equity, better group and organizational performance, individual skill development, an inclusive organizational culture, and greater organizational commitment to diversity, inclusion, and equity.

Chapter 3 (Designing Structured Inclusive Interaction Practices) delves into the six workgroup and organizational practices for prejudice reduction and meaningful adaptive contact among diverse individuals. These practices are an extension of contact theory that has been developed, empirically investigated, and revised over six decades, yet remains underutilized in organizations. Practice one, *pursuing a shared task-orientation or mission*, identifies the importance of workgroup members having a common goal or overarching focus, one not necessarily focused on diversity and inclusion, which enables the workgroup members to coalesce as they strive for enhanced performance outcomes.

The second practice, *mixing members frequently and repeatedly*, begins with ensuring a diverse membership. The mixing of members within a workgroup, team, or organization enables individuals to reduce self-segregation and increase engagement with diverse others. Repeated interactions of diverse members create a sense of comfort, often following an initial period of discomfort, as individuals begin to learn the value of each other's unique perspectives. This creates a balance of uniqueness and belonging, which contributes to the ability of the individuals and the group to overcome the anti-inclusionary social forces mentioned above, thereby enabling the group to perform at a higher level.

Practice three, *collaborating with member interdependence*, is predicated on the commitment to a common pursuit and the willingness to work interdependently with others of equal status. When members are committed to a shared task purpose or mission, collaborate with equal status, and are interdependent in their collaborating, they are able to foster a superordinate group identity that creates a sense of "we" without necessarily submerging their primary group identities. This superordinate identity, which can exist in tandem with the primary identity, leads to lower intergroup bias.

Handling conflict constructively is the fourth practice. This practice is predicated on turning differences into advantages, which requires procedures for routinely negotiating the tensions that naturally arise when differing perspectives are put forth.

Practice five, *exhibiting interpersonal comfort and self-efficacy*, draws from the knowledge that in diverse workgroups and teams, individuals can experience anti-inclusionary forces that inhibit inclusive interactions, including self-segregation, interaction discomfort, stereotyping and stigmatizing, and implicit bias. Workgroup members can also experience cognitive stress in the form of inconsistency between the stereotypes they hold of a group and the behaviors they are observing, which creates apprehension about interacting with diverse others. Reducing this apprehension and cognitive dissonance relies upon individuals adjusting their perceptions of members of other groups.

Practice six, *ensuring equal insider status to all members*, builds on the practice of repeated and frequent member interaction and suggests the importance of three combined relational elements: bringing diverse members into frequent interaction, both around formal tasks and in informal socializing; equal standing among workgroup members in terms of participation and mutual respect in task decisions; and the interactions being collaborative. Until all workgroup and team members feel valued and of equal standing with others in terms of insider status and decision-making, the group performance will be negatively impacted. Individuals strive to feel valued for their independent contributions to the group and for being a valued team member.

The preceding six practices, shaping the norms that govern formal and informal interactions in the workgroup and organization, can gradually produce comfort and self-efficacy in communicating with others, leading to increasingly effective and equitable interactions. Without such comfort and skill, willingness to continue to interact and adjust perceptions will erode.

At the conclusion of Chapter 3, we describe how inclusion is created and sustained by enacting the six practices and how these provide group and organizational conditions for prejudice-reducing, adaptive contact among diverse individuals. Subsequently, the chapter provides the logic for why the six practices, ideally, will operate in combination *as a set*. Knowledge and the ability to foster these practices provide the capability for organizational change. In Chapter 9, we will discuss practical ways to implement the practices, drawing on knowledge reviewed in the earlier chapters of the book.

Chapter 4 (Exclusionary Forces: Widespread Social Practices that Inhibit Inclusion) delves into the evidence from various academic disciplines on societal forces that inhibit inclusion. The persistence of problems in achieving inclusion indicates that complex, ubiquitous impediments exist. To produce inclusion, four key anti-inclusionary practices found to be widespread in societies must be overcome: self-segregating, interacting uncomfortably, stereotyping and stigmatizing, and making decisions influenced by implicit bias. These phenomena impede positive, inclusive interactions, often leading to homogeneous groupings, overemphasis on differing identities, stigmatizing of other groups, and reduced performance by stigmatized individuals. Strategies to achieve meaningful inclusive interactions must recognize and deal with the four anti-inclusive practices. The anti-inclusionary social phenomenon of self-segregating occurs when diverse individuals differentiate and distance themselves socially, even when in physical proximity. The phenomenon of interacting with discomfort often occurs as a result of a lack of experience due to self-segregating. It involves cross-cultural communication apprehension, the fear of communicating with diverse others. The third anti-inclusionary social practice is stereotyping, which categorizes members of particular groups as incompetent and cold, leading them to be stigmatized as unproductive and unhelpful. These stereotypes are increasingly sustained and manifested in practice by the fourth anti-inclusionary phenomenon, making decisions on the basis of implicit bias, cognitions of bias that are less conscious but more pervasive than overt racism or sexism.

Chapter 5 (The Performance Issue: How Overcoming Exclusion Matters for Workgroup Effectiveness) examines evidence from several bodies of research bearing on how the negative relational practices that inhibit inclusive interactions can potentially be avoided or overcome by programs and practices that suppress implicit bias, such as accountability in managers' personnel decisions, or promote inclusion for all team members, such as cross-functional training. Evidence indicates that implementing indirect approaches to inclusive interactions, ones *not* labeled as "diversity" initiatives, can skirt stereotyping and stigmatizing by promoting specified conditions for producing high performance in diverse workgroups.

Chapter 6 (Structured Interaction Practices for Adaptive Behavioral Learning) is predicated on well-established evidence from numerous settings that frequent positive contact extended over time overcomes prejudices and discomfort. Overcoming prejudices depends on individuals engaging in practices that provide them with the willingness and ability to work through interaction discomfort and continue to engage with different others until their stereotypes change and their interaction skills increase. Once adaptive learning occurs, people experience social integration and information elaboration. Social integration fosters feelings of safety, trust, and justice among workgroup members. Information elaboration enhances perspective taking, cooperative interdependence, and decision-making. Taken together, adaptive learning and skill development counter the anti-inclusive practices of self-segregating and interacting anxiously. This chapter integrates concepts and findings from contact theory, practice theory, and organizational socialization to identify norms and routines that create adaptive learning. Contact theory suggests that simply placing diverse individuals in contact with one another does not guarantee meaningful interactions. Rather, inclusive practices that members follow and in which they become invested through their speech, movements, and emotions lead to adaptive learning and the development of a common in-group identity, sustaining *inclusive engagement* among members of a workgroup or team.

Chapter 7 (Merit, Accountability, and Transparency Practices to Address Equity and Performance) draws attention to the importance of organizations adopting accountability and transparency practices that ensure equitable rewards for members of underrepresented groups. In addition, we propose a need for accountability practices to monitor inclusive engagement. Evidence indicates that reward inequities still persist despite decades of attention by organizations, the legal system, and regulatory bodies. The major cause of inequities appears not to be related to lower performance evaluations but to the flawed translation of those evaluations into reward decisions influenced by bias. Organizational studies indicate that fair employment practices combined with transparency and accountability practices can counter inequities in reward decisions.

Chapter 8 (Sustainable Inclusion: Multiple Outcomes for Individual, Workgroups, and Organizations) addresses how inclusive interactions, combined with practices for transparency and accountability, can lead to increased workgroup and organizational performance overall and equity for historically underrepresented groups. Engaging in inclusive interactions is a step toward addressing structural and systemic injustices, building social connections across differences that expand awareness, diversify social capital, draw on otherwise untapped human capital, and share power. As found in programs that promote cross-functional teams, inclusive interactions can increase equity in the workplace through job rewards that result from making visible the contributions of individuals whose work would otherwise be discounted. In addition to fostering equity and improving group and organizational performance, individuals, as a result of their exposure to positive, inclusive engagements with diverse others and adaptive learning, will develop individual skills that replace the negative, anti-inclusive forces. Organizations committed to creating an inclusive culture will reap the benefits of becoming known as a comfortable place to work, increasing the recruiting and retention of members of underrepresented groups.

In Chapter 9 (Case Examples: Practices for Inclusive Actions and Accountability), we provide examples that can guide and critique the process of designing effective strategies for implementing the inclusive interaction practices. Focusing on actual cases, the chapter illustrates how, when implemented, the practices increase individual and collective, social, and performance benefits. Here, we present examples of diverse workgroups, teams, and organizations that have promoted social practices that achieve the multi-level outcomes to varying degrees. The examples cover a range of contexts and highlight the opportunities for instituting the six inclusive interaction practices in various forms that fit a particular organization or workgroup.

Our final chapter, Chapter 10 (Performance Through Diversity and Inclusion: Leveraging Organizational Practices for Equity and Results), concludes the book by addressing the feasibility of the Framework for Inclusive Interactions in a multitude of organizational types. Describing an extended case of successful organizational change, the chapter highlights the need for intentionality in moving to implement the structured inclusive interaction practices. Embracing the practices and developing adoption strategies may not be without challenges but leads to an inclusive culture that benefits individual status, skills, and unit performance.

Reading these chapters will guide you in developing and structuring inclusive interaction practices in order for your workgroups and organizations to optimize their performance and equity. Structuring practices for inclusion enables workgroup members to be transformed through adaptive learning and personal growth, with an inclusive culture becoming the norm. As you read this book, we anticipate that you will be visualizing your workgroup experiences and contemplating how to structure inclusive interaction practices. We suggest that you use our Framework for Inclusive Interactions as a roadmap or flowchart for implementing the kind of change that enables organizations and workgroups to achieve sustainable inclusion.

PART I OVERVIEW

Leveraging the framework for inclusive interactions to improve performance and equity

In Part I, readers will find a presentation of the book's intent and its framework for organizations to achieve equity and performance from diversity and inclusion. As a prelude to this section, we present here a summary of the book's logic so that, from the start, the reader can engage critically with its main ideas.

The current situation in the United States and other advanced economies is a slowing, plateauing, and even regressing of progress on reducing discrimination and benefitting from diversity. There has been a reawakening of the reality that inequitable, unjustified treatment of those from historically underrepresented groups, including women, continues. Workplaces experience tensions and underutilization of talent that harms performance. How can this be, given that anti-discrimination legislation has been in place for over 50 years and many organizations have been pursuing diversity initiatives since the 1990s? One issue, as discussed in the Preface, is that academics have done poorly on integrating research-based evidence across their varying academic disciplines, and academics and managers have done poorly on communicating with each other to develop and apply research-based evidence that is relevant to organizational action. More and better collaboration can occur. A second issue, discussed in the following chapters, is an overreliance on, and overconfidence in, a legally driven compliance approach to diversity that included organizations adopting fair employment practices. These increased diverse representation but failed to control the operation of bias in many personnel decisions. We will see that research now clearly indicates that:

- Some diversity efforts commonly relied upon by organizations and promoted by many advocates are ineffective.

DOI: 10.4324/9780367822484-1

- Inequities arise from managers' decisions on hiring, pay, and promotions due to the decisions being influenced by unconscious bias against those from underrepresented groups, including women.
- The implementation of fair employment practices, some effective in curbing discrimination and some not, provides organizational members, including leaders, with the belief that meritocratic practices are being followed.

The consequence is that leaders and many members believe that their organization's current practices are fair and adequate while inequitable decisions continue to be made.

The overreliance on particular diversity approaches and the narrow focus of much research fails to deal with system-wide complexities that have existed for decades and centuries. Knowledge is needed that copes with the complexities by specifying the various places in the employment system—the loopholes—where problems persist and thwart current efforts. By taking a systems perspective and integrating research-based evidence from a variety of fields, we attempt to identify these holes and specify feasible, effective options for managers and organizations.

Synthesizing research from various academic disciplines and applied fields, this book offers practice-based, evidence-informed guidance for leaders and managers and for applied research:

- The effects of diversity on equity and performance depend on the social conditions in an organization, conditions such as task-based interdependence that shape the behavior of organizational members toward each other and their work.
- Leaders can implement particular *inclusive practices* that structure social conditions such that the organization's members learn to interact professionally and effectively. They engage with reduced discomfort and reduced prejudices by becoming familiar and sharing personal experiences with each other, and they make decisions using procedures that control their remaining unconscious biases.
- Inclusive practices can be created by particular workgroup and organizational programs such as cross-functional teams that are not normally viewed as diversity-focused.
- Combining inclusive practices at the workgroup and team level with transparency and accountability practices at the organizational level enables simultaneous improvements in equity and performance, leveraging members' differing talents, encouraging positive views of diversity, and increasing members' commitment to the organization. The combination of inclusive and accountability practices covers the variety of holes in the employment system that permit discrimination problems to persist, enabling organizations to sustain diversity and inclusion and make the organization attractive to talented members from all backgrounds.

The three chapters in Part I examine the current situation and present an evidence-based framework to guide more effective managerial action. The Introduction chapter (The elusive goal: Diversity and inclusion for equity and performance) describes the historical backdrop of the current state of diversity and inclusion in organizations and presents the impetus for this book. Chapter 1 (Doing better: Achieving equity and performance from diversity) reviews effective and ineffective approaches to diversity, including a discussion of diversity training. Chapter 2 (The framework: Improving performance and equity through inclusive interaction practices) presents an overview of the Framework for Inclusive Interactions, the book's central framework that identifies processes for achieving equity and performance from diversity.

INTRODUCTION

The elusive goal: Diversity and inclusion for equity and performance

The unrealized opportunity: Diversity with inclusion

The increased recognition that societies and their organizations have fallen short on equality for members of underrepresented groups and women leads to the focus of this book: A recalibration to a *practice-based* and *evidence-informed* approach to diversity, equity, and inclusion in order to produce positive, productive change in bottom-line organizational performance and in equity for all organizational members, including those from underrepresented groups. In many countries, many of us citizens believed that we had come a long way in overcoming problems of discrimination. But had we? It is now clear that progress has occurred in some limited aspects and not in others. Consider an early 1950s performance evaluation for a female lawyer in the United States Air Force's Office of Staff Judge Advocate:

> The problem of a female dealing with male subordinates poses some difficulties, but this officer, with poise and tact, has maintained necessary relationships without hard feelings.
>
> Although this officer is considered outstanding, her sex precludes promotional opportunities within this command.

Today, seeing the phrase "her sex precludes promotional opportunities" explicitly stated in a performance evaluation can strike us as shocking. For well over half a century in the United States, since the passage of the Civil Rights Act in 1964, that phrase would be deemed discriminatory and illegal. Nevertheless, have more fundamental issues, such as the difficulty some men (and we now know, some women) experience in being subordinate to women executives, changed? Recent research has found that subtle discrimination, emanating from fundamental problems of interaction, produces stronger discriminatory effects on the career success, turnover,

DOI: 10.4324/9780367822484-2

and mental health of minorities and women than does overt discrimination.[1] Organizations that employ these individuals pay a price by forgoing the high performance of talented individuals, as indicated by a later evaluation of the same female lawyer:

> During a 3-month absence of the Staff Judge Advocate, this officer filled that position in an admirable manner, guiding Staff Judge Advocates of lower commands through a trying period characterized by a lack of competent lawyers and beset with problems of extreme legal technicity.

The female lawyer's talents were utilized well during that period, but she then returned to her prior, less consequential role. Consider that this scenario played out innumerable times across the economy. It still does today, not only on the basis of gender but also race, ethnicity, age, disabilities, religion, and other characteristics that trigger implicit bias and result in talent being underutilized and treated inequitably. A recent estimate based on research evidence is that, in a single year with approximately six million job openings being filled in the United States, gender bias alone results in one million fewer women than men being hired into new positions for which they are equally qualified.[2] In some areas, we are regressing rather than improving. For example, the employment of women in science, technology, engineering, and math (STEM) occupations trended up strongly from 1999 to 2003, but then plateaued subsequently.[3]

The persistence of inequalities has been even worse for Black Americans. Analysis of data from the Bureau of Labor Statistics by members of the Federal Reserve Bank of San Francisco revealed that the Black–White wage gap has not decreased but, rather, increased over the past four decades.[4] In 1979, the average hourly earnings for Black men was 80 percent that of White men ($15/hour vs. $19/hour) but had regressed to 70 percent by 2016. For Black women, the regression in progress was more severe, with the Black–White earnings ratio being 95 percent in 1979 and falling to 82 percent in 2016.

> For college and post-college graduates, the Black–White earnings gap for men and women has increased over recent decades.

Statistical analyses showed that only a portion of these earnings gaps can be explained by measurable factors, such as occupation and education. Substantial gaps remain after controlling for these and other factors—age, part-time status, and state of residence—leading the authors to conclude:

> Perhaps more troubling is the fact that the growth in this unexplained portion accounts for almost all of the growth in the gaps over time. ... This implies that factors that are harder to measure—such as discrimination, differences in

school quality, or differences in career opportunities—are likely to be playing a role in the persistence and widening of these gaps over time.[5]

The Center for Employment Equity used equal opportunity (EO) report data to grade industries on various diversity dimensions, including total employment, managerial representation, occupational segregation, and pay gaps as well as to assign an overall grade across the four dimensions.[6] Some of the findings from their executive summary include:

> For all demographic groups except for Asians, high wage industries tend to have worse employment records. High-wage industries hire more men and generate high gender pay gaps. Larger African American–White wage gaps and higher segregation of African Americans from Whites are also found in high wage industries. … 47.8% of industries receive overall failing … or near failing grades. In these industries, mean wage gaps tend to be over 20%.

Other analyses[7] indicate that measures of racial prejudice, such as objection to interracial marriage, account for part of the Black–White wage gap in the U.S. economy. At the organizational level, research findings discussed in Chapter 7 suggest that many of the problems underlying the persistence and growth of disparities for women and underrepresented groups stem from biased personnel decisions on hiring, career development, and promotions. That bias, overt in the 1950s and more implicit in recent years, is still producing racial, ethnic, and gender disparities today, often in ways that are less visible and less conscious on the part of decision-makers.

> Bias that was more overt in the 1950s is more implicit today, still producing racial, ethnic and gender disparities.

In societies around the world experiencing dramatic inequalities, it appears that relying primarily on a legalistic approach has fallen short. So, too, have voluntary organizational efforts to promote diversity in terms of numerical representation. These approaches fail to touch the more fundamental problems of achieving equitable and productive interactions in the workplace. Interactions among differing people, and the biases, stereotypes, and discomfort that drive such interactions, underlie the disparities in personnel decisions. These interpersonal interaction issues persist in a manner vexing and even tiring to many of us, regardless of our backgrounds.

> Many people, particularly Whites, thought society had moved beyond racism and many women thought society had moved beyond sexism.

Those believing that we had moved beyond these and other "isms" now realize they were mistaken. The Me-Too movement has brought significant attention to the ongoing issues of gender-based mistreatment and harassment in the workplace, and gender discrimination issues have been widened to encompass transgender and gender non-binary individuals. Furthermore, where race is concerned, contemporary events surrounding police brutality against Blacks and protests against racial injustice inspired by the Black Lives Matter movement in the United States and echoed around the world suggest that we are, indeed, not living in post-racial societies. Women and members of underrepresented groups are tired of enduring treatment based on stereotypes. Many people from all backgrounds walk on eggshells when interacting with diverse others, afraid to offend those with different beliefs, ideas, and cultures. Poorly executed diversity training has contributed to this diversity fatigue and uneasiness by unfairly burdening people of color, women, and other members of underrepresented groups with teaching others about bias and discrimination. This often puts Whites, males, and members of dominant groups on the defensive, thus making them less responsive to diversity initiatives. At the same time, accompanying these understandings and emotions is the realization that we and our organizations must do better.

Social movements encourage people to have *more* conversations, whether comfortable or not, about race, ethnicity, prejudice, culture, inequality, differences, and so on. Within organizations—those adopting the proper culture and inclusive practices, we argue—such conversations can more organically and productively emerge in everyday work settings than in training settings.

When these conversations occur, do we have the knowledge and support that enable us to do better? Why do we continue to see such disparities in employment among various racial and ethnic groups and women and a severe lack of representation from these groups among top leadership in organizations, corresponding with an overrepresentation of those from historically underrepresented groups at the bottom of the organization? There is a broad consciousness among the public and organizational leaders that the challenges in addressing equity and performance through diversity and inclusion continue to be embedded in institutional and organizational structures and processes. However, while it is widely recognized that institutionalized disparities are prevalent, less known is that organizational and, by extension, societal economic performance is suffering as well, and that organizational performance gains from diversity require more than diverse representation.

> While diverse organizational membership is a step toward more inclusive organizations, performance gains from diversity require more than diverse representation.

Awareness that social and performance problems continue to exist is a useful first step but only a first step. Identifying the underlying sources of the problems and how they have been reproducing themselves over the decades is necessary if leaders and managers are to effectively deal with them. Also important is identifying improved approaches to bringing about structural change in organizations.

The stakes for organizations and societies

The economic stakes of leading on diversity and inclusion are increasingly high. With demographics changing within societies and many organizations operating globally, workforces are more and more diverse. Organizations that secure high performance from their diverse workforces gain a competitive advantage in effectiveness.

> Organizations that can leverage a diverse workforce for higher performance gain a competitive advantage.

Basic economic theory holds that organizations that exhibit a "taste for discrimination"[8] in their personnel decisions and ongoing functioning will suffer compared to organizations that base their functioning more purely on performance-based criteria. That is, the optimal allocation of human capital results in improved performance at the level of an organization and, by extension, an economy as a whole.

The economic costs for organizations and societies are opportunity costs—the forgoing of higher performance from failing to use the best human capital available for particular jobs. This process of exercising a taste for discrimination, of foregone performance, has been documented repeatedly in both field and laboratory experimental studies. As we noted above, regarding millions of hiring decisions per year, many employers make decisions based on bias against qualified members of underrepresented groups, keeping them underrepresented. Research shows that bias, today often more unconscious than the overt prejudice illustrated at the beginning of this chapter, still produces large disparities in final managerial decisions on who is hired, how much they are paid, and which members are chosen to be promoted.[9] Opportunity costs occur not only in these areas of hiring, personnel development, promotions, and turnover, but also in reduced individual and workgroup performance. The research covered in Chapters 4 through 7 reveals problems in each of the following areas:

- Treatment in the workplace that exhibits a taste for discrimination in the form of stereotyping and stigmatizing members of underrepresented groups leads to reduced self-efficacy and performance from those individuals and loss of their talents due to higher turnover (Chapter 4).
- Failure to incorporate the perspectives and expertise of diverse members inhibits the elaboration of information needed for better decision-making in workgroups (Chapter 5).

- Despite the supposed promulgation of fair employment practices in organizations, rewards are inequitably distributed in terms of developmental opportunities and promotions (Chapter 7).

The other side of this economic coin is that organizations that figure out how to achieve inclusion—that is, properly hire, develop, allocate, and organize the talents of all members—will produce not only greater equity but also higher organizational effectiveness. These inclusive organizations will be able to incorporate differing skills and perspectives that may critically impact their success and potentially their survival. They will be operating with an "integration and learning perspective"[10] that transforms diversity into performance across the organization, rather than from the less productive perspectives of conforming with the law or steering diverse individuals primarily into functions that relate to diverse populations of customers.

For organizations and societies, there are other stakes beyond the economics:

- From recent experience, we now know that the limited gains that women and people of color have achieved in organizations may be capped or eroded if inclusion's benefits are not realized.
- As equity and social justice issues repeatedly come to the forefront in public discourse, organizations will encounter more diversity conflict and reputational disadvantages if they are not able to meaningfully rather than superficially address inclusion and equity.

While optimizing human capital allocations will result in improved economic performance and higher effectiveness and efficiency,[11] optimizing this allocation additionally provides equity, serving the ends of social justice and reflecting good business ethics. With an eye toward both equitable outcomes and organizational performance, the Framework for Inclusive Interactions that we present later in this chapter provides a fresh, ethical, and alternative approach to diversity and inclusion in organizations in a manner that meets the interests of key stakeholders—that is, in a way that achieves the ethical managing of human differences in organizations.

> Organizations advancing diversity and inclusion will reap both individual and collective benefits, as opposed to those organizations failing to adapt to the realities of diversity.

The realities: Representation and legal compliance are not enough

Both recent experience and research tell us that successful treatment of diversity by an organization rests on meaningful inclusion of members whose gender, race, or other characteristics differ from those of dominant group members. In the past, a business case for diversity has been conceived on too limited a basis, involving the addition of new members as a means to reach various underserved markets to increase revenue and market share or to enhance innovation leading to other market advantages. Further, the business case was built upon the instituting of employment practices that complied with legal requirements. We now have enough experience with these approaches to know their severe limitations. As we cover in this book, research reveals that simply creating a more diverse workgroup does not lead to higher creativity or performance.

> Research reveals that simply having a more diverse workgroup does not automatically lead to higher creativity or performance.

Nor does simply instituting several fair employment practices lead to a meritocracy that incentivizes and rewards the most capable organizational members. Without attending to the treatment of members of underrepresented groups on the job—to whether the interactions among all members are inclusive and productive, to whether rewards are truly distributed in a meritocratic manner—the unfair reasons for their being underrepresented in the first place will reproduce their under-representation over time.

Sustainable inclusion

Central to doing better is overcoming social practices of exclusion—such as stereotyping—that are ubiquitous in our societies and that impede productive interactions among members. Recognizing the need to institute inclusive practices that overcome exclusion, this book seeks to inform leaders and researchers on how to proceed from diversity to what we term *sustainable inclusion*, a state of the organization in which diversity is leveraged for a combination of enhanced equity and organizational performance, with both of these being sustained over time. Understanding this state requires defining what we mean by diversity and inclusion. Recently, "organizations have begun to use the term *diversity and inclusion* to underscore the need for compositional diversity and institutional belonging."[12] However, the concept of sustainable inclusion points to a further distinction between the two. *Diversity* refers to organizational efforts to enhance the demographic representation of its members, both overall and in managerial and leadership positions. We refer to this as *representational diversity*[13] or, sometimes more simply, as *diversity*. *Sustainable inclusion* inherently subsumes the concept of representational diversity but goes well beyond it. To continue to produce beneficial effects over time, inclusion must involve practices more deeply embedded in an organizational culture that reaches down to the level of workgroups, a deeper level than is reached by the limited practices aimed at representation. Sustainable inclusion points to practices and policies that make up an *inclusive culture* that provides the opportunity, supports the motivation, and enhances the ability of all organizational members to integrate their perspectives into key organizational decisions and work processes.[14] Sustainable inclusion produces high levels of equity, retention of talent, skill development, and commitment among organizational members. To be sustainable, meaningful inclusion both requires and supports an inclusive culture that evolves over time to adapt to societal changes.

Sustainable inclusion involves practices and policies comprising an *inclusive culture* that provides the opportunity, supports the motivation, and enhances the ability of all organizational members to integrate their perspectives into key decisions and work processes.

Developing sustainable inclusion is a more complex and long-term proposition than representational diversity, involving the evolution of a particular type of organizational culture, one that some organizations have shown is practical to attain. Without it, an informed manager will understand that deeply embedded structural problems will continue, as they have in the past.

Evidence-informed management for sustainable inclusion

Searching for guidance on how organizations can do better in leveraging diversity, we have discovered that there is much that researchers and leaders can learn from each other. Diversity researchers have produced knowledge that has been far too little applied by organizations. At the same time, some organizations and occupational groups have pursued and refined performance-improvement programs that achieve inclusion in ways unknown to most researchers and policymakers.

In this book, we synthesize knowledge and findings from published reviews of various bodies of research across several disciplines and organizational fields. The synthesis is captured in a framework that emphasizes routine practices that managers can intentionally structure to foster inclusive interactions in their organizations. The practices are not necessarily new ones. In fact, they have been refined and used successfully in some organizations. However, they require careful design by organizational leaders and workgroup managers who are informed by knowledge of social and organizational behavior, by managerial expertise shared among an industry's members, and by the intricacies of the particular organizational situation.[15] With this knowledge, informed and savvy leaders and managers in all sectors—business, nonprofit, and government—can produce sustainable inclusion and its performance and social benefits. (See Box I.1 on research-based evidence for management practice.)

BOX I.1: PRODUCING EVIDENCE FOR EVIDENCE-INFORMED MANAGEMENT

Managers can apply research-based evidence to better guide effective organizational programs, combining that evidence with understandings of their particular organizational situations. We rely on two key approaches to identifying and applying the knowledge from research-based evidence: (1) transdisciplinary synthesis of bodies of diversity research and (2) evidence-informed management. First, we recognize that the dynamics involved in organizational diversity, inclusion, equity, and performance are complex and have been investigated in a variety of academic disciplines. Accordingly, we review research that has produced knowledge about the dynamics from disciplines that can significantly inform management and organizational practice—sociology, economics, social psychology, psychology, and communication studies. Second, the book presents research-based evidence—from these multiple scholarly disciplines—for the purpose of providing organizational leaders with knowledge to evaluate and diagnose their current actions and to creatively develop improved actions for diversity, inclusion, equity, and performance.

Doing better than we have in the past calls for an analysis of the anti-inclusionary forces that are producing the shortcomings organizations are experiencing. Doing better also requires identifying practices that can counter those forces. Research-based evidence provides valuable guidance on both scores, explaining in detail social forces that continue to reproduce inequality in organizations despite societal and organizational efforts, and identifying well-intentioned diversity practices currently in use that fail to counter these forces as well as revealing practices that are more effective

Leaders at all organizational levels can be informed by this evidence and combine it with knowledge of their workgroups, organizations, and communities to generate effective change that simultaneously benefits both equity and bottom-line performance. In this evidence-informed analytical process, they can identify where social and performance costs are incurred in their organizations. An important aspect of leveraging this evidence is using it to update our beliefs and understandings (Box I.2).

BOX I.2: UPDATING OUR PRIOR KNOWLEDGE

To succeed with diversity and inclusion, a human challenge is to update our beliefs and understandings, whether we are managers, students, educators, or researchers. We should "update our priors," a term used in Bayesian statistics, the prior probabilities that we ascribe to a situation, based on new evidence. Consider how this applies to several aspects of inclusion discussed in this book:

1. As individuals who possess stereotypes about a particular group, when we have frequent positive interactions with members of that group, we tend to update our priors and see that group in a more positive way.
2. As individuals whose past experiences have taught us to distance ourselves from different others, we update our priors on how to behave after being socialized into a new, inclusive organizational setting, becoming more comfortable with different others.
3. As individuals (including researchers and diversity staff members) with beliefs about which diversity practices in organizations are effective, we update our priors when we learn about evidence indicating that some are ineffective and others that we had never considered to be diversity practices are effective.

The evidence: Confounding effects of contemporary diversity efforts

Drawing on convincing evidence from research, this book specifies sources of persistent inequities and reduced performance. The sources are often unconsciously followed and difficult-to-see social practices, such as making decisions based on implicit bias. Such practices, largely untouched by most current diversity initiatives, are *anti-inclusive*. They prevent the inclusion of differing others by creating tension, distancing, and disparaging across subgroups.

Without knowledge of anti-inclusive practices, it is difficult for managers to understand that many widely relied-upon approaches to diversity and inclusion in organizations have limited or even harmful effects.

For instance, diversity and inclusion initiatives that seem highly encouraging, such as training approaches strongly advocated by the human resources department and key leaders, never actually get implemented or backfire due to poor planning and/or implementation, or because they are based on faulty assumptions and are not accompanied by changed practices on the job. Such common initiatives are undermined by long embedded but often subtle everyday practices among organizational members, causing consternation even among diversity and inclusion advocates. Rather than helping, these initiatives end up increasing conflict and resentment among people from various identity groups, harming both equity and performance, thereby contributing to the *regression* of progress now evident in organizations and in society more broadly. Fortunately, we now have knowledge that enables the design of more effective initiatives.

Effective approaches

Organizational efforts that have been effective for diversity and inclusion include some (but certainly not all) practices that are specifically targeted for diversity and inclusion. Surprisingly, and with great promise, some practices that are not targeted at diversity but, instead, purely at mission or performance attainment have also been found to be effective for diversity. We know about effective approaches from studies by Alexandra Kalev, Frank Dobbin, and colleagues that examined changes over time in the proportions of minorities and women in managerial positions in over 800 U.S. firms.[16] For example, college recruitment programs and mentoring programs, diversity task forces, and diversity managers have been cited as approaches that have yielded positive diversity and inclusion results. On college recruitment programs, Dobbin and Kalev[17] found that:

> Five years after a company implements a college recruitment program targeting female employees, the share of White women, Black women, Hispanic women, and Asian-American women in its management rises by about 10%, on average. A program focused on minority recruitment increases the proportion of Black male managers by 8% and Black female managers by 9%.[18]

Similarly, mentoring programs were effective:

> Mentoring programs make companies' managerial echelons significantly more diverse: On average, they boost the representation of Black, Hispanic, and Asian-American women, and Hispanic and Asian-American men, by 9% to 24%. In industries where plenty of college-educated nonmanagers are eligible to move up, like chemicals and electronics, mentoring programs also increase the ranks of White women and Black men by 10% or more.[19]

The explanation given for these positive effects on representation is that recruiting and mentoring programs serve to engage managers in problem solving around diversity ("How can we increase diversity?"), putting managers in the mode of increasing diversity and inclusion. Further, this body of research indicated that promoting social accountability practices such as diversity task forces and diversity managers was effective in increasing managerial representation among underrepresented groups.

The foregoing approaches—recruitment, mentoring, diversity task forces, and managers—are diversity specific and should be expected to boost diversity. Less expected but highly promising are findings that creating self-managed teams and providing cross-training, which are not diversity specific but do address inclusion, had similar positive effects—increasing the managerial representation of underrepresented groups.

> Programs that involve inclusion for all members, whether from underrepresented groups or not, advance the status of underrepresented group members.

Ineffective approaches

In contrast, some types of diversity efforts that are explicitly focused on diversity and adopted on a wide scale have been found to be ineffective and even countereffective. One such type is *mandatory* diversity training, one of the most common approaches to diversity and inclusion in organizations. Esen[20] estimates that 67 percent of U.S. organizations and 74 percent of Fortune 500 organizations invest in diversity training programs. Thus, substantial organizational resources have been poured into diversity training as a way of leveraging beneficial organizational outcomes from diversity. However, diversity training has had mixed results in organizations. As shown in the study by Alexandra Kalev and colleagues,[21] across a large number of organizations and across decades, diversity training has been found to be not just generally ineffective but also detrimental for some groups. In a more recent study, they reported that:

> … five years after instituting required training for managers, companies saw no improvement in the proportion of White women, Black men, and Hispanics in management, and the share of Black women actually decreased by 9%, on average, while the ranks of Asian-American men and women shrank by 4% to 5%. Trainers tell us that people often respond to compulsory courses with anger and resistance—and many participants actually report more animosity toward other groups afterward.[22]

> Diversity training has been found to be not just generally ineffective but also detrimental for some groups.

Thus, diversity training did little to increase the managerial representation of many underrepresented groups and even decreased representation among some. As we discuss further in Chapter 1, some types of training can be useful when properly combined with practices for inclusion. As with most efforts involving diversity, the effects of training are complex. While mandatory training is highly problematic, *voluntary* training for managers can be effective. For instance, in their wide-ranging, decades-long study of over 800 workplaces, Dobbin and Kalev also found that voluntary diversity training led to significant increases in diverse management representation.

Diversity training also suffers from "short-termism:" "The positive effects of diversity training rarely last beyond a day or two."[23] Further, diversity training frequently suffers from a lack of connection to organizational mission and goals, with no accountability for post-training implementation. Having said this, we are quick to point out that not *all* types of training related to diversity and inclusion are problematic. Particular types of training can be valuable when combined with inclusive practices; we discuss this issue in Chapter 1.

Other organizational approaches that have been implemented to address bias and discrimination have been ineffective as well. For example, Dobbin and Kalev[24] found that companies that prescribed mandatory written tests in hiring had *decreases* of 4 to 10 percent in the representation in managerial jobs held by White women, African American men and women, Hispanic men and women, and Asian American women over the next five years, and group differences in test-taking skills do not explain these disparities. Further, performance ratings do little to enhance diversity within the management ranks for these underrepresented groups. In fact, "studies show that raters tend to lowball women and minorities in performance reviews,"[25] and there is a further bias against members of underrepresented groups as performance evaluations are translated into pay, promotion, and termination decisions.[26] Another practice designed to ensure fairness, grievance procedures, has actually not been helpful for diversity. Even though nearly half of all midsize and large companies have such procedures, Dobbin and Kalev[27] found that with grievance procedures:

> … many managers—rather than change their own behavior or address discrimination by others—try to get even with or belittle employees who complain. Among the nearly 90,000 discrimination complaints made to the Equal Employment Opportunity Commission in 2015, 45% included a charge of retaliation—which suggests that the original report was met with ridicule, demotion, or worse.[28]

Many organizations have been expending resources on common approaches to diversity, such as mandatory diversity training, that have been proven to be ineffective.

Social behavior around diversity is not as simple as current organizational initiatives assume. These initiatives frequently produce unintended consequences that organizations fail to address. For instance, while conceptually affirmative action programs are not typically considered "diversity" programs, many organizations combine their efforts on equal employment opportunity and affirmative action with diversity efforts. The research by Kalev and colleagues shows that, over several decades, affirmative action programs have had positive impacts on progress for underrepresented groups. However, there are confounding factors, social dynamics that caution whether and how diversity efforts should be designed and communicated. Recent research discussed in Chapter 4 suggests that highlighting affirmative diversity efforts and their beneficiaries can have negative consequences. These findings urge us to consider how explicitly labeled "diversity programs" can, unintentionally, stigmatize those from underrepresented groups.

Being informed by evidence on diversity interactions

In the field of medicine, the most sound knowledge to guide practice comes from systematic reviews that develop guidelines for doctors by examining and synthesizing the findings from a body of studies. In the area of diversity (and as we discuss in Chapter 6), reviews of a large body of studies that span many decades have produced strong evidence that can guide managers. The evidence is that diversity interactions lead to prejudice reduction, especially under particular conditions.[29] In our synthesis, we incorporate this knowledge on the efficacy of positive intergroup contact and the practices that favor it. For reasons that are not clear, this knowledge has not previously informed managerial action on diversity.

Is lack of progress due to complacency?

Given that we now have much knowledge that can guide leaders, including knowledge on effective alternative options to currently dominant diversity initiatives, why have so many organizations continued to rely on approaches that are ineffective or countereffective? With the persistence of discriminatory treatment and inequitable outcomes in many countries now being recognized as a societal problem, this question begs an answer. Societal complacency is one answer. An explanation offered for such complacency is the prevalence of particular beliefs held by management educators, managers, and public policymakers concerning market-based economic systems, beliefs that some analysts are now claiming to be myths.[30] The beliefs are that: markets are efficient; human resource management systems in organizations are meritocratic; and globalization is a positive force. The second belief bears directly on organizations that have increased their efforts for representational diversity, as through enhanced recruitment and reformed personnel evaluation procedures. Such efforts and reforms reinforce beliefs that organizations now have fair employment practices, that personnel practices in one's own organization are meritocratic. These beliefs engender satisfaction with diversity efforts among members at all levels, from leaders on down. The plateauing of progress and the persistence of personnel decisions influenced by bias, as noted above, indicates that such satisfaction is out of step with the realities.

A practice-based approach: Why is it necessary?

A major reality revealed by research is that key practices in organizations, ones left untouched by effective practices such as expanded recruitment, account for major inequities in employment outcomes. Even when performance evaluations for members of underrepresented groups are reasonably equitable, large disparities continue in promotion, pay, and termination decisions that are supposedly based on those evaluations.[31] Organizational practices that permit unmonitored discretion to workgroup managers making personnel decisions, such as for pay and promotions, enable the continued operation of biases similar to that in this chapter's opening scenario from the 1950s. Similarly, at the workgroup level, social practices of stereotyping and stigmatizing by majority group members not only aid in the persistence of these biases, they also reduce the performance and self-competence of the individuals targeted by the stigmatizing,[32] harming workgroup performance. If inequities, poor allocation of human capital and stereotyping are to be managed effectively, practices of exclusion at the level of the manager and workgroup must be addressed. This calls for countervailing practices that foster the inclusion of all members' talents and hold individuals accountable for their behavior and decisions. These countervailing practices must reach the workgroup level, with practices there being understood as what members *do* in their habitual, everyday interactions and decision-making.[33]

The workgroup level is precisely where practice-based approaches to other organizational challenges have proven to be highly successful in transforming organizations. Examples include quality management programs such as ISO 9000 in manufacturing, and agile teams in high-tech, fast-paced organizations. These programs specify distinctive workgroup and team practices that organizations have adopted to improve their performance. Parallel to initiatives such as ISO 9000 and agile teams, we need more programs involving organizational practices for inclusion and accountability—programs that build on and extend change initiatives that research is now revealing to be successful in producing and sustaining inclusion.

By using a practice-based approach, successful programs focus on how organizational members actually behave—in particular, whether they behave inclusively. In contrast, many currently dominant approaches to diversity management treat attitudes as the main problem, attempting to address biased attitudes directly through rhetoric, education/training, or sanctions. These attempts ignore that biased attitudes are activated, or not, by everyday social practices in the workplace. The approach we are led to by various bodies of evidence is *behavior-centric*. It does not dispute the pervasive nature of biased attitudes. It recognizes them and identifies how to address them by structuring particular organizational practices to counter anti-inclusive practices and shape inclusive behavior, simultaneously producing high workgroup performance and equity for diverse members and changing biased attitudes *over time*. As behavior, first, and then attitudes change due to new inclusive practices, a culture that supports sustainable inclusion emerges at the workgroup level.

A practice-based, evidence-informed framework for leveraging diversity

By structuring proper practices at the workgroup level, practices for inclusive interactions, and accountable decision-making, organizational leaders and individual workgroup managers influence the skills and comfort of members dealing with their diversity, their differences. Over time, members of diverse workgroups and teams move from feelings of discomfort to comfort, learn from one another, accept each other's unique qualities, form a sense of group belonging and, as a result, improve performance and equity. Our Framework for Inclusive Interactions[34] captures the dynamics of this process. It is the central feature of this book, intended to be used by leaders and managers in organizations in all sectors—business, non-profit, and government—to produce performance and social benefits from diversity. As depicted in Figure I.1, the Framework also serves as a guide to the later chapters of the book, where each element in the Framework, and the research-based evidence behind it, is discussed.

> Our Framework for Inclusive Interactions is useful for leaders and managers in organizations in all sectors to produce performance and social benefits from diversity.

The Framework illustrates how organizations that have in place *organizational conditions that support inclusion*, with a demonstrated commitment to leveraging diversity for high performance and equity, can move beyond demographic representation to intentionally structure key practices that will foster *sustainable inclusion*. We contend that the *structured inclusive interaction practices* specified in Figure I.1 allow diverse organizational members to engage in positive, ongoing *inclusive interactions* that overcome the otherwise common *anti-inclusive practices* of stereotyping and stigmatizing, self-segregating, interacting anxiously, and making decisions based on implicit bias. Managers and leaders can initially structure and then keep vibrant particular practices for inclusion for all members, creating and sustaining an environment within which productive interactions can flourish. The structured inclusive interaction practices, discussed and illustrated in more detail in Chapter 3, are:

1. pursuing a *shared task* orientation or mission;
2. *mixing* members frequently and repeatedly;
3. *collaborating* with member interdependence;
4. *handling conflict* constructively;
5. engaging in interpersonal *comfort* and *self-efficacy*; and
6. ensuring *equal insider status* for all members.

These practices represent inclusion in action. As organizational members follow these practices to engage with each other in workgroups and teams, they avoid *anti-inclusive practices* (Chapter 4) and undergo *adaptive learning* in which they experience social integration that is inclusive. They also expand the amount and quality of task-relevant information through perspective taking and cooperative interdependence in order to produce improved team decision-making (Chapter 5). *Adaptive learning* (Chapter 6) is an ongoing process with members continually adjusting

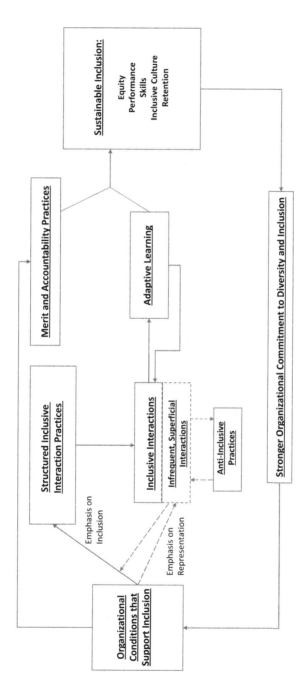

FIGURE I.1 The Framework for Inclusive Interactions: Overview

their interactions to comply with norms of inclusion and to achieve high performance. That learning, together with organizational *accountability and transparency practices* (Chapter 7) that hold all members accountable for behaving inclusively and that foster equitable decisions on the part of managers, leads to an evolving inclusive culture that represents *sustainable inclusion* (Chapter 8). Unlike a conception of diversity that is focused on statistical representation, sustainable inclusion is characterized by a set of beneficial outcomes that are continually reproduced over time: equity, individual skill development, an increased valuing of diversity and inclusion that represents an inclusive culture, and enhanced employee commitment and team performance at all levels. In that sense of reproduction, the Framework can be thought of as a flow diagram, capturing the dynamics that lead from representational diversity to increases over time in sustainable inclusion with its beneficial outcomes, and, through feedback, to the reduction of anti-inclusive practices and the evolution and vitality of inclusive practices. In a continual, ongoing manner a *stronger organizational commitment to diversity and inclusion* is built.

> The Framework is like a flow diagram, capturing the dynamics leading from representational diversity to sustainable inclusion and its benefits, and, through feedback, to the reduction of anti-inclusive practices and to the ongoing vitality of inclusive practices.

In short, based on integrating evidence from multiple bodies of research, we are led to the conclusion that organizations can achieve performance and equity through sustained, positive inclusive interactions among diverse organizational members (including staff, managers, and leaders), deploying specific organizational practices aimed at sustaining comfortable interactions, high performance, and accountable behavior. Sustained inclusion is the means to simultaneously achieve performance and equity. The book's Framework provides managers with guidance on how to achieve these dual outcomes, educators and students with insights from across a broad range of research studies, and researchers with issues worthy of further investigation concerning social conditions and practices in a range of organizations.

Addendum: Key terminology and language

In this book, we strive to be inclusive in our use of language. At the same time, when citing research, we generally prefer to use the same terms the authors use in their work. For example, much of the research cited here uses the term "minorities" to refer to groups that are in the numerical minority in a particular setting (organization or geographic location). In citing this research, we tend to retain the terminology of the authors, but more generally, we use the term "underrepresented groups" to refer to such groups. Further, practice is mixed with reference to whether or not to capitalize "Black" and "White" when referring to groups identified by race. We have chosen to capitalize all terms referring to particular groups (e.g., Black, White, Hispanic, Latino, etc.). Also, while we recognize that there are differences in terms of what authors mean by "people of color", we use that term here broadly to apply to members of historically underrepresented and marginalized groups who are nonwhite.

Similarly, we recognize that the term "gender" reflects a continuum of identities that do not necessarily correspond to the male/female biological binary. However, when citing research that examines gender differences in particular phenomena, we discuss that research using the same terms as in the original work. More generally, when discussing gender wage inequity or gender discrimination, we typically employ the terms "women" and "men" rather than "female" and "male", unless referring to studies where the authors used those latter terms. Finally, we sometimes refer to "race and ethnicity" rather than simply "race," recognizing that concerning particular social dynamics, members of some ethnic groups (e.g., Latinos/Latinx) are treated similarly to those of particular races (e.g., Blacks).

The term "diversity" is one of the most commonly used terms in organizational studies but also one that is saddled with a variety of disparate interpretations that often create confusion in discourse on the topic, as well as in practice. We recognize that many use the term "diversity" as an umbrella term to refer to a variety of organizational practices and policies related to dealing with demographic differences among workforce members. Here, we use the term "representational diversity,"[35] or simply "diversity," to refer to the degree to which people of color and women, who have been historically underrepresented in organizations in higher status occupations and managerial and executive leadership levels, are currently represented in the organization. In other words, representational diversity focuses on the numbers of these organizational members at various levels.

While some elements of diversity and inclusion significantly overlap, diversity and inclusion can be separated.[36] We differentiate between representational diversity and inclusion here using Nishii's (2013) definition of a "climate for inclusion" which has three elements: (1) *Fairly implemented employment practices and diversity-specific practices* that help to eliminate bias, (2) *Integration of differences*, which has to do with expectations and norms around openness with which diverse employees can enact and engage core aspects of their whole selves such that they are integrated into the organization, and (3) *Inclusion in decision-making,* which refers to the extent to which diverse member perspectives fundamentally affect the organization and its work, even if such perspectives challenge or upset the status quo.[37] Quinetta Roberson's research identifies organizational attributes for inclusion that include collaborative work systems and processes for conflict resolution and accountability, revealing inclusion in practical terms to be:

> The way an organization configures its systems and structures to value and leverage the potential, and to limit the disadvantages, of differences.[38]

Thus, our view of inclusion encompasses *organizational practices, organizational processes*, as well as *organizational culture*. We prefer using the term *culture* to *climate* here in that the former suggests a longer-term organizational change process, which we believe more closely reflects the dynamics we discuss in our Framework. Thus, this definition moves the notion of inclusion from one representing how individuals *feel* about their experiences to one recognizing the critical role that structured organizational practices play in creating a sustained culture wherein diverse members' knowledge, skills, and abilities are recognized, valued, and contribute to the core work of the organization. We use the term *sustained inclusion* to emphasize the ongoing embedding of inclusion in the form of an inclusive culture. This culture contributes to beneficial outcomes for individuals, workgroups, and the organization.

Finally, in defining equity, we recognize that equity can be defined at various levels—the individual, group, or organization/system. Generally, equity has to do with fair treatment and impartiality, regardless of the level. In this book, we are focused on the individual and organizational levels. At the individual level, equity can refer to one's perceptions of rewards received in exchange for the work effort expended, as compared to others.[39] At the group level, equity can reflect the degree of inequality in outcomes, such as gender pay inequity or racial leadership inequity. It can also refer to treating members of historically marginalized groups in a way that fosters equity in outcomes, which is not the same as treating everyone the same, or equally. We see equity and inclusion as interacting effectively. For inclusion to be sustained, we need particular inclusive interaction practices for all organizational members *and* accountability practices for managers and leaders, holding them responsible for progress toward equity. Equity calls for the righting of systemic and structural injustices. To achieve equity and other benefits of inclusion, it is important to discuss and elevate practices that can move us from diversity to equity.

Notes

1 Jones, K. P., Peddie, C. I., Gilrane, V. L., King, E. B., & Gray, A. L. (2016). Not so subtle: A meta-analytic investigation of the correlates of subtle and overt discrimination. *Journal of Management, 42*(6), 1588–1613.

2 Kurdi, B., Seitchik, A. E., Axt, J. R., Carroll, T. J., Karapetyan, A., Kaushik, N., Tomezsko, D., Greenwald, A. G., & Banaji, M. R. (2018). Relationship between the Implicit Association Test and intergroup behavior: A meta-analysis. *American Psychologist, 74*(5), 569–586.

3 National Science Foundation. (2014). *Has employment of women and minorities in S&E jobs increased?* https://nsf.gov/nsb/sei/edTool/data/workforce-07.html

4 Daly, M., Hobijn, B., & Pedtke, J. H. (2017). Disappointing facts about the black-white wage gap. *FRBSF Economic Letter, 26*, 1–5. https://www.bls.gov/opub/mlr/2017/beyond-bls/the-unexplainable-growing-black-white-wage-gap.htm

5 Ibid, p. 4.

6 Tomaskovic-Devey, D., Brummond, K., Han, J., & Davidson, S. (2012). *Private sector industry disparities: A report on evidence of systemic disparities for women, African Americans,*

Hispanics, Asians and Native Americans. Prepared for the U.S. Equal Employment Opportunity Commission. Center for Employment Equity. https://www.umass.edu/eeodatanet/private-sector-industry-disparities-report-evidence-systemic-disparities-women-african-americans

7 Charles, K. K., & Guryan, J. (2008). Prejudice and wages: An empirical assessment of Becker's the economics of discrimination. *Journal of Political Economy, 116*(5), 773–778.

8 Becker, G. S. (1971). *The economics of discrimination* (2nd ed.). University of Chicago Press.

9 Shwed, U., & Kalev, A. (2014). Are referrals more productive or more likeable? Social networks and the evaluation of merit. *American Behavioral Scientist, 58*(2), 288–308.

10 Ely, R. J., & Thomas, D. A. (2001). Cultural diversity at work: The effects of diversity perspectives on work group processes and outcomes. *Administrative Science Quarterly, 46*(2), 229–273; Thomas, D. A., & Ely, R. (1996). Making differences matter: A new paradigm for managing diversity. *Harvard Business Review, 74*(5), 79–90.

11 Becker, G. S. (2013). *The economic approach to human behavior*. University of Chicago Press.

12 Newkirk, P. (2019). *Diversity, Inc: The failed promise of a billion-dollar business*. Bold Type Books. (Emphasis in original, p. 15.)

13 Weisinger, J. Y., & Salipante, P. F. (2005). A grounded theory for building ethnically bridging social capital in voluntary organizations. *Nonprofit and Voluntary Sector Quarterly, 34*(1), 29–55.

14 Nishii, L. H. (2013). The benefits of climate for inclusion for gender-diverse groups. *Academy of Management Journal, 56*(6), 1754–1774; Nishii, L. H., Khattab, J., Shemla, M., & Paluch, R. M. (2018). A multi-level process model for understanding diversity practice effectiveness. *Academy of Management Annals, 12*(1), 37–82.

15 Rousseau, D. M. (2012). Envisioning evidence-based management. In D. M. Rousseau (Ed.), *The Oxford handbook of evidence-based management* (pp. 3–24). Oxford University Press.

16 Dobbin, F., & Kalev, A. (2016). Why diversity programs fail. *Harvard Business Review, July-August*, 1–8; Dobbin, F., Schrage, D., & Kalev, A. (2015). Rage against the iron cage: The varied effects of bureaucratic personnel reforms on diversity. *American Sociological Review, 80*(5), 1014–1044; Kalev, A., Dobbin, F., & Kelly, E. (2006). Best practices or best guesses? Assessing the efficacy of corporate affirmative action and diversity policies. *American Sociological Review, 71*(4), 589–617..

17 Ibid.

18 Ibid, p. 5.

19 Ibid, p. 5.

20 Esen, E. (2005). *Workplace diversity practices survey report*. Society for Human Resource Management.

21 Kalev et al. (2006). "Best practices or best guesses?"

22 Dobbin & Kalev (2016). "Why diversity programs fail."

23 Ibid, p. 2.

24 Ibid.

25 Ibid, p. 4.

26 Castilla, E. J. (2012). Gender, race, and the new (merit-based) employment relationship. *Industrial Relations: A Journal of Economy and Society, 51*(S1), 528–562.

27 Dobbin & Kalev (2016). "Why diversity programs fail."

28 Ibid, p. 4.

29 Paluck, E. L., Green, S. A., & Green, D. P. (2019). The contact hypothesis re-evaluated. *Behavioural Public Policy, 3*(2), 129–158; Pettigrew, T. F., & Tropp, L. R. (2006). A meta-analytic test of intergroup contact theory. *Journal of Personality and Social Psychology, 90*(5), 751–783.

30 Amis, J. M., Mair, J., & Munir, K. A. (2020). The organizational reproduction of inequality. *Academy of Management Annals, 14*(1), 195–230.

31 Castilla (2012). "Gender, race, and the new (merit-based) employment relationship."

32 Leslie, L. M., Mayer, D. M., & Kravitz, D. A. (2014). The stigma of affirmative action: A stereotyping-based theory and meta-analytic test of the consequences for performance. *Academy of Management Journal, 57*(4), 964–989.

33 Janssens, M., & Steyaert, C. (2019). A practice-based theory of diversity: Respecifying (in) equality in organizations. *Academy of Management Review, 44*(3), 518–537.

34 Bernstein, R. S., Bulger, M., Salipante, P., & Weisinger, J. Y. (2019). From diversity to inclusion to equity: A theory of generative interactions. *Journal of Business Ethics, 167*(3), 395–410.

35 Weisinger & Salipante (2005). "A grounded theory for building."

36 Roberson, Q. M. (2006). Disentangling the meanings of diversity and inclusion in organizations. *Group & Organization Management, 31*(2), 212–236.

37 Nishii, L. H. (2013). The benefits of climate for inclusion for gender-diverse groups. *Academy of Management Journal, 56*(6), 1754–1774.

38 Roberson (2006). "Disentangling the meanings of diversity and inclusion in organizations."

39 Adams, J. S. (1965). Inequity in social exchange. In L. Berkowitz (Ed.), *Advances in experimental social psychology* (Vol. 2, pp. 267–299). Elsevier.

1

DOING BETTER

Achieving equity and performance from diversity

How did we get where we are currently, and what represents a realistic and promising way forward? Diversity training has been a dominant approach. This chapter investigates the history of that training in the United States and provides an overview of knowledge gained from that history and this book's integration of research-based evidence. We identify often-hidden practices that impede diversity and inclusion and suggest how to counter them by concentrating on on-the-job behavior and organizational practices.

The ongoing evolution of diversity efforts

Rohini Anand and Mary-Frances Winters[1] have reviewed the evolution of corporate diversity training in the United States in a fashion that helps us understand the challenges and opportunities that now confront many societies. Their analyses of the period from the 1960s to the 2000s, summarized in this section, show the progression of training approaches—primarily in forward-thinking organizations—from a focus on compliance with equal employment opportunity/antidiscrimination laws to a contemporary focus on increasing numbers of underrepresented groups and creating inclusive organizational cultures for equity and organizational effectiveness. These analyses, combined with relatively recent research, help us in assessing their efficacy.

As Anand and Winters[2] specify, the challenge for U.S. organizations during the 1960s and 1970s was *compliance* with legal requirements for equal employment opportunity and, among government contractors, with Affirmative Action guidelines. During this time, the Black–White wage gap narrowed as Blacks made meaningful strides in education and wages rose among lower and middle classes.[3] During the 1980s, as women and minorities took advantage of new occupational opportunities, organizations took an *assimilation* perspective on the

DOI: 10.4324/9780367822484-3

integration of members of protected classes into new roles in the workplace. Training emphasized the need to support the adjustment of women and minorities to existing organizational cultures. The view was that they would learn to fit in with those cultures rather than the cultures changing to take better advantage of a diversity of members.

However, the concept of diversity expanded in the 1990s. Following a reduction in compliance enforcement by the U.S. federal government during the 1980s, some organizations voluntarily took on diversity. Diversity began to be seen as a demographic necessity, notably highlighted by the publication of the Hudson Institute's *Workforce 2000* in 1987.[4] Its statistics showed net new entrants into the labor market by 2000 being women, minorities, and immigrants. Affirmative Action had already plateaued in helping women and minorities. Furthermore, the labor market had begun to shift, with returns to labor—the wages and rewards that workers received—favoring high-skill jobs requiring college education or beyond. The result was increased inequality in the U.S. labor force. Groups such as Blacks, whose members were dominantly in lower-level jobs, regressed in their relative earnings despite increases in their educational attainment at the high school level.[5]

During the 1990s, it became clear that members of underrepresented groups were experiencing difficulties in advancing in their careers, and the focus of some organizations shifted to helping particular groups in corporate life. Also, the concept of diversity was broadened by incorporating secondary dimensions such as education and communication style. This expansion presented a concern, continuing today, that the focus on the most serious societal problems—ones associated with the visible differences of race, ethnicity, gender, age, and physical disabilities—were being diluted. Roosevelt Thomas made the case for "diversity" as imperative for business survival, noting that Affirmative Action alone was not designed for the long-term task of creating organizational cultures geared toward upward mobility of all kinds of employees, including White males. Anand and Winters suggest that despite diversity training that brought White males into the fold, "White men were not viewed as having valid issues about their place in the new more diverse workplace. They were primarily viewed as the problem and in need of 'fixing.'"[6]

Reactions to diversity training among majority group members were increasingly recognized as an issue. Although the focus on "diversity" was supposed to be different from compliance, in practice, many organizations combined them in training. Thus, training approaches were broad and varied in intensity and length. Diversity training backlash ensued against the backdrop of the Bakke case and concerns about "reverse discrimination." As we review later in the book, research revealed that Affirmative Action, as well as other organizational signals that minorities and women were the focus of efforts to improve their status, were associated with organizational members stereotyping and stigmatizing the women and minorities around them.[7] Anand and Winters[8] point out that some negative consequences of diversity training for these groups and the organization then began to be recognized, with a realization that stereotyping and stigmatizing lead to reduced self-confidence and performance among group members, and to loss of talent due to turnover and failure to advance. These negative aspects of diversity training do not mean that it must be avoided. Rather, as we discuss below based on substantial evidence, while training on its own should not be expected to produce attitude change that persists, it can lead to useful cognitive and behavioral learning.

Diversity training can be designed to contribute as one piece of a comprehensive program for diversity and inclusion.

Beyond training: Contemporary paradigms for managing diversity

A more recent focus in some organizations is that diversity can lead to learning that enables individuals and organizations to be adaptive. We see this view as representing what many have termed the *business case* for diversity. From the 1990s and continuing to the present, diversity training began to vary more across organizations in ways that roughly correspond to three paradigms that help to clarify the business case. The paradigms categorize differing organizational approaches to diversity:[9]

1. *discrimination and fairness*, focusing on equal opportunity and compliance;
2. *access and legitimacy*, celebrating differences to attract multicultural talent and serve diverse markets; and
3. *learning and effectiveness*, valuing different approaches to work that produce continual learning and greater organizational effectiveness.

The first paradigm reflects a compliance approach, with little attention to performance issues. We view the second and third paradigms as pursuing the business case, with the third paradigm constituting the strongest form of the case—an organizational focus on producing deeper, dynamic capabilities for improved performance and adaptation through diversity. This focus is tied to inclusion, which Anand and Winters define as "creating organizational environments that work for everyone."[10] As such, inclusion shifts the focus to benefits for all organizational members.

The intent is for all members, whether from majority or other groups, to learn to work with and gain valuable perspectives from others different from themselves, significantly transforming, in a positive way, the work being done. Anand and Winters note that, in training, the corresponding focus is the development of cross-cultural competence, defined as a:

> continuous learning process to develop knowledge, appreciation, acceptance and skills to be able to discern cultural patterns in your own and other cultures and be able to effectively incorporate several different world views into problem solving, decision making and conflict resolution (from Hewitt proprietary diversity training materials).[11]

In this view of the business case for diversity, learning is continual, ongoing. We note that identity plays a role, with the organization benefiting from members using particular parts of their distinctive identities to make contributions to organizational success.

> Through inclusion, or integration, the organization and all of its members benefit in terms of ongoing learning that produces greater effectiveness.

Historically, and continuing into the present, corporate initiatives on diversity have relied heavily upon training. However, serious questions have been raised about the efficacy of such training, especially training that is more cognitive and attitudinal than behavioral and skills focused. A meta-analytic review by Bezrukova, Spell, Perry, and Jehn[12] of over 250 studies found that the initial learning impacts on training participants were greater for cognitive learning (for instance, knowledge about other cultures) than for behavioral and attitudinal learning. Similarly, another meta-analytic review by Kalinoski, Steele-Johnson, Peyton, Leas, Steinke, and Bowling[13] of 65 studies found smaller impacts of diversity training on attitudinal outcomes than on cognitive- and skills-based outcomes. This review also investigated whether particular conditions in the training affected attitudinal outcomes, finding that social interaction in the form of task interdependence among participants during the training was strongly associated with positive attitudinal outcomes. Were the participants diverse, this finding is highly consistent with the view that particular types of structured interactions lead to prejudice reduction, as specified in our Framework.

A central concern for managers is whether learning that occurs during training carries over to actual behavior in workgroups. Does the learning translate into behavior that makes a difference in terms of inclusion?

> A central issue for managers is whether learning that occurs during training translates into changes in on-the-job behavior that make a difference in terms of inclusion.

Findings from the Bezrukova et al.'s[14] review are not encouraging. Only the cognitive learning was stable, while the smaller positive effects for attitudinal and behavioral learning decayed over time. These findings are not surprising since the difficulties associated with off-the-job training have been recognized for generations. For example, in the 1950s, human relations training designed to increase managers' considerateness toward their subordinates led on average to less, not more considerateness.[15] The explanation was that the trained managers became more aware of considerateness issues, then went back to their workgroups and emulated their own superiors' on-the-job behavior, with that behavior being low in considerateness. This finding bears an eerie resemblance to findings of backlash being associated with mandatory, short-term diversity training that attempts to deal with deep social and organizational culture issues.

The ability of diversity training to carry over to the job depends on the organizational and workgroup context. Extending from their systematic review of diversity training, Alhejji, Garavan, Carbery, O'Brien, and McGuire[16] proposed that an organization's dynamic capabilities affect this ability, with changes in job behavior depending on the organization's flexibility and its capacity to absorb new knowledge. At a more concrete level, the meta-analytic findings by Bezrukova et al.[17] indicated that training's learning effects were greater when the training was combined with other diversity initiatives, when it included skills development as well as awareness, and when it was conducted over an extended time.

> Diversity training's learning effects can be greater when the training is combined with other diversity initiatives, when it includes skills development as well as awareness, and when it is conducted over an extended time.

The review by Kalinoski et al.[18] similarly found stronger effects from extended training and also that training conducted by a direct manager/supervisor produced significant attitudinal outcomes, in contrast to a lack of attitudinal effects when the trainer was an internal staff member. These findings are consistent with the view that connections to the job and learning that extends over time support changes in behavior. When interpreting their findings, Bezrukova et al.[19] draw on contact theory, discussed in Chapter 6, by pointing to the role of interactions among a diverse group of members during extended training—sometimes, months-long—as leading to learning.

> Diversity training that includes diversity interactions extended over time is more effective in terms of learning.

The limitations of diversity training appear to be more severe than indicated by its effects on individuals' learning. Learning is but an intermediate step between training and the desired outcomes of improved organizational performance and greater equity for members of underrepresented groups. Examining changes over time (1971–2002) in the odds of women and minorities holding managerial jobs, analyses of data from over 800 organizations revealed that diversity training did not increase the odds for women and minorities, and it significantly decreased the odds for Black women.[20] In contrast to the null and negative effects of training, some other diversity initiatives—including diversity managers, enhanced recruitment efforts, and open posting of jobs—increased the odds for members of underrepresented groups to move into management.[21] Putting these findings on employment outcomes for underrepresented groups together with the historical evolution of training and findings from the body of studies on training, it is clear that heavy organizational reliance on diversity training, as commonly practiced, has been problematic in achieving equity and performance from diversity.

> Over-reliance on diversity training in organizations, as commonly practiced, has made achieving equity and performance from diversity challenging.

Combining business and social justice imperatives

Organizational problems with diversity extend beyond the limitations of training. As is evident from statistics showing slowed and plateaued progress for members of underrepresented groups, the business case for diversity has not advanced their benefits as much as was anticipated and claimed. The case was pursued not only through training, with its flaws, but also through other initiatives that have been conceived too simplistically. There were claims and beliefs that representational diversity, sometimes called workgroup heterogeneity, would lead to workgroup effectiveness in general, particularly where tasks involved creativity. As is detailed in Chapter 5, we now know from a large body of studies that representational diversity alone is as likely to lead to decrements as to increments in performances. Researchers examining workgroup performance are increasingly attributing the differences between poorer vs. improved performance from diversity to differing conditions in the workplace, including more vs. less collaborative conditions that affect whether diverse members are included in problem-solving, decision-making, and conflict resolution.

Put simply, representational diversity without inclusion is inadequate to achieve the business case. Nor is it adequate to achieve a *social justice case* for diversity, a case that recognizes historical societal impediments and its discriminatory legacy operating in the present. It is expected that nonprofit and public sector organizations would rely less on the business case and more on the social justice case. However, due to the strength and persistence of exclusionary social practices in our societies, a multipronged approach to diversity is necessary, one that focuses not only on representational diversity but also on antidiscrimination and inclusion.[22]

> A multipronged approach to diversity—one that focuses not only on representational diversity but also on antidiscrimination and inclusion—is necessary.

Increasingly, progressive for-profit organizations have been looking for ways to embrace the social justice case. This approach emphasizes procedural fairness, equity, equal opportunity, compliance, and enhanced individual and organizational learning.[23] In contrast, the commonly applied business case for diversity does not address intergroup inequality.[24] It focuses mostly on leveraging diversity differences to enhance organizational performance and pays less attention to the equity of rewards received.

By pursuing not only improved performance, but also social justice in terms of equitable treatment and rewards for all their members and learning and adaptation for the organization, we believe that organizations are more likely to effectively address issues of discrimination and inclusion and better achieve the business case.

And vice-versa: Organizations that focus on the social justice case, such as many nonprofit and governmental organizations, can gain from combining it with the business case to better ensure a focus on inclusion of diverse members in ways that benefit both those members and the organization's mission. Our Framework encompasses evidence-based practices to achieve, simultaneously, the business and social justice cases.

> Our evidence-based practices Framework helps to achieve, simultaneously, the business and social justice cases for diversity.

An emergent, refined understanding of inclusion

Organizational struggles with achieving performance and equity from diversity, whether through training or other efforts, have led to a focus on inclusion and to a more refined understanding of what inclusion is and requires. Most fundamentally, inclusion is understood as being part of an organization's culture,[25] embedded in the taken-for-granted ways that members act. Drawing on the work of several scholars, O'Donovan's contemporary review of diversity and inclusion emphasizes several aspects of a culture of inclusion. One aspect is a feeling of *belonging* among *all* employees:

> Inclusion concerns helping employees who do not feel that they belong to the mainstream of the organization to feel they belong, while also helping those employees who do feel they belong to continue to do so.[26]

Inclusion, then, deals with emotions. It involves efforts to draw in new members and create a sense of attachment and commitment while not alienating existing members who would otherwise resist diversity and inclusion. O'Donovan further specifies that the differences that individuals bring to the organization are "integrated into the very fabric of the organization's culture" (p. 74) and that inclusion is transient and operates at both the individual and organizational levels. We see these aspects of inclusion being facilitated by socialization practices, discussed below as part of workgroup members' adaptive learning. Particular types of socialization practices enable diverse newcomers to influence existing practices by bringing to bear their distinctive expertise and perspectives. The ability to do that depends on the organizational culture fostering flexibility and choice through particular types of behavior:[27] members valuing and using each other's ideas, partnering within and across departments, and exhibiting commitment to each other and to the organization's goals.

In ways that other treatments of inclusion do not, our Framework addresses these behaviors of inclusion in terms of workgroup *practices* that either impede or foster inclusive behavior. Some of the inclusive interaction practices in the

Framework represent the direct behaviors of inclusion, namely, comfortable interactions among individuals respected as having equal status in contributing to the organization's work. The Framework's other inclusive practices support and encourage that type of inclusive behavior. Through the design of tasks and operating procedures, they structure work and work roles such that various members mix frequently and have routine mechanisms for productively managing tensions that may arise among them.

The foregoing discussion of inclusion omits one important aspect of inclusion, an aspect noted in this book's preceding chapter as follows: fairly implemented employment practices and diversity-specific practices that recognize historical disparities and help to eliminate bias.[28] Inclusion in terms of everyday behavior in the organization's work will be meaningless to members of underrepresented groups if personnel practices of recruitment, pay, development, and promotion distribute rewards in inequitable ways common in history. Research reveals that such inequities in rewards remain persistent, rooted in decisions that involve implicit (largely unconscious) bias, discussed in Chapter 4, and in beliefs that our organizations operate as meritocracies, as critiqued below. Consequently, leaders' practical understanding of inclusion must include assessment of practices for holding managers accountable for their personnel decisions, practices that we incorporate within our Framework for Inclusive Interactions.

Integrating knowledge to guide inclusive practices in organizations

History, as discussed above, makes clear that organizations remain challenged in achieving diversity and inclusion. Diversity initiatives alone are inadequate to achieve the benefits of diversity. More comprehensive programs are required, containing multiple elements that favor members following *pro-inclusive practices* over anti-inclusive ones. This book brings together knowledge from several disciplines that inquire into the determinants and consequences of inclusive interactions. It further draws on several different contextual fields in which we have situated our own research on diversity: for-profit organizations, nonprofit organizations, public sector organizations, higher education, medicine, and mixed-income communities. That research enables us to illustrate how various phenomena revealed by research operate in a range of organizations.

When a problem is complex and persistent, as diversity and inclusion issues have proven to be, a transdisciplinary integration of knowledge is a highly valuable prerequisite for evidence-informed management (Box 1.1). Complex problems are multilevel, cutting across the levels of individuals, groups, and institutions. Each level is the primary focus of one social science discipline—respectively, psychology, social psychology, and sociology. Furthermore, complex problems are sensitive to differing contexts in terms of varying industries, workforces, and societal events. For managers, being evidence-informed means being knowledgeable about phenomena and opportunities at multiple levels.

BOX 1.1: A TRANSDISCIPLINARY REVIEW FOR EVIDENCE-INFORMED MANAGEMENT

This book draws on empirical findings and well-supported theories from multiple disciplines and organizational settings. Our goal is not to collect and analyze a readily definable body of literature, as in a systematic review of material from a single discipline.[29] Rather, we seek to identify a range of bodies of knowledge known to us, as management researchers, from our own and other academic disciplines' differing fields of research focus. As a creative enterprise, the review can make no claim to being comprehensive. Rather, the review's contribution is a *cross-disciplinary synthesis* in the form of a framework to guide practical, feasible managerial action. Such a transdisciplinary review is defined by several characteristics:[30]

1. Inquiring into a specified phenomenon—here, how exclusion and inclusion are produced at the interpersonal, group, and organizational levels;
2. Integrating the reviewers' (authors) varying perspectives into the constructive process of the inquiry;
3. Crossing paradigms rather than remaining within one paradigm;
4. Viewing the central phenomenon—inclusive interactions—and its composite subphenomena—overcoming anti-inclusive forces and generating adaptive learning—as a complex system with rich and problematic interrelationships.

To bolster the rigor and validity of evidence that managers and researchers can use in an evidence-informed approach, we focused on systematic reviews of entire bodies of research on key topics that inform our Framework. Systematic reviews increase validity by drawing together as much relevant empirical research as can be located, rather than authors picking and choosing which research studies to include. Systematic reviews are also capable of producing knowledge about questions not addressed by the individual studies—such as whether particular features of a context influence a finding—by comparing findings across an entire set of studies. We combined the knowledge from many systematic reviews conducted in various disciplines and contexts with findings from our own past research and with newly conducted interviews of managers and professionals from the private, nonprofit, and public sectors. Some interviewees were in positions having specific responsibility for diversity, equity, and inclusion, while most were on the firing line—line managers, executives, and internal consultants. Throughout this book, pseudonyms are used to identify all interviewees to protect their identity.

According to the principles of *evidence-informed management*,[31] research-based evidence should be combined with local knowledge:

1. the decision-maker's experience;
2. the problem context, which here refers to the decision-maker's local situation; and
3. diagnostic evidence from the problem context.

This means that there are many ways to apply our Framework, presented in detail in Chapter 2, and its six inclusive interaction practices, described in Chapter 3, to create an effective program. Effective application calls for local knowledge and creativity to apply the evidence-based conceptual knowledge in the Framework to the actual situation.

> We intend to produce knowledge for evidence-informed use by line and staff managers, executives, and researchers—use that realistically reflects the complexities of diversity and inclusion while guiding improved approaches for achieving equity and performance.

What have we learned?

The transdisciplinary synthesis of research-based evidence detailed in Chapters 4 through 8 draws together the knowledge that experts in various disciplines have put forward. Our synthesis of this knowledge provides cogent explanations for the historical challenges with diversity, equity, and inclusion that organizations have experienced and is substantiated by numerous contemporary statistics on the persistence of large racial, ethnic and gender disparities. We can think of these challenges as residing in social and organizational practices that enable inequitable disparities to be reproduced again and again over time.

The essence of the explanation for the ongoing reproduction of disparities is the continuing presence and operation of what we label throughout this book as *anti-inclusive practices*. These practices create a self-fulfilling prophecy that particular other groups are incapable of or not worthy of career success. Chapter 4 pursues these exclusionary practices in greater depth. Here, consider a partial accounting for how various exclusionary practices interact in the form of a vicious cycle that repeats over time.

An anti-inclusive practice that appears to permeate all societies is self-segregating, where we most often choose to associate with individuals similar to ourselves. By reducing interactions with different others, we remain unfamiliar with them. Lack of familiarity is then expressed in the second anti-inclusive practice, interacting with discomfort and anxiety. For members of some underrepresented groups, anxiety is likely to be well-founded in terms of past experiences of discriminatory treatment and exclusion from valuable interactions. Whatever its source, unfamiliarity or self-protection, discomfort serves to perpetuate our self-segregating. Lack of interaction with individuals from particular groups enables the continuance of the third anti-inclusive practice—stereotyping and stigmatizing those whose visible and cultural characteristics lead some to see them as members of low-status groups or that they are in competition with them. That stigmatizing impedes our ability to collaborate effectively with different others and induces anxieties in those others, hampering their ability to perform up to their talents. Furthermore, that stereotyping and stigmatizing underlie the continuance of the fourth anti-inclusive practice, using implicit bias to make decisions, particularly personnel decisions affecting the equity of rewards. In recent decades we have learned from numerous research studies that subtle discrimination emanating from largely unconscious, implicit bias is ubiquitous. Humans use a process of categorizing each other as a frequently functional way to make their interactions efficient and safe. Dysfunctional categorizing takes the form of inappropriate application of negative stereotypes, ones that can be held quite unconsciously. Frequently, these stereotypes are associated with emotions of competition or fear, arousing prejudice toward particular individuals that we encounter, simply based on their surface characteristics. We have learned that this dysfunctional categorizing is embedded and expressed in everyday social practices in organizations—in interpersonal interactions and in managerial personnel decisions, producing inequitable decisions on performance evaluations, developmental opportunities, and promotions.

Over time, the interplay of the four anti-inclusive practices represents a vicious cycle that reproduces unjust disparities in organizations, crowding underrepresented groups into low-status jobs and slowing advancement to higher status positions. Furthermore, as an additional spur to the reproduction of inequalities at a societal level, those disparities within organizations create disincentives for members of underrepresented groups to invest in education or pursue careers in higher status occupations.

In effect, the challenge at the organizational level comes down to two phenomena: (1) problems with interpersonal interactions due to self-segregation, interaction anxieties, and stereotyping and stigmatizing and (2) the operation of implicit bias in managers' personnel decisions. So, why have these not been better identified and addressed in organizations? What are the sources of a de facto complacency in tackling underlying problems? On this issue, research is beginning to make some headway but it is still quite speculative. Based on emerging findings about bias in personnel decisions and a failure of current accountability practices, some researchers are pointing to beliefs that are widely held by managers and much of the public in developed economies but that, to some degree, are myths.[32] The first myth is about organizational efficiency being assured by market forces. If decision-makers consistently exercise a taste for discrimination,[33] as through the operation of pervasive implicit bias in hiring and wage decisions, there is, in effect, collusion rather than competition[34] among organizations regarding the utilization of underrepresented groups in the labor market. The second myth is about the existence of a meritocracy, in which human resource management practices are supposed to ensure that rewards are allocated according to performance-based merit. However, research over several decades has consistently indicated that members of underrepresented groups do not receive hiring and performance evaluation outcomes that are equitable compared to others who have the same qualifications and performance. The strength of those research findings clearly identifies the belief in meritocracy as a myth. The third myth concerns globalization being a positive force that lifts all boats. This is counter-indicated by the actions of multinational organizations that favor members of economically dominant cultures and exploit other labor. The three beliefs can be understood as creating a view among organizational leaders and policymakers that the existing institutional conditions in their economies are legitimate. That legitimacy contributes to their continuing to make decisions, including how diversity and inclusion are pursued, that enable anti-inclusive practices to be under-identified, reproducing inequities.

For managers and policymakers who are now more aware and ready to address shortcomings in their organizations' pursuit of inclusion, we have learned from recent research that there are organizational practices and programs that can interrupt the vicious cycle of anti-inclusive practices. Many of these, such as expanded recruitment, were discussed in the Introduction. Most intriguing, perhaps, are programs that are not aimed at diversity for underrepresented groups but, rather, as inclusion for organizational members in general, such as cross-job training and cross-functional, semi-autonomous teams, including international teams. With managerial commitment to address on-the-job practices and decisions, progress can resume. We illustrate that with a case in the section below, titled, "A Practical Case about Changing Practices."

A more promising way forward

For organizations to advance beyond the bounds of currently common diversity efforts, we suggest that managers (and researchers) frame their thinking along the lines of four basic questions:

1. What is needed to produce behavioral change on the job?
2. How can equity and performance be pursued without stimulating anti-inclusive practices?
3. What is the nature of individual learning and competence about diversity that sustains equity and performance?
4. How can synergies for inclusion be realized from efforts at both workgroup and organizational levels?

To outline a new path forward, we consider our answers to each of these questions in turn.

Question: What produces behavioral change on the job?
Answer: Culture change through practices shaping social behavior.

The recognition that racial, ethnic, gender, and other disparities result from deep-seated social phenomena has increased in many societies. Addressing the ways that these societal realities invade organizations is central to managers succeeding with diversity. Consequently, effective managerial action is aided by a realization that the pursuit of inclusion involves change at a deep, cultural level in organizations. As described by Stella Nkomo,[35] inclusion reflects basic assumptions, understood as theories-in-use that underpin the habitual practices followed every day by organizational members. We agree with the view that inclusion resides at the deep level of organizational culture; however, we do critique and challenge the implications for organizational change that have been offered regarding how to achieve inclusion. The focus on mental models leads to reliance on educational approaches. This seems to be, especially for academics whose lives revolve around education, the most direct way to address assumptions. We want to make people aware of their beliefs that underpin their everyday practice, changing their beliefs so that they change their behavior. However, as discussed above, we know from research and experience that awareness training often produces negative reactions and that the net effect of diversity training as commonly carried out is either null or negative for some underrepresented groups in terms of their representation in managerial positions.

We propose a different approach, one that is more promising based on research evidence from our own research and more broadly from research on key behavior theories. In this book, culture and the assumptions underpinning it are seen as residing in social practices, in what individuals *do together*. This perspective and its underlying theory, discussed in Chapter 6, separate what people *are*—their views of themselves—from what they *do* with others in particular contexts. From this view, what is important is *practice*, the behavior that people habitually exhibit when they are together in a particular situation. This perspective accords with managerial interest in learning about "best practices"—for example, practices for continuous quality improvement or agile software development—effective practices for the tasks in their particular functional areas. The bottom-line for diversity and inclusion is what happens on the job every day when tasks are performed and more occasionally when decisions are made that involve individuals' development and advancement. As Nkomo states:

> At the group level, we might infer the existence of inclusiveness by how the group draws on and uses its diversity to perform tasks, using the talents of all its members.[36]

Leaders and managers can assess inclusion by asking themselves: Are all workgroup members guided by prevailing, routinized practices in the workplace such that they include and engage all their coworkers and make personnel decisions that are fair and equitable?

A common challenge to this practice-oriented approach is that individuals will not change their behavior in ways that are at odds with their fundamental beliefs. If this is so, the result will be constant resistance to new practices. However, proceeding from research-based evidence, we propose the power of social contexts to shape behavior and, over time, to alter the implicit understandings that guide that behavior. Everyday experience supports this view since, as members of complex, modern societies, we behave somewhat differently in the various social contexts that we experience—being with our parents, or our children, or at work, or in a religious ceremony or a civic, political setting. We can be who we are while behaving in concert with norms for interaction that vary across those settings. The two bodies of research that we rely upon for this view and discuss further in Chapter 6 are contact theory and cognitive dissonance theory. Studies testing contact theory indicate that repeated interactions with others different from oneself, under particular conditions, lead over time to prejudice reduction. Cognitive dissonance theory is well-supported in its insight that individuals justify their behavior by adjusting their attitudes to fit that behavior. When workgroup practices continually shape organizational members' behavior to be inclusive, we can expect attitudes consistent with inclusion to follow.

Q: How can managers pursue diversity without stimulating anti-inclusive behavior?
A: Emphasizing pro-inclusive practices that benefit all.

Taking what has been learned from Affirmative Action and diversity training efforts, we know that a major challenge facing organizations is how to successfully leverage diversity without engendering the backlash and stigmatizing that results from some members feeling that underrepresented groups are being favored.

> Organizations and workgroups should treat diversity training as a supplement to initiatives that emphasize practices for inclusion and accountability, rather than seeing such practices as supplements to diversity training. The practices for inclusion and accountability that managers can ensure include engaging frequently in comfortable, respectful, collaborative, conflict-handling, task-productive mixing with their various coworkers.

That stigmatizing of their coworkers from underrepresented groups then results in lower performance due to several effects noted earlier in this chapter. One approach to this challenge is to treat diversity training as a supplement to initiatives that emphasize inclusion and accountability practices, rather than seeing such practices as supplements to diversity training. While common diversity training essentially sees the challenge as residing in the individual, leading to negative reactions from some individuals, a practice approach sees the problem as social. That approach does not ask people to change who they are but, rather, what they do in particular organizational circumstances. Rather than engaging in self-segregating, stereotyping, and stigmatizing practices, managers can ensure (as we have discovered through our interviews that some do) that workgroup members frequently engage in comfortable, respectful, collaborative, conflict-handling, task-productive mixing with their various coworkers. Managers can ask for this social behavior on the basis of either the business imperative or the moral imperative or, better, both. The business case can be framed as requiring the inclusion of all members and as producing benefits for all members, not only reducing the perceptions of a competitive threat but also motivating managers to promote inclusive practices. In some organizations, as Deirdre O'Donovan puts it:

> It is likely that only business reasons, specifically reasons that highlight potential improvements in the organization's bottom line, will result in the long-term motivation critical to managing diversity.[37]

This book's focus on inclusion and accountability practices provides a way to finesse issues of backlash and stigmatizing, countering these anti-inclusive practices with pro-inclusive ones. As we discuss further in the next two chapters and illustrate with a case about changing practices later in this chapter and additional cases in Chapter 9, the inclusion and accountability approach involves (a) focusing on inclusion as applying to and benefiting all members; (b) identifying practices, such as constructive conflict management, that foster inclusion and are promoted as being the basis for strong workgroup and team performance; and (c) achieving accountability through social practices that hold all members to inclusive norms for behavior that raise workgroup performance and managers to decision-making procedures that control bias. (See Box 1.2 for a case example illustrating practices for inclusion that benefit all members.)

A critique for a practice-oriented approach is that it is unrealistic to presume that deeply embedded social practices can be changed through managerial action, that the practices such as frequent mixing specified in our Framework can be implemented. However, much organizational experience proves the contrary, as do various bodies of research, our own past research, and the reports of managers interviewed for this book. Many organizational programs that specify particular interaction practices have been widely and successfully adopted by organizations, locally and globally, programs that fundamentally changed the ways in which members carried out their jobs. These include quality improvement programs, cross-functional training, international virtual teams, and teams for agile software development. Furthermore, key elements of all these programs are inclusive practices to ensure that members contribute to team performance. These past organizational successes provide confidence that, with organizational and managerial commitment (discussed below), programs involving inclusive practices are readily feasible.

Organizational and managerial commitment to programs involving inclusive practices is readily feasible.

BOX 1.2: A CASE OF INTERNATIONAL JOINT VENTURES WITH DIVERGENT RESULTS

A comparison of three international joint ventures between American and Japanese companies[38] illustrates key phenomena that we discuss in subsequent chapters of the book and demonstrates the feasibility and potency of practices for inclusion that benefit all members, as specified in our Framework:

1. pursuing a *shared task* orientation or mission;
2. *mixing* members frequently and repeatedly;
3. *collaborating* with member interdependence;
4. *handling conflict* constructively;
5. engaging in interpersonal *comfort* and *self-efficacy*; and
6. ensuring *equal insider status* for all members.

The comparison across the ventures also shows that representational diversity—that is, simply emphasizing demographic representation in a workgroup—is insufficient to benefit from diversity. Rather, instituting seemingly mundane interaction practices that apply to and benefit all members can make a dramatic difference in achieving success.

The three early-stage joint ventures—JVA, JVB, and JVC—were in the Midwest of the United States. They each had nearly equal ownership by the American and Japanese partners. The partners sought to learn from each other's manufacturing technologies and expand their reach into new markets. In terms of the practices specified in our Framework, the joint ventures started with the advantage of the first two practices: an important shared purpose and opportunities for frequent mixing of American and Japanese technical personnel on the job. However, JVA and JVB experienced significant cross-cultural tensions. Their contact experiences led the American engineers and technicians to create stereotypes of their Japanese counterparts as sometimes untrustworthy and less competent. These negative characterizations exactly fit the two dimensions specified by a body of research on stereotypes discussed in Chapter 4,[39] lack of warmth and lack of competence. More importantly, the stereotypes illustrate the operation of categorization. As captured by the categorization-elaboration model presented in Chapter 5,[40] the negative *categorizations* impeded the *elaboration* (surfacing and sharing) of knowledge for decision-making, undermining the learning goal of the venture. In sharp contrast, JVC's technical personnel said that accounts of such cross-cultural tensions and impediments to performance in JVA and JVB were "unrealistic" in their experience and did not accurately characterize Japanese technical personnel. The question for both conceptual understanding and for managerial practice then becomes: What was different about JVC that accounts for successful collaboration and lack of prejudice? Why did Americans in JVC make different sense of their interactions and develop different understandings of their Japanese counterparts than Americans in JVA and JVB?

The answer lies in the everyday behavior, the interaction practices, experienced by the personnel in JVC, and the productive relationships that resulted from these practices. Particular practices for conflict-handling and collaboration in JVC turned the types of cultural collisions that occurred in all three joint ventures into productive and learning experiences rather than into tensions that impeded learning. JVC's practices kept the focus on the technical issues of manufacturing performance rather than on the personal character of the other party. The key practices were two-fold:

1. A morning meeting (each morning) to set agendas and address issues from the preceding day.
2. "Running a trial" as a procedure for resolving differences in proposals for addressing a particular production problem. Sometimes this involved the practice of "prototyping," creating two different prototypes corresponding to differing proposals for a piece of machinery, then seeing which worked better.

It is difficult to say that one of these practices was for conflict-handling and the other for collaborating with interdependence. Rather, the combination of the two accomplished conflict-handling and collaborating. How the personnel handled conflict (their engineering differences) was how they collaborated, and vice-versa. This combination embedded a *joint problem-solving* focus in the interactions across the national cultures. The workplace culture was inclusive due to the evolution of practices that addressed tensions constructively, rapidly, and with a results focus. At JVC, the practices of the morning meeting and running engineering trials were ways of collaborating comfortably, respectfully, interdependently, and productively, achieving the practices of interacting comfortably and with equal status specified in our Framework.

At JVC, an engineering culture evolved that was a hybrid of the two national cultures, permitting situated learning[41] as they *engaged jointly* with each other in their work tasks. The parallel is striking to the case of a Finnish organization's international technical personnel discussed in Chapter 6. There, the members developed interaction practices that enabled them to use code-switching (switching into a mother tongue not understood by others present) to better solve technical problems without inciting the interpersonal tensions associated with code-switching in other organizations.[42]

The interaction practices at JVC produced understandings of appropriate behavior for which individuals can be held accountable. While practices for inclusive interactions and for accountability are depicted in our Framework as separate, for simplicity's sake, the JVC case suggests that they are favorably linked when inclusive interactions are achieved. At JVC, American personnel developed tacit understandings about Japanese members' behaviors that were characteristic of and appropriate within Japanese culture and within the joint venture workplace. When Americans at JVC were presented with scenarios (anonymized) of cultural collisions recounted by Americans at other joint ventures, the JVC members noted that the behavior characterized of particular Japanese personnel was aberrant, an individual, personality characteristic rather than a cultural characteristic. From their own direct, positive interaction experiences, Americans at JVC understood the behavior to be inappropriate within Japanese culture. The members at JVC, but not those at JVA and JVB, had engaged in adaptive learning that diminished negative stereotyping and taught them the nature of productive, inclusive behavior that was appropriate and expected in their diverse workplace. Through an effective combination of practices for interaction and accountable behavior, the result was better achievement of the venture's learning goal. Cultural collisions were not impediments but, rather, opportunities for two types of learning—social and technical—and, as a consequence, higher workgroup effectiveness that benefited all members.

Q: What learning about diversity sustains equity and performance?
A: Adaptive learning through inclusive practices.

Whether for diversity and inclusion or any other change in organizational culture, a practice-oriented approach requires learning. Workgroup members need to learn the interaction skills and behaviors that enable them to follow the practices. Developing the skills and behaviors that are adapted to the inclusive practices requires time. As discussed in Chapter 6, findings from the large body of studies on contact across differing individuals indicate that the practices that we have labeled as inclusive favor the reduction of prejudices over time.[43] Similarly, high frequencies of such contact, termed diversity interactions, that are positive result not only in reduced prejudiced behavior—that is, in more inclusion—but also in personal development of broader skills, including leadership skills.[44] In effect, adaptive learning produces benefits for the organization in terms of performance-enhancing inclusive behavior, consistent with the learning and integration paradigm of diversity noted above, but also produces benefits for all members in terms of interaction and leadership skills.

Learning new practices involves socialization, as discussed in Chapter 6. Members adapt to new sets of inclusive practices guided and modeled by their managers and, initially, by the inclusive behavior of some coworkers more than others. As socialization proceeds, they develop routines involving behavior specific to situations that arise in their particular work context. For example, in an international organization, members developed inclusive communication practices about language "code-switching" to prevent some team members from becoming defensive when other team members had to switch into their native tongue in order to understand and discuss a particular technical issue.[45] Practices such as these evolve as tasks and membership morph over time. For new members, *personal-identity socialization*[46]—a form of socialization that emphasizes the incoming member's personal identity and the distinctive contributions that the individual can make given their particular expertise and perspectives—hastens their socialization and their adaptive learning. Perhaps more importantly, the new skills, knowledge, and views that incoming members bring, when activated by the existing inclusive practices in the workgroup, contribute to the further evolution of those practices. In this way, the nature of inclusion being for all and ever-developing is sustained by the addition and personal-identity socialization of new members. This approach is an improvement over the decades-old pursuit of assimilation. Instead, there is *enculturation* that takes advantage of the talents of newcomers.

Adaptive learning involves a fundamental change in perspective that stems from what the organizational members actually, habitually do—what they are to do according to the norms embedded in the practice. The learning is adaptive in three senses: The nature of the skills and behavior learned are adapted to the inclusive practices; the learning enables members to adapt to each other across their differences; and the workgroup and organization adapt to new task, technology, and market changes.

Much of adaptive learning resides in tacit knowledge, knowing how to behave in a social context in order to appear competent to others and accomplish a desired end, termed *practical consciousness* by Anthony Giddens.[47] The learning is dominantly experiential, gained through experience rather than cognitive learning. Consider cultural competence, described (as noted above) by Anand and Winters in part as an individual "being able to discern cultural patterns in your own and other cultures."[48] This implies that the culturally competent individual possesses cognitive knowledge about other cultures' ways of thinking and acting, a view found in the scholarly literature on cultural differences. Our own research in international joint ventures[49] reveals that, in work settings, cultural competence does not reside in cognitive learning about the mental models of other cultures, as might be emphasized in some cross-cultural training. Rather, cultural competence resides in the interaction practices that members use in their daily work. Competence lies in developing and following particular practices, such as a daily team meeting and practices for language code-switching, that enable differences to arise and be dealt with productively. This competence-through-practices is hence both individual and collective.

> Training and workgroup norms that focus on behavioral practices for effective cross-cultural interaction, rather than on mental understandings of another culture, are important tools for adaptive learning in the form of cultural competence.

Socialization is never complete. Adaptive learning of inclusive behavior requires continual reinforcement. As recounted by one of our interviewees, in his organization team members were held accountable for respectful, inclusive behavior toward others by managers and fellow members calling out inappropriate behavior. They reminded the transgressing members to pay attention to values statements on their employee badges that specified mission-appropriate behavior. In a case of persistent transgressions, members can be transferred or dismissed.

In adaptive learning that occurs through following inclusive practices, consistent with both the business and social justice cases for diversity, the emphasis is on learning how to function well and respectfully together, what to *do* together, not on how one should think. An analogy from everyday life exhibits this phenomenon: Consider how some parents successfully deal with a child's inappropriate behavior. Rather than attempting to discern the child's mental models, "psych out" the child, figuring out what they must be thinking and then directly challenging that thinking, they use practices, such as modeling desirable behavior and using "time-outs" and explanations of the value of appropriate behavior. The first approach typically incites continued resistance while the latter contributes to the child gradually learning alternative ways to behave. In a work setting, one of our interviewees emphasized how young engineers new to their workgroups were able to learn appropriate inclusive behavior. However, if you were to ask them to articulate the *reasons* for that behavior, they would not be able to explain it.

For inclusion to continually evolve to reflect changes in personnel, markets, and technology, adaptive learning should be ongoing. This nature of adaptive learning can aid managers in timing particular diversity and inclusion efforts. In this regard, a key question is whether and how adaptive learning about inclusion generalizes. Studies on contact theory do indicate such generalizing, from one "other" group to another, to a degree. However, in particular contexts, learning that enables an individual to adapt to some groups may be easier than adapting to other groups. An example from one of our interviews concerned international teams in a technical field. A North American–based organization placed female managers in leadership roles on these teams. Team members across a number of countries had relatively little difficulty adapting to their ethnic differences, but gender differences were more challenging. Male team members in one country created high tensions due to an unfamiliarity (to put it nicely) in dealing with women in superior organizational positions. Organizations that recognize such challenges to adaptive learning might have some situations where they can stage inclusion such that the inclusive behaviors are embedded, starting with locally easier differences. Managers can then request training for their teams that is specialized to issues and behavioral skills for dealing with the inclusion of the particular, less-easy differences. Whether customized training is used or not, the need for members to adapt to more challenging differences can be emphasized as consistent with the already-embedded behavioral practices of inclusion, such as exhibiting comfortable, interdependent collaboration and, as one interviewee put it, members learning to leave their biases at the door when they walk into the building.

Q: How can synergies for inclusion be created?
A: Through mutually reinforcing managerial and organization-level initiatives.

Pursuing diversity and inclusion through establishing workgroup practices can be initiated and sustained at two levels: the workgroup and the organization as a whole. Combining and coordinating action at both levels can be most potent, with an eye on the workgroup level as primary. The workgroup is where inclusion must be practiced by workgroup members and managers. When organization-wide diversity initiatives, such as diversity training, fail to change behavior in workgroups, those initiatives can be deemed as failures. In contrast, as we discovered from the interviews for this book, a primary focus on the workgroup level can be liberating for individual managers concerned with performance and equity. Within their span of discretion workgroup managers can institute inclusive interaction practices, those specified in our Framework, in terms of how the workgroup is structured and tasks are pursued. For instance, one of our managerial interviewees had created three semi-autonomous teams, repeatedly reinforced norms on how their members would interact and make decisions, and established procedures to coordinate interdependent activities within and across the teams. These practices established not only inclusive treatment for all members but also a record of world-leading performance in their professional field.

> Individual managers can take the initiative and seize opportunities to achieve higher performance and equity from diversity in their workgroups.

Examples such as this, and the case presented immediately below, indicate that top management support is not a *necessary* precondition for success in establishing inclusion in particular workgroups. Accordingly, our Framework is designed for application at the workgroup level as well as the organizational level. However, thoughtful action by top management can encourage effective initiatives by workgroup managers and help to spread successful initiatives more widely throughout the organization. O'Donovan outlines a repetitive four-stage process for diversity management and learning at the organizational level: (1) analysis that assesses diversity throughout the organization; (2) planning that establishes key objectives for diversity and communication to increase member buy-in; (3) implementation that concentrates on the accomplishment of organizational objectives, in part by identifying policies and procedures in need of change; and (4) monitoring and evaluation that tracks the success of revised and new procedures.[50]

This process is well-suited to supporting and learning from bottom-up efforts by individual managers. With resource support from top management, such as worker training on interactions skills that is specialized to the workgroup's particular functional area, such as sales,[51] those managers most committed to producing diversity and inclusion's benefits can take the lead in instituting inclusive practices in their workgroups, such as interdependent reliance on each other's expertise, and in making equitable personnel decisions. Top management can then critically evaluate the levels of success achieved, identifying effective practices, and promoting these practices and the managers who initiated them. From these experiences, managers at both workgroup and organizational levels can share the knowledge they have gained, not only with others in their organization but also with colleagues in their field, spreading the knowledge to other organizations in their industry or sector.[52] The process becomes one of top management supported experiential learning, adjustment, and scaling up of successes, with workgroup managers and specialized support staff, such as organization development specialists and industrial counselors, able to exercise discretion to achieve performance and equity goals. This process mirrors how effective practices in other domains—such as scrums for agile software development—have been refined and customized to achieve success at the workgroup level.

A practical case about changing practices

As an illustration of practical progress on both equity and performance that results from addressing interaction practices on-the-job, consider a case involving a program for cross-functional collaboration. In this case of a bottom-up initiative, presented in more detail in Chapter 10, operations staff analyzed that women and underrepresented group members were crowded into support groups with much lower status than the mainly White male scientific professionals in their division of the organization. On the basis of performance difficulties, the internal consultants from the division's operations unit sold top administrators on creating a task force to address problematic interactions between the professionals and support staff. The task force's membership was diverse in terms of ethnicity, race, gender, and job function. Such a task force corresponds well with the types of cross-functional collaboration that a study of more than 800 organizations has revealed to lead to the progression of women and minorities into managerial positions.[53] Over the course of a year the task force in the scientific group met to produce a set of recommendations to increase cross-functional effectiveness. However, according to the consultant who approached us after hearing about our focus on inclusion, it was the process of task force members with different backgrounds using inclusive interaction practices (as specified in our Framework) that produced improved, more functional interactions and relationships. On-the-job interaction practices that displayed respect for individuals across the workgroups were formed in the task force, representing the development of inclusion among the diverse members. During and after completion of the task force's formal efforts, the practices of inclusion started among members of the task force spread to other members of the various workgroups. The practices shaped on-the-job behavior that was more inclusive.

Highly pragmatic managerial action can counter anti-inclusive practices to produce inclusive treatment and career development of diverse individuals, simultaneous with improved effectiveness for the organization.

We can also see that this successful first step needs to be followed by a process that spreads it to other organizational units. That scaling up will depend on continuing top management support, in this particular case, predicated primarily on the business case. And follow-up monitoring would be needed to assure that rewards were being equitably distributed.

The periods required for inclusion vary with the organizational level, as suggested by this case. At the level of the diverse task force itself, interactions became more comfortable and inclusive in about six months. The spread of those interactions to other members of the division took additional months, and the still-to-be-done scaling up may require several years if similar task forces are formed in other divisions. Only at the end of that process can the organization be judged to have achieved embedded practices that represent an inclusive culture, a culture that will continue to evolve as members come and go and technologies and tasks change.

A major impediment to leveraging diversity is that the interaction and decision-making practices that were identified by internal consultants as problematic and in need of remedy in this case are typically not recognized as the source of inequities. The everyday practices of non-inclusive interaction—self-segregation, uncomfortable interactions, stereotyping and stigmatizing, and making decisions influenced by implicit bias—are subtle rather than blatant forms of discrimination. Being unconscious or taken-for-granted by many individuals, everyday practices have tended to fly "under the radar" of most diversity and inclusion efforts. Knowledge of their impact is critically important. That knowledge opens the door to effective efforts since, once they are identified, managers are in a position to change the anti-inclusive social practices in their organizations. However, as confirmed by the limited success of historical efforts at improving diversity and inclusion, and as illustrated by the case above, changing these seemingly mundane practices requires more than good intentions and educational approaches. Effective change efforts benefit from managerial action that is informed by analysis within the organization, by the experience of other organizations in a field, and by research-based evidence on effective workgroup practices.

While continuing research can make a larger impact on organizations by being more applied and focused on interactions and personnel decisions, we already know enough to do far better than in the past. At the same time, managerial action and research should be cognizant of the complexities of diversity and inclusion but also sufficiently straightforward to be implemented, refined, and accepted by the wide range of members typical in organizations. In the next chapter, we portray what we already know in a convenient framework designed to guide effective managerial action. The Framework captures the most potent complexities yet identifies a practical way forward, a way that promises to revitalize progress in an area sorely needed in our societies.

Notes

1 Anand, R., & Winters, M.-F. (2008). A retrospective view of corporate diversity training from 1964 to the present. *Academy of Management Learning & Education*, 7(3), 356–372.
2 Ibid.
3 Bayer, P., & Charles, K. K. (2018). Divergent paths: A new perspective on earnings differences between black and white men since 1940. *The Quarterly Journal of Economics*, 133(3), 1459–1501.
4 Johnston, W. B., & Packer, A. E. (1987). *Workforce 2000: Work and workers for the 21st century*. Hudson Institute.
5 Bayer & Charles (2018). "Divergent Paths."
6 Anand & Winters (2008). "A retrospective view of corporate diversity training," p. 359.
7 Leslie, L. M., Mayer, D. M., & Kravitz, D. A. (2014). The stigma of affirmative action: A stereotyping-based theory and meta-analytic test of the consequences for performance. *Academy of Management Journal*, 57(4), 964–989.
8 Anand & Winters (2008). "A retrospective view of corporate diversity training."
9 Thomas, D. A., & Ely, R. (1996). Making differences matter: A new paradigm for managing diversity. *Harvard Business Review*, 74(5), 79–90.
10 Anand & Winters (2008). "A retrospective view of corporate diversity training," p. 362.
11 Ibid, p. 362.
12 Bezrukova, K., Spell, C., Perry, J., & Jehn, K. (2016). A meta-analytical integration of over 40 years of research on diversity training evaluation. *Psychological Bulletin*, 142(11), 1227–1274.
13 Kalinoski, Z. T., Steele-Johnson, D., Peyton, E. J., Leas, K. A., Steinke, J., & Bowling, N. A. (2013). A meta-analytic evaluation of diversity training outcomes. *Journal of Organizational Behavior*, 34(8), 1076–1104.
14 Bezrukova et al. (2016). "A meta-analytical integration of over 40 years of research."
15 Fleishman, E. A. (1953). Leadership climate, human relations training, and supervisory behavior. *Personnel Psychology*, 6(2), 205–222.
16 Alhejji, H., Garavan, T., Carbery, R., O'Brien, F., & McGuire, D. (2016). Diversity training programme outcomes: A systematic review. *Human Resource Development Quarterly*, 27(1), 95–149.
17 Bezrukova et al. (2016). "A meta-analytical integration of over 40 years of research."
18 Kalinoski et al. (2013). "A meta-analytic evaluation of diversity training outcomes."
19 Bezrukova et al. (2016). "A meta-analytical integration of over 40 years of research."
20 Kalev, A., Dobbin, F., & Kelly, E. (2006). Best practices or best guesses? Assessing the efficacy of corporate affirmative action and diversity policies. *American Sociological Review*, 71(4), 589–617.
21 Dobbin, F., Schrage, D., & Kalev, A. (2015). Rage against the iron cage: The varied effects of bureaucratic personnel reforms on diversity. *American Sociological Review*, 80(5), 1014–1044.
22 Nkomo, S. M. (2014). Inclusion: Old wine in new bottles. In B. M. Ferdman & B. R. Deane (Eds.), *Diversity at work: The practice of inclusion* (pp. 580–592). Jossey-Bass.

23 Bond, M. A., & Haynes, M. C. (2014). Workplace diversity: A social–ecological framework and policy implications. *Social Issues and Policy Review, 8*(1), 167–201.

24 Linnehan, F., & Konrad, A. M. (1999). Diluting diversity: Implications for intergroup inequality in organizations. *Journal of Management Inquiry, 8*(4), 399–414.

25 Nkomo (2014). "Inclusion: Old wine in new bottles."

26 O'Donovan, D. (2018). Diversity and inclusion in the workplace. In C. Machado & J. P. Davim (Eds.), *Organizational behaviour and human resource management* (pp. 73–108). Springer, p. 74.

27 Ibid, citing Gasorek (2000).

28 Nishii, L. H. (2013). The benefits of climate for inclusion for gender-diverse groups. *Academy of Management Journal, 56*(6), 1754–1774.

29 Hammersley, M. (2001). On 'systematic' reviews of research literatures: A 'narrative' response to Evans & Benefield. *British Educational Research Journal, 27*(5), 543–554; Tranfield, D., Denyer, D., & Smart, P. (2003). Towards a methodology for developing evidence-informed management knowledge by means of systematic review. *British Journal of Management, 14*(3), 207–222.

30 Montuori, A. (2013). Complexity and transdisciplinarity: Reflections on theory and practice. *World Futures, 69*(4-6), 200–230.

31 Rousseau, D. M., & Gunia, B. C. (2016). Evidence-based practice: The psychology of EBP implementation. *Annual Review of Psychology, 67*, 667–692.

32 Amis, J. M., Mair, J., & Munir, K. A. (2020). The organizational reproduction of inequality. *Academy of Management Annals, 14*(1), 195–230; Castilla, E. J. (2008). Gender, race, and meritocracy in organizational careers. *American Journal of Sociology, 113*(6), 1479–1526.

33 Becker, G. S. (1971). *The economics of discrimination* (2nd ed.). University of Chicago Press.

34 Hirschman, A. O. (1970). *Exit, voice and loyalty: Responses to decline in firms, organizations and states.* Harvard University Press.

35 Nkomo (2014). "Inclusion: Old wine in new bottles."

36 Ibid, p. 588, citing Chatman (2010).

37 O'Donovan (2018). "Diversity and inclusion in the workplace," p. 89.

38 Weisinger, J. Y., & Salipante, P. F. (2000). Cultural knowing as practicing: Extending our conceptions of culture. *Journal of Management Inquiry, 9*(4), 376–390.

39 Fiske, S. T., Cuddy, A. J., & Glick, P. (2007). Universal dimensions of social cognition: Warmth and competence. *Trends in Cognitive Sciences, 11*(2), 77–83.

40 van Knippenberg, D., De Dreu, C. K., & Homan, A. C. (2004). Work group diversity and group performance: An integrative model and research agenda. *Journal of Applied Psychology, 89*(6), 1008–1022.

41 Lave, J. (1993). The practice of learning. In J. Lave & S. Chaiklin (Eds.), *Understanding practice: Perspectives on activity and context* (pp. 3–32). Cambridge University Press; Lave, J., & Wenger, E. (1991). *Situated learning: Legitimate peripheral participation.* Cambridge University Press; Wenger, E. (1998). *Communities of practice: Learning, meaning, and identity.* Cambridge University Press.

42 Ahmad, F., & Barner-Rasmussen, W. (2019). False foe? When and how code switching practices can support knowledge sharing in multinational corporations. *Journal of International Management, 25*(3), 1–18.

43 Pettigrew, T. F., & Tropp, L. R. (2006). A meta-analytic test of intergroup contact theory. *Journal of Personality and Social Psychology, 90*(5), 751–783.

44 Bowman, N. A., & Park, J. J. (2015). Not all diversity interactions are created equal: Cross-racial interaction, close interracial friendship, and college student outcomes. *Research in Higher Education, 56*(6), 601–621.

45 Ahmad & Barner-Rasmussen (2019). "False foe?"

46 Cable, D. M., Gino, F., & Staats, B. R. (2013). Breaking them in or eliciting their best? Reframing socialization around newcomers' authentic self-expression. *Administrative Science Quarterly, 58*(1), 1–36.

47 Giddens, A. (1984). *The constitution of society: Outline of the theory of structuration.* University of California Press.

48 Anand & Winters (2008). "A retrospective view of corporate diversity training," p. 362.

49 Weisinger & Salipante (2000). "Cultural knowing as practicing."

50 O'Donovan (2018). "Diversity and inclusion in the workplace."

51 Anand & Winters (2008). "A retrospective view of corporate diversity training."

52 Nowotny, H., Scott, P., & Gibbons, M. (2003). Introduction: "Mode 2" revisited: The new production of knowledge. *Minerva, 41*(3), 179–194.

53 Kalev, A. (2009). Cracking the glass cages? Restructuring and ascriptive inequality at work. *American Journal of Sociology, 114*(6), 1591–1643.

2

THE FRAMEWORK

Improving performance and equity through inclusive interaction practices

The evidence-based Framework for Inclusive Interactions presented here is designed to guide leaders at all organizational levels, when combined with their knowledge and experience, in meeting and overcoming challenges that have plagued organizational efforts to leverage diversity for equity and performance. As stated in the preceding chapters, we see the key diversity challenge for organizations as having diverse representation without inclusion. Further, we have noted the ongoing challenges with performance and equity due to inadequate organizational approaches to diversity and inclusion. We have asserted that critical aspects of overcoming these challenges involve countering ubiquitous *anti-inclusive practices* in favor of a specific set of *structured inclusive interaction practices* designed to foster inclusive behaviors. Following these practices leads to the sort of learning—*adaptive learning* about how to interact productively across differences—that is necessary to create *sustainable inclusion*.

Our Framework for Inclusive Interactions (Figure 2.1) represents these dynamics. This practice-based model captures the complexities of moving from representational diversity to inclusion, which involves individual, workgroup, and organizational level processes. (See Box 2.1 for our definition of the term *workgroup*.) Further, it emphasizes the important role of *social practices* in leveraging diversity for inclusion, performance, and equity. In focusing on social practices, and specifically on practices at the workgroup level where key actions and decisions reside, we draw attention to what workgroup members *do* together, guided by behavioral norms and work practices. We have argued earlier that prevalent diversity and inclusion approaches—ones that attempt to change attitudes that are then presumed to lead to changes in behavior, such as common types of diversity training—can fall short. In contrast, practice-based approaches have a history of practicality and success in

DOI: 10.4324/9780367822484-4

organizations, as demonstrated by the widespread adoption of programs such as ISO 9000 for quality management and agile teams for software development.

BOX 2.1: WORKGROUPS

In this book, we are using the term *workgroup* to represent any group or team that functions within any business, nonprofit, governmental, social, or voluntary organization. For example, this may include workplace teams, boards of directors, sport teams, student teams, divisions, departments, sections, service organizations, etc. The Framework for Inclusive Interactions may be applied to all of these and many more. The independent nature of a workgroup, encompassing the idea that individuals are coming together with a common work purpose, is an important precursor to inclusive interactions.

Like such programs, a practice-based approach to inclusion emphasizes daily, routine patterns of behavior that shape workgroup members' interpersonal interactions, the meanings they give to them, and their joint engagement to accomplish work. It is expected that, *over time*, productive inclusive interactions, including behaviors leading to adaptive learning, will lead to changed attitudes, such as prejudice reduction. Hence, we recognize that the process highlighted by this Framework represents a cultural change in the organization. Our interviews and research tell us that managers and staff at various organizational levels, not only leaders at the top, can initiate and produce such change.

Practice-based approaches have a history of practicality and success in organizations.

The Framework guides managers and leaders to develop and maintain *structured inclusive interaction practices* (Chapter 3). These practices facilitate engagement among diverse organizational members through positive, sustained interactions that overcome the otherwise common *anti-inclusive practices* (Chapter 4) of stereotyping and stigmatizing, self-segregating, interacting with discomfort, and making personnel decisions based on implicit bias. This engagement leads to the *adaptive learning* (Chapter 6), which, along with key *merit and accountability practices* (Chapter 7), is crucial in moving toward *sustainable inclusion* (Chapter 8) in organizations, reflecting equity, individual skill development, an increased valuing of diversity and inclusion, and enhanced employee commitment and team performance at all levels. As seen

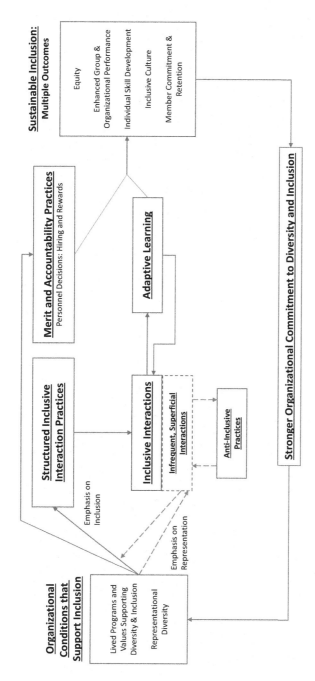

FIGURE 2.1 The Framework for Inclusive Interactions

in Figure 2.1, the core of this model involves this particular set of inclusive inter-action practices:

1. Pursuing a *shared task* orientation or mission;
2. *Mixing* members frequently and repeatedly;
3. *Collaborating* with member interdependence;
4. *Handling conflict* constructively;
5. Engaging in interpersonal *comfort* and *self-efficacy*; and
6. Ensuring *equal insider status* for all members.

Structured practices for inclusive interactions

The key to the Framework for Inclusive Interactions is the set of structured inclusive interaction practices.

The key to our Framework for Inclusive Interactions is the set of practices that workgroup managers and leaders can intentionally structure in order to promote inclusive behaviors within the workgroup while fostering sustainable inclusion and enhancing performance. Without inclusive interactions, diverse workgroups will engage in the most basic type of interaction—infrequent, superficial interactions—in which diverse individuals commonly experience discomfort. Such discomfort often leads to underrepresented group members choosing to leave the organiza-tion, ultimately reducing representational diversity and heterogeneity within the workgroup. Conversely, the Framework proposes that when high-performing workgroups adopt the practices of inclusive interaction, several multilevel outcomes are achieved simultaneously. Representational diversity will be sustainable, as underrepresented group members remain with the organization and the emergent inclusive culture becomes instrumental in attracting those from underrepresented groups and others to join the organization. In Chapter 3, we describe how inclu-sion has been created and sustained in particular organizations by enacting the six practices for inclusive interaction and how these practices lead to prejudice-reducing, adaptive learning among diverse members. In addition, we provide logic for why the six practices should operate in combination, *as a set*, in a synergistic fashion (Box 2.2).

For maximum benefit, the six inclusive interactions practices should operate together, synergistically, as a set.

BOX 2.2: SWISS CHEESE: APPLYING A COMBINATION OF APPROACHES

The Swiss cheese model, first conceived of by James Reason, highlights the need for multiple barriers with respect to risk management—in this case, barriers against the operation of anti-inclusive, biased practices. Each barrier is likely to be fallible, or have holes, just as each slice of Swiss cheese has holes. By overlaying multiple layers of Swiss cheese, the holes are covered, reducing the likelihood of a major accident or catastrophe. Applying the Swiss cheese model to the Framework illustrates the necessity for the multiple practices to align. One slice of Swiss cheese is not enough. That is, the effectiveness of the Framework for Inclusive Interactions goes up with the addition of each additional structured inclusive interaction practice or slice of cheese. Maximum effectiveness is reached when all the specified practices for inclusive interactions, plus those for accountability, are in place. Inclusive culture results from the multiple, complementary practices that favor inclusion and equity.

Unfortunately, if a Swiss cheese-eating mouse is introduced, the impact of the stacked layers is eroded by new holes chewed through the multiple overlapping layers of cheese. This cheese-eating mouse, as applied to the framework, emphasizes the point that inclusive culture—composed of multiple complementary structured inclusive interaction practices—is in-the-making, needing to continually evolve to overcome new risks (or holes). The risks in the framework represent the anti-inclusive practices of self-segregation, interaction discomfort, stereotyping and stigmatizing, and implicit bias. Carefully laid layers of Swiss cheese are necessary to fortify against such risks.

Source: Roberts, S. (2020, December 5). The Swiss cheese model of pandemic defense. *The New York Times*. https://www.nytimes.com/2020/12/05/health/coronavirus-swiss-cheese-infection-mackay.html

We recognize that implementing all six practices takes time, with the practices building on one another. However, during this transitional period, as the practices become normative behaviors, positive, inclusive interactions take place, which impacts sustainable inclusion and workgroup performance. In Chapter 9, we present various cases involving workgroup or organizational adoption of the practices, while Chapter 10 covers strategies that organizations and managers may use to develop these practices. The strategies, under the scope of management, must be fluid and developed respecting the context, nature and, mission of each organization and workgroup. We are making a distinction between the six practices, as stated in a general fashion in the Framework for Inclusive Interactions, and the specific strategies that a particular organization will use to customize and enact them. Local knowledge, existing organizational culture, prior attempts at diversity and inclusion,

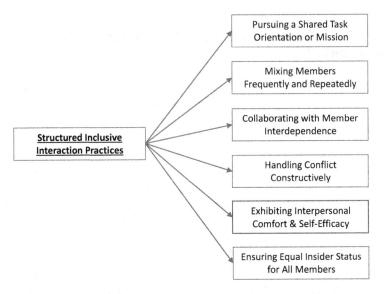

FIGURE 2.2 Structured Inclusive Interaction Practices

and many other factors will determine the best strategies to successfully design and implement the structured inclusive interaction practices. The six practices, as shown in Figure 2.2, represent what members are actively, routinely, and habitually doing in diverse workgroups and teams.

Practice one: Pursuing a shared task orientation or mission

A shared task orientation is the overarching focus of the workgroup, typically without highlighting diversity. The shared task orientation provides opportunity for bonding within the workgroup as members strive for enhanced performance outcomes. In other contexts, the shared orientation may be a shared purpose, such as an organizational or workgroup mission. Pursuing a shared task orientation or mission can help to foster a superordinate workgroup identity that transcends but coexists with their primary group identities.

Practice two: Mixing members frequently and repeatedly

Members engage with diverse others often and over extended periods. Mixing of members within a workgroup or team enables individuals to reduce self-segregation and engage with others with whom they are likely to have discomfort initially but then develop familiarity over time. During our interviews, we heard about the importance of social interactions among diverse members from nonprofit boards, workgroups across the business, governmental and voluntary sectors, and higher-education extracurricular groups.

Practice three: Collaborating with member interdependence

Through proper job and task definitions and teamwork norms, members achieve a sense of belonging. Working interdependently, members learn the value of others' distinctive traits, knowledge, and skills. This creates a balance of uniqueness and belonging that contributes to the ability of the individuals in the workgroup to avoid anti-inclusive social practices such as stereotyping and stigmatizing that inhibit performance and equity.

Practice four: Handling conflict constructively

Some level of tension over differences in diverse workgroups is both to be expected and to be embraced as a corollary of well-considered decisions. When tensions arise, members engage in routinized procedures that value members' inputs, manage emotions, and elicit information, enabling productive decisions. In a financial services firm, for example, an internal consultant was available to workgroups to assist with conflict handling.

Practice five: Engaging in interpersonal comfort and self-efficacy

In diverse workgroups, new members can experience communication apprehension and interaction discomfort when communicating with diverse others. They can also experience cognitive stress in the form of inconsistency between the stereotypes they hold of a particular identity group and the behaviors they observe of particular coworkers from that group. Reducing this apprehension and cognitive dissonance, or stress, relies upon individuals gaining skills of effective interaction by modeling the exhibited effective interaction practices of the other workgroup members. Over time, as new members are absorbed into the workgroup and follow the foregoing five practices, they develop not only comfort in interacting with other members but also self-efficacy in their ability to interact productively. Without such comfort and self-efficacy, willingness to continue to interact erodes.

Practice six: Ensuring equal insider status for all members

Until all workgroup members feel valued and of equal standing with others, with their knowledge and skills being sought and respected, inclusion and performance will be negatively impacted. Individuals strive to feel valued for their independent contributions to the workgroup and for being a valued workgroup member. Failing that, individuals are likely to withdraw psychologically or exit the workgroup or organization. The overarching identity stemming from a shared task or mission orientation, combined with the frequent mixing of members, sets the stage for avoiding ingroup vs. outgroup dynamics that would undermine equal insider status.

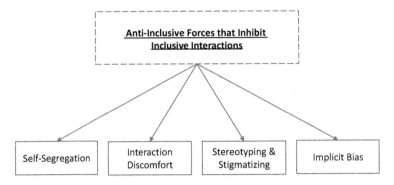

FIGURE 2.3 Anti-Inclusive Forces that Inhibit Inclusive Interactions

Overcoming anti-inclusive practices that inhibit inclusive interactions

Often overlooked by those seeking to leverage diversity for inclusion leading to performance and equity are the exclusionary practices that act to inhibit inclusive interactions. Figure 2.3 illustrates four exclusionary, or anti-inclusive social practices identified by substantial bodies of research: self-segregation, interaction discomfort, stereotyping and stigmatizing, and making decisions based on implicit bias. These anti-inclusive practices explain why many workgroups and organizations have not been successful in achieving sustainable inclusion and equity. Left unchecked, these phenomena impede positive development of inclusive interactions, producing homogeneous subgroupings with an overemphasis on differing identities, ingroup formation, and stigmatizing of other groups. These complex, ubiquitous social impediments can be expected to occur by default, so they must be anticipated and addressed by establishing countervailing practices, such as the six described above. Chapter 4 further examines the major anti-inclusive social practices, and how they impede inclusive, productive interactions.

Self-segregation

Self-segregation is the phenomenon of diverse individuals differentiating and distancing themselves socially, even when in physical proximity. This phenomenon is often referred to as "birds of a feather flocking together."[1] The process of individuals seeking to interact most often with similar others and least often with different others is ubiquitous in social life. It provides one explanation for the research finding that diversity in workgroups most often fails to lead to improved performance.

Interaction discomfort

Many individuals naturally experience anxiety when interacting with members of unfamiliar identity groups. Norms of political correctness heighten the anxiety due to fear of saying the wrong thing, producing yet stronger motivation to avoid such interactions and a felt awkwardness in superficial interactions that the individual cannot avoid. (See Box 2.3 for two examples illustrating interaction discomfort.) Some individuals, due to a history of being stereotyped and stigmatized because of their own group membership, may avoid interactions with members of other identity groups.

BOX 2.3: DISCOMFORT IN INTERACTIONS

Participating in positive inclusive interactions over time allows for trust to develop within the workgroup. Phillip, a young White man who is a member of a 13-member diverse cohort participating in an 18-month leadership fellowship, spoke of the many months it took for the fellowship group to develop sufficient trust to begin benefiting from their diverse membership. He spoke of the fear he felt that held him back from being 100 percent honest initially with the group because he was afraid of saying the wrong thing and being labeled as insensitive. His initial fear and hesitancy took several months to overcome, during which time the group engaged in many bonding moments, such as a weekend in a local forest singing, eating, dancing, and drinking together, or as Phillip said, having "authentic personal one-on-one time talking about things other than race." As a result of such interactions Phillip was able to "learn and make mistakes in front of others to grow through this uncomfortable situation."

In another example, Ron, an Assistant Chancellor for Equity and Inclusion at a large Western public university, noted discomfort as a necessary part of interactions with diverse others, saying that, "when you have people bridge with one another, you need capacity for empathy, cultural humility, being able to sit with discomfort." Ron would like to see workgroups make time for member storytelling, "which involves persons' history, experiences—sharing our stories—how people can be partner and ally in doing this work." The structured inclusive interaction practices provide opportunity for sharing and learning. In both these examples, it took patience and time to allow for the groups' members to achieve a level of comfort and trust.

Stereotyping and stigmatizing

Stereotyping erodes inclusion when diverse individuals engage with one another. Unfortunately, research finds that common attempts to increase diversity, such as diversity training, often increase negative stereotyping of underrepresented groups, discouraging and hampering interactions among diverse members. Those who are stereotyped feel stigmatized and their performance suffers.

Making decisions based on implicit bias

Implicit biases are attitudes understood to be largely unconscious and pervasive in society. They involve stereotypes about members of various identity groups and underlie decisions about how to behave toward and reward or sanction members of those groups. Members of a particular group itself may even hold such biases. These biases cause individuals, who often express that they are not prejudiced, to unconsciously act in discriminatory ways toward others. For majority group members, biases are often triggered by a perception of competitive threat—of an underrepresented group being favored over their own group—and for an underrepresented group's members, these biases can often be internalized, leading to increased feelings of being stigmatized.

Overcoming the anti-inclusive practices is critical to creating effective inclusive interactions. Carrying the inclusive practices means that as members go about their work or engage with each other informally, they skillfully perform in ways consistent with inclusion rather than with negative stereotypes and anti-inclusive practices that might otherwise strongly affect their behavior. Consistent with the characteristics of practices specified in practice theory (Chapter 6), by following structured inclusive interaction practices, members routinely act, speak, understand, and feel emotions in a manner that enables the differing perspectives and skills of their fellow members' to be included in decision-making.

An important point about developing these practices is that managers and leaders have the flexibility to structure these practices in such a way to not only take advantage of key research evidence but also to integrate local management knowledge of the organizational environment. As such, our Framework does not instruct specifically, for example, *how* to mix diverse members or *how* to handle conflict constructively. We believe that the most effective implementation of these practices follows the evidence-informed approach (Chapter 1), relying on the best research evidence available *and* on local knowledge. Once practices are developed, the challenge for leaders becomes how to maintain the practices' vitality and relevance for inclusion of all members, thereby creating and sustaining an environment within which such interactions can continue to thrive.

We have stated that these practices represent inclusion in action. As organizational members engage in these practices with each other in workgroups and teams, they develop adaptive learning in which they experience social integration—reflecting safety, trust, and justice—and expand the amount and quality of task-relevant information by perspective taking and cooperative interdependence in order to produce improved team decision-making. Adaptive learning is an ongoing process wherein members continually adjust their behavior and interactions to comply with norms of inclusion and to achieve high performance. (See Box 2.4 for an example of how adaptive learning impacted a member of a leadership fellowship.) However, as represented on the right-hand side of Figure 2.1, that adaptive learning alone does not get organizations to an inclusive culture or to higher performance. The learning on the part of individual members has to be coupled with organizational merit and accountability practices. These have three components: accountability for outcomes (rewards and sanction) being based on merit; transparency in opportunities (such as for development and advancement) and in the processes for outcome accountability; and a behavioral accountability component, holding individuals accountable for behaving inclusively. Structured inclusive interaction practices, along with accountability and transparency practices, lead to an emergent inclusive culture that is central to sustainable inclusion.

> Sustainable inclusive culture is dependent on both the structured inclusive interaction practices at the workgroup level and accountability and transparency practices at the organizational level.

The benefits of sustainable inclusion are continually reproduced over time: equity, individual skill development, an increased valuing of diversity and inclusion, and enhanced employee commitment and team performance at all levels. As these outcomes are achieved, leader and member commitment to diversity and inclusion are strengthened. In effect, the Framework depicted in Figure 2.1 captures the dynamics of a virtuous cycle that reproduces sustainable inclusion's beneficial outcomes over time. As such, it can be thought of as a flow chart to help organizations see how they can progress from representational diversity to inclusive and accountability practices to sustainable inclusion.

The starting point for the Framework, *organizational conditions supporting inclusion*, recognizes that many—though not all—organizations have experienced at least some degree of success in recruiting a diverse membership or workforce (representational diversity). Even for those that have not had such success, we maintain that this Framework can still serve them well. Maintaining an inclusive culture as part of sustainable inclusion efforts can lead to stronger organizational commitment to diversity and inclusion, which will, in turn, help to attract and retain members

BOX 2.4: ADAPTIVE LEARNING

Phillip, who shared his experiences as a member in the leadership fellowship (see Box 2.3), emphasized to us how much he had learned about diverse members during his frequent interactions with his cohort. His ability to learn about himself and diverse others, he noted, was based on the group's willingness to allow him to make mistakes which were followed by compassion rather than condemnation. Phillip felt that this kind of compassion allowed him to come to the realization that "I am a White man, born a White man, and I am here to learn. I was not responsible for slavery, but I want to learn to be an advocate and want to fight for change, however that may look." This example suggests that, through becoming a carrier of the practices in his fellowship group, understandings that he gained about particular others in the group and about equity were generalized to his broader social world.

of underrepresented groups, thereby enhancing representational diversity. This dynamic is indicated by the feedback loop, *stronger organizational commitment to diversity and inclusion*, from *sustainable inclusion* to *organizational conditions*. According to Elizabeth, an African American Audience and Access Coordinator at a large Midwest museum, inclusion was often seen as an end goal, particularly by those not working in diversity roles. Elizabeth, a Black woman, felt this was counter to the need for inclusion to be embedded into the culture. *Inclusion must be "an iterative, ongoing process."*

Further, it is now fairly common for organizations to have visible diversity statements, to include diversity and inclusion among their key organizational values, and/or to have existing programs supporting diversity and inclusion (lived programs and values supporting diversity and inclusion). This awareness and activity around diversity and inclusion lays the groundwork for organizations to move through the flow depicted in the Framework. So, too, does top management providing resources to managers and staff at all levels to support their well-informed diversity and inclusion efforts. Ron, Assistant Chancellor for Equity and Inclusion, echoed the importance of lived organizational values, where organizational leaders model the behaviors and values with respect to diversity, inclusion, equity, interpersonal interactions, and performance.

The dotted line arrow in Figure 2.1, from *organizational conditions* to the *infrequent superficial interactions* box, denotes how overemphasizing representational diversity can often lead to infrequent, superficial interactions. That is, organizations can have a diverse membership, but without an environment that facilitates positive, sustained inclusive interactions, realizing sustainable inclusion outcomes can be very difficult. Members in this situation may not have adequate opportunities and support to develop productive inclusive interactions and thus do not achieve the adaptive learning needed for inclusion and sustainable inclusion.

> Even in diverse organizations, if an environment that facilitates positive, sustained inclusive interactions does not exist, sustainable inclusion will not be realized.

In contrast, the solid line arrow in the figure, from *organizational conditions* to *structured inclusive interaction practices*, denotes how emphasizing inclusion leads managers and leaders to consider how to intentionally structure particular interaction practices. The goal is to develop practices and behavioral norms that support productive inclusive interactions leading to the adaptive learning that fosters inclusion and sustainable inclusion.

For organizations that initially pursue an emphasis on representational diversity, finding that members engage mostly in infrequent, superficial interactions that do not counter the anti-inclusive forces mentioned earlier, the dotted line arrow from *infrequent superficial interactions* going back to meet the line reflecting an emphasis on inclusion shows that these organizations can ultimately redirect their efforts toward inclusion and the six inclusive interactions practices.

Finally, the arrow from *organizational conditions* to *merit and accountability practices* (Chapter 7) highlights the importance of holding members accountable for key personnel decisions that minimize bias, particularly in hiring and rewards, to ensure equitable developmental opportunities and rewards for members of underrepresented groups. In addition, transparency regarding this accountability, including monitoring relevant metrics or goals, is critical for accountability effectiveness. As indicated earlier, one key reason research has revealed for persistent inequities is the role of bias in impacting performance evaluations, particularly in how those evaluations are translated into reward decisions for members of underrepresented groups.

Also as discussed earlier, the structured inclusive interaction practices are the anchoring point for the Framework. Organizations that are successful in developing and maintaining these practices will experience members' adaptive learning about how to achieve productive interactions with each other across their differences. The more adaptive the learning, the more this learning informs members' inclusive interactions, resulting in a positive reinforcing cycle, as indicated by the arrows in Figure 2.1. But also, this adaptive learning is the critical step in moving the organization toward an inclusive culture reflected in sustainable inclusion (Chapter 8).

> The structured inclusive interaction practices facilitate adaptive learning and this learning informs members' inclusive interactions, resulting in a positive reinforcing cycle.

Adaptive learning, along with the aforementioned merit and accountability practices for key personnel decisions, ultimately lead organizations to sustainable inclusion. *Sustainable inclusion* is represented by multiple outcomes. When a workgroup or organization achieves sustainable inclusion, individuals have learned new behavioral skills that benefit them in their interactions with diverse others, they are more skilled at handling conflict, and perhaps most significantly, the workgroup culture produces and reproduces these behaviors as embedded in the members' routine practices of interpersonal interaction. New members are socialized by the inclusive culture in ways that produce their learning and skill for interacting productively across valued, task-relevant differences. Over time, both group performance and individual equity in terms of inclusion and rewards are improved and sustained. Members' retention and commitment to the organization follows from the inclusive culture. Members respect one another, listen, contribute to the group, and focus on performance.

As one can see, the Framework identifies *three relevant sets of practices*: First and foremost, *structured inclusive interaction practices* that facilitate diverse members' engagement with each other; second, the *anti-inclusive practices* noted earlier, such as stereotyping and stigmatizing; and third, *merit and accountability practices* employed by the organization to monitor whether inclusion and equity are being achieved.

At any one time, the combining or entangling of these three types of practices determines whether, when, and where inclusion, and its attendant outcomes of equity and performance, occur in the organization.

The next chapter, Chapter 3, describes and illustrates real-life examples of the inclusive interaction practices. Central to our Framework of Inclusive Interactions, these practices foster behaviors among workgroup members that create a positive inclusive culture where members are valued and respected, adaptive learning occurs, and sustainable inclusion flourishes.

Note

1 McPherson, M., Smith-Lovin, L., & Cook, J. M. (2001). Birds of a feather: Homophily in social networks. *Annual Review of Sociology*, 27, 415–444.

PART I SUMMARY

Leveraging the framework for inclusive interactions for performance and equity

It is astonishing that in the decades since the passage of the Civil Rights Act in 1964, so little progress has been made with respect to equity and inclusion in organizations. As a result, organizations continue to experience challenges with respect to how people interact with people who are different from themselves. This lack of progress hampers the workgroups and organizations in their ability to excel and to provide equitable opportunities. The persistence of inequalities, particularly among underrepresented groups, highlights that the approaches taken have more often than not failed to ensure sustainable inclusion and its associated benefits of equity and performance. The economic stakes for organizations and societies that do not incorporate differing skills and perspectives are high due to the increasingly diverse nature of global demographics. It is clearly time to move beyond legal compliance and representational diversity to recognize and strive for equity and sustainable inclusion.

Efforts to recruit members of historically underrepresented groups are a necessary first step. However, achieving full inclusion remains a challenge, where anti-inclusionary practices (self-segregation, interaction discomfort, stereotyping and stigmatizing, and implicit bias) must be replaced with structured inclusive interaction practices (pursuing a shared task orientation or mission, mixing members frequently and repeatedly, collaborating with member interdependence, handling conflict constructively, exhibiting interpersonal comfort and self-efficacy, and ensuring equal insider status for all members), and merit and accountability practices (personnel decisions that ensure equitable hiring and rewards). The Framework for Inclusive Interactions provides a flow-chart for workgroups and organizations to implement in order to achieve sustainable inclusion.

Understanding of contemporary and historic approaches to diversity and inclusion highlights why greater progress has not been realized (Introduction):

DOI: 10.4324/9780367822484-5

- We need to acknowledge that progress for members of underrepresented groups remains poor. Diversity needs to be leveraged, through the adoption of inclusive interaction and accountability practices, for the benefit of organizations and societies.
- Contemporary diversity initiatives remain lacking primarily because they often do not properly address the anti-inclusive practices. In addition, diversity initiatives often focus on education and not on engaging in positive inclusive interactions, resulting in increased tensions, while often reinforcing stereotypes and biases.
- Effective approaches must replace ineffective approaches to fostering meaningful inclusive interactions. It is imperative to be equitable when considering promotion, pay, and termination decisions.
- Use a practice-based approach to focus beyond representational diversity on how organizational members interact inclusively with one another. Positive inclusive behaviors must be "lived" in order for the anti-inclusionary forces to be challenged and attitudes to change—resulting in a culture that supports sustainable inclusion.

Where are we currently with respect to diversity, equity, and inclusion? What represents a realistic and promising way forward? Do the currently used approaches to diversity, equity, and inclusion result in improved performance and sustainable outcomes? (Chapter 1):

- Moving beyond "checking the box" of diversity training to managing inclusion for all members, such that everyone learns to work with and gain valuable perspectives from others different from themselves, significantly transforming, in a positive way, the work being done.
- Acknowledging that contemporary explanations for the historical challenges with diversity, equity, and inclusion that organizations have experienced is substantiated by the persistence of large racial, ethnic, and gender disparities.
- Workgroup members, over time, will learn the interaction skills and behaviors that enable them to follow the inclusive interaction practices.
- The challenge to achieving sustainable inclusion at the organizational level comes down to three phenomena: (1) problems with interpersonal interactions due to self-segregation, interaction anxieties, and stereotyping and stigmatizing, (2) implementation of the structured inclusive interaction practices, and (3) the operation of implicit bias in managers' personnel decisions.
- A different, more promising approach evolves from what individuals *do together*. This perspective separates what people *are*—their views of themselves— from what they *do* with others in particular contexts. From this view, what is important is *practice*, the behavior that people habitually exhibit when they are together in a particular situation. Inclusive interactions occur on the job every day when tasks are performed and when decisions are made. Experiencing repeated, positive, meaningful interactions leads to individuals' development and adaptive learning.

- Adaptive learning results from engaging in inclusive practices where the emphasis is on learning how to function well and respectfully together, what to *do* together, not on how one should think.
- Managerial and organizational-level initiatives that support the structured inclusive interaction practices provide a foundation for adaptive learning, equitable personnel decisions, and sustainable inclusion.

The Framework for Inclusive Interactions provides a practice-based model for overcoming the challenges often associated with diverse workgroups. Implementing a specific set of inclusive interaction practices designed to foster inclusive behaviors leads to the sort of learning— adaptive learning about how to interact productively across differences—that is necessary to create sustainable inclusion (Chapter 2):

- The Framework, unlike the majority of existing diversity and inclusion approaches, is focused on changing behaviors through the establishment of structured inclusive interaction practices, which then leads to adaptive learning and attitude changes that overcome the common anti-inclusive practices.
- The particular set of inclusive interaction practices includes:
  1. pursuing a *shared task* orientation or mission;
  2. *mixing* members frequently and repeatedly;
  3. *collaborating* with member interdependence;
  4. *handling conflict* constructively;
  5. engaging in interpersonal *comfort* and *self-efficacy*; and
  6. ensuring *equal insider status* for all members.
- Along with equitable merit and accountability practices, the inclusive inter-action practices move toward sustainable inclusion in organizations, reflecting equity, individual skill development, an increased valuing of diversity and inclusion, and enhanced employee commitment and team performance at all levels.

PART II OVERVIEW

Moving from diversity to inclusion: Evidence-based guidance for making diversity and inclusion work

This section of the book relies heavily on reviews of research conducted by experts in various academic disciplines and on large-scale research studies. The focus is on social barriers to diversity and inclusion, on programs that produce inclusion, and on cognitive and behavioral learning that sustains inclusion. We know with a high degree of certainty what these forces of exclusion are and how they operate. From this research, we see that sustaining diversity and inclusion requires organizational actions that deal with natural social forces that, otherwise, produce distancing and exclusion. These social phenomena are natural in the sense that they are useful in simplifying life for individuals by reducing mental effort about what to pay attention to and how to pursue their interests. Because they are natural, they are ubiquitous, influencing all of us.

The phenomenon of self-segregation pushes individuals (us) to associate with others similar to themselves (ourselves). Associating with similar others serves a valuable protective and learning function for members of underrepresented groups seeking to cope with a lack of inclusion. In general, however, self-segregating over the years leads us to be less comfortable and skilled at interacting with dissimilar, unfamiliar others. The distancing that results from self-segregation and inter-action discomfort means that we have less opportunity to question whether the assumptions, the stereotypes held about those others are accurate and whether they apply to particular individuals. Negative stereotypes of low competence and unlikeability—ascribed to members of groups of lower status who are seen as com-peting for scarce resources, such as jobs and promotions—then persist and serve to stigmatize those members. Even negative biases that are held implicitly, at a

DOI: 10.4324/9780367822484-6

relatively unconscious level, produce at least the same degree of discriminating behavior as does overt discrimination. Estimates based on findings from an entire body of research studies indicate that our societies, economies, organizations, and individuals pay a high price for these biases in terms of poor use of millions of people's talents and poor service to large numbers of organizational clients.

Given the four exclusionary forces of self-segregation, interaction discomfort, stereotyping and stigmatizing, and implicit bias, it is no surprise that disparities in occupational status and wages have persisted for generations, nor that recent research studies have countered the myth that workgroup diversity typically leads to greater creativity and performance. As often as it does, it does not. The managerial challenge is to create the conditions where diversity does produce higher performance through strong utilization of all organizational members' perspectives, skills, and knowledge.

In recent years, both research and managerial experience with particular organizational programs point to practical opportunities for producing high performance and equity from diversity. Particular sets of organizational practices, acting in combination, foster prolonged intergroup contact that produces reductions in prejudiced behavior and attitudes. In contrast, efforts that attempt to change attitudes through mandatory training and educational efforts have been found to be ineffective and harmful to some groups. Taken as a whole, research from a variety of academic fields and sectors of the economy provides a consistent message: Adaptive learning in the form of prejudice reduction and familiarity with otherwise dissimilar others can be produced by managerial practices that shape workgroup members' interactions to be frequent and positive. These practices overcome exclusionary forces by pushing all workgroup members to interact with and become familiar with each other, and to behave in ways that prevent the triggering of negative bias. Repeated, positive interactions sustain the surfacing of perspectives that produce better decisions, raising workgroup performance. Combined with an organizational commitment to equitable merit and accountability practices, sustainable inclusion, with its multi-level outcomes, may be achieved.

The chapters in Part II are built around what we can learn from research-based evidence. Chapter 3 (Designing structured inclusive interaction practices) introduces the six inclusive interaction practices necessary to foster inclusive behaviors in workgroup members. In Chapter 4 (Exclusionary forces: Widespread social practices that inhibit inclusion) the exclusionary forces that inhibit inclusive interactions—self-segregation, interaction discomfort, stereotyping and stigmatizing, and implicit bias—are presented. Chapter 5 (The performance issue: How overcoming exclusion matters for workgroup effectiveness) examines options for overcoming the exclusionary forces while creating behavior change that enables diversity to be a path to greater performance. Adaptive learning, discussed in Chapter 6 (Structured interaction practices for adaptive behavioral learning), occurs as a result of managerial commitment to fostering prolonged, positive inclusive interactions with diverse others through performance-oriented programs. The final contribution to sustainable inclusion, presented in Chapter 7 (Merit, accountability and transparency practices to address equity and performance), is the need for equitable merit and accountability practices that counter biased personnel decisions. Chapter 8 (Sustainable inclusion: Multiple outcomes for individuals, workgroups, and organizations) discusses the beneficial outcomes that individuals, workgroups, and organizations can expect from sustainable inclusion.

3
DESIGNING STRUCTURED INCLUSIVE INTERACTION PRACTICES

This chapter delves into the workgroup and organizational practices for fostering positive, meaningful, inclusive interactions among members of diverse workgroups to produce equity and high performance. Figure 3.1 indicates where the interaction practices fall within the Framework for Inclusive Interactions. The six *structured inclusive interaction practices* shown in Figure 2.2 in Chapter 2 are: (1) pursuing a shared task orientation or mission, (2) mixing the members frequently and repeatedly, (3) collaborating with member interdependence, (4) handling conflict constructively, (5) engaging in interpersonal comfort and self-efficacy, and (6) ensuring equal insider status for all members. We consider Practices 5 and 6 fundamental to inclusion. When members routinely follow them, inclusion is achieved in terms of actual behaviors. The preceding four practices (1–4) are necessary to foster and continually support the last two practices.

We draw here from research studies and extensive interviews of diverse members experiencing the six practices cognitively, emotionally, and habitually. We describe how inclusion is created and sustained by enacting these six practices and how they provide workgroup and organizational conditions for reducing prejudice and adaptive learning among diverse individuals, as described in subsequent chapters.

A valuable parallel exists between inclusion that aids diversity and equity and inclusion that aids workgroup performance. Achieving inclusive interactions may apply to all mission or task-relevant differences that individuals bring to the workgroup. This type of inclusion is often found, implicitly or explicitly, in specified operating principles of semi-autonomous teams or cross-functional teams (Chapter 5) or nonprofits with a core value of fellowship (Chapter 8), without any reference to surface-level diversity. The performance-based pursuit of inclusion and the incorporation of differences to achieve greater effectiveness can benefit all employees, enabling them to more fully express themselves in their work and generate better decision-making and performance for the team.[1] Seeking the

DOI: 10.4324/9780367822484-7

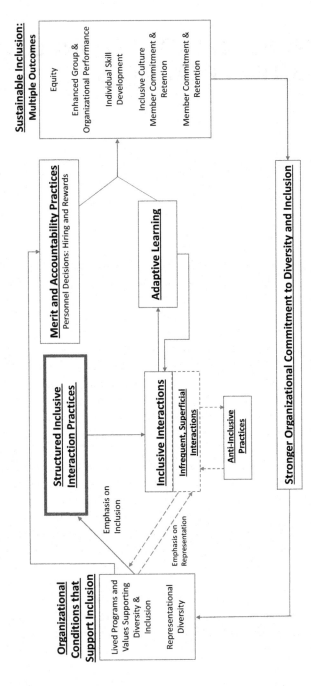

FIGURE 3.1 The Framework for Inclusive Interactions: Structured Inclusive Interaction Practices

performance benefits associated with incorporating differences through inclusive practices can move organizations toward programs that improve performance across the organization, including cross-job training and agile teams.

> Achieving inclusive interactions may apply to all mission or task-relevant differences that individuals bring to the workgroup.

The research presented in this book demonstrates that many organizations stand not only to improve equity but also to gain effectiveness by adopting practices for inclusion that reach into workgroups throughout the organization. The six structured inclusive interaction practices we propose are eminently feasible and well worth the effort involved to enact them. Some managers or workgroup leaders may even find that several of the practices are already integrated into routines or norms. Others may realize that much work remains. As we present the practices below, you may find yourself asking, "How do I bring these practices into my organization?" The response to this inquiry will be unique to your workgroup and organization, and the implementation process will be addressed in further detail in Chapters 9 and 10. In this chapter, we highlight examples of how these practices—some implemented at the organizational level and others at the workgroup level—look in various organizational contexts. As you read the practices and examples, you will observe how very different types of workgroups across the sectors have adopted each practice. You will also find that many of the examples address more than one practice. We hope that as you read these examples, you will observe that there is no one *right way* to enact each practice. Each practice can be adapted to the particular organizational situation, increasing its practicality and effectiveness. Every workgroup and organization is distinctive and operates within a larger set of organizational values and norms.

> As you read this chapter, we challenge you to think about what strategies you would use to implement the practices within your situation.

The practices in our Framework have their basis in research-based evidence on intergroup contact theory (Chapter 6). Seven decades of this research[2] have refined our understandings of effective and ineffective contact.[3] The accumulated findings support the importance of positive contact[4] and shared goals across subgroups[5] as a path to reducing prejudice and conflict. The theory specifies several social, situational conditions as important:

> Prejudice ... may be reduced by equal status contact between majority and minority groups in the pursuit of common goals. The effect is greatly enhanced if this contact is sanctioned by institutional supports (i.e., by law,

custom or local atmosphere), and provided it is of a sort that leads to the perception of common interests and common humanity between members of the two groups.[6]

These social conditions are woven through the six inclusive interaction practices we specify.

In the descriptions and examples of inclusive interaction practices that follow, it is understood that no single practice will ensure inclusion. For example, the practice of mixing members frequently and repeatedly can as readily lead to increased tensions as to increased understandings and familiarity. However, combining that practice with practices for shared task orientation, constructive conflict handling, and engaging comfortably favors positive results from mixing. The goal of a set of practices for inclusive interactions is to create a *high frequency of high-quality diversity interactions*. It is the combination of high frequency and high-quality interactions (or "positive interactions") that are personally meaningful to the individuals, either (formally) in terms of accomplishing a task or (informally) becoming more engaged with dissimilar individuals that produces positive developmental changes.[7] Furthermore, it is the set of complementary practices that is most likely to produce this combination of frequent, positive interactions.

> The goal of the set of practices for inclusive interactions is to create a *high frequency of high-quality diversity interactions*.

Practice 1: Pursuing a shared task orientation or mission

Strongly shared task orientation or mission provides a common interest as a foundation for meaningful inclusive interactions and guides those interactions toward ends perceived as organizationally legitimate by members. The shared purpose may be at the organizational or workgroup level and may change focus as workgroups tackle new projects. Ideally, the strongly shared task orientation or mission creates a superordinate purpose that brings together individual interests and provides a common in-group identity that becomes more salient than other identities as members work together.[8]

Pursuing a shared task orientation or mission contributes to workgroup members' sense of belonging. Belonging is often fostered by the individual members broadening their identification to that of the workgroup. This recategorizing within the group is consistent with the common in-group identity model,[9] which proposes that intergroup bias "can be reduced by factors that transform members' perceptions of group boundaries from 'us' and 'them' to a more inclusive 'we.'"[10] This phenomenon is further developed in social identity theory,[11] which suggests that individual identity is "based on symbolic attachment to the group as a whole." Social identities, however, are complex and also contain a personal component that involves both defining oneself and building individual-level self-esteem[12] in order to balance assimilation and differentiation[13] and build both a sense of belongingness and uniqueness.[14]

> Shore et al. argue that "uniqueness will provide opportunities for improved group performance when a unique individual is an accepted member of the group *and* the group values the particular unique characteristic."[15]

Examples of pursuing a shared task orientation or mission

"What is our mission?" is a frequent question posed by Gary, director of a medical research unit at a major medical center. Gary manages two very diverse semi-autonomous employee workgroups assembled into one unit. The workgroups are composed of either pre-medical school students (referred to as the JV Team) or post-medical school students (referred to as the Fellows). These groups are composed of members joining the research unit from all over the world for one to three years to hone their research skills, so socialization and enculturation are continuous processes that the manager works on. The gender, ethnic and racial diversity of both teams vary as members join and depart, but the workgroup is consistently very diverse by both these measures. Because these teams function semi-autonomously, Gary transfers greater responsibility for mission attainment directly to the group and its members. The Fellows arrive with cross-cultural sensitivity that is an integral part of medical school training, while members of the JV Team, fresh out of college, have not necessarily experienced a level of sustained or meaningful diversity interactions. Hence, it is important to help them develop a superordinate ("we") identity that encourages interactions.

Key to developing that superordinate identity is that each new member is onboarded by Gary, the director, who emphasizes the following: (1) the mission, (2) the importance of collaboration within the team, and (3) the expectation that you will be treated fairly, reinforcing Practice 3 (collaborating with member interdependence) and Practice 6 (ensuring equal insider status for all members) as well. Established in 1985, the mission of the research group is to be among the world's leading clinical research sites. The emphasis on the mission is repeated at unit meetings, where the director likes to give "pop quizzes," asking the unit members to recite the mission and its three fundamental aspirations—"publish more peer-reviewed clinical research than any other comparable organization; recruit more extra-mural clinical research funding than any similar department; and train clinical investigators, including residents, fellows, and faculty." These quizzes, a practice that fits the unit's knowledge-producing focus, keep the emphasis on the mission and group performance outcomes. The research unit's strong focus on mission, and the reliance on collaboration to achieve it, serves to enhance inclusion without any explicit emphasis on the entire workgroup's diversity. In contrast, highlighting the desire to promote diversity can promote stigmatizing,[16] discussed in Chapter 4.

Given the differing national, ethnic, and gender identities in the workgroup, the message of diversity being valued is implicit and tied to the workgroup's effectiveness in achieving its mission.

The research unit's purpose is to conduct world-class research. This shared task orientation is clear and frequently reinforced by Gary, demonstrating support for the goals by the unit's director and shared among members. Due to this ongoing practice of the manager and workgroup members reiterating the goals and their importance, each of the members clearly knows what they are expected to accomplish, how it relates to their individual career interests, how their work supports the success of the entire unit, and that, in accordance with intergroup contact theory, they are supported by authority. Within the teams, leaders and members are responsible for attending to the prescribed practices. The actions and behaviors by the director and team members has resulted in the research unit having succeeded in achieving its mission.

Across a society's sectors, a multitude of firms and organizations represent millions of workgroups, each with a unique mission or purpose. In the above example and the ones that follow, the shared task orientation or mission provides a common identity that drives productive interactions and relationships among the workgroup members. In diverse workgroups, strongly shared task orientation sets the stage for collaboration. Therefore, organizational action leading to inclusion starts with managers promoting programs—that is, sets of practices—and emphasizing the underlying organizational purposes and values that guide their enactment, with an emphasis on mission accomplishment that connects with various individuals' interests and skills and with which they can identify.

> Shared task orientation or mission provides a common workgroup identity that drives productive interactions and relationships among members.

Shared task orientation with a clear, simple mission is also exemplified in our study of a coeducational (extracurricular) voluntary service fraternity that has thousands of members performing community service in chapters on hundreds of U.S. campuses. Its formally stated purpose—Service, Leadership, and Fellowship—is to develop leadership, promote friendship, and provide service to humanity, a mission shared among members. Students in this organization typically participate each week in an organizational meeting, community service, and a fellowship activity. Students are drawn to the association to engage in community service, which includes such activities as organizing the American Cancer Society's Relay-for-Life event on campus, mentoring local youth, and helping immigrant families. Fellowship activities are optional and purely social in nature. A Black woman member of the service fraternity summarized the transcendent identity power of shared purpose within this nonprofit organization when she said, "It didn't really occur to me that there were mostly White people or that anyone was different from me, really. Cause we're all there for the same purpose and that was service, and the races or ethnicities are not in the forefront of my mind." Another student, an Asian man, emphasized the importance of doing the service work as an impetus for interactions: "We all have common interest in doing the work, so that's the big thing." Within the fraternity, members from dominant and underrepresented groups credited the sense of purpose as more significant for facilitating conversation and building meaningful diversity interactions than commonality of skin color or cultural or ethnic background, indicating that participation in the service fraternity inspired a sense of community that transcended cultural differences among members.

> "We all have common interest in doing the work, so that's the big thing." (Service fraternity member, Asian Man)

In both of the above examples, the service fraternity and the medical research unit, inclusion for diversity is not a stated part of the purpose. The experience of interacting with diverse others is secondary to the workgroup's purpose. In speaking with the national CEO of the service fraternity, he and the organization's board were surprised and happy to hear that meaningful, intercultural interactions were a by-product of the activities that were occurring in the individual campus chapters. Experiencing positive interactions with diverse others as a by-product of the mission highlights the power of non-diversity-focused practices on inclusive interactions.

During an interview with a supervisor trainer, Richard, who works in Human Resources at a large military base, we were told, "Mission is key!" This particular facility employs thousands of civilians with a mission to "Maintain, modernize and retire our force's equipment." With the recent arrival of a new Commanding Officer (CO), the first female CO, a new graphic strategic framework was developed that emphasizes its vision, mission, results, strategies, and values surrounded by the guiding principles and organizational values of integrity, teamwork, ingenuity, excellence, and service (to the organization and community). According to Richard, when supervisors internalize these values, he observes fewer problems and greater teamwork. Richard emphasizes to new supervisors that these managers must "articulate the strategic framework to their team and focus on their small area" within the larger community of the military base. Contributing to the framework's success occured when the CO and top administrators asked the workforce for their input as they created the updated document. According to Richard, the new strategic framework is "well accepted," but, "if a supervisor does not buy-in, then the job is probably not right for them and they should leave." Though, he further explained that it might take some time, saying that the supervisors, "don't have to believe, but they must behave and then they come around."

The military base has had a history of diversity-related issues. Some supervisors have difficulty working with diverse teams and exhibit anti-inclusive behaviors. For Richard, this new strategic framework aids him in his role as a trainer of supervisors to emphasize the need to create diverse teams by focusing first on behavior and adopting inclusive practices, then subsequent attitude change to enhance performance outcomes. This is made easier by the fact that the CO "leads and lives this daily [with actions that are] infectious and inspiring." Wouldn't it be great if we could all "be lifelong learners and continually build relationships and inspire?" said Richard. The idea that behavior leads to believing is consistent with our model and its emphasis on structuring inclusive practices such that they change behavior, challenge existing stereotypes, and then lead to adaptive learning.

Predicating all six of the inclusive interaction practices is the organizational commitment to diversity and inclusion, as seen on the left side of Figure 3.1. The practice of pursuing a shared task orientation or mission needs to be supported by leaders as well as shared among members in order to promote inclusive interactions. Gary and Richard highlighted the fact that their work is made easier if the institutional leaders "model behaviors and live the values of the organization." As Richard told us, it is important that the organization's leadership is diverse and "walks the walk and talks the talk" with respect to diversity, equity, and inclusion. This was also emphasized by Richard, the director of the medical research unit, who expects all of the leadership, at the unit and team levels, including himself, to "lead from the front … working the hardest and treating everyone well" in order to achieve their goals and mission.

> The practice of pursuing a shared task orientation or mission needs to be supported by leaders as well as shared among members in order to promote inclusive interactions.

These examples exemplify the strength of workgroup shared task orientation or mission as being central to fostering inclusive interactions, as specified by contact theory's conditions of common goals and interests. The structured inclusive interaction practice, pursuing a shared task orientation or mission, acts to unify workgroups toward the superordinate goal of performance. While none of the stated missions or purposes included diversity, the strength of the mission or purpose was sufficiently strong to bring diverse members together and keep them focused on workgroup outcomes and performance. The adherence to the practice of shared task orientation or mission achievement fosters workgroup and organizational identities that transcend subgroup identities, enabling members to have positive interactions in which subgroup differences are less salient, but wherein members bring their differing perspectives and skills to bear on the task. The examples demonstrate some of the themes of this book—the need for a common workgroup identity, the value of non-diversity-focused approaches to inclusive interactions, and that support from authority for inclusion begins with the shared purpose. This practice is foundational and supports the other practices by transcending and incorporating individual interests. But alone, this practice of pursuing a shared task orientation or mission is unlikely to be enough to sustain inclusion.

> The value of non-diversity-focused approaches to inclusive interactions with support from authority begins with a shared task orientation or mission.

Practice 2: Mixing members frequently and repeatedly

The Framework for Inclusive Interactions draws a distinction between inclusive interactions that are effective and positive and those that are infrequent and superficial. By preserving unfamiliarity, the latter reinforce members' uncomfortable feelings and the desire to self-segregate, to remain apart, preventing inclusion. Dissuading clique formation and intentionally designing tasks and assignments that create different combinations of workmates over time pushes members who may have only limited experience working with diverse coworkers to engage with those others. We recognize that some workgroups are already structured in ways that mix members repeatedly and frequently due to the members' respective tasks. For other workgroups, members must be made to interact with one another to counter the natural desire to self-segregate. Repeated, frequent contacts are key to changing superficial interactions to inclusive interactions. (Box 3.1 provides examples of how to mix workgroup members repeatedly and frequently.) Through repeated, frequent positive interactions, members develop an attachment to the group as a whole ("we"). As a result of the frequent, repeated interactions, members also undergo adaptive learning.

> Structuring practices that mix members within a workgroup inhibits self-segregation and pushes members to engage with diverse others.

According to Crisp and Turner,[17] the key for adaptive learning to occur and stereotypes to be eroded is that individuals must be willing and able to interact repeatedly with members of the other group (Chapter 6). We argue that the full set of structured inclusive interaction practices presented here provides that willingness and ability, enabling diversity interactions that are of high frequency and, due to shared task orientation, highly meaningful, providing a continued pattern

---

BOX 3.1: MIXING MEMBERS

Mixing members repeatedly and frequently is important for establishing inclusive interactions and may be achieved in a multitude of ways:

1. Cross-functional activities and team projects;
2. Random assignment to workgroups or within workgroup activities;
3. Virtual meetings for global teams;
4. Social interactions among members, such as picnics, parties, regular group or subgroup meetings, catered or pot-luck lunches, community service projects, etc.;
5. Establishing common meeting places for formal and informal interactions;
6. Incorporation of onboarding practices in which meaningful conversations occur.

---

of adaptive, cross-differences contact. When repeated sufficiently, the positive contact produces inclusion and its associated benefits for workgroup members.

For adaptive learning to occur individuals must be willing to interact repeatedly with members of other groups, a willingness that can be created by frequent mixing and enacting the other inclusive practices.

When combined with the other specified practices, frequent and repeated mixing results over time in increasingly skillful and comfortable interacting. This process, through individual and collective learning in the workgroup, allow for initial, superficial interactions to become inclusive interactions, involving prejudice reduction and learning that is developmental rather than superficial.[18] To overcome psychological barriers to interacting with dissimilar others, practices that structure opportunities for mixing, even those that "force" members to interact (see Box 3.2), are critical.

Intentional, structured mixing aids in controlling the potentially negative effects of cliques and in-group–out-group tensions. Even if cliques are internally diverse, they manifest self-segregation. When combined with power differences, they counter the inclusive practice of equal insider status for all members. Managers and team leaders can design mixing practices that intentionally build community and minimize clique formation.

BOX 3.2: FORCED INTERACTIONS WITH DIVERSE OTHERS

In conducting the interviews for this book, and other inclusion and diversity research, the authors repeatedly heard the term "forced," as in being "forced" to engage with diverse others. In all cases, the interviewees then told us that they had experienced positive, inclusive interactions due to these forced interactions. The use of the word "forced" was prevalent, particularly by students and young adults, who had had only limited diversity interactions but were pleasantly surprised by their individual reactions to experiencing interactions with diverse others. "Forced" was used in the context of being put into a situation where they experienced interactions with diverse others. These individuals implied that this was not something they sought out. For example, college students who joined a diverse extra-curricular club engaged together in activities. There was no way to participate in the activities without interacting with diverse others. For many members, this was their first sustained, deep-level interaction with those different from themselves. Engaging with diverse others was not forced by the leadership but resulted from the norms of the workgroup. In the organizations where we heard about being "forced," circumstances were created that compelled diversity interactions because workgroup tasks were structured for member interdependence. In some circumstances, the members were thrown together, as described by the students completing activities together or compelled to work together to complete a task or project, as reported in an engineering firm. These workgroup members did not have a choice but to engage with diverse others; yet, we repeatedly heard how these experiences were positive. Being "forced" to engage in these interactions was expressed as a positive experience, not the way we are accustomed to using this "forced" term. These interviewees' workgroups had adopted the set of structured inclusive interaction practices, which enabled the "forced" interactions to be positive, inclusive interactions.

Examples of mixing members frequently and repeatedly

Space design

One method of creating repeated interactions among diverse members is the careful design of physical spaces. For example, in the medical research unit described above in Practice 1, Gary, the director, insisted on having a kitchen large enough to be used as a lunchroom. The result? "Waves of groups using the space as they were freed up to eat lunch together." In addition, Gary insisted during the design phase that all office doors be glass, with everyone having access to all of the offices in order to limit isolation and foster collaboration.

> One method of promoting frequent and repeated interactions among diverse members is through the careful design of physical spaces.

Two additional examples highlighting the importance of space come from university students interviewed about the circumstances under which they experience inclusive interactions on campus at a "commuter" school. The students repeatedly mentioned that inclusive interactions were inhibited by the lack of a student union and cafeteria. They simply did not know where to go to hang out or eat while on campus. As a result, they attended classes and left campus, limiting social and interaction opportunities. In another example, Ron, an administrator for a Western U.S. public university, stressed the importance of a physical place to promote a sense of belonging and ownership as well as a place that allows for repeated diverse interactions and different types of engagements. To achieve this, his university was expanding and relocating its Center for Equity and Inclusion, adjacent to other important campus units to increase traffic to the center. In addition, Ron expressed hope for creating a new Center for Faculty Inclusion to increase engagement and interaction among the faculty and provide a place to discuss diversity, inclusion, and equity issues. Without engagement and interaction, Ron felt that students and faculty would not build an understanding of others' identity and lived experiences.

A counterexample comes from research on mixed-income housing communities, which found only a limited number of mixed-income residential developments included the intentional design of physical spaces that encouraged positive resident interaction between income groups; fewer still included either intentional community building programming or inclusive managerial practices.[19] However, the low-income residents of the properties that did include physical and social opportunities for community building reported stronger social relationships and lower social isolation when compared to low-income residents of the properties lacking these additional opportunities for interpersonal interaction. We find from research covered in Chapter 4 that lacking the community-building practices, physical mixing alone is likely to produce more cross-income conflict than do spaces not promoting mixing.

Enculturation, not assimilation

In the medical research unit described above, new members are brought into the existing teams—JV or Fellows—that have particular ways of interacting that have evolved over time and become embedded within each team. These normative ways largely reproduce themselves now, with limited reinforcement by the unit leaders. In this example, the workgroup started from an initial point in time and persisted with frequent mixed interactions long enough to produce adaptation and learning. The interactions, in this case, are structured according to particular practices or norms that not only lead to adaptation but also enable the interaction behaviors to become institutionalized. Once the practices and behaviors are embedded, adaptive learning occurs organically for new members such that the new members rapidly become enculturated to the team's expectation of inclusive behaviors. Shared mission and the other practices foster the insider, equal status identity. Then, the tricky part is for the workgroup to maintain that status and identity while still offering different perspectives and skills, rather than members being totally assimilated to one identity group's perspectives and ways. With some members graduating from the teams each year and new members coming in, socialization is especially important. Some group members, particularly the Fellows, are preconditioned for inclusion and have less adaptive learning to do than others. Other team members come in with less preparation for interacting and engaging with diverse others. According to Gary, "they learn by doing," alongside others in their team, which is indicative of behavior preceding attitudinal change. Under a set of norms of inclusion established in their workgroup, repeated interactions with diverse others, within the team and beyond, results in high levels of comfort and diversity-related skills.

Norms of inclusion within a diverse workgroup enable members to achieve high levels of comfort and diversity-related skills.

Rotating work assignments is one way to structure the practice of mixing the members frequently and repeatedly. In the campus service fraternity, members signed up for service work assignments using signup sheets and emails, ensuring that the individuals were mixing with an ever-changing set of members. In addition, the frequent coming together enabled, "constant interacting … constant socialization." Within the service fraternity, the concept of fellowship, or socializing together, among the members is so important that fellowship, along with service and leadership, is one of the central tenets of the national organization. Welcoming or onboarding practices are particularly important aspects of mixing for new members, particularly for those who may be hesitant about interactions with diverse others. For new attendees of the university service fraternity, "It was like an open door, so welcoming. I mean, they really don't have a strict way of taking members, as long as you are willing to give back to the community… It was more of a family, an open-arms community. It was very welcoming", said a Black male alumnus of the service fraternity. This was reflected in the organization's policy that "everybody's welcome" who is committed to engaging in community service.

The organization had instituted social practices that facilitated this feeling of welcoming, including activities that "forced" members to interact together (Box 3.2). This included new members interviewing all existing members for half an hour each, participating in a longer-term community service project with other new members, being assigned "big brothers" as mentors, and sitting in a circle during meetings in order to reduce self-segregation and clique formation. As the above-mentioned alumnus put it, "This enabled me to learn about and get to know someone from a different background." For many members, at the two predominantly White universities where we conducted interviews, this often represented the first time that the White members had interacted with someone from a different race or ethnicity, which they often mentioned as being both impactful and significant. According to the newest members of the group, these welcoming practices "forced you to know everyone," using the term "forced" in a good way.

For both the service fraternity and the members of the medical research unit, there is an emphasis on the value of fellowship and informal social interactions. While this is clearly stated in the student service fraternity, it is also central to the research unit, as evidenced by the use of a dedicated space for eating lunch together, numerous formal and informal social activities, and strong acculturation of newcomers by the existing group members. In these and other examples, the fellowship-centered behaviors lack explicit diversity labeling, consistent with the idea that member perception of a program as being aimed at helping a target group engenders stereotyping and stigmatizing of and by that group,[20] inadvertently strengthening exclusionary processes.

The examples provided here demonstrate the necessity, but not the sufficiency, of providing the opportunity for diverse individuals to interact together frequently. An interview with Amy, a woman with 30 plus years of civil engineering experience, provided us with an example of what we do *not* mean by mixing of members repeatedly. She told us how, as a woman, she had often been used strategically to demonstrate that her firm was diverse. Amy was often asked to attend meetings with male members of her firm when they met with potential partners with whom they were seeking contracts, government officials, or community partners. For example, she was taken with her male partners to a meeting with the Head of the Board of Engineering, who is a Black woman. Amy clearly understood that she was being used as "window dressing" but noted that she had "benefitted from diversity" because of the opportunities that presented themselves as a result of attending these meetings.

Mixing members frequently and repeatedly highlights the importance of enabling diverse others to interact with one another. In some situations, managers and workgroup leaders may find that the mixing occurs with little effort, while in other situations, it may take more effort and implementation of additional inclusive practices to bring diverse others together. For example, when diverse individuals are assigned to the same team to achieve an outcome with a particular deadline, these group members know that they must work together. A Black employee working at a high-tech company emphasized the time and performance pressure the workgroups experienced that kept them focused on outcomes. While this practice, mixing members frequently and repeatedly, appears simple, it is often up to the managers and leaders to create the opportunities and reinforce the practices needed for diverse members to have positive, rather than negative, interactions with one another.

It is the responsibility of managers to generate and sustain the opportunities and practices by which differing members have positive interactions with each other.

However, high-quality interactions that are only occasional are likely to be insufficient to produce adaptive learning.[21] Without a high frequency of high-quality interactions, it is likely that the workgroup members will not experience sufficient interactions to overcome preexisting stereotypes.[22] Interactions of moderate frequency extend the time over which adaptive learning is likely to occur, if it occurs at all, while mixing members frequently and repeatedly enables diverse workgroup members to spend time together experiencing sufficient positive interactions to overcome anti-inclusive practices, build trust, and ultimately, perform at a higher level.

Practice 3: Collaborating with member interdependence

Combined with Practice 1, the goal of this practice is to achieve an overarching workgroup identity that becomes salient by focusing on individuals collaborating to attain shared mission. Being collaborative, with member interdependence, and valuing individual members' uniqueness and belonging allows for workgroups to incorporate diverse perspectives and skills into decision-making, raising performance.[23] In two examples presented below of cross-functional teams in a large engineering firm and a financial services company, we draw attention to a study of organizational change programs that confirms the promise of cross-functional job restructuring. Alexandra Kalev[24] studied the impact of organizational diversity and inclusion policies that are not explicitly or formally focused on promoting diversity by examining the diversity impacts of creating cross-functional work teams to enhance organizational effectiveness. Given that one substantial source of workplace inequality is job segregation, with minorities and women overrepresented in job functions with lower status and fewer upward mobility opportunities, Kalev proposed that change efforts in the form of cross-functional collaboration can counter job segregation, thereby improving outcomes for these groups. She found that (1) cross-functional teams, but not within-function teams, and (2) cross-training but not within-job training, are associated with increased odds of managerial positions being held by White and Black women and Black men. The positive outcomes are attributed to relational processes that restructure interactions from separated to collaborative relations, eroding stereotypes and group boundaries, and increasing positive assessments of women's and minorities' capabilities, as well as their networking opportunities. Ultimately, these outcomes lead to improved chances for job transfer and upward mobility and highlight that indirect approaches to formulating inclusive interactions may reap the benefits of inclusion.

Interdependent collaboration in cross-functional teams: Two examples

In the first example, the engineering firm introduced above, success is measured by the quality of the work, client satisfaction, and on-time project completion. To accomplish this, the firm creates teams based on the various types of skills needed to perform the specific job tasks to complete very large multiyear projects. These projects often take a decade to complete, and the teams work together on various phases of the project, typically for about a year, then reconfigured as the next phase of the project is tackled. Engineers are assigned to teams based on their skill sets and experiences, for example, drilling skills, road work, etc. When the workgroups are configured, "the qualifications for what needs to be done is the most important consideration, not diversity," despite the fact that the firm is very diverse with Whites being in the minority and women making up 25 percent of employees, said Amy, a senior engineer. Despite this organizational level diversity, management remains "White guys, but even this is changing ... Knowledge and skills are expected, even forced, because for each phase of the projects different types of engineers are needed, so they ... must collaborate." Amy elaborated by saying that "the new person in the group must prove themselves technically as engineers; they must demonstrate that they are able to complete the work competently. This may take six months or more." One exception to this occurs when the firm brings together experts from all of their offices to write proposals. These workgroups typically are together for only one month, with "the time frame to trust being very fast because of the established professional expertise."

In this situation, the workgroup members are collaborating while being valued for their individual knowledge and skillsets. Amy shared with us that "interacting with diverse others ... still depends on qualifications. Being able to depend on whomever it is to follow through on assignment and be reliable, dependable. They need to have demonstrated that." In discussing the need for team collaboration, she told us how working with diverse others meant "forced time and listening to one another," which led to "building of skills within the group and the achievement of a comfort level." She finds that as a result of these experiences her "stereotypes are challenged." One suggestion Amy has for her firm is "that within the organization there needs to be more opportunities for groups to interact with other teams to help achieve the organizational purpose and for getting to know one another." This particular engineering firm does host a number of social events providing interactions with one another both internal and external to the workplace. Amy expressed gratitude for being "forced" to work with diverse others and how she grew to understand the value of these interactions for themselves and for the workgroup. As noted above in Box 3.2, the word "forced" was prevalent in our interviews and research, particularly by those who had only limited prior exposure to diversity interactions.

The second example of cross-functional team collaboration comes from a large financial services company. "With time, I came to hold the view that diverse groups were higher performing. More creativity, and better results, were possible with a diverse group. I always focused on the results," said the top-level executive in charge of national and global/regional divisions. "But," George went on to say, "most investors don't care about any of this unless somehow it manages to impact enterprise value." After 30 years of experience managing thousands of people, George said that at the culmination of his career, he built a highly diverse group in a multinational setting in a multimillion-dollar operation. In the diverse workgroups, "performance was high, better than the rest of the industry." Unfortunately, the diversification of the groups came at a cost.

> It was a massive challenge to manage. There was creative conflict, but also destructive conflict. [This was because] the organizational culture had a lot of negative aspects I couldn't eliminate. Performance was high, but the climate of high tension eventually led to a breakdown in the group. The level of conflict was too intense to sustain.

This example demonstrates the necessity for organizational support of diversity, inclusion, and equity, as discussed above in Practice 1 (pursuing a shared task orientation or mission) and in Practice 4 (handling conflict constructively), discussed below.

In the diverse workgroups, "performance was high, better than the rest of the industry." (George)

George expressed a concern that many of the financial services managers who are worried about their own retention are less likely to invest in diversity and accept the time it takes for diverse workgroups to be successful. But for those that did, the "teams were highly productive and diverse, proving that both can be achieved. The clarity of the goal, plus time pressure, created an environment where people came together very effectively. Differences of opinion were handled without fallout and the teams kept moving forward." George continued saying, "the skill of the leader of these teams is important, of course. The thought occurs that if associates have the opportunity to work in a setting such as this, then they will be more effective members of a diverse executive team as they move forward in their careers." However, George acknowledged that "managers have differing tolerance for risk" and therefore some are more likely to take the easier path, using homogeneous teams.

Gender roles inhibiting collaboration

In some of the interviews, we heard that collaboration is inhibited by traditional gender roles. "Women are not given a fair chance," Richard from the military base commented, reflecting on how many of the men doubt the abilities of the women employees. Yet, within the base, women work as welders, crane operators, and other traditionally male jobs. Richard repeatedly hears that there are male employees who say, "women are not strong enough, not capable enough, or are wallflowers," despite the fact that many of the women at the base are doing traditionally "men's work" such as welding and crane operation. Working with five generations of employees, Richard likes to ask, particularly of the supervisors from underrepresented groups, "is this a place where you want your sons and daughters to work? If not, why not?

What do we need to change?"While this is indicative of the work still to be done in order to improve the culture of the facility, it is important to see Richard nudging the supervisors to form diverse teams to achieve the repeated mixing necessary for adaptive learning and performance benefits.

The attitude toward women at the military base is consistent with what we heard from our interviews at the engineering firm and financial services company. Conflict within the workgroups in these organizations is more commonly associated with gender and national diversity. The financial services company executive told us, "The problems were not ethnic but gender-based, possibly due to cultural background beliefs." In the engineering firm, we heard how cultural differences were used to justify a lack of respect for women in leadership. For example, we heard of a male engineer from a very patriarchal country who had gender-biased views, which the interviewee, a woman, ascribed to his cultural upbringing. (Box 3.3 examines how generational differences impact collaboration.)

BOX 3.3: GENERATIONAL DIFFERENCES

Working in human resources at the military base, Richard added to our discussion of diversity generational differences. At the base, he told us that there are five generations of employees with many examples of people in their late twenties supervising older employees. Richard has found that generational differences are often easier for him to deal with than those involving race or gender. However, when issues did arise, he would ask the older employees, "is this a place you would want your children to work?" He found that this response frequently shifted their perspectives.

At the engineering firm we studied, we heard two extremes with respect to age diversity. In Amy's firm, the age of the engineers tends to be older with lots of overt resentment toward the millennials whom they perceive as not "putting in their time." She continued by saying, "All they (millennials) want is vacation and promotion without working." The baby boomers were additionally vocal about the "women and men with children who put in far fewer hours but did not make similar adjustments when those without children needed time off." It was clear that there was resentment by the baby boomers of the millennials and a resistance to afford the millennials equal insider status. Amy followed these statements by saying that, "within the workgroups, status and influence in decision-making is based on who has the skills and expertise for that particular task," indicating that proving oneself professionally is vital to erode these baby boomers' stereotypes.

> "We are suspicious of bubbly personalities until they prove themselves," said Amy, referring to how the baby boomers view the younger engineers in the firm. They wanted the younger engineers to be as serious and work as hard as they had.

In contrast to Amy's firm, John, an engineering manager in a high-tech firm, told us that in his team, where the members ranged in age from 23 to 69, "there is lots of banter and no issues when the oldest and younger ones communicate." John attributes this to the fact that the young hires were interns before they were permanently hired, during which time they learned the firm's behavioral norms and expectation of professionalism. "Seamlessness, it is amazing how folks work together. It is amazing." What makes one firm have generational tension and the other not? John attributes his firm's success to a lack of tolerance for such behavior, "when conflict occurs, it is shut down very quickly," by the team leader or other members. Here, the norms of the organization dictated that exhibiting unconstructive conflict, in this case, along generational lines, led to an immediate intervention to stop the offensive behavior.

Decision-making with respect to collaboration

When collaborating, "it is easy to say that the group needs to rally behind a given decision once it is taken," but that is easier said than done. The point here is that to the extent a group brings diverse perspectives to the table, the challenges involved in getting the group to agree on a way forward increase. As noted above by George from the financial services company, working with diverse teams does bring additional managerial challenges. Workgroup leaders need to focus on the long-term outcomes and be willing to initially sustain a potentially higher level of member conflict. Echoing George, above, Richard, the military base supervisor trainer, finds there is often a perceived "tradeoff between delivering results and maintaining a diverse culture—to achieve both is hard work and well worth it if the team continues to outperform the competition." When managers view diversity and performance as a trade-off or an "either or," they are likely to sacrifice diversity in the name of pursuing results. The Framework for Inclusive Interactions introduces managers to the structured inclusive interaction practices, which enable them to pursue long-term performance gains by instituting practices that eliminate the trade-offs.

Collaborating with member interdependence results in respect for all members as a result of the collaboration and coordinating to optimize performance. As a result of the mission or task orientation, the mixing and frequent interactions, and social interactions, the workgroup members value one another for their contributions and learn to deal with inclusive decision-making in a constructive manner. Because stereotypes and biases are likely to be brought into the organization from the broader society, achieving collaboration and sustaining it can be challenging. Support from authorities and use of the other practices described here are important if these challenges are to be overcome and, with time, prejudices reduced.

Practice 4: Handling conflict constructively

Much of our Framework's approach is about structuring interactions such that inclusion, equity, and performance are maximized and unconstructive conflict is minimized. When diversity-related conflict does occur, or when tensions arise around behavior or due to differing ideas on task-related decisions, there should be procedures and skills for dealing constructively with the conflicts. In diverse groups, conflict can be of two types, which sometimes overlap.

The first, personalized conflict, concerns personal treatment—the way that people behave with each other, typically reflecting stereotypes and/or clashes involving personal differences. The second is substantive conflict, concerning differences around how tasks or workgroup goals are pursued. When tensions are personalized, the conflict-handling procedure could involve recourse to a skilled, mutually-trusted individual whose counsel is sought. George, the executive in the financial services company, noted that when one particular trusted person who was an expert in mediating conflicts left the organization, there was a substantially diminished capacity to handle interpersonal tensions. The same interviewee recounted an experience where, despite continuing high performance in an international team, a few men continually created tensions in dealing with their women peers. The executive said that, in retrospect, while he could have dismissed these individuals, which would have "made a significant statement about his commitment to diversity and inclusion, doing so would have put a material dent in the performance of the workgroup." George continued by saying that "some level of conflict is inherent in organizations and that natural conflict is important to sustained high performance." Managing conflict, he said, was very challenging as he attempted to balance performance with his diversity and inclusion goals noting that "successful managers and team leaders need to optimize consistently and dynamically across objectives and constraints." Instances of personalized conflict involving intolerance for identity-based differences call for offending members to be held accountable through practices for accountable behavior (discussed in Chapter 7). In cases where a combination of conflict-handling practices and accountability practices prove insufficient to manage interpersonal conflicts, dismissal may be a necessary last resort and a signal of top management's commitment to diversity and inclusion.

When tensions are substantive, task-related, resulting from members' differing perspectives and expertise, they can be embraced as opportunities for workgroup performance to benefit from diversity. As cases arise, the opportunities can be recognized by the lead manager or members in regular team meetings. Standard operating procedures can turn those tensions into better decisions by offering agreed-upon paths to resolve the conflict. In an international joint venture, engineers from two different countries routinely identified differences that had arisen the day before in a daily morning meeting and resolved them by running trials or building prototypes to ascertain the best approach.[25] In a study of industry associations, the organizations judged to be the most successful overall in the association field were found to resolve impasses by assigning task forces or consultants to generate additional knowledge used to make an ultimate decision. Such standardized procedures de-personalize tensions and lead to better thought-out and accepted decisions.[26]

Examples of handling conflict constructively

Various approaches to conflict management existed within the organizations we interviewed. Perhaps most inspiring is the establishment by the new Commanding Officer (CO), the first woman in this position at the military base where we interviewed Richard, of a new internal office to investigate all unfair work practices and report directly to her. The CO made it clear to the 14,000 employees that she wanted a "safe environment for all." The office was established with two counselors, with plans to hire more, and a hotline to simplify reporting. We heard from the military base and engineering firm that conflicts should be resolved at the lowest levels, employee-to-employee. Richard emphasized that "this is easier when people feel comfortable. Though sometimes conflicts can't be resolved due to mental biases." But if this fails, "then the conflict goes up the chain of command with the goal of compromise and collaborate." To facilitate conflict resolution, the supervisors spend one day of the five-day management training on how to handle conflict—at which point Richard quickly interjected that this could be both "good and bad, destructive and constructive"—and typically centered on dealing with difficult behaviors.

> Conflict can be both "good and bad, destructive and constructive" (Richard).

When Richard sees race-related issues arise, he feels that this may be related to the fear some Whites have as they lose their dominance in the United States. Richard is concerned that those Whites who interpret this as being outnumbered are more fearful that others are being favored. In such cases, organizational emphasis on inclusion and on addressing the problems of *all* members around shared organizational goals can be useful. Richard explained that "we have fearful Whites because in the United States, they are becoming a minority." Speaking specifically about the supervisors in his classes, Richard teaches how to identify what needs people have that are not being addressed. This he feels is "often 100 percent of the problem." The difficulty for Richard is in getting his supervisor trainees to identify the specific problem. The emphasis, he said, should be on letting people tell their story, explain their perception of the problem, and make sure all involved are speaking the same language. We heard a similar comment from Ron, the administrator for a Western U.S. public university, who acknowledged "increased diversity means increased conflict." Ron elaborated by saying that, "we want the university to embrace [diversity], we want shared connections to each other's humanity," which comes with storytelling and learning each other's history. The caveat is the need, he felt, for a shared language, which may need to be taught in order to become an organizational norm. In conclusion, Ron said, "beyond the interactions ... are the policies that govern the interactions."

Alternatively, in the leadership fellowship, presented below, when the cohorts formed, one of the first tasks was to collectively write policies that dealt with governance and respect for one another. This model works because of two things: first, the cohort model ensured that everyone joined simultaneously and there were no prior members from whom to learn the organizational norms, and second, the group had the luxury of time as they were not profit-driven. This approach, which takes time, may be challenging for some managers to adopt and sustain in the workplace.

In the engineering firm, the majority of the conflict arises between their contractors and the firm's employees. Conflict handling is driven by formal agreements among the different project partners. These formal arrangements with the contract organizations include sections for how to resolve issues, "beginning at the lowest levels prior to going up the chain," which is the same approach to conflict resolution employed at the military base and common in many organizations. In the engineering firm, Amy revealed that, "within the company [conflict], goes to human resources (HR) and G-d knows what happens." She is concerned that "HR exists to keep the company out of litigation" and is not genuinely interested in resolving conflicts. Returning to the financial services company example, George suggested that it would have been useful in dealing with diverse workgroups to "have an industrial psychologist internal to the organization to advise the leader—someone trusted by everybody. The goal is to have a trusted organizational expert who can advise one-on-one, be a good listener, and provide frank feedback to the leader and the team—both as a group and individually." During our interviews, we observed a fear of litigation that drives the need for policies and trusted advisors.

> A daily huddle or stand-up meeting provided a mechanism for workgroup members to check in, clarify member responsibilities, air grievances, and address potential conflicts.

In a number of organizations we studied, we found that the use of a daily huddle or stand-up meeting provided a quick way for everyone in the workgroup to check in, clarify member responsibilities, and enable potential conflicts to be addressed. For example, we heard from a Black manager at a major banking firm that the members have a 15-minute stand-up meeting each morning, in addition to the more traditional weekly meetings. The manager felt that these meetings significantly contributed to the positive culture and lack of serious conflict. The medical research unit meets together weekly or bi-weekly, but the Fellows and JV Team meet every workday afternoon in a "team huddle" in order to quickly review how the clinical research trials were progressing, to divide up the tasks for the following day, reconfigure who is working on which trial because members must conduct their research in teams of two as each medical trial requires a "blinded" and "non-blinded" team member. While the team huddle provides an opportunity to air grievances and assess how the members are working together, the repeated shifting of the members into subgroups enables all team members to repeatedly interact with one another. Given that the Fellows and JV Team members have self-selected to join the group and see the opportunity as a great honor and benefit to their future, "bad behavior" is not observed, and Gary reports never having had to resolve a diversity or inclusion related issue.

Elizabeth, an outreach coordinator at a Midwest contemporary art museum, agreed that inclusion is still a challenge: "People accept that diversity is not the end; but then, when looking for inclusive options, often there is 'identity erasure.'" In other words, diversity and inclusion plans, such as those implemented at the museum, seemed to ignore identity-based conflict issues that staff members were having. For example, people of color did not appear to have the space to discuss real diversity-related issues affecting them, such as microaggressions. She went on to say that leadership was focused more on institutionalizing diversity, equity, inclusion, and access than on interpersonal conflict. Thus, *ignoring* conflict can also be challenging with inclusive interactions.

Some level of tension is to be expected if diversity is to lead to better decisions and performance, as we will consider further in Chapter 5. Everyday practices for constructively handling those task- and interpersonal-related tensions improve interaction comfort and performance. However, when tensions arise due to member behavior that is not inclusive, other conflict-handling practices, such as counseling and holding members accountable (Chapter 7), may be necessary.

Practice 5: Engaging in interpersonal comfort and self-efficacy

In diverse workgroups and teams, individuals can experience exclusive forces (Chapter 4) that inhibit inclusion including self-segregation, interaction discomfort, stereotyping and stigmatization, and implicit bias, which increases apprehension and cognitive dissonance, or stress, in the form of inconsistency between the stereotypes they hold of diverse group members and the behaviors they are observing. Reducing this discomfort and stress relies upon individuals adjusting their perceptions of those from the other group(s). Implementing the above practices can gradually produce comfort and self-efficacy in communicating with others, leading to more and more effective inclusive interactions. Comfort reflects an individual's fit within a group or social setting that enables appropriate behaviors when engaging with dissimilar others.[27] Without such comfort and skill, willingness to continue to interact and adjust perceptions will erode, resulting in lowered performance and equity outcomes.

Comfort is the "felt ease, safety, and self-efficacy of interacting appropriately with diverse others."[28] Within a diverse group or social setting, the member exhibits appropriate behaviors because feeling comfortable allows one to mitigate the need to be constantly self-moderating and fit within the group.

Comfort is significant for its ability to mitigate the need to be constantly self-moderating with dissimilar others. This empowers individuals within a group to engage with dissimilar others, disclose personal information and ask sensitive questions, and ultimately, become familiar with and learn from each other and alter the way that they behave, avoiding actions or comments that disrespect others and gaining communication skills. Individual behavior results from the continuous interaction among cultural structure, individual cognitive and affective processes, biology, and social environment.[29] Becoming comfortable with interpersonal interactions enables the acquisition of cultural competency that includes learning socially acceptable behaviors and how to negotiate the institutional structures of dissimilar cultures, races, and ethnicities. For workgroup members to experience and exhibit interpersonal comfort and self-efficacy, workgroup managers will, ideally, create opportunities for individuals to develop enough comfort in diverse interactions to learn and acquire behavioral skills that reflect cross-cultural competence. Comfort among workgroup members is not easy to achieve. At the military base, Richard said that as an organization, they often deal with disruptive behaviors and hostilities. Because of the "forced" diversity, supervisors must ask "if the hostilities are due to the resistance to diversity? We are very diverse. Do people feel comfortable? Not yet." According to Richard, "We are trying, but we need to break down barriers and biases and create relationships." Doing so requires, according to our Framework, following the practices described above. That is, the practice of engaging comfortably and with self-efficacy in a diverse workgroup depends on time spent by members experiencing the structured interaction practices of shared mission, frequent mixing, collaboration, and constructive conflict handling.

Understanding interpersonal comfort and self-efficacy

The self-efficacy of diverse members is at risk when they are stigmatized. Managers can address this problem proactively. In the medical research unit Gary routinely reinforced in his JV and Fellows teams the need for the members to treat each other and all those they interacted with in their professional duties warmly. This simple managerial practice contributed to maintaining comfortable inclusive behavior by addressing and controlling an important dimension of stereotyping: the stigmatizing of dissimilar others as cold and difficult to work with.[30] Being stigmatized is associated with anxieties that lead to diminished performance levels as assessed not only by others but also by the stigmatized individuals themselves.[31] That is, self-efficacy is diminished by inappropriate behavior that disrespects individuals, and that causes their discomfort. The discomfort felt by stereotyped members then is not something that is simply a nuisance but, rather, an organizational reality that hampers individual and workgroup performance. According to John, an engineering manager in a high-tech firm, this was recognized by leaders of the firms for which he had worked. They strongly promoted values statements and provided tools to apply the values in order to control non-inclusive behavior that produced interpersonal tensions, because these tensions disrupted team performance. A consequence was that managers and team members followed useful practices for behavioral accountability, having learned when and how to call out and end disrespectful behavior and interpersonal tensions when they arose.

Self-efficacy is also at play in workgroups in terms of members' skills in interacting with dissimilar others comfortably. Comfort among diverse members was identified in Janice McCabe's study of a multicultural sorority.[32] McCabe linked the sustaining of its diverse membership and its promotion of multiculturalism to specific practices among its members, including recognizing and valuing differences, teaching and learning about differences, and bridging differences via diversity interactions and organizational alliances. Within the sorority, these social practices were embedded in routinized behavior, enabling members to achieve a level of comfort in the interactions with diverse others. In our study of a college service fraternity, we[33] observed similar social practices that lead to intercultural comfort. The service fraternity's practices created among diverse members a close, equal status community where meaningful ties and comfort developed. Members reported that they experienced attitudinal change within the close community of the fraternity as a result of their experiencing comfort, direct interactions, and observations. Furthermore, these members reported strong feelings of belonging to the group and social identification with the group due to the perception of similarity strongly related to feeling safety and comfort,[34] respect for individual differences, and friendships that developed across diverse groups.

For individuals' personal development, comfort facilitates adaptive contact and learning, building social competence, and bolstering one's sense of efficacy.[35] Development of self-efficacy takes engaging in repeated shared task orientation experiences over time, as new information and experiences are acquired.[36] Self-efficacy enables individuals to become more flexible, adaptable, and able to adopt appropriate behaviors when engaged in diversity interactions. With respect to the service fraternity, we adopted the term intercultural comfort, defined as the "felt ease, safety, and self-efficacy of interacting appropriately with ethnically different others."[37] For these students, adopting the particular social practices described above enabled members to build intercultural comfort and overcome communication apprehension. These practices sustained Crisp and Turner's[38] four conditions for intercultural learning, discussed further in Chapter 6: perceptions of stereotype inconsistencies, motivation to engage, ability to engage, and repetition. Under these conditions, the service fraternity members formed close heterogeneous communities in which fellowship and comfort enabled individuals to learn from their differences.

Cross-group power issues apparent in our larger society are, in many situations, one source of interaction discomfort. These were addressed through self-disclosure practices within the leadership fellowship. According to Phillip, they were being taught the "true history of America, genocide of Native Americans, and slavery with real numbers" by listening "to stories of those in these affected groups." Through this process, Phillip "found out what being White means to me." One exchange he shared with us was when a member of the cohort told him, "I am Black and will die Black, but not you, who can reinvent yourself as a person in power, Black men cannot change." Phillip attributed the changes he experienced to "hearing about the trials and tribulations persons of color experience in a raw organic way." This storytelling was extraordinarily powerful for him. However, this and other self-disclosures by members, he felt, would not have occurred outside the "safe bubble" of the cohort, where trust had been fostered as a result of the repeated, frequent interactions. This trust, he said, enables one to speak and to endure harm while learning from diverse others. Once the trust was established, he knew he could come to the group "with imperfections and be accepted and loved" because "we are all comfortable enough to call something out, we know the other person wants to learn and change."

Relatively few workgroups will require the high level of self-disclosure experienced in the leadership fellowship, but some level of self-disclosure is valuable in many workgroups since it is a path to reducing bias.[39] A level of comfort is needed to generate disclosures, and those disclosures, in turn, increase interpersonal comfort. This comfort often extends relationships beyond formal organizational activities into personal social contexts and friendships. In the leadership fellowship, mothers with young children found that their relationships transcended racial differences and extended beyond the fellowship into their personal lives. At the military base, Richard, found that "informal interactions make teams better, builds comfort, and eases re-bonding when teams are reconfigured." And the students participating in the service fraternity spoke of deep friendships that included becoming roommates with diverse others.

Examples of engaging in interpersonal comfort and self-efficacy

Prior to experiencing feelings of comfort, many of our interviewees noted that they had often experienced discomfort. In Chapter 4, we highlight the inhibiting factors that individuals commonly experience in encounters with diverse others, including self-segregation, interaction discomfort, stereotyping and stigmatizing, and implicit bias. Phillip of the leadership fellowship said the "hardest part was overcoming fear. I am here to learn and make mistakes in front of others and grow through this uncomfortable situation."

Prior to joining the fellowship, Phillip thought he understood diversity issues but found this was not true when he was placed into this diverse group. "I am White, though raised in diverse New Mexico, I am a White man and born White man, and I am here to learn. I was not responsible for slavery, but I want to learn and be an advocate and want to fight for change, however that may look. I will make mistakes, [but in this group I know that will be] followed with compassion." "Don't condemn me," Phillip said, "enable me to be a better person and this had to come from someone who was a person of color." To get to a place of comfort, Phillip indicated that it took him about six months to, "learn how ignorant you are [and be able] to overcome fear and discomfort." Experiencing comfort within the group enabled him to reflect that instead of needing to "change [his] mind, I needed to change my actions through deep conversations with those around me," which he attributed to the safe bubble of the fellowship. We recognize that this example—the leadership fellowship—is quite extreme due to the group's personal developmental mission. We include this example to illustrate what is capable of happening through comfort and self-disclosure. It shows the power of comfort and the possibilities for this level of adaptive learning to occur among some workgroup members.

> Interviewees typically reported that it took about six months for them to overcome discomfort and be ready to learn.

Within the medical research group, comfort with diverse others is critical to mission achievement. In the health care institution, the Fellows and JV Team members must interact not only with one another but also with patients, doctors, and other medical personnel from diverse races and ethnicities. When asked about how these interactions impact the team members, Gary, the director, simply said, "we expect excellence—work hard but in a warm, friendly, learning environment. Friendly is also what we hear from the [JV Team] students." Feeling comfortable in diverse interactions is part of learning how to appropriately make a case to the patients for volunteering in a trial. "Over the time spent here," said Gary, "the Fellows and JV Team rapidly learn to be comfortable in [patient] interactions, to be convincing." Adding to the sense of comfort within the group is the unit philosophy that "there is only limited tolerance for competition." This unit's norm is one of collaboration, discussed above in Practice 3, as opposed to competition. Collaboration facilitates building comfort and contributing to the positive team culture.

> Transitioning from discomfort to comfort enables adaptive learning and individual skill development to occur.

The examples above illustrate a transition from discomfort to comfort. It is only through this transition that adaptive learning and individual skill development occurs. The shift from discomfort to comfort is the result of repeated, positive interactions with diverse others over a period of time. Comfort in interacting with diverse others is a necessary prerequisite for attitudinal change and the adaptive learning that will impact sustainable inclusion and performance. Developing comfort in interactions with diverse others takes time and patience, which in today's climate of "now," as George, the financial services executive told us, is difficult to sustain, despite the tremendous impact on performance outcomes he observed when he instituted these practices into his workgroups. For Phillip, from the leadership fellowship and Amy, the engineer, overcoming fear and establishing comfort among diverse workgroup members took them about six months. Comfort evolves from the time spent together experiencing strong, positive interactions under the conditions of these inclusive interaction practices.

This practice of engaging in interpersonal comfort and self-efficacy and the practice below, ensuring equal insider status for all members, are the most fundamental to accomplishing and sustaining inclusion. Becoming comfortable within the workgroup is most commonly an individual achievement that supports the collective achievement of equal status (Practice 6). The highlighting of equal status and comfortable interactions as most important is that they lead most directly to inclusion, equity, and performance. These two practices are the products of and the reason for the other practices. In other words, Practices 1–4 are supportive and enabling of these last two practices, which curtail biases, enable the integration of differences, and include all members in decision-making—supporting all aspects of Nishii's definition of inclusion (Introduction).

> Facilitating equal status and engaging in comfortable interactions are highlighted as the most important practices in that they lead most directly to inclusion, equity, and performance.

Practice 6: Ensuring equal insider status for all members

Ensuring equal insider status is fundamental to the inclusive engagement of organizational members. Put another way, being equally included is the most basic aspect of inclusion. Without it, the stigmatizing of underrepresented group members prevalent in society leads to their being excluded from important workgroup functions and decisions and to their experiencing reduced self-esteem and performance (Chapter 5). Due to experiences of discrimination in the broader society, members of underrepresented groups are especially susceptible to signs that they are not welcome[40] or valued.

> The most basic aspect of inclusion is being equally included.

What, exactly, does ensuring equal status entail? What is meant by "equal"? Drawing on Gordon Allport's[41] seminal specification of conditions favoring the reduction of intergroup prejudice, a contemporary social condition of equal status has been described in the following terms, terms that we see as inadequate for today's organizations:

Both groups must engage equally in the relationship. Members of the group should have similar backgrounds, qualities, and characteristics. Differences in academic backgrounds, wealth, skill, or experiences should be minimized if these qualities will influence perceptions of prestige and rank in the group.[42]

This specification includes two dimensions. One is based on backgrounds, where differences in characteristics that underlie formal status, socioeconomic status as seen in the broader society, confer rank. If a workgroup is composed of members, diverse and otherwise, who come from similar academic and wealth backgrounds, then this dimension of equal status will be present. However, these are relatively static characteristics of the individuals involved, and organizational practices are not static but dynamic and interpersonal. Practices are what people do together, routinely by habit (Chapter 6). Practices for inclusive engagement involve particular ways that they relate to each other in their everyday interactions, how they behave toward each other. The nature of organizational practices accords better with the other dimension in the above specification, "engage equally in the relationship," which can apply across differences in socioeconomic status and attendant characteristics of education, wealth, and experiences. This behavioral, engaging-in-the-relationship meaning of equal status is especially relevant when a diverse workgroup includes members from different job categories and socioeconomic backgrounds (including education and wealth), as in a cross-functional team with members from design, marketing and production, or a workgroup with members playing different technical and support roles.

Practices that ensure equal status do not mean equality in formal authority. Even in organizational situations involving semi-autonomous, self-directed teams, there exists a larger hierarchy of authority charged with making final decisions. Ensuring equal status in the workgroup means members having a respected voice in the decision-making process. This voice is important not only for equity but also for performance, elaborating perspectives, and information leading to better workgroup decisions (Chapter 5). Minority views are encouraged and respected, whether "minority" refers to an underrepresented group member or to someone who is by nature quiet and hesitant to speak up. Through their inclusive engagements with each other, the group considers multiple perspectives when coming to an important decision, with no dominant clique or subgroup carrying more weight. Workgroup members are understood as bringing complementary skills and experiences to the table, with their expertise in their role being sought and respected. It is in this behavioral sense that the practice of ensuring equal status is fundamental to inclusion, to inclusive engagement among organizational members.

Workgroup members are understood as bringing complementary skills and experiences to the table, with their expertise in their role being sought and respected.

Workgroups that create equal status communities share, or grow to share, a moral culture that embodies practices for equal status. Members treat each other as insiders, respecting each other's ideas and skills, whether meeting informally over lunch or more formally in a daily workgroup huddle where each member gets to voice concerns and ask questions. In the interviews conducted and the research examined for this book, we found that practices for equal status included communicating and consulting with each other, sharing information, and making decisions in ways that exemplify warmth, respect for competence, and self-disclosure. Equal status experiences and relationships are described with phrases such as partnership, not dependency; expertise that enriches the other; learning from each other; bicultural competency; interacting as peers; leaving one's cultural authority at the door; respect and reciprocity,[43] and being professional. Practices for ensuring equal status are on display in many formal and informal activities ranging from everyday one-on-one task discussions to periodic planning meetings, to infrequent group retreats, to occasional social engagements such as picnics and parties. (Box 3.4 provides an example of how some workgroups have used language justice to ensure equal insider status for all members.)

Examples of ensuring equal insider status for all members

Sharing Voice Promotes Equal Insider Status. "All voices will be heard" became the goal of the leadership fellowship, according to Phillip, as it worked together to establish ground rules for their cohort. This included drafting "community agreements" that addressed conflict management, respect, what will and will not be tolerated, and a voting process. "These agreements established ways in which we can maintain respect and integrity. [They are] not punishments, but [establish] how we stick together as a team." This kind of workgroup collaboration and valuing of all members facilitates inclusive interactions. This leadership fellowship, with the time-limited existence (18 months) of each cohort, was our only example of the workgroup writing their own policies.

BOX 3.4: LANGUAGE JUSTICE: CREATIVE APPLICATION OF EQUAL INSIDER STATUS

If a workgroup has a broadly shared commitment to the pursuit of inclusion, the diverse members will choose to address, as opposed to submerge or avoid, dealing with tough issues that will arise. Here, we provide such an example of how some workgroups have applied the practice of ensuring equal insider status for all members through the use of language justice.

In considering inclusive interactions and engagement, we would like you to consider how you communicate in your workgroup. *Language justice* is a term that is used to signify an organizational commitment to ensure that all voices are welcomed, heard, respected, and valued. This means having processes in place that allow all people to have equal access to information and an equal ability to participate. For some workgroups, this has meant ensuring tools are in place to help people connect across different languages, cultures, races, ethnicities, or immigration experiences. This may mean that translation services* need to be provided so that all members get to have their voices heard, be part of the discussion, and communicate with one another.

There is a business case for language justice because it builds better relationships, enables everyone to bring their full selves to the workgroup, creates a stronger sense of belonging, and allows all stakeholders to feel welcome. Below we provide examples of how to improve communication and information accessibility that are often used when inclusion is being pursued seriously. Communication issues commonly arise in diverse workgroups, particularly within those that are recently formed. When a workgroup is seriously committed to inclusion, addressing, rather than submerging or avoiding, communication challenges become the behavioral norm. We invite you to consider the examples below for ensuring language justice within your workgroups. Chapter 6 elaborates on the use of the technique of code-switching.

Therefore, we suggest you consider the following questions and reflect on how they may impact your workgroup:

- What kind of language are we using? For example, are we using academic vs. formal language?
- Are we engaging in code-switching?
- What is the workgroup's communication style, and is that accessible to all in attendance?
- What kinds of body language are being expressed, and is this offensive to others from different cultures or ethnicities?
- Are we consciously thinking about temporality and respecting each other's time?
- Is information being presented in a way that enables those with different learning styles to take advantage of the materials being provided?
- What are we doing to build trust and create a safe place for everyone to work together?
- What kinds of nonverbal interactions are the workgroup members engaging in? Are they appropriate and in support of the organization's task orientation or mission?

A few things to think about to improve the language justice within your workgroup:

- Speak in short phrases, avoid idioms, slang, professional jargon
- Define terms or acronyms

- Speak in the first person
- Address one another directly
- Be present at all times during the meeting
- Debrief or summarize after meetings or discussions

* Translation services prevent simple communication misunderstandings. For example, "debrief" may be interpreted to mean taking off your underwear to someone who is unfamiliar with English!

Power and Equal Insider Status. "Power is a big issue," said Ron, the university administrator, when discussing how students, staff, and faculty interact together. To overcome this, he strives to acknowledge:

> The differential factors and considerations that impact [minoritized groups'] sense of place, sense of belonging, and how they are seen by others [due to the] complex web of things operating in the background... So, team leaders should know about multiple identities, lived experiences, and institutional experiences [of the group members] and how these impact how they operate with others.

Ron suggested that there are "sets of skills needed for work team leaders and others" with a particular focus on enabling storytelling opportunities.

> Pedagogically speaking, with the use of [diversity, equity, and inclusion] best practices in development and training, it's not so much the cognitive learning but also the *affective*, the emotional. When having people bridge with one another, you need the capacity for empathy, cultural humility, being able to sit with discomfort. The work within any kind of training program that involves the most promise involves storytelling, which involves a person's history, experiences—sharing our stories—how people can be partner and ally in doing this work.

The self-disclosure that comes from interaction comfort can move some of this emotional work from the training setting to everyday workgroup interactions.

Ultimately, a workgroup needs to establish norms for behaviors and "community agreements with shared voice" that may be framed by asking, "how committed is the organization to diversity, equity, and inclusion?" (Ron)

Structuring interactions to ensure equal status and shared power are found within the service fraternity, where members rotated committee assignments and leadership positions. Because of the emphasis on teaching leadership skills in the organization, the students were unable to serve a second term or new leadership position until all members had assumed a leadership role. Structured interactions were employed to reduce the formation of cliques, and in the case of boards of directors, the formation of the well-recognized dominant coalitions that centers power within a smaller subgroup of the members. Cliques and dominant coalitions violate the practices of ensuring equal status for all members and mixing members repeatedly. An example of how disruptive cliques and dominant coalitions can be is commonly found in the executive committee of boards. In some cases, these committees that are typically charged in the organization's by-laws with only dealing with emergencies that may arise between formal board meetings, become very controlling and may, for example, prohibit potential agenda items from coming to the whole board or withhold information from board members to influence a decision. Without implementing Practice 6 (ensuring equal status) and Practice 2 (mixing members repeatedly), it is easier for cliques to form and, particularly in the case of boards of directors, power to become controlled by a few and not shared by all members.

The interaction practices work together

The practices described in this chapter foster inclusive interactions at the interpersonal level that are the key to achieving performance benefits. At the individual level, the benefit is learning about diverse others and developing self-efficacy and interaction skills that benefit collaborations and may be transferable to other diverse workgroups. The examples provided in this chapter demonstrate that inclusive interactions are created and sustained by these structured inclusive interaction practices that provide opportunities for prejudice reduction and adaptive learning, discussed in the subsequent chapters.

> Adopting and implementing sustained, structured, inclusive interaction practices provide opportunities for prejudice reduction and adaptive learning.

The examples also tell us that challenges arise and must be anticipated and dealt with skillfully and over time. In workgroups where the dynamic phenomena of exclusion predominate by default rather than being countered by effective practices, diversity efforts will be unsuccessful. When appropriately designed organizational practices are used, these phenomena are mitigated, enabling strong inclusive interactions that enhance diverse individuals' willingness and ability to engage repeatedly and improving sustainability, diversity, and performance outcomes. Without implementing the six specified practices and combining them with practices that hold members responsible for behaving inclusively, anti-inclusive dynamics will likely stifle the frequency and quality of diversity interactions. Weak, superficial interactions will dominate, as opposed to the frequent, meaningful interactions necessary to progress toward inclusion and sustainable diversity.

The earlier discussion about mixed-income housing provides a clear example of the frequent inadequacy of a single inclusive practice. While space for mixing is important, it is not a guarantee of residents engaging in inclusive interactions. Bringing together groups with substantially different statuses, as in mixed-income housing, makes prejudice reduction more difficult. What matters are whether or not inclusive interactions occur in these spaces, whether or not there are social structures, norms, and practices to shape those interactions and ensure that members interact comfortably and are given equal status in decision-making. In addition to the common spaces, there could be shared involvement in the governance of the community, along with norms of how to behave when in that governance process. Governance bodies within the mixed-income housing development may need to focus on how to create and support opportunities for the inclusive interactions to occur in order to mitigate the anti-inclusive social practices that heighten negative categorization, conflict, and anxieties. Actively promoting inclusive interaction practices across income groups, and addressing challenges along the way, enables more positive interactions and relationships to develop over time.[44] While residents must be willing to engage with diverse others and the physical space for these interactions must be provided, the supportive authority role of the property managers and governors plays an important role in the nature of social ties that develop among residents. Housing developments with common spaces but without enacted inclusive interaction practices are analogous to homogeneous workgroups, such as having both male and female work teams but not gender-mixed teams. These gender-separate teams may keep identity-based conflicts lower but reproduce segregation and categorization, causing problems when the groups do need to interact. Ultimately, given the social realities in most communities, the structured inclusive interaction practices need to work in combination within an organization.

Figure 3.2 highlights the impact of the structured inclusive interaction practices on interactions. Creating opportunities for workgroup members to engage in the inclusive interaction practices structured by their managers and organization creates strong interactions that foster adaptive learning. If the practices are not in place, the likelihood is that the interactions will be weak, consistent with the 60 percent null or negative performance outcomes of implementing diversity that a large body of research has revealed.[45] A vicious cycle occurs when inhibiting attitudes lead workgroup members to avoid interactions, enabling the persistence of prejudices. If, on the other hand, the set of inclusive interaction practices enable workgroup members to experience comfortable interactions, a virtuous cycle of adaptive learning is fostered. In this situation, the benefits of diverse interactions are experienced, reinforcing further inclusive interactions.

As structured inclusive interaction practices are implemented, managers should be focused on producing two workgroup behavioral processes over time. The first is positive social integration across identity groups based on perceptions of interpersonal

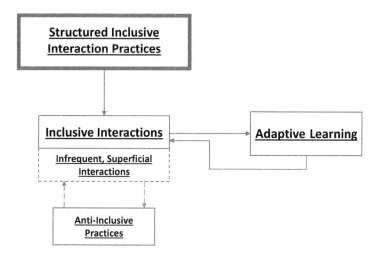

FIGURE 3.2 The Impact of Structured Inclusive Interaction Practices

comfort, psychological safety, trust, and justice. The second is an enhanced ability of the workgroup members to engage in insider status interchanges that elaborate perspectives and information relevant to interdependent work tasks. Both of these processes—social integration and information elaboration—will be elaborated upon in Chapter 5. Next, however, we turn to the nature and consequences of social practices that undermine inclusion, ubiquitous practices that create the need for organizations and their managers to devote conscious attention to structuring the practices for inclusive interactions described in this chapter.

Notes

1 van Knippenberg, D., De Dreu, C. K., & Homan, A. C. (2004). Work group diversity and group performance: An integrative model and research agenda. *Journal of Applied Psychology, 89*(6), 1008–1022.

2 Pettigrew, T. F., & Tropp, L. R. (2006). A meta-analytic test of intergroup contact theory. *Journal of Personality and Social Psychology, 90*(5), 751–783.

3 Dovidio, J. F., Glick, P., & Rudman, L. A. (Eds.). (2005). *On the nature of prejudice: Fifty years after Allport.* Blackwell; Paluck, E. L., Green, S. A., & Green, D. P. (2019). The contact hypothesis re-evaluated. *Behavioural Public Policy, 3*(2), 129–158.

4 Allport, G. W. (1954). *The nature of prejudice.* Addison-Wesley.

5 Sherif, M., & Sherif, C. W. (1953). *Groups in harmony and tension.* Harper.

6 Allport, G. W. (1954). *The nature of prejudice,* Addison-Wesley, p. 281.

7 Bowman, N. A. (2013). How much diversity is enough? The curvilinear relationship between college diversity interactions and first-year student outcomes. *Research in Higher Education, 54*(8), 874–894.

8 Gaertner, S. L., Mann, J., Murrell, A., & Dovidio, J. F. (1989). Reducing intergroup bias: The benefits of recategorization. *Journal of Personality and Social Psychology, 57*(2), 239–249.

9 Gaertner, S. L., Dovidio, J. F., Anastasio, P. A., Bachman, B. A., & Rust, M. C. (1993). The common ingroup identity model: Recategorization and the reduction of intergroup bias. *European Review of Social Psychology, 4*(1), 1–26.

10 Ibid, p. 1.

11 Roccas, S., & Brewer, M. B. (2002). Social identity complexity. *Personality and Social Psychology Review, 6*(2), 88–106, 89.

12 Brewer, M. B., & Gardner, W. (1996). Who is this "we"? Levels of collective identity and self representations. *Journal of Personality and Social Psychology, 71*(1), 83.

13 Brewer, M. B. (1991). The social self: On being the same and different at the same time. *Personality and Social Psychology Bulletin, 17*(5), 475–482.

14 Pickett, C. L., Gardner, W. L., & Knowles, M. (2004). Getting a cue: The need to belong and enhanced sensitivity to social cues. *Personality and Social Psychology Bulletin, 30*(9), 1095–1107.

15 Shore, L. M., Randel, A. E., Chung, B. G., Dean, M. A., Holcombe Ehrhart, K., & Singh, G. (2011). Inclusion and diversity in work groups: A review and model for future research. *Journal of Management, 37*(4), 1262–1289 (p. 1265, italics in original).

16 Harrison, D. A., Kravitz, D. A., Mayer, D. M., Leslie, L. M., & Lev-Arey, D. (2006). Understanding attitudes toward affirmative action programs in employment: Summary and meta-analysis of 35 years of research. *Journal of Applied Psychology, 91*(5), 1013–1036; Leslie, L. M., Mayer, D. M., & Kravitz, D. A. (2014). The stigma of affirmative action: A stereotyping-based theory and meta-analytic test of the consequences for performance. *Academy of Management Journal, 57*(4), 964–989.

17 Crisp, R. J., & Turner, R. N. (2011). Cognitive adaptation to the experience of social and cultural diversity. *Psychological Bulletin, 137*(2), 242–266.

18 Halualani, R. T. (2008, 2008/01/01/). How do multicultural university students define and make sense of intercultural contact? A qualitative study. *International Journal of Intercultural Relations, 32*(1), 1–16.

19 Joseph, M. (2013). *National Initiative on Mixed-Income Communities.* Case Western Reserve University. https://case.edu/socialwork/nimc/

20 Leslie et al. (2014). "The stigma of affirmative action."

21 Bowman (2013). "How much diversity is enough?"

22 Crisp & Turner (2011). "Cognitive adaptation."

23 van Knippenberg et al. (2004). "Work group diversity and group performance."

24 Kalev, A. (2009). Cracking the glass cages? Restructuring and ascriptive inequality at work. *American Journal of Sociology, 114*(6), 1591–1643.

25 Weisinger, J. Y., & Salipante, P. F. (2000). Cultural knowing as practicing: Extending our conceptions of culture. *Journal of Management Inquiry, 9*(4), 376–390.

26 Engle, M. T. (2012). Balanced conflict, better decisions. *Associations Now, The Volunteer Leadership Issue*(January), 89–91.

27 Noble, G. (2005). The discomfort of strangers: Racism, incivility and ontological security in a relaxed and comfortable nation. *Journal of Intercultural Studies, 26*(1–2), 107–120.

28 Bernstein, R. S., & Salipante, P. (2017). Intercultural comfort through social practices: Exploring conditions for cultural learning. *Frontiers in Education*, Vol. 2, Article 31, p. 9. doi:10.3389/feduc.2017.00031. http://journal.frontiersin.org/article/10.3389/feduc.2017.00031/full?&utm_source=Email_to_authors_&utm_medium=Email&utm_content=T1_11.5e1_author&utm_campaign=Email_publication&field=&journalName=Frontiers_in_Education&id=272155.

29 LaFromboise, T., Coleman, H. L., & Gerton, J. (1993). Psychological impact of biculturalism: Evidence and theory. *Psychological Bulletin, 114*(3), 395–412.

30 Fiske, S. T., Cuddy, A. J., Glick, P., & Xu, J. (2002). A model of (often mixed) stereotype content: Competence and warmth respectively follow from perceived status and competition. *Journal of Personality and Social Psychology, 82*(6), 878–902.

31 Leslie et al. (2014). "The stigma of affirmative action."

32 McCabe, J. (2011). Doing multiculturalism: An interactionist analysis of the practices of a multicultural sorority. *Journal of Contemporary Ethnography, 40*(5), 521–549.

33 Bernstein, R. S., & Salipante, P. (2015). Comfort versus discomfort in interracial/interethnic interactions: Group practices on campus. *Equality, Diversity and Inclusion: An International Journal, 34*(5), 376–394; Bernstein & Salipante (2017). "Intercultural comfort through social practices."

34 Noble (2005). "The discomfort of strangers."

35 Jones, J. (1995). *Affects of process.* The Analytic Press.

36 Gist, M. E., & Mitchell, T. R. (1992). Self-efficacy: A theoretical analysis of its determinants and malleability. *Academy of Management Review, 17*(2), 183–211.

37 Bernstein & Salipante (2017). "Intercultural comfort through social practices," p. 9.

38 Crisp & Turner (2011). "Cognitive adaptation."

39 Kenworthy, J. B., Turner, R. N., Hewstone, M., & Voci, A. (2005). Intergroup contact: When does it work, and why. In J. F. Dovidio, P. Glick, & L. A. Rudman (Eds.), *On the nature of prejudice: Fifty years after Allport* (pp. 278–292). Blackwell.

40 Spencer, K. B., Charbonneau, A. K., & Glaser, J. (2016). Implicit bias and policing. *Social and Personality Psychology Compass, 10*(1), 50–63.

41 Allport, G. W. (1954). *The nature of prejudice.*

42 Wikipedia. (2020). *Contact hypothesis.* https://en.wikipedia.org/wiki/Contact_hypothesis

43 Seidl, B., & Friend, G. (2002). Leaving authority at the door: Equal-status community-based experiences and the preparation of teachers for diverse classrooms. *Teaching and Teacher Education, 18*(4), 421–433.

44 Levy, D. K., McDade, Z., & Bertumen, K. (2013). Mixed-income living: Anticipated and realized benefits for low-income households. *Cityscape, 15*(2), 15–28.

45 Joshi, A., & Roh, H. (2009). The role of context in work team diversity research: A meta-analytic review. *Academy of Management Journal, 52*(3), 599–627, discussed in Chapter 5.

4

EXCLUSIONARY FORCES

Widespread social practices that inhibit inclusion

Why is it that diversity has proved so challenging for organizations? To answer that question, this chapter brings together evidence from several different academic fields to identify exclusionary forces that workgroups, teams, and organizational members experience when attempting to turn diversity into beneficial outcomes. The challenge of achieving sustainable inclusion, with its attendant equity and performance benefits for workgroups, is complex. Due to this complexity, the limitations and lack of progress of many well-intended approaches are no surprise. Here, as illustrated in Figure 4.1, we introduce the exclusionary forces as a set of practices that some or many organizational members follow, inhibiting inclusive interactions and adaptive learning. These forces have been identified in various large bodies of empirical studies.

In this chapter, we will see that exclusion is caused by social forces that are ubiquitous. In their most basic forms, these forces are natural, serving everyday human needs related to pursuing self-interest and reducing cognitive complexity. Exclusionary forces are felt at the organizational and workgroup levels.

Exclusionary forces are ubiquitous natural human phenomena felt at the organizational and workgroup levels.

Their persistence in workgroups is strengthened by occupational grouping at the societal level—grouping on the basis of race, ethnicity, gender, and age, such as women in nursing and men in engineering. The several exclusionary forces interrelate and feed on each other, impeding diversity interactions from becoming inclusive interactions. Each force leads to homogeneous groupings, overemphasis on differing identities, and failure to utilize the knowledge and skills of underrepresented groups. The

DOI: 10.4324/9780367822484-8

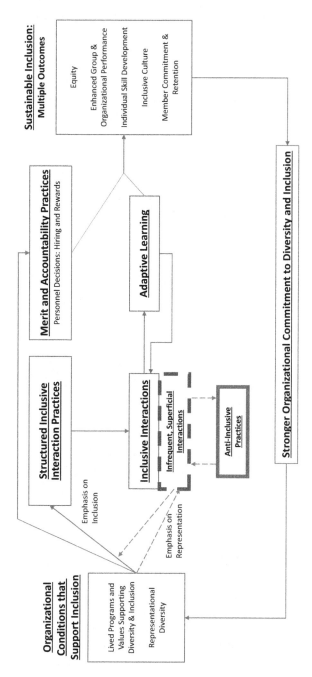

FIGURE 4.1 The Framework for Inclusive Interactions: Exclusionary Forces that Inhibit Inclusive Interactions

reality for organizations and workgroups is that these detrimental outcomes can be expected to occur by default unless group and organizational strategies are instituted to counter them and drive positive, meaningful inclusive interactions.

Figure 4.2 illustrates the exclusionary forces as four *anti-inclusive practices* that inhibit inclusive interactions and adaptive learning. Three of the practices involve individuals' active social behavior: self-segregating into interactions with individuals similar to oneself; experiencing discomfort and anxiety when interacting with someone seen as dissimilar; and stereotyping and stigmatizing a dissimilar other as incompetent and unfriendly. These behaviors represent the triggering into action of the fourth force, implicit bias. That unconscious bias also underlies the practice of managers making inequitable personnel decisions on pay and promotions for members of underrepresented groups. These four practices, then, often do not operate as overt discrimination. Rather, they can be more subtle and widespread, representing largely unconscious attitudes and behavior that are not felt by the acting individual as discriminating or harmful. Ironically, research findings discussed below indicate that subtle discrimination has greater detrimental effects than overt discrimination and that even small amounts of implicit bias produce large errors in personnel decisions, creating dramatic societal differences in hiring members of underrepresented groups.

Subtle discrimination has greater detrimental effects than overt discrimination.

Separately and in combination, the four exclusionary forces produce diversity interactions that are less frequent and more anxiety-producing than interactions with similar others, inhibiting the adaptive learning among workgroup members required to leverage diversity successfully. Failure to understand why and how exclusion is widespread leads a society to suffer reduced equity across its members and lowered performance across its organizations, producing economic costs borne not only by its underrepresented members but by all its members and organizations.

Anti-inclusive practices can be countered.

Fortunately, research reveals that anti-inclusive practices can be countered. In this chapter and the next, we note strategies that are ineffective and those that are effective and practical, as revealed by research evidence. Effective strategies require understanding and acknowledging the operation of each of the four anti-inclusive practices, which we present here in four sections. In these sections, we present overviews of the research-based evidence, more details on the evidence, illustrative cases and examples, and implications for effective organizational action. The objective of this chapter, and those immediately following, is not to provide a comprehensive analysis of the research. Rather, it is to utilize expert systematic

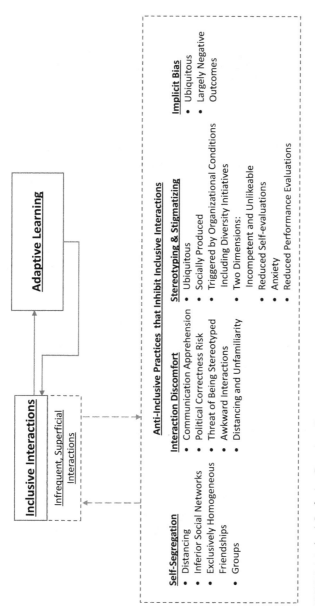

FIGURE 4.2 Anti-Inclusive Practices Summary

reviews of that research[1] to draw out key findings that can guide organizations in understanding the need to mitigate the exclusionary forces' negative effects, which dominant contemporary efforts have failed to do.

Box 4.1 provides a primer on the nature and value of systematic reviews. The primer provides an overview for those interested in how evidence from a set of related research studies is analyzed and synthesized. However, the main point is that, as in the field of medicine, synthesizing and pooling the findings from a number of studies provides more reliable and valid evidence upon which to base practice. In this book, we prefer to rely on the findings and conclusions from systematic reviews when available, rather than on the findings from individual studies.

BOX 4.1: SYSTEMATIC REVIEWS FOR EVIDENCE-INFORMED MANAGERS: A PRIMER[2]

Literary systematic reviews

- are built around a specific question, such as whether accountability practices reduce the impact of gender bias on hiring and pay;
- perform an exhaustive search for all studies whose findings bear on that question, including unpublished studies;
- draw together the relevant studies, either or both quantitative and qualitative studies;
- specify criteria for selecting in and, possibly, weeding out studies based on their methods—for example, selecting only laboratory studies with experimental designs that permit conclusions about causality, or only studies done in actual organizational settings;
- assess agreements and disagreements in findings across the studies;
- engage in interpretations, seeking to explain the reasons for disagreements;
- propose implications for further research and for managerial practice.

Meta-analytic reviews

- are similar to systematic literary reviews in all the above ways except draw only on quantitative studies having analyses that specify the strength of relationships among the study's variables.
- Are able to pool the data from all the included studies to produce results based on a large population size, rendering higher statistical confidence.
- Propose a net effect from the group of studies, even when individual studies have produced divergent findings.
- May identify contextual factors that varied across the studies and that statistically explain differences in the effects found.

Self-segregating as an exclusionary dynamic

Self-segregating, commonly known by the saying "birds of a feather flock together" and termed *homophily* in sociological literature,[3] is a natural human behavior. Even when physically proximate to dissimilar others for long periods of time, individuals tend to associate instead with people most clearly similar to themselves. Self-segregating by ethnicity, race and social class is ubiquitous in modern societies. In the United States, its extent has remained stable for decades and operates even in residentially integrated settings.

> *The Evidence.* A review of research[4] finds that interactions across individuals of differing income and ethnicity are infrequent and superficial in mixed-income housing developments. They become even less frequent over time.[5] Bringing different groups into proximity in mixed-income housing, including in spaces where architectural design encourages interaction, typically leads to tensions and a lack of cross-group social ties.[6] Efforts that create proximity but leave interactions to natural social processes fail. For example, plans to create inclusive organizations of residents failed to be enacted.[7]

Interactions across individuals that differ in income and ethnicity are infrequent and superficial in settings with intentionally diverse membership, such as mixed income housing developments and schools.

> Attesting to the widespread nature of self-segregating behavior, in U.S. General Social Surveys over 85% of Whites report knowing an African-American, but well fewer than 2% report a close relationship with an African-American.[8] Distancing can start at an early age. In a field experiment involving elite primary schools in India, richer students were found to be willing to sacrifice monetary rewards to avoid interacting with poorer students.[9] With racial homophily in the U.S. being stable over several decades,[10] self-segregation has persisted even in supposedly desegregated settings. Public schools have become more, not less, segregated.[11] Many other examples illustrate this persistence of homophily in various types of organizations—voluntary, public sector, and businesses. For instance, approximately half of Girl Scout troops in two stably integrated U.S. communities were found to be either homogeneously White or homogeneously Black.[12] And, students in an affluent community's integrated high school self-segregated into racially homogeneous academic tracks.[13]

Self-segregation is natural and widespread because it can serve positive purposes, but it imposes costs of reduced connections that are valuable for collective performance and pursuing opportunities.

The Evidence. For groups that experience discrimination, homogeneous groups provide protection. For groups in general, homophily simplifies the development of trust. It can contribute to the formation of valuable affinity and support groups, as noted in Chapter 2. However, self-segregating has a major downside regarding social networking and the development of social capital for pursuing business opportunities. Homophily strongly determined the ethnic and gender composition of teams starting new businesses,[14] and friendship networks in an MBA program were found to be racially homogenous due in part to exclusionary pressures from dominant group members.[15] Homophily's effects on achieving cooperation in large groups, as in mass political movements, appear to be curvilinear, moderate levels being helpful but too much homophily impeding success.[16]

When social structures leave individuals to their own volition, self-segregating behavior is the expected outcome.

Implications for inclusive practice. Self-segregating behavior is so ubiquitous and stable over time that all leaders must be concerned with its effects in their organizations, even within seemingly integrated situations. When social structures leave individuals to their own volition, self-segregating behavior is the expected outcome. It takes only one group desiring similarity for self-segregation to occur. Self-segregating behavior need not be countered in all situations. For members of underrepresented groups, it can aid the formation of support groups that provide safety and valuable sharing of knowledge on how to manage difficult situations. However, organizational leaders should expect that self-segregating behavior is leading to distancing and lack of valuable social networking across gender and ethnic groups, and across functional areas requiring coordination, such as between White male scientists and female and minority support staff in the scientific group case presented earlier, in Chapter 1. As we will see next, self-segregating leads to uncomfortable interactions with dissimilar others, directly impeding the development of inclusive behavior and its attendant equity and performance benefits.

Self-segregating leads to uncomfortable interactions with dissimilar others, directly impeding the development of inclusive behavior and its attendant equity and performance benefits.

Interacting with discomfort: Anxiety and communication apprehension

Discomfort in diversity interactions takes the form of apprehension about how to communicate with a dissimilar other. For dominant group members, this apprehension can be heightened by social norms of political correctness. Members of underrepresented groups have more opportunities to develop familiarity with dominant group members than the reverse, but they can be anxious about being stereotyped. When interactions do occur, clumsiness inhibits learning. Discomfort and self-segregating reinforce each other, as unfamiliarity and anxiety in the interactions lead to avoiding future interactions, preserving unfamiliarity and anxiety.

> Discomfort in diversity interactions leads to avoidance of dissimilar others that inhibits learning.

The Evidence. Anxiety in diversity interactions can take the form of cross-cultural communication apprehension.[17] For members of both dominant and underrepresented groups, anxiety can be experienced in interactions governed by organizational norms of political correctness and propriety, creating increased risk when interacting with dissimilar others.[18] Members of a society's most populous group, by definition, have fewer opportunities for interacting with minority group members and gaining familiarity, while many minorities have more opportunities, frequently unavoidable, for interacting with dominant group members.[19] Consequently, minority group members are more likely to develop bicultural communication skills. However, their discomfort and anxiety may be triggered by knowing that the dominant group member is uncomfortable or, more ominously, by the threat of being negatively stereotyped by that individual,[20] based on past experience of discrimination.

Self-segregation and communication apprehension operate recursively, reinforcing each other over time. Self-segregating behavior produces unfamiliarity, uncertainty and anxiety in interactions, and these feelings, in turn, provide an incentive to avoid future contact.[21] When contact does occur, clumsiness in the interaction works against the interaction being adaptive, since unfamiliarity and uncertainty persist.[22] Examples of this can be observed when dominant workgroup members are fearful of asking diverse members questions, such as about heritage or cultural history and traditions, as they perceive these topics to be politically incorrect or insensitive.[23]

> Self-segregation and interaction discomfort reinforce each other over time. Avoidance preserves unfamiliarity that leads to clumsiness in interactions, and that discomfort leads to avoiding future interactions.

Implications for inclusion and organizational effectiveness. Discomfort and self-segregating form a vicious cycle that results in a continuing lack of meaningful interactions across members of differing ethnicity, race, gender, and other personal characteristics. Though for different reasons, members of both dominant and underrepresented groups are likely to be anxious about their interactions with each other. When interactions are uncomfortable, norms of political correctness heighten avoidance and make the fewer interactions superficial ones, as depicted in Figure 4.1. These norms can create barriers to discussing and implementing an equity lens[24] when inclusive interaction practices are lacking. By not asking each other serious questions and engaging in self-disclosure, individuals do not progress to greater familiarity and adaptive learning about how to interact most productively. Superficial interactions then have problematic consequences for performance in workgroups, with decreased chances of all members' knowledge and skills being tapped, especially when individuals are distracted from a task-focus by "the burden of regulating their own behavior."[25]

Stereotyping and stigmatizing

Self-segregating and experiencing interaction discomfort are relatively self-focused and unaggressive social practices. However, the unfamiliarity and anxiety that they engender can serve as a foundation for more outwardly negative dynamics based on prejudice—the stereotyping and stigmatizing of members of underrepresented groups. Unfamiliarity leads to stigmatizing through the process of a person acting on the basis of unconscious implicit biases, discussed in the next section of this chapter, or from more conscious biases. Self-segregating, interaction discomfort, and even stereotyping are insufficient to cause stigmatizing.[26] The intervention of a *negative bias* transforms self-segregating, discomfort and stereotyping into stigmatizing. Understanding these social processes requires defining two key concepts:

> Stereotype: A widely held but fixed and oversimplified image or idea of a particular type of person or thing (Oxford Dictionary, www.lexico.com).
>
> Stigmatize: Describe or regard as worthy of disgrace or great disapproval (Oxford Dictionary, www.lexico.com).

Stereotypes can represent either a positive or a negative bias, while stigmatizing is singularly negative and exclusionary since it involves the act of disgracing.

Why is stereotyping common?

Whether positive or negative, stereotypes involve prejudging another through the normal and functional process of *categorization*. Creating categories simplifies decisions and makes for greater human efficiency. While they oversimplify, creating categories that stereotype others can be understood as necessary for individuals in everyday life. They bound rationality,[27] reducing the time and effort needed to make a decision and act.

The Evidence. Brain studies[28] indicate that judgments that are individualized (to one particular person) rather than stereotyped involve the activation of a more complex neural network. Even with more cognitive resources activated, individuating is less effective when focused on members of racial out-groups rather than on members of an in-group. However, the process of categorization has potential for inaccuracy and prejudice since gross categories are more efficient than fine-grained ones, the categories are resistant to change from evidence, "us" vs. "them" emotions are created on the basis of in-group vs. out-group categorization, and observed behavior is interpreted in ways that favor the in-group.[29]

Being socially produced, negative stereotypes and stigmatizing can be mitigated

While held and acted upon by individuals, stereotypes are produced and revised by a social process—by individuals in a particular group generating and sharing beliefs. Since it involves disgracing, stigmatizing is similarly and necessarily a social process.

> *The Evidence.* Laboratory research shows that stereotypes can be modified by social messages.[30] And, when social conditions lead a person to be motivated to be more accurate in their observations, individuals do see subgroup differences within an out-group, "limiting the tyranny of categories."[31]

Implications for organizations. Understanding that stereotyping and stigmatizing are social is critical to enhancing inclusion in organizations. Being social means that social practices in a particular organization can dampen or amplify negative stereotyping and stigmatizing, making them less vs. more present and less vs. more relevant to members of workgroups. Consistent with our Framework's emphasis on social practices, social factors can thwart negative stereotyping. However, without some intentional structuring of countervailing social practices, organizations can expect that negative stereotypes and stigma in the general society will be present in their workplaces or teams, inhibiting inclusion and performance within heterogeneous workgroups and across workgroups having differing compositions.

Organizational conditions that trigger stigmatizing

Stereotypes and stigma are triggered into decisions and actions by particular situations that arise in everyday life. Some actions that result from stereotyping protect individuals but diminish their inclusion and developmental opportunities, as in an example from one of our interviews.

> Stereotypes and stigma are triggered by situations that arise in everyday life.

A young female Asian engineer was denied the opportunity to go to a job site by her older female engineering supervisor. The rationale was based on stereotypes regarding the individuals involved, namely, a fear of sending a young, vulnerable woman to a rough, male-dominated job site, despite knowing that "she was just as good as the men." In this case, the stigma was attached to the males involved, not the member of the underrepresented group.

Research has focused on one main factor that can trigger stigmatizing against members of underrepresented groups: The nature of diversity initiatives in organizations—their design and how they are communicated to members. From that research, we conclude that some stigmatizing is likely to result from any initiative perceived as diversity-focused. The conditions that trigger stigmatizing can be illustrated by three examples:

A simple statement such as "Affirmative Action Hire" on the bottom of a job candidate's application can trigger stigmatizing by the individual doing the hiring, even when, for example, a new hire is presented as holding an MBA from Harvard University.[32]

Within higher education, the practice of releasing funding for "opportunity hires"—jumping on the chance to hire a faculty member of color—may lead to stigmatizing the individual hired as opposed to rejoicing in the hiring of a highly-qualified person.

Within faith-based nonprofits, including universities, those who are members of the particular organization's faith report feeling the stigma of being an "opportunity hire" because of their religious affiliation.

BOX 4.2: CONFIDENCE IN RESEARCH FINDINGS

Research studies vary in their validity, in the confidence that we can place in their findings. Experimental studies conducted in laboratory settings are able to control on alternative explanations for their findings. They are termed to be high on *internal validity* for testing causal effects, with high confidence in the findings having actually occurred in the particular manipulated laboratory situation. However, since lab studies' findings may not carry over well to the more complex real world, field studies in actual organizations are superior in *external validity*, with their findings being more clearly applicable to organizational settings. Higher-quality field studies approach laboratory studies in establishing causality when they measure effects over time and perform analyses that control on alternative explanations. When findings converge between laboratory studies and field studies, when they *cross-validate*, we can have higher confidence that the effects of the studied elements are both causal and applicable to particular organizational settings.

Two large systematic literature reviews, presented below, used meta-analytic techniques to pool (combine) and analyze data from many individual studies. The reviews investigated ways in which diversity initiatives, in the form of Affirmative Action Programs, stigmatize members of groups who are seen as the intended beneficiaries. More broadly, this research informs us about the effects of any form of diversity initiative, whether labeled as affirmative action or not. In the reviews, stigmatized groups were termed "targets" of the program, and other organizational members "non-targets." Our confidence in the findings of these reviews and their reflecting actual organizational realities is high since they consistently found similar results both from carefully controlled laboratory studies that are high in internal validity (causation, as described in Box 4.2) and from field studies in organizations that are high in external validity (applicability in the real world). The reviews are particularly relevant for organizational policy and design because they investigated situational factors, factors amenable to managerial manipulation.

The first of these two reviews by David Harrison and colleagues[33] found that attitudes opposing or in favor of an organization's diversity program varied in expected ways according to the ethnicity, race, gender, self-interest, personal experience of discrimination, racism, sexism, and political ideology of the member. Of greater interest for designing organizational practices, the researchers identified the influence on these attitudes of a program's *prescriptiveness*, the degree to which a program prescribed an influence on job-outcome decisions for target individuals. Prescriptiveness ranged from the weakest level of enhancing opportunity through recruitment efforts to middle levels of prohibiting discrimination and allowing tie-breaking when qualifications are equal, to the strongest level, preferential treatment.

Definition of *Prescriptiveness*: the degree to which a program prescribed an influence on job-outcome decisions for target individuals.

The Evidence. For some studies in the meta-analysis, prescriptiveness was measured in terms of perceived fairness, while for most of the studies, prescriptiveness was assessed in terms of the type of program, as described above. Across the 110 studies in the meta-analysis, prescriptiveness consistently affected the strength of the relationships between personal characteristics and supportive vs. unsupportive attitudes toward programs. For example, the difference between the supportive attitudes of Blacks and Whites was approximately four times greater for programs with the highest measured prescriptiveness than for programs with low prescriptiveness. Regarding how particular individuals justified their opposition to a program, the review found stronger results of this type when a study used measures of "modern racism"[34]—defined as explanations for negative beliefs about other groups that the individual intended to be plausible and nonprejudicial rather than racist—than when a study measured overtly racist beliefs.

The meta-analysis also investigated whether members of an organization are influenced by how a diversity program is presented to them. Programs that were only tacitly defined were associated with stronger negative attitudes than those providing explicit knowledge of the program's approach. And, justifying the program only on the basis of lack of representation decreased its support.

Implications for practice. It is not surprising that individuals' support for diversity programs varied by race, gender, and other characteristics, but the lack of shared attitudes among organizational members can create tensions that undermine the very purpose of the programs, as we will see below. The findings based on a study's use of modern racism scales indicate that leaders should not expect that a lack of observed, overt racism indicates that programs are being accepted and supported by members. Members can justify unsupportive attitudes toward a diversity program in more subtle ways, through espousing beliefs about a group's inferiority that are based on explanations that are intended by the individual to be nonprejudicial. Fortunately, organizations can lessen the differences across their members through the choices they make on how diversity initiatives are designed and communicated. According to the findings, organizational communication on the prescriptiveness of a program should be explicit, not tacit. Regarding prescriptiveness, a program that emphasizes broadening the applicant pool and whose purpose is stated to be locating and hiring the most qualified applicants to provide the greatest skill, knowledge, and energy to workgroups will make sense to a broad range of current organizational members.

> How diversity initiatives are designed and communicated can lessen the differences across organizational or workgroup members.

Stigmatizing content

> The two primary categories of negative stereotypes are *low competence* and *lack of warmth*.

Stigmatizing members of underrepresented groups rests primarily on the two categories that the stereotype content model[35] identifies: *low competence* and *lack of warmth*. The model proposes that an individual from one group who sees another group as having low status justifies this as deserved because the group lacks competence, while high-status groups are seen as having earned it through competence and hard effort. That is, low perceived status of a group triggers stereotypes of low competence being applied to all members of that group. The other category, lack of warmth, is seen as triggered by a different perception, that the other group is being favored in receiving rewards.

The Evidence. The two categories differentiated stereotypes of various groups, as rated by student and non-student samples that were approximately 70% White. Poor Whites and poor Blacks were rated as low in competence and warmth. Housewives were rated most highly on warmth but low on competence. Groups rated high in competence were the rich, Jews, feminists, businesswomen, Asians, Northerners, and Black professionals, but they were rated (respectively) only low to moderate in warmth. As proposed in the model, the ratings of competence were predicted by the stereotyped group's social status, while lack of warmth was predicted by perceived competition between the rater and the specified group over jobs, power, and resources.

> A group with low social status is stereotyped as low in competence, while a group seen as a competitor is stereotyped as difficult to work with.

Negative stereotypes about competence can be a problem not only within an organization but also in its efficient use of external resources. An example:

Black entrepreneurs reported that they needed to make special efforts to prove their competence before being chosen to provide services or products to dominantly White organizations, while White entrepreneurs were often chosen simply on the basis of a referral.[36]

Implications for Organizations. A lack of representational diversity in the society as a whole plays a role in stigmatizing: Underrepresentation in high-level jobs and overrepresentation in low-level jobs defines a group as low status, opening the group's members in any organization to the stigma of low competence. The members of underrepresented groups in the organization who are most successful, such as businesswomen and Black professionals, may be seen positively in terms of competence, but not as positively on warmth because others perceived them as posing a threat to their interests. The main problem is clear: negative stereotypes impede the recognition and proper utilization of talent because members of stereotyped groups are stigmatized as difficult to work with and/or lacking in competence.

> Negative stereotypes impede the recognition and proper utilization of talent due to the stigma or perception of being difficult to work with.

Stigmatizing's impacts on members of underrepresented groups

Stigmatizing based on negative assessments of competence and warmth has serious, self-fulfilling consequences on the perceived job performance of members of underrepresented groups, inhibiting inclusion of these members. A second meta-analytic review of studies on affirmative action programs by Lisa Leslie and her co-researchers[37] was designed to investigate and explain an unintended consequence of these programs: That they lowered rather than raised performance evaluations of their intended beneficiaries. This review of studies found that greater prescriptiveness in a diversity program was associated with stronger negative stereotyping of underrepresented group members and with lower performance evaluations, both in formal evaluations and, more insidiously, in the members' self-evaluations. The detrimental effect on self-evaluations is consistent with stereotype threat theory[38]—confirmed by studies carried out in a variety of societies—which holds that negative stereotyping presents a personal threat to those who are stereotyped.

> *The Evidence.* Parallel to the first meta-analytic review's focus on program prescriptiveness, this review[39] examined the perceived extent of affirmative action. In two separate sets of analyses, the review related this extent to evaluations of targets' performance by non-targets and by the targets themselves. The analyses for non-targets revealed that the association between an individual's perception of the program and an evaluation of targets' performance was fully explained (mediated) by two stereotypes. The two stereotypes represent the low competence and lack of warmth categories of the stereotype content model.
>
> A second set of analyses in the review aggregated studies that investigated self-perceptions held by targets of affirmative action programs. The analyses provided a partial explanation for a telling phenomenon—that the perceived extent of a diversity program is associated with the targets' lowered self-evaluations of their own performance. A number of systematic meta-analytic reviews has confirmed stereotype threat: Spencer et al.[40] provide an overview of research on stereotype threat, including meta-analyses by Lamont et al.[41] and Nguyen and Ryan.[42] The reviews covered a wide range of stereotyped groups in a variety of settings, including non-U.S. contexts that were not characterized by affirmative action programs.[43] Being negatively stereotyped by others negatively influences not only self-evaluations of performance but also workplace attitudes, such as turnover intentions among older workers, and mental health.[44]

A case: The experience of being repeatedly stigmatized

Even those in the most prestigious occupations are the targets of frequent stereotyping. As but one example reported in the media, consider Black women physicians: "More than a dozen Black women interviewed said that they frequently heard comments from colleagues and patients questioning their credibility and undermining their authority while on the job … sometimes hampering teamwork, creating tensions that cost precious time during emergency procedures."[45] Being stereotyped by patients is a societal issue but being stereotyped by colleagues is a sign of an organization inadequately managing inclusion. One incident is illustrative: A Black woman in the second year of her residency approached an attending physician to report on her patients. The attending mistook her for an electrocardiogram technician, even though she was the only Black resident in her class. "How could he not know who I am?" she asked. These experiences are not isolated. As another Black women professor of medicine recounted, "After the twelve-thousandth time, it starts to impede your ability to be successful. You start to go into scenarios about your self-worth. It's a head trip."[46]

> For Black women physicians, being stereotyped by their patients is a societal issue, but when they are stereotyped or disrespected by their colleagues, it is a sign of an organization inadequately managing inclusion.

Implications for organizations and individuals. What can be learned by integrating the findings from these two meta-analyses by the Harrison and Leslie research teams? Both reviews support the view that diversity programs with moderate or high levels of prescriptiveness trigger perceptions of threat among both targets and non-targets. However, these threats differ. For non-targets, the perceived threat is of targets competing for workplace rewards, a threat that leads to some degree of opposition in the form of negative stereotyping that lowers assessments of the warmth of the program's intended beneficiaries. That stereotyping by others then represents a threat to targets, a threat commonly experienced as repeated aggressions that lead to reduced self-confidence and, consequently, reduced performance. Negative stereotyping and its associated threats of stigmatizing— lowered performance and heightened anxiety—represent serious exclusionary forces, making it more difficult for diverse workgroups to practice inclusion and achieve high performance.

Taking the two reviews together also leads to a conclusion critically important for leaders: Opposition to inclusion is malleable. Opposition from some dominant-group members in the form of stereotyping and stigmatizing will be heightened or lessened by the nature of a diversity program. However, consider an additional finding in the second review: Individuals who perceived a high extent of preference, regardless of the actual extent of preference, were more likely to stigmatize targets than were those who perceived a lesser extent for the program. Consequently, a more refined conclusion from integrating the two reviews is that low prescriptiveness in a diversity program, as it is designed and communicated, reduces the amount of stigmatizing, but even within a less prescriptive program, organizational leaders should expect that some individuals perceive the program as sufficiently preferential that they are stigmatizing its targets' competence and warmth. These findings instruct us on the importance of a diversity initiative's design and communication. They further imply that managers should be ready to address and mitigate residuals of stigmatizing that are likely to occur.

A further refinement in applying the findings described above is suggested by an example from higher education:

> Recruiting for a diverse student body has been debated and challenged in the courts for decades. Some universities grant acceptance to the top tier (some established percentage) of students from all of the state's high schools. With so many high schools being homogeneous, this practice ensures the acceptance of an equitable percentage of highly talented students from underrepresented groups. Once on campus, these students are often stereotyped by others as only accepted because of their underrepresented status. Feeling stigmatized, they engage less with dissimilar others.

A program designed to provide equity and enhance opportunity for underrepresented groups may, in fact, create discomfort and challenges for those students. Does this mean that leaders should abandon diversity initiatives, and that underrepresented groups would actually benefit from organizations doing so? Evidence suggests not. As we will see in Chapter 5, the effects of formal programs over time are that they benefit underrepresented groups. The implication is not that diversity initiatives should be abandoned, which would "throw the baby out with the bath water," to use a colloquial saying. Rather, the threats that diversity programs engender among various employees, targets and non-targets alike, need to be anticipated and mitigated through effective program design and communication. In their review, Lisa Leslie and colleagues conclude that stigmatizing "is a real-world phenomenon with the potential to derail organizational efforts to create and maintain a diverse workforce,"[47] but they further suggest that organizations emphasize diversity efforts as having the potential to benefit all organizational members through improved performance. As specified in this book's framework, we would add that the way to make such an emphasis real is to adopt practices for inclusive interactions and accountable behavior that overcome prejudice in the workplace.

The threats that diversity programs engender need to be anticipated and mitigated through program design and communication.

Does information on an individual's capabilities overcome stereotyping?

Might it be possible to eliminate negative stereotyping and stigmatizing in a simpler way, not through program design and implementing inclusive practices but by providing evidence of the capabilities of the particular members of underrepresented groups in the organization? Harrison and colleagues, the authors of the first meta-analytic review discussed above, suggest that "stigmatization can be greatly reduced by providing observers with incontrovertible evidence of the target individual's competence."[48] Leslie and colleagues suggest an additional condition: To prevent low self-assessments of competence by targets, those individuals must be convinced that non-targets recognize that they are qualified. A few studies have investigated the issue of whether clarifying a target's qualifications can dampen stigmatizing, and their findings are mixed, inconclusive.

> *The Evidence.* While some studies support the value of providing proof of competence, one laboratory study[49] found that even when the superior qualifications of a minority hiree were made clear, these qualifications were ignored in subjects' attributions of why the person was hired, especially when the affirmative action policies of the organization were made explicit. A field experiment on hiring found that providing a higher quality resume widened rather than reduced the gap in call-backs between Whites and Blacks.[50]

The implications for sufficient action. These mixed findings support the suggestion that the evidence of competence be incontrovertible, and even that may be insufficient. Leslie and colleagues note a further problem: Making clear an individual's competence might counter stereotypes of low competence, but that clarity is unlikely to affect stereotypes of low warmth, which are triggered by targets' competitiveness. That is, perceiving targets as competent can increase the likelihood of seeing them as cold, as found in views toward businesswomen and Black professionals in the stereotype content studies.[51]

An example illustrates why providing information on objective qualifications is alone insufficient to overcome the effects of negative stereotypes:

> An interviewee for this book mentioned the significance of dominant group members saying that during selection interviews, they are assessing the applicant for "fit" within the workgroup. Rejecting an applicant based on "fit," she felt, provided a too-easy way to eliminate otherwise qualified applicants from underrepresented groups. "Fit" enables members to not have to justify why they are unhappy with an applicant.

Simply providing evidence on an individual's qualifications and competence will not be the "silver bullet" that eliminates stereotyping and stigmatizing. For goals of both performance and equity, what is required is a shift in behavior—that when interactions occur and decisions are made, organizational members behave by individuating rather than generalizing from stereotypes. As we discuss below, studies that provide resume information and measure call-backs indicate that stereotyping is the default mode, even when individuating information is available, but that this default outcome can be overcome by conditions that provide the decision-maker with the motivation and capacity to use the individuating information.[52] Similarly, Charles Stangor,[53] reviewing the history of social psychological research on prejudice, casts doubt on strategies aiming to directly change stereotyped beliefs. Instead, he sees research as favoring a reduction of the categorization *process* itself through intergroup contact: "Stereotyping and prejudice are reduced significantly when the members of the different groups are able to perceive themselves as members of a common group, to see each other similarly, and to make friends with each other."[54] Thus, organizational conditions that shape how people behave with each other, relate to each other, and make decisions will determine the degree of stereotyping. We consider this focus on malleable organizational conditions further in the next section, on bias that is implicit.

> Organizational conditions that shape how people behave with each other, relate to each other, and make decisions will determine the degree of stereotyping.

Behavior based on implicit bias

As in the preceding sections on exclusionary forces, the intent in this section on bias held implicitly, mostly subconsciously, is not to provide a general overview of research findings. Instead, the discussion identifies how research findings, as analyzed and reported in systematic literature reviews across several fields, inform us about whether and when implicit bias produces exclusionary and performance-harming interactions and decisions, as well as what conditions can counter those effects. We will see that even small biases can have dramatic impacts, resulting in disparities that harm organizational and societal productivity. Of greatest importance for our focus on producing positive, adaptive interactions, research indicates that negative implicit bias need not lead to negative decisions but, rather, that it can be controlled. Somewhat surprisingly, despite implicit bias being framed as subconscious, particular situational conditions lead to more conscious decision-making and reduce the likelihood that an assessor will translate an implicit bias into an unfounded, detrimental action.

> Small biases can have dramatic impacts, resulting in disparities that harm organizational and societal productivity.

The nature and prevalence of implicit bias

Self-segregation, interaction discomfort, stereotyping, and stigmatizing can be understood as manifestations of the broader concept of bias. Bias is typically defined as a preference. Anti-inclusive practices involve preferences that interfere with being impartial in behavior and decisions, corresponding to the economically costly operation of a *taste for discrimination.*[55] Implicit bias affects personal decisions such as whom to associate with, whom to feel anxious about and avoid, whom to favor, and whom to denigrate. A useful set of distinctions is made by Susan Fiske,[56] with stereotypes understood as cognitive bias, discrimination as behavioral bias, and prejudice as emotional bias.

> When considering biases, Susan Fiske suggests that we consider stereotypes as cognitive bias, discrimination as behavioral bias, and prejudice as emotional bias.[57] Therefore, prejudice is a better predictor of discriminatory behavior than stereotypes.[58]

The role of prejudice, of emotional bias, is seen particularly in the negative stereotyping of members of an out-group as cold and difficult to work with, the dimension of stereotyping stemming from the perception of a competitive threat from an out-group. This threat arouses emotions that trigger stereotyping and stigmatizing. Similarly, prejudice as emotional bias is evident in interaction discomfort and communication apprehension. Emotional biases (prejudices) predict discriminatory behavior better than cognitive biases (stereotypes),[59] implying that discriminatory behavior can be reduced by practices that cause individuals to be less emotional and more rational in their decision-making.

Individuals may be quite unaware of the biased emotions and cognitions that lead them to anti-inclusive behavior and decisions. Research informs us that seeing stereotyping and stigmatizing as overt forms of discrimination, with individuals quite conscious of their biases, is increasingly inadequate. Overt displays of discrimination are seen as inappropriate by large segments of American society, and many societal members do not believe themselves to be racist or sexist. However, contemporary research indicates that bias is still widespread, operating in the less overt, more subtle form of implicit bias. Implicit bias is one "that operates beyond individuals' conscious awareness and may exist even among individuals who genuinely believe themselves to be unbiased."[60] Implicit bias is deeply embedded in society. It can be held by a person who, by any reasonable standard, is not racist or sexist. Consider a personal example from a prominent social scientist who has studied implicit bias in, and done consulting with, police forces:

> When discussing the widespread nature of implicit bias, Black psychologist Jennifer Eberhardt[61] recounts a disturbing personal experience: Her five-year-old son saw a man and commented that he looked like his father. Professor

Eberhardt thought not, but the man was the only Black male on the plane that they were traveling on. He was behaving the same as a large number of White males there. Then, her son asked, "Is he going to rob the plane?" (pp. 3-4).

> Implicit bias creates disparities and harms organizations through poor allocation of human talent and poor treatment of an organization's clients.

Implicit bias has been demonstrated to create disparities and harm organizational effectiveness in two ways: poor allocation of human talents within an organization and poor treatment of an organization's clients. Training and mentoring opportunities have favored White males,[62] and health care professionals secure information from and treat members of minority groups less effectively. We know of these types of effects with high certainty because implicit bias has been studied extensively in several academic fields, most notably psychology, human resource management, and health care, producing a large number of studies that enabled the nine systematic literature reviews that we draw upon here.

> Implicit bias allows individuals to assess others who possess the same qualifications and exhibit the same behavior as unequal.

In employment studies, implicit bias takes the form of differential assessments of individuals who possess the same qualifications and exhibit the same behavior. Implicit bias operates as an exclusionary force when an assessor fails to individuate when judging an individual; that is, when the assessor fails to base an assessment on actual characteristics of the individual and, instead, relies on stereotypes based on visible factors such as ethnicity, race, gender, and age. The stereotypes, the biases, are robust against conscious desires to avoid them and favor the young, the rich, and Whites.[63]

Seemingly small biases have large employment impacts

Implicit bias resides in the individual but has been shown to influence not only interpersonal interactions but also managerial decisions that exclude other individuals from employment opportunities and rewards.[64] These effects can be quite subtle. For instance, a manager may ask for assistance from a colleague whom the manager knows to be competent and will get the job done, rather than trying someone new and of a different ethnicity, race or gender who has never been given such an opportunity. Somewhat less subtle is implicit bias in a company's hiring of a supplier, as noted in an example above, where a White manager might be satisfied by a fellow manager's referral to a White supplier but require data or firsthand experience to assess competence before hiring a Black supplier. Companies and organizations that receive government contracts are often required to compensate for such biases by regulations for hiring a mandated percentage of minority-owned businesses as contractors. These give minority-owned businesses a chance to prove themselves and receive further work opportunities. However, the deck may be stacked against them. Consider the following example from one of our interviews:

> The interviewee reported that the organization was forced to hire minority-owned businesses even if these businesses were not as qualified and inhibited work outcomes. But, are these assessments unbiased? As noted above with regard to the degree of prescriptiveness of diversity initiatives, the presence of programs seen as favoring one group leads others to stereotype and stigmatize that group as incompetent and cold, leading to discounting the capabilities of capable individuals. The program triggered the attitude of implicit bias into the behavior of stigmatizing. The interviewee did note that many of the minority-owned businesses were quite good, but the mandates were seen as limiting their hiring options and impacting performance.

In effect, the policy remedy for implicit bias in hiring failed to eradicate the bias, instead triggering it into stigmatizing that creates impediments for productive interactions once a minority-owned business is hired.

The operation of subtle biases has been investigated in many research studies and found to have substantial detrimental effects on underrepresented group members. Researchers have also performed *audit studies* in which fictitious applicant resumes indicating equal qualifications are sent to potential employers and the percentage of call-backs for various groups are compared. The evidence is compelling that subtle, implicit bias has large detrimental impacts on underrepresented groups, larger than overt discrimination.

> *The Evidence.* A meta-analysis by Jones and colleagues[65] of 90 analyses in empirical studies finds that subtle discrimination has detrimental effects on the career success, turnover, and psychological health of members of underrepresented groups. These effects are larger than the effects of overt discrimination. Subtle discrimination takes the form of interaction behavior that is exclusionary, such as ending conversations prematurely, avoiding eye contact, and being unhelpful or hostile. The perception that such interaction behavior is largely inconsequential for organizational performance is seriously flawed. Implicit bias has been repeatedly demonstrated by research to lead to hiring and promotion decisions that ignore or discount qualifications. A meta-analysis of field experiments on implicit bias[66] finds that, since 1989, there is no evidence of a decline in hiring bias against Blacks, while there has been a possible slight decline for Latinos.

> Implicit bias has been repeatedly demonstrated to lead to hiring and promotion decisions that ignore or discount qualifications.

Implications for organizational effectiveness. Biased hiring and personnel development decisions reduce future organizational performance. Even small errors in hiring decisions can dramatically impact organizational performance, equity, and social justice, as is evident from the analysis in Box 4.3. A seemingly small amount of gender bias renders one in six hiring decisions erroneous, preventing the proper employment of half a million women in just one year, with the hiring organizations bearing higher wages and the opportunity costs of lower performance.

BOX 4.3: BIAS IN HIRING

Using statistics of 5.7 million job openings in the United States in 2017 and an estimate of bias that is consistent with the findings from systematic reviews, Kurdi and colleagues[67] published (in the *American Psychologist*, one of the top-ranked psychological journals) an estimate for one societal effect of gender bias:

> If one assumes that an equally qualified man and woman applied for each job, an $r=.10$ relationship between implicit gender bias and hiring decisions would result in the hiring of 3.36 million male candidates compared to 2.34 million female candidates. (p. 15).

This quite modest correlation between gender bias and hiring decisions results in inequities affecting many hundreds of thousands of individuals every year, and biases based on ethnicity or race can affect hundreds of thousands more.

Persistence of inequities

Implicit bias is a potent explanation for why, despite decreases in explicit or overt racism and sexism over recent decades, inequities in personnel decisions have persisted. Progress has been made in some fields, but not in general.

The Evidence. Regarding gender bias, one extensive experimental audit study[68] finds a consistent bias in favor of one underrepresented group: In STEM fields (biology, engineering, economics, and psychology) faculty members, both men and women, were found to have a 2:1 preference for hiring women for tenure-track faculty positions when presented with candidates having equal qualifications. This finding, as well as research findings showing lack of disparities in reward and promotion decisions for women in STEM faculty positions, was attributed to decades-long efforts to promote the value of women in STEM occupations.

More general reviews indicate this one study's findings to be quite unique. One meta-analysis[69] found that ratings of promotion potential were higher for men despite job performance ratings that favored women. Another[70] found that bias in favor of men persisted across experimental studies published from the 1970s to the 2000s, with no clear shifts over that time period. Men evidence implicit bias against women in both male and female occupational categories, while women do not show bias against women in male-dominated jobs but do, surprisingly, in female-dominated occupations, perhaps reflecting men holding specialized and managerial roles in those occupations.

Across studies, the average size of the negative effect that bias has on decisions appears to be quite small. However, as the example above shows, this relatively small effect can have dramatic consequences every year for job outcomes among underrepresented groups. An example from the nonprofit sector, where we might expect more sensitivity to social justice issues than in the business world, makes clear that the implications of the research evidence about bias are a reality in many corners of society.

> In the U.S. nonprofit sector, boards of directors have remained overwhelmingly White (about 82 percent) over the past dozen years,[71] being out of step with the demographic composition of the general population and the clients served. Additionally, BoardSource found that among nonprofit CEOs, 90 percent are White, 72 percent female, and 56 percent are 50–64 years old, while board chairs were also 90 percent White, but only 42 percent are female, and 43 percent are 50–64 years old.

The long-term disparity between the diversity representation of clients and that of leadership, we were informed by an interviewee, implies a lack of commitment to or knowledge about how to increase leadership diversity. Nora, a consultant who is a lawyer and specializes in nonprofit board member diversity, equity, and inclusion, emphasized the need to be deliberate about recruiting board members in order to overcome this diversity disparity, which may have detrimental effects on client services.

With respect to nonprofit boards, the recruiting of new board members must be deliberate in order to overcome diversity disparity, which may negatively impact the provision of client services.

Implicit bias and interactions

Studies in health care provide insights on the nature of impacts that implicit bias has on diversity interactions. Relations between health care providers and their patients point to dysfunctions in their interactions and the effects that these have on medical treatment decisions.

> *The Evidence.* Hall and colleagues'[72] review of studies on ethnic bias among health care professionals finds that bias triggers particular forms of deficient interaction with Black and Latino patients. These include providers displaying "dominant communication styles, fewer demonstrated positive emotions, and infrequent requests for input."[73] These patients, in comparison with White patients, report being less respected. They perceive the provider as being less collaborative. A provider's dominant approach decreases the patient's voice and results in a limited understanding of the patient's situation. The providers' biases are "automatically activated and applied most often when people are busy, distracted, tired, and under pressure."[74]

The poor interaction, then, takes the form of a lack of positive, meaningful inclusive interactions that distances the patient and may result in inappropriate treatment decisions by the provider with the implicit bias. The finding that bias is most triggered into behavior when individuals are under time pressure is a reflection of stereotyping being a way to reduce cognitive effort in response to situational demands. Even individuals being generally aware that they have implicit bias and should control it is insufficient to actually control it in pressurized instances common in many situations.

When is implicit bias (not) triggered into actions and decisions?

Fortunately for organizations, and consistent with our Framework for Inclusive Interactions, conditions can be created to bring implicit bias to a more conscious and controllable level. These conditions include learning situations, the displaying of prescribed practices, and being held accountable for one's decisions.

> *The Evidence.* The activation of implicit bias into behavior is subject to situational conditions. A meta-analysis of psychological studies relating implicit bias to measures of ethnic discrimination[75] concludes that "how implicit biases translate into behavior—if and when they do at all—appears to be complex and hard to predict."[76] The meta-analysis investigating the largest number of studies states that relationships between implicit attitudes and behavior "may, at least in part, arise due to situational factors rather than stable individual differences."[77]

Despite the strict meaning of its label, implicit bias seems to be subject to conscious introspection in particular organizational conditions, as when individuals are held accountable for their behavior or are in a learning situation, such as students engaging in prescribed practices.

Implicit bias may be countered when individuals are held accountable for their behavior.

The Evidence. A study of medical students[78] found a lack of disparate decisions across groups when performing prescribed medical tasks. Similarly, nursing students showed less bias than qualified nurses.[79] A meta-analysis of gender bias in employment decision-making concludes that organizational conditions produce variation in the effects of implicit bias.[80] Even subtle differences in conditions, such as an individual requesting an immediate vs. a delayed meeting, can produce differences in responses based on bias.[81] Across experimental studies, less bias in employment decisions was found among experienced professionals and also when individuals were held accountable for their decisions or were provided with job-relevant individuating information clearly indicating competence.[82] Situations that enable learning about others as individuals counter impressions based on group membership.[83]

Implications for organizational control of bias. Across different fields of studies, then, findings point to the moderating role of situational conditions that organizations can establish, making implicit bias controllable. Implicit bias, per se, is not the problem.

Implicit bias, per se, is not the organizational problem. Failing to institute conditions that control it is the problem.

Leaders should assume that they and their fellow organizational members of all backgrounds carry these biases. They should be concerned not with its existence but with its potential consequences for poor decisions and poor interactions, a problem that can be avoided by organizations creating conditions where interaction behavior and decisions are more conscious, intentional, and unbiased. Consider a case in higher education:

In a medical school, training on implicit bias produced a valuable difference in outcomes for members of underrepresented groups.[84] The outcome in this case was the diversity composition of a class of students entering the school. All faculty and student members in the school took a Black–White Implicit Association Test, making them aware of their implicit biases. The incoming class that entered the year following that exercise was the school's most diverse in history. Key features in this case are that the training focused on a particular type of decision and involved all individuals who could influence those decisions. The training created a socially shared expectation that the recruitment and selection decisions would be made in a fashion that controlled implicit bias.

Unlike types of diversity training that can trigger backlash among participants who believe that they are being labeled as racist or sexist (as covered in Chapter 1), the concept of implicit bias means that individuals need not be blamed for their biases since they are framed as ubiquitous, subconscious, and lacking intentionality. At the same time, their impact on decisions can be stressed, with training focused on effective decision-making behavior and on instituting standard operating procedures that inhibit the bias from affecting outcomes. An example is prescribed patient interviewing practices taught to medical students. For managers and human resource management staff, an example of proper procedures is not relying on unstructured interviews in selection decisions since research has firmly established that these have low validity.[85] As noted above regarding reliance on "fit" when making selection decisions, biased decisions are likely without prescribed interview protocols. According to Nora, the nonprofit diversity, equity, and inclusion consultant, among nonprofit boards the result was that existing board members selected new members that were, most often, similar in demographic composition to the current board. Proper procedure is to base decisions on structured interviews and on specific qualifications that have been validated as predictors of job performance.[86] However, training alone provides little assurance that awareness of implicit bias and of practices to counter it in decision-making, such as structured interviewing, will actually result in those practices being followed on the job. Broader sets of workgroup conditions and practices that favor inclusion over exclusion are primary, with training then playing a valuable, complementary role.

The findings in this chapter concerning conditions that permit vs. mitigate stereotyping and stigmatizing, whether based on overt or implicit attitudes, underlie the Framework in this book, emphasizing the importance of organizational practices that suppress the triggering of prejudice into behaviors and decisions.

Conclusion: Refining our beliefs about achieving diversity and inclusion

When combined with the evidence presented in Chapter 1 on diversity training, the research-based evidence covered in this chapter and summarized in Figure 4.2 should cause us to examine two common beliefs more critically than we have in the past. The beliefs are as follows:

1. Formal diversity efforts in organizations improve outcomes for members of underrepresented groups.
2. Society has tackled discrimination and has made good progress in reducing it.

> Research informs us that particular types of diversity efforts carry a high risk of triggering stereotyping and stigmatizing that threatens members of underrepresented groups in terms of their self-confidence and performance and, consequently, the performance of the workgroups and organizations in which they function.

The design and communication of diversity efforts bear on these effects, and even well-conceived designs are likely to engender stigmatizing behavior on the part of some members that perceive their interests as threatened.

Concerning progress on discrimination, we should not be deluded into believing that discrimination is less a problem than previously or that reductions in overt discrimination mean greater equity and performance. Research indicates that subtle discrimination, often residing in implicit bias held by members from all backgrounds, is widespread and that it produces detrimental effects at least as large as overt discrimination. Not only are small amounts of implicit bias estimated to produce large disparities in employment outcomes for underrepresented groups but, once in the workplace, additional disparities occur through the demonstrated detrimental effects of stereotyping and stigmatizing on members of those groups.

The research covered here explains, but only in part, how and why equity problems and performance dysfunctions remain so wicked, persistent, and widespread. Social forces of exclusion, including self-segregation and interaction discomfort, are natural. They are deeply embedded in societal life, often subtle and implicit, and are difficult to see and recognize. Despite societal and organizational efforts to counter them, they enable disparities and dysfunction to persist.

> The four exclusionary forces—self-segregation, interaction discomfort, stereotyping and stigmatizing, and implicit bias—overlap and feed on each other.

Absent effective and extended efforts to deal with them, they reproduce inequity and unmet expectations over time. They produce self-fulfilling prophecies,[87] such as a negative stereotype of low group competence leading to a failure to use individuating information on potential hires, leading to underrepresentation in higher status jobs, leading to reinforcement of the negative stereotype. Across organizations and societies, the result is reduced equity and effectiveness due to flawed allocation of human talents and poor treatment of particular clients, suppliers, and customers.

On the positive side, research has generated knowledge that points to paths for interrupting these types of processes and achieving performance and equity. The basic knowledge is that situational conditions influence whether the ubiquitous exclusionary forces actually produce detrimental effects. The findings strongly suggest that managers can create and sustain particular practices in their organizations and workgroups that counter forces such as implicit bias and stereotyping, preventing their triggering into exclusionary behavior and flawed decisions. This view is confirmed by evidence that we turn to next, evidence on the effects that various organizational programs have on performance and equity in organizations.

WORKSHEET and MEMO TO SELF

SOCIAL FORCES OF EXCLUSION: PRESENT VS. COUNTERACTED

Search for recurring patterns from your organizational experience:

Where have you observed exclusionary forces operating?

In which cases were biases operating through overt discrimination? Through implicit bias?

Under what conditions were the forces operating, affecting interactions and decisions?

What decisions and performance outcomes were affected? Were costs visible or hidden (opportunity costs)? Was anyone concerned about them? Who?

What were the longer-term effects of these forces – leadership quality? Retention of talent? Ongoing conflict?

Where have you observed these forces *not* operating and inclusion being achieved?

In those cases, what practices and procedures counteracted the forces?

MEMO TO SELF—Opportunities I see for improving my organization:

Notes

1 Briner, R. B., & Denyer, D. (2012). Systematic review and evidence synthesis as a practice and scholarship tool. In D. M. Rousseau (Ed.), *The Oxford handbook of evidence-based management* (pp. 112–129). Oxford University Press.

2 Ibid.

3 Lazarsfeld, P. F., & Merton, R. K. (1954). Friendship as a social process: A substantive and methodological analysis. *Freedom and Control in Modern Society, 18*(1), 18–66; McPherson, M., Smith-Lovin, L., & Cook, J. M. (2001). Birds of a feather: Homophily in social networks. *Annual Review of Sociology, 27*(1), 415–444; Stark, T. H., & Flache, A. (2012). The double edge of common interest: Ethnic segregation as an unintended byproduct of opinion homophily. *Sociology of Education, 85*(2), 179–199; Stearns, E., Buchmann, C., & Bonneau, K. (2009). Interracial friendships in the transition to college: Do birds of a feather flock together once they leave the nest? *Sociology of Education, 82*(2), 173–195.

4 Levy, D. K., McDade, Z., & Bertumen, K. (2013). Mixed-income living: Anticipated and realized benefits for low-income households. *Cityscape, 15*(2), 15–28.

5 Joseph, M., & Chaskin, R. (2010). Living in a mixed-income development: Resident perceptions of the benefits and disadvantages of two developments in Chicago. *Urban Studies, 47*(11), 2347–2366.

6 See, for example, Crul, M., Steinmetz, C. H., & Lelie, F. (2020). How the architecture of housing blocks amplifies or dampens interethnic tensions in ethnically diverse neighbourhoods. *Social Inclusion, 8*(1), 194–202.

7 Levy et al. (2013). "Mixed-income living."

8 Green, D. P., & Wong, J. S. (2009). Tolerance and the contact hypothesis: A field experiment. In E. Borgida, C. M. Federico, & J. L. Sullivan (Eds.), *The political psychology of democratic citizenship* (pp. 1–23). Oxford University Press.

9 Rao, G. (2019). Familiarity does not breed contempt: Generosity, discrimination, and diversity in Delhi schools. *American Economic Review, 109*(3), 774–809.

10 Smith, J. A., McPherson, M., & Smith-Lovin, L. (2014). Social distance in the United States: Sex, race, religion, age, and education homophily among confidants, 1985 to 2004. *American Sociological Review, 79*(3), 432–456.

11 Kozol (2005), cited in Green, D. P., & Wong, J. S. (2009). Tolerance and the contact hypothesis: A field experiment. In E. Borgida, C. M. Federico, & J. L. Sullivan (Eds.), *The political psychology of democratic citizenship* (pp. 1–23). Oxford University Press.

12 Weisinger, J. Y., & Salipante, P. F. (2005). A grounded theory for building ethnically bridging social capital in voluntary organizations. *Nonprofit and Voluntary Sector Quarterly, 34*(1), 29–55.

13 Ogbu, J. U. (2003). *Black American students in an affluent suburb: A study of academic disengagement.* Routledge.

14 Ruef, M., Aldrich, H. E., & Carter, N. M. (2003). The structure of founding teams: Homophily, strong ties, and isolation among US entrepreneurs. *American Sociological Review, 68*(2), 195–222.

15 Mehra, A., Kilduff, M., & Brass, D. J. (1998). At the margins: A distinctiveness approach to the social identity and social networks of underrepresented groups. *Academy of Management Journal, 41*(4), 441–452.

16 Centola, D. M. (2013). Homophily, networks, and critical mass: Solving the start-up problem in large group collective action. *Rationality and Society, 25*(1), 3–40.

17 Neuliep, J. W., & McCroskey, J. C. (1997). The development of intercultural and interethnic communication apprehension scales. *Communication Research Reports, 14*(2), 145–156.

18 Barreto, M., & Ellemers, N. (2005). The perils of political correctness: Men's and women's responses to old-fashioned and modern sexist views. *Social psychology quarterly, 68*(1), 75–88; Ely, R. J., Meyerson, D. E., & Davidson, M. N. (2006). Rethinking political correctness. *Harvard Business Review, 84*(9), 78–87.

19 McPherson, M., Smith-Lovin, L., & Cook, J. M. (2001). Birds of a feather: Homophily in social networks. *Annual Review of Sociology, 27*(1), 415–444.

20 Steele, C. M., Spencer, S. J., & Aronson, J. (2002). Contending with group image: The psychology of stereotype and social identity threat. *Advances in Experimental Social Psychology, 34*, 379–440.

21 Kim, M. S. (2012). Cross-cultural perspectives on motivations of verbal communication: Review, critique, and a theoretical framework. In M. E. Roloff (Ed.), *Communication Yearbook 22* (pp. 51–90). Routledge; Lin, Y., & Rancer, A. S. (2003). Ethnocentrism, intercultural communication apprehension, intercultural willingness-to-communicate, and intentions to participate in an intercultural dialogue program: Testing a proposed model. *Communication Research Reports, 20*(1), 62–72.

22 Neuliep & McCroskey (1997). "The development of intercultural and interethnic communication apprehension scales."

23 Bernstein, R. S., & Salipante, P. (2017). Intercultural comfort through social practices: Exploring conditions for cultural learning. *Frontiers in Education*, Vol. 2, Article 31. doi:10.3389/feduc.2017.00031. http://journal.frontiersin.org/article/10.3389/feduc.2017.00031/full?&utm_source=Email_to_authors_&utm_medium=Email&utm_content=T1_11.5e1_author&utm_campaign=Email_publicatio n&field=&journalName=Frontiers_in_Education&id=272155.

24 Forman, T. A. (2004). Color-blind racism and racial indifference: The role of racial apathy in facilitating enduring inequalities. In M. Krysan & A. E. Lewis (Eds.), *The changing terrain of race and ethnicity* (pp. 43–66). Russell Sage Foundation.

25 Fiske, S. T. (2005). Social cognition and the normality of prejudgment. In J. F. Dovidio, P. Glick, & L. A. Rudman (Eds.), *On the nature of prejudice: Fifty years after Allport* (pp. 36–53). Blackwell Publishing, p. 47.

26 van Knippenberg, D., De Dreu, C. K., & Homan, A. C. (2004). Work group diversity and group performance: An integrative model and research agenda. *Journal of Applied Psychology, 89*(6), 1008–1022.

27 Simon, H. A. (1996). *Sciences of the artificial.* MIT Press.

28 Freeman, J. B., Schiller, D., Rule, N. O., & Ambady, N. (2010). The neural origins of superficial and individuated judgments about ingroup and outgroup members. *Human Brain Mapping, 31*(1), 150–159.

29 Fiske (2005). "Social cognition and the normality of prejudgment."

30 Santos, A. S., Garcia-Marques, L., Mackie, D. M., Ferreira, M. B., Payne, B. K., & Moreira, S. (2012). Implicit open-mindedness: Evidence for and limits on stereotype malleability. *Journal of Experimental Social Psychology, 48*(6), 1257–1266.

31 Ibid, p. 40.

32 Resendez, M. G. (2002). The stigmatizing effects of affirmative action: An examination of moderating variables. *Journal of Applied Social Psychology, 32*(1), 185–206.

33 Harrison, D. A., Kravitz, D. A., Mayer, D. M., Leslie, L. M., & Lev-Arey, D. (2006). Understanding attitudes toward affirmative action programs in employment: Summary and meta-analysis of 35 years of research. *Journal of Applied Psychology, 91*(5), 1013–1036.

34 Ibid, p. 1023.

35 Fiske, S. T., Cuddy, A. J., Glick, P., & Xu, J. (2002). A model of (often mixed) stereotype content: Competence and warmth respectively follow from perceived status and competition. *Journal of Personality and Social Psychology, 82*(6), 878–902.

36 Watt, R. M. (2015). Trust by design: The affective and cognitive antecedents among African Americans, building long-term business relationships. Doctor of Management [dissertation]. Case Western Reserve University, Cleveland, OH.

37 Leslie, L. M., Mayer, D. M., & Kravitz, D. A. (2014). The stigma of affirmative action: A stereotyping-based theory and meta-analytic test of the consequences for performance. *Academy of Management Journal, 57*(4), 964–989.

38 Steele et al. (2002). "Contending with group image."

39 Leslie et al. (2014). "The stigma of affirmative action."

40 Spencer, S. J., Logel, C., & Davies, P. G. (2016). Stereotype threat. *Annual Review of Psychology, 67*(1), 415–437.

41 Lamont, R. A., Swift, H. J., & Abrams, D. (2015). A review and meta-analysis of age-based stereotype threat: negative stereotypes, not facts, do the damage. *Psychology and Aging, 30*(1), 180–193.

42 Nguyen, H.-H. D., & Ryan, A. M. (2008). Does stereotype threat affect test performance of minorities and women? A meta-analysis of experimental evidence. *Journal of Applied Psychology, 93*(6), 1314–1334.

43 e.g., Appel, M., Weber, S., & Kronberger, N. (2015). The influence of stereotype threat on immigrants: Review and meta-analysis [Original Research]. *Frontiers in Psychology, 6* (Article 900); Picho, K., Rodriguez, A., & Finnie, L. (2013). Exploring the moderating role of context on the mathematics performance of females under stereotype threat: A meta-analysis. *The Journal of Social Psychology, 153*(3), 299–333.

44 von Hippel, C., Kalokerinos, E. K., & Henry, J. D. (2013). Stereotype threat among older employees: relationship with job attitudes and turnover intentions. *Psychology and Aging, 28*(1), 17–27.

45 Goldberg, E. (2020, August 11). For doctors of color, microaggressions are all too familiar. *The New York Times.* https://www.nytimes.com/2020/08/11/health/microaggression-medicine-doctors.html

46 Ibid.

47 Leslie et al. (2014). "The stigma of affirmative action," p. 982.

48 Harrison et al. (2006). "Understanding attitudes toward affirmative action programs in employment," p. 1030.

49 Resendez (2002). "The stigmatizing effects of affirmative action."

50 Bertrand, M., & Mullainathan, S. (2004). Are Emily and Greg more employable than Lakisha and Jamal? A field experiment on labor market discrimination. *American Economic Review, 94*(4), 991–1013.

51 Fiske et al. (2002). "A model of (often mixed) stereotype content."

52 Fiske (1998), cited in Smith, E. R., Miller, D. A., Maitner, A. T., Crump, S. A., Garcia-Marques, T., & Mackie, D. M. (2006). Familiarity can increase stereotyping. *Journal of Experimental Social Psychology, 42*(4), 471–478.

53 Stangor, C. (2009). The study of stereotyping, prejudice, and discrimination within social psychology: A quick history of theory and research. In T. D. Nelson (Ed.), *Handbook of prejudice, stereotyping, and discrimination* (pp. 1–12). Psychology Press.

54 Ibid, p. 11.

55 Becker, G. S. (1957). *The economics of discrimination.* University of Chicago Press.

56 Fiske, S. T. (2020). Prejudice, discrimination and stereotyping. In R. Biswas-Diener & E. Diener (Eds.), *Noba textbook series: Psychology.* DEF Publishers.

57 Ibid.

58 Fiske (2005). "Social cognition and the normality of prejudgment."

59 Ibid.

60 Banks, R. R., Eberhardt, J. L., & Ross, L. (2006). Discrimination and implicit bias in a racially unequal society. *California Law Review, 94*(4), 1169–1190. (p. 1170).

61 Eberhardt, J. L. (2019). *Biased: Uncovering the hidden prejudice that shapes what we see, think, and do.* Viking.

62 Bertrand, M., & Duflo, E. (2017). Field experiments on discrimination. In A. V. Banerjee & E. Duflo (Eds.), *Handbook of economic field experiments* (Vol. 1, pp. 309–393). North-Holland.

63 Banaji, M. R., Bazerman, M. H., & Chugh, D. (2003). How (un) ethical are you? *Harvard Business Review, December*, 3–10.

64 Bias in reward decisions and accountability practices to control it are discussed in Chapter 7.

65 Jones, K. P., Peddie, C. I., Gilrane, V. L., King, E. B., & Gray, A. L. (2016). Not so subtle: A meta-analytic investigation of the correlates of subtle and overt discrimination. *Journal of Management, 42*(6), 1588–1613.

66 Quillian, L., Pager, D., Hexel, O., & Midtbøen, A. H. (2017). Meta-analysis of field experiments shows no change in racial discrimination in hiring over time. *Proceedings of the National Academy of Sciences, 114*(41), 10870–10875.

67 Kurdi, B., Seitchik, A. E., Axt, J. R., Carroll, T. J., Karapetyan, A., Kaushik, N., Tomezsko, D., Greenwald, A. G., & Banaji, M. R. (2018). Relationship between the Implicit Association Test and intergroup behavior: A meta-analysis. *American Psychologist, 74*(5), 1–18.

68 Williams, W. M., & Ceci, S. J. (2015). National hiring experiments reveal 2:1 faculty preference for women on STEM tenure track. *Proceedings of the National Academy of Sciences, 112*(17), 5360–5365.

69 Roth, P. L., Purvis, K. L., & Bobko, P. (2012). A meta-analysis of gender group differences for measures of job performance in field studies. *Journal of Management, 38*(2), 719–739.

70 Koch, A. J., D'Mello, S. D., & Sackett, P. R. (2015). A meta-analysis of gender stereotypes and bias in experimental simulations of employment decision making. *Journal of Applied Psychology, 100*(1), 128–161.

71 BoardSource. (2017). *Leading with intent: 2017 index of nonprofit board practices.* BoardSource.

72 Hall, W. J., Chapman, M. V., Lee, K. M., Merino, Y. M., Thomas, T. W., Payne, B. K., Eng, E., Day, S. H., & Coyne-Beasley, T. (2015). Implicit racial/ethnic bias among health care professionals and its influence on health care outcomes: A systematic review. *American Journal of Public Health, 105*(12), e60–e76.

73 Ibid, p. e61.

74 Ibid.

75 Oswald, F. L., Mitchell, G., Blanton, H., Jaccard, J., & Tetlock, P. E. (2013). Predicting ethnic and racial discrimination: A meta-analysis of IAT criterion studies. *Journal of Personality and Social Psychology, 105*(2), 171–192.

76 Ibid, p. 185.

77 Kurdi, B., Seitchik, A. E., Axt, J. R., Carroll, T. J., Karapetyan, A., Kaushik, N., Tomezsko, D., Greenwald, A. G., & Banaji, M. R. (2018). Relationship between the Implicit Association Test and intergroup behavior: A meta-analysis, *American Psychologist*, p. 15.

78 Haider et al. (2011), as cited in Hall et al. (2015). "Implicit racial/ethnic bias among health care professionals."

79 Linden & Redpath (2011), cited in FitzGerald, C., & Hurst, S. (2017). Implicit bias in healthcare professionals: A systematic review. *BMC Medical Ethics, 18*(Article 19), 1–18.

80 Koch et al. (2015). "A meta-analysis of gender stereotypes and bias," p. 142.

81 Milkman et al. (2012), as cited in Bertrand, M., & Duflo, E. (2017). Field experiments on discrimination. In A. V. Banerjee & E. Duflo (Eds.), *Handbook of economic field experiments* (Vol. 1, pp. 309–393). North-Holland.

82 Davison, H. K., & Burke, M. J. (2000). Sex discrimination in simulated employment contexts: A meta-analytic investigation. *Journal of Vocational Behavior, 56*(2), 225–248.

83 Lacksley et al. (1980), as cited in Stangor, C. (2009). The study of stereotyping, prejudice, and discrimination within social psychology: A quick history of theory and research. In T. D. Nelson (Ed.), *Handbook of prejudice, stereotyping, and discrimination* (pp. 1–12). Psychology Press.

84 Capers, Q. I., Clinchot, D., McDougle, L., & Greenwald, A. G. (2017). Implicit racial bias in medical school admissions. *Academic Medicine, 92*(3), 365–369.

85 For instance, see Kausel, E. E., Culbertson, S. S., & Madrid, H. P. (2016). Overconfidence in personnel selection: When and why unstructured interview information can hurt hiring decisions. *Organizational Behavior and Human Decision Processes, 137*, 27–44.

86 Koch et al. (2015). "A meta-analysis of gender stereotypes and bias."

87 Bertrand & Duflo (2017). "Field experiments on discrimination."

5

THE PERFORMANCE ISSUE

How overcoming exclusion matters for workgroup effectiveness

Since the social forces producing distancing and exclusion are natural and pervasive, savvy organizational leaders, managers at all levels, and researchers must consider whether and how an increasingly diverse workforce can produce high performance. Overcoming exclusion by experiencing *inclusive interactions* is the main focus of this chapter, as depicted in Figure 5.1. This chapter discusses a series of questions that people in these roles, as well as researchers, should ask. Addressing these questions by drawing on research from several different academic fields provides insight into the realistic possibilities for organizations to achieve high performance and individual equity by taking informed, creative action. We ask the following questions and use evidence from field- and laboratory-based research to respond to these questions and identify promising approaches:

> *Inevitability vs. Promise*: Do exclusionary forces mean that organizations will suffer decreased performance from diversity in workgroups, or is diversity a path to greater effectiveness?
>
> *Efficacy*: Which interventions are more promising for achieving benefits from diversity: attitude-change efforts or programs that promote prolonged, inclusive interactions, and why?
>
> *Intent*: How do some organizational programs produce inclusion for diverse members without being diversity-focused?

The conclusions from considering these questions will help leaders become optimistic about their prospects for creating and sustaining conditions that lead to higher economic performance and individual equity. Marianne Bertrand and Esther Duflo, the latter author being the recipient of the Nobel Prize in Economics in 2019, state from their review of field experiments on discrimination that there is promising research "ripe for the picking,"[1] while a review of psychological research has

DOI: 10.4324/9780367822484-9

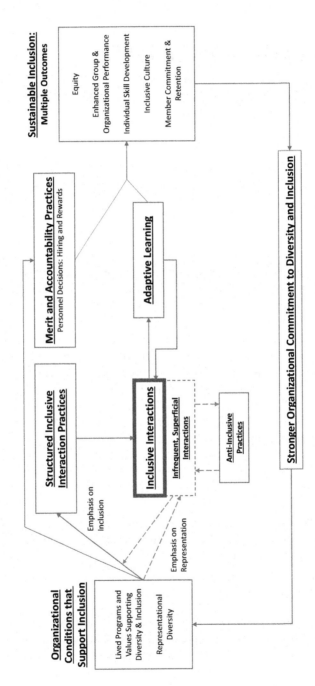

FIGURE 5.1 The Framework for Inclusive Interactions: Inclusive Interactions

identified approaches worthy of widespread implementation and evaluation, similar to clinical trials in medicine.[2] Accordingly, organizational leaders can use evidence-informed approaches as they seek to produce inclusion.

The question of inevitability

Do exclusionary forces mean that organizations will suffer decreased performance from diversity in workgroups, or is diversity a path to greater effectiveness?

The discussion in Chapter 4 suggests two contrasting answers to this question:

1. In the default case of organizational inattention to them, exclusionary forces will impede performance and equity.
2. Decreased performance is not inevitable. Whether exclusionary forces impede performance depends on workgroup social conditions, since the forces themselves are social. Diversity's path to greater effectiveness is through improved workgroup decision-making.

Direct research on the effect of diversity on workgroup performance presents and explains both answers: The odds are neither in favor of nor against increased performance from diversity. Increases or decreases depend on workgroup conditions that can be established and maintained through habitual group practices. A basic explanation is found in the categorization-elaboration model (CEM).[3] That model identifies two competing forces associated with workgroup diversity, as described in Box 5.1.

BOX 5.1: THE CATEGORIZATION-ELABORATION MODEL

Categorization is a negative force operating through implicit bias, stereotyping, and stigmatizing. It harms performance by producing social tensions and a lack of social integration among workgroup members.

Example: Stigmatizing Hispanic executives as tokens and difficult to work with.

Elaboration of information is a positive force that improves performance through better decision-making. Elaboration calls for the knowledge and perspectives of all workgroup members to be included in decisions.

Example: A woman automotive engineer convincing her fellow engineers to test the effects of its seatbelts and safety bags on shorter drivers.

The take-away: To achieve high performance from diversity, create positive social ties among workgroup members and promote the inclusion of diverse members' knowledge and perspectives.

The two contrasting forces of categorization and information elaboration explain the mixed odds for producing success from workgroup diversity that have been revealed by research evidence. Here, we discuss what has been learned about these forces and the conditions that affect their relative balance, determining whether or not elaboration triumphs over categorization. We draw primarily from two major meta-analytic literature reviews and a systematic descriptive review, all three identifying important workgroup conditions. These conditions relate to the practices outlined in the Framework presented in Chapter 2 and to conditions specified by intergroup contact theory to be discussed in Chapter 6.

> Categorization and information elaboration are two contrasting forces that represent the challenges of achieving performance and equity success in diverse workgroups.

Exclusion vs. inclusion in the performance of diverse workgroups

Each of the exclusionary forces discussed in the preceding chapter—self-segregation, interaction discomfort, stereotyping and stigmatizing, and implicit bias—represents human behavior that can have a functional basis for individuals. As such, these forces can be expected to occur, by default, in any organizational setting. When they occur, they directly impede the frequency and effectiveness of interactions. Individuals distance themselves from others, and when they do interact, the interactions are more superficial, uncomfortable, guided by stereotypes, and they stigmatize some individuals. These default exclusionary forces work against interdependence and collaboration in and across workgroups, harming both performance and equity. These forces provide an explanation for the reality that

> When actions are not taken to inhibit the exclusionary forces, a self-fulfilling process is established: A recurring cycle of weak interactions and exclusionary forces prohibit progress toward sustainable inclusion and its benefits of performance and equity.

heterogeneity in workgroups does not, in general, lead to improved performance compared to homogeneous groups,[4] even for innovative, creative performance as had been hypothesized in earlier research and accepted as conventional wisdom (Box 5.2). Figure 4.2 (Chapter 4) highlights the components of the exclusionary forces and how, if unaddressed, they lead to further weak interactions. The exclusionary forces inhibit strong, positive, meaningful interactions that foster adaptive learning about how to work together effectively.

> *The Evidence.* Analyzing data from over 8,000 teams in 39 studies, the effects of diversity on performance are perfectly mixed,[5] as noted above. The same result of inconsistent effects (that is, no general effect of diversity on

performance) is consistently reported by other systematic reviews.[6] The validity of this finding is heightened by the fact that these reviews used differing criteria to select their samples of empirical studies. Their findings indicate that merely achieving representational diversity in a workgroup is as likely to lead to decrements in performance as to increments; whether decrement or increment depends on the situational conditions in the workgroup.[7]

BOX 5.2: THE EFFECTS OF DIVERSITY ON PERFORMANCE

The empirical findings on the effects of diversity on performance are striking for their symmetry: Across all studies included in a major meta-analytic review of diversity's effects on workgroup performance, approximately 20 percent found a positive effect of diversity on performance, 60 percent no effect, and 20 percent a negative effect.[8]

The shared conclusion from the several systematic reviews is that more must be known about the conditions that lead to performance increments rather than decrements. Fortunately, research has moved toward just such a focus, identifying factors that influence the performance effectiveness of diversity in positive rather than negative ways, given the ubiquitous exclusionary social forces that exist.

The multilevel (organizational, workgroup, and individual) framework presented in this book indicates that various factors intervene as *moderating boundary conditions* and *mediating processes* to determine whether representational (numerical) diversity leads to higher or lower workgroup performance. See Box 5.3 for definitions of these terms and an example.

BOX 5.3: MEDIATING AND MODERATING PROCESSES

Mediating processes describe how and why individuals interact as they do. For example, communication apprehension is a process that mediates (intervenes) between a workgroup's diversity and the quality of interpersonal communication among its diverse members.

Moderating boundary conditions are characteristics of the broader situation. They are at the workgroup, organizational, or societal levels, beyond the boundary where the interpersonal interactions occur. Boundary conditions moderate the interpersonal interactions by affecting mediating processes—that is, how individuals interact—increasing or decreasing the influence of an exclusionary force on performance. For example, a workgroup-level boundary condition of high task interdependence among members can suppress the

> exclusionary mediating process of self-segregation, preventing superficial interactions across diverse workgroup members.
>
> Boundary conditions are important because they can be changed by managers and organizational leaders in order to produce inclusion and performance.

Recent meta-analytic reviews of research have emphasized the need to focus on moderating conditions and mediating processes. As is captured by the categorization-elaboration model, a common theme among these reviews is that diversity produces both negative processes (e.g., conflict among members and increased tension) and positive processes (e.g., incorporation of more perspectives) in workgroups.

> *The Evidence.* To investigate the effects of cross-cultural diversity, one research approach investigates the boundary conditions that influence team processes that, in turn, produce team convergence vs. divergence.[9] This approach recognizes that divergence can have the positive effect of increased creativity, but that the convergent processes of effective communications, satisfaction, and social integration are also required to overcome potential losses due to conflict. Findings indicate that the moderating conditions of a workgroup's tenure, geographical dispersion, size, and task complexity influence the convergent and divergent processes.

> In diverse workgroups, convergent processes of effective communications, satisfaction, and social integration are required to overcome potential losses due to conflict.

The workgroup conditions and processes identified in this research can be initiated and sustained by managers in order to increase the odds that diversity will lead to better team functioning. An increasingly common example would be managers initiating daily "huddles" (a moderating condition) during which differing views are surfaced and discussed (a mediating process) in order to reach better decisions (a performance outcome).

The effects of diversity on performance, then, depends on situational contingencies—in the terms defined above, on moderators. A large number of contingencies have been identified in systematic reviews of empirical studies relevant to the categorization-elaboration model.

> *The Evidence.* Situational contingencies include virtual vs. face-to-face communication, task complexity, the degree and nature of workgroup member interdependence, team tenure, and mindsets toward diversity;[10] networks

and team interaction processes, including friendship ties across subgroups, and differences in perceptions of team climate, conflict, and other team processes;[11] growth-oriented strategy, uncertainty, norms of interpersonal conduct, organizational climate for justice, and inclusive leadership.[12]

These many contingencies reflect conditions that vary from one organizational situation to another, whether by intentional design or not. By intentionally attending to these conditions, managers can stimulate interaction processes among workgroup members that reduce categorization and enhance information elaboration.

Interaction processes in top management teams

Following the outlines of the categorization-elaboration model, Hyuntak Roh and associates[13] were able to specify particular interaction processes in a meta-analytic review of over 50 studies of diversity in top management teams.

> *The Evidence.* Using the advanced statistical method of structural equation modeling that tests causal linkages, Roh and associates[14] examined two types of diversity—that due to demographic differences, our main focus in this book, and task-oriented (also known as job-related) diversity, such as that arising from differences in education. They found that task-oriented diversity led to both categorization and information elaboration, while demographic diversity was only weakly (but still statistically significantly) related to information elaboration but more strongly related to categorization (the greater the diversity, the greater the categorization). As we would expect, the analyses identified the relational conflict that results from this categorization as hampering firm performance. This meta-analysis further revealed that the challenge varies with national culture and industry characteristics:
>
> > The findings emphasize the prevalence of social categorization among executives and also the importance of managing those categorization-based interactions especially … in individualistic, resource-scarce, or stable environments … to affect firm performance in a positive direction.[15]

Categorization phenomena operate in teams even at the highest levels of organizations, confirming the performance challenge of diversity. As with the prior research on workgroup diversity and performance, the implication is that demographic diversity is at least as likely to lead to decrements as to increments in performance unless proper interaction processes are in place. But what are those processes?

Proper interaction processes increase the odds that demographic diversity will produce increments in performance.

The meta-analyses by Roh and co-researchers confirmed six team processes as linking diversity to higher performance, the first three aiding information elaboration and the latter three handling social categorization:

1. Communication and information exchange
2. Task-related debate
3. Comprehensive information search
4. Team cohesion
5. Behavioral integration
6. Strategic consensus

In terms of our Framework, we see all of these processes as resting on inclusive practices. Without those practices, such as collaboration and equal status, these processes of interaction are unlikely to occur reliably.

> Diversity without inclusive practices is likely to lead to relational conflict and impaired team processes that detract from performance.

The conclusion here from a large body of organizational studies—that the performance effects of diversity are contingent on situational conditions—validates the parallel conclusion from the findings discussed in Chapter 4 for stigmatizing and implicit bias. These findings across several bodies of research underlie our Framework's specification that inclusion that leads to performance is determined by particular practices at the organizational and workgroup levels.

> Research findings clearly imply that factors under managerial control can be used to leverage high performance from diversity.

Managerial control over exclusionary forces through sets of practices

As research on diversity's effects on performance has progressed over time, it has increasingly pointed to the importance of social processes and practices governing intergroup contact and to *combinations* of group and organizational-level factors that influence these processes and practices.

> *The Evidence.* Grouping the factors that moderate the effects of diversity on performance into three categories—organizational strategy, leadership, and human resource practices—the most wide-ranging systematic review[16] makes the point that many contingencies *interact* to affect performance. The contingencies reside at multiple levels, from individual to group to organizational.

The researchers who performed the reviews and integrated the knowledge to be gained from them specified important implications for action. Researchers and organizations should attend to sets of practices[17] and make a "contextual diagnosis" to customize practices to their situation.[18]

The categorization-elaboration model provides guidance for this customizing by specifying the goals of these practices, no matter their particular form: decrease group bias and increase information elaboration for improved decision-making,[19] while decreasing individuals' uncertainty in interactions in order to avoid anxiety and unproductive conflict.[20] The practices specified in this book's Framework for Inclusive Interactions directly address these goals.

> *An Information Technology Example.* For teams in an information technology company, Daan van Knippenberg and colleagues[21] illustrate a desired set of practices for information elaboration. For cross-functional project teams— teams intended to operate across different functions—they specify high performance to depend on members doing the following:
>
> - Sharing representation of the task as requiring elaboration
> - Injecting one's expertise—"informing the team on the basis of their own expertise about the different issues involved"
> - Understanding the implications of others' perspectives—"carefully processing the perspectives introduced by other team members to understand the implications for their own areas of expertise"
> - Feeding back the implications to the team
> - Integrating perspectives to design products.

This example specifies social processes that can be established as recurring habitual practices, with the practices operating in tandem as a set. Their combination is designed to accomplish an important organizational goal. Note that this set of practices fulfills five of the six practices specified in the book's Framework and illustrated in Chapter 3: Sharing a mission; repeatedly, frequently mixing members; collaborating with member interdependence; handling conflict constructively; and ensuring equal insider status. Following these five practices for the goal of informed team decision-making should produce over time the Framework's remaining practice, exhibiting and experiencing comfort and self-efficacy.

> *An example: Board Practices.* Research on diversity and inclusion in nonprofit boards of directors[22] provides another example of sets of practices that foster high performance from diversity. Some of the identified practices are board and organizational policies that operate as favorable boundary conditions at the organizational level. These include:
>
> - Incorporating diversity into the organization's core values;
> - Conducting diversity trainings;
> - Developing a plan to become representatively diverse.

These organizational policies address representation but are weak on inclusion. Other effective board practices that have been identified as transforming diversity into board effectiveness operate as mediating processes to foster inclusion. The practices represent norms that characterize the direct interactions between members of the dominant group and those from underrepresented groups:

- Initiating social interactions with board members from underrepresented groups, taking an interest in each other's backgrounds, sharing personal ideas, feelings, and hopes, and becoming friends.
- Valuing the contributions from members of underrepresented groups.
- Members of underrepresented groups participating in developing the board's most important policies.

Note in this example that each of the specified interaction practices counters an opposite social practice that is to be expected otherwise, based on the ubiquitous exclusionary forces discussed in Chapter 4. The introduction of the indicated boundary condition policies and mediating processes changed the impact of diversification from being negative to positive in terms of the ability of the board to perform its governance role. We discuss more about the fit between these board practices and our Framework in Chapter 8.

Managing the right tensions: Avoiding too little conflict, avoiding the wrong conflict

Both nonprofit and business boards are commonly criticized for being too homogeneous and club-like, for favoring agreement and failing to identify and work on difficult issues facing the organization.[23] Failing to adequately question each other may be a problem in workgroups throughout organizations. The findings above on performance from diverse workgroups point to the need for some differences and tensions—those that contribute to elaborating information and making better decisions—and for the avoidance of others, those that involve categorization that leads to intergroup tensions and stigmatizing.

> Simply erring on the side of conflict reduction may result in manageable levels of tension but poorer decisions and lower workgroup performance.

The common situation of erring on the side of conflict reduction is identified by L. David Brown[24] as one of too little conflict, illustrated in Figure 5.2. There is a range of conflict within which the workgroup or board or organization performs best. Below that range, members may feel comfortable but are insufficiently critical or energized to collectively perform at a higher level. And, when tensions rise too

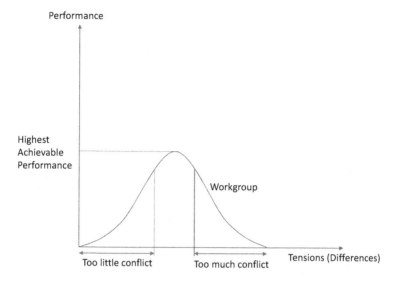

FIGURE 5.2 Managing Tensions in a Workgroup

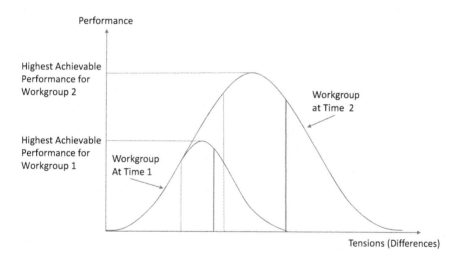

FIGURE 5.3 Progression to More Productive Handling of Differences

high, performance suffers, as indicated by the decline in performance that occurs to the right of the bolded line in the figure. Consider the implications of the categorization-elaboration model, which desires to have it both ways: Low levels of tension arising from categorization and high levels of (well-managed) tension around performance-relevant differences. Figure 5.3 portrays a workgroup at two different times. Starting from Time 1, when the diverse workgroup can only cope with low levels of tensions, the group develops over time a state of improved social integration combined with expression of differences. By Time 2, the workgroup benefits from higher levels of the right kinds of tensions, conflict with constructive, performance-enhancing ends. This shift represents an organization development process that, with adequate time, produces sustained inclusive practices that involve higher but well-managed tensions arising from performance-relevant differences. In Chapter 9, we present two cases—from an international joint venture and from a high-tech firm—where interpersonal tensions are reduced and task-related tensions are constructively managed.

From moderators to managerially structured practices prolonged over time

> Time is a key element in the ability of particular practices to overcome exclusionary forces.

As in the information technology (IT) teams and board examples above, the effects of diversity on inclusion and performance come down to sets of practices that are sustained over time at the workgroup level. Practices can vary in their effects in the long term vs. the short term. For instance, problems in terms of self-segregation and interaction discomfort that may appear in the early days of a heterogeneous workgroup or team's functioning can be overcome over time by particular team practices and norms, leading to performance equal to or greater than that in homogeneous groups. In particular, norms of political correctness in diversity interactions tend to produce interaction discomfort and self-segregation for individuals in general settings, such as occasional interactions on college campuses.[25] However, in mixed-gender teams, this norm has been found to promote team members' creativity by reducing the uncertainty of diversity interactions.[26]

> With appropriate practices, familiarity and comfort evolve over time.

The recent recognition by researchers of the importance of practices should provide actionable guidance for managers, leaders, and policymakers. However, much of the research and theory on these practices has focused on moderating factors—such as diversity climate and mindsets—that are somewhat distant from managers' actions. A meta-analytic review of research in social service organizations has found that members' perceptions of their organization's climate of inclusion are quite strongly related to their perceptions of beneficial outcomes, such as their satisfaction and assessments of the organization's performance.[27] These findings support the importance of inclusion. However, the implications for leaders' actions are somewhat vague, since organizational efforts are specified at an abstract level, as "diversity management and climate of inclusion."[28]

Workgroup conditions in the form of social practices are a more concrete and practical concept. As we have seen, studies investigating the effects of diversity on workgroup performance have led increasingly to the realization that what matters are such conditions. However, research has made surprisingly little use of a long-established and well-tested theory that specifies social conditions for effective diversity interactions—namely, intergroup contact theory,[29] discussed in the next chapter. The several conditions specified by this theory are practical. They can be put into action by managers. However, only the theory's condition of cooperative interdependence has been addressed much in organizationally oriented research. The fuller set of conditions specified by intergroup contact theory is strongly reflected in the practices in our Framework. Guillaume et al.'s[30] review uses elements of contact theory to explain particular findings that do not fit well with the categorization-elaboration model. That comprehensive review moves the conversation in the literature from abstract moderators to more concrete organizational practices, especially emphasizing the importance of integrative team processes. The review finds these processes and the diversity mindsets that accompany them to be more important than more distant concepts, such as a climate of civility.

Managerial control with constructive tensions

The question addressed in this section has been whether exclusionary forces make decreased performance inevitable as workgroups become more diverse. The research on workgroup diversity and performance tells us that the answer is not only "No," but that performance can be heightened by diversity. With categorization overcome by inclusive interaction practices, the conflict phenomenon that is more likely to be present is tension across diverse workgroup members due to differences in their perspectives, knowledge, and skills. As seen through the lens of the categorization-elaboration model, these tensions are a desired and integral part of workgroup functioning. The workgroup elaborates information in order to make better decisions and achieve higher performance. Where the valuable tensions are too low, the workgroup's performance may suffer.[31]

> The challenge is to adopt appropriate conflict management practices to constructively manage tensions, not eliminate them, so that the workgroup can benefit from its differences.

If members of underrepresented groups were simply assimilated into the majority group's way of thinking about and performing the workgroup's tasks, information elaboration and performance would suffer.

The clear implication from research evidence on conditions that are associated with higher performance in diverse workgroups is that organizational leaders can, if they are sufficiently patient, embed workgroup practices to produce higher performance through diversity in perspectives and knowledge. Extending from Guillaume and colleague's conclusions,[32] we propose that managers should customize the six organizational practices specified in Chapter 2's framework such that the practices produce and reproduce two workgroup behavioral processes over time: (1) positive social integration across identity groups based on perceptions of psychological safety, trust and justice rather than stigmatizing and anxiety-riddled interactions and (2) information elaboration and perspective-taking relevant to interdependent work tasks.

The question of efficacy

Which interventions are more effective for producing adaptive learning: Attitude-change or behavior-change efforts?

Reasons to favor behavior change over attitude change efforts were discussed briefly in Chapter 2. The theory of cognitive dissonance[33] holds that individuals will experience cognitive tension when their behavior does not match their attitudes, and that their attitudes will adjust to comply with their behavior. However, given the pervasiveness of implicit bias and stereotyping, does this process work in the case of diversity? Must organizations, instead, directly address implicit bias and stereotyping through formal attitude-change interventions? Here we consider the research evidence on this issue. We conclude that particular types of behavior-change interventions are both feasible and more promising, calling for persistence and creativity by organizational leaders rather than too-easy reliance on short-term, off-the-job attitude-change interventions.

Given the general findings that diversity training fails to deliver on its intentions, as discussed in Chapter 1, and that implicit bias is ubiquitous despite many organizational members having been exposed to diversity training over several decades, the prospects for direct attitudinal interventions to reduce bias seem poor. Nevertheless, efforts have continued to be made due to societal institutions, including governmental regulatory bodies and courts, being attuned to such interventions.

> A bottom-line way to judge the efficacy of various diversity efforts is to examine job outcomes for underrepresented groups.

In a study of over 750 firms, Alexandra Kalev, Frank Dobbin, and colleagues[34] used Equal Employment Opportunity Commission data on changes from 1971 to 2002 in the share of White women, Black women, and Black men in managerial positions. They found important differences in efficacy overall, as well as differences in impacts on the three underrepresented groups. Overall, efforts to reduce managerial bias were least effective.

> *The Evidence.* Diversity training had no significant effects on managerial positions for White women and Black men, but a significant negative effect for Black women. Including diversity measures in managers' performance appraisals produced a positive effect for White women, no effect for Black women, and a negative effect for Black men. A pattern of differences across groups also emerged for organizational programs designed to counter a group member's social isolation through within-group networking (support groups). Such programs were useful for White women but had a strong negative effect for Black men. Mentoring was greatly valuable for Black women but not for others.
>
> Paluck et al.'s[35] systematic review of prejudice reduction efforts in the field of psychology similarly finds a lack of supportive findings for instructional (training and education) efforts, with those poor results possibly being due to efforts failing to be guided by theories of learning or prejudice reduction. Also discouraging for attitude-change approaches, their review found a lack of evidence for a reduction in implicit bias producing a reduction in prejudiced behavior. Psychological studies overall do not provide clear evidence that attitude-oriented interventions reduce prejudice, especially in real world settings. For example, a lab experiment where individuals were instructed to suppress stereotypes found, instead, that such instructions had the opposite effect. And, simply providing an individual with information inconsistent with their stereotype is ineffective because the information is ignored, distorted, forgotten, or attributed away.[36]

Plainly put, direct efforts to change managerial attitudes were ineffective and even harmful for some groups. In contrast, accountability efforts and initiatives that engaged managers in diversity-promoting behavior were effective.

> *The Evidence.* In Kalev and colleagues' study,[37] the efforts with the most beneficial effects and without negative effects for any of the three groups were programs that established organizational responsibility, holding the organization accountable for progress. Affirmative action plans benefited White women and Black men, while having a diversity committee, staff devoted to diversity, and a targeted recruitment policy had significant beneficial effects for all three groups. These organizational accountability efforts can be understood as requiring changes in the decision-making behavior of managers responsible for hiring, developing, and promoting members of underrepresented groups.

The differences that Alexandra Kalev and colleagues discovered in the impacts of particular diversity efforts on the three underrepresented groups, and especially the negative impacts, seem to be little recognized in organizational practice. Their findings imply that some continuing diversity efforts are dysfunctional for inclusion and equity.

A number of common diversity efforts are hampering rather than benefiting inclusion and equity.

The continued reliance on diversity training may be partially due to a belief in the value of education on the part of educators and diversity officials, as well as its simplicity of implementation as a "check off the box" exercise. Drawing on their findings, Dobbin and Kalev[38] propose that organizations should instead focus on changing managerial behavior through managers being incorporated into accountability efforts such as diversity task forces. The reasoning is that, through the cognitive dissonance between their pro-diversity behavior on a task force and their biased attitudes, their attitudes will gradually change to be more in line with their behavior.

Studies of accountability approaches that focus on behaviors and decisions do show reductions in the effects of bias. Meta-analytic reviews are persuasive on this point.

The Evidence. Steven Spencer and colleagues'[39] meta-analysis of experimental studies found reductions in the effects of gender bias on employment ratings (e.g., for hiring) when individuals were motivated to behave more carefully, "when participants felt accountable for their decisions, believed their decisions had real-life consequences, or were reminded of equity norms" (p. 139). The contextual conditions surrounding the behavior promoted less-biased decision-making. Similarly, with regard to ethnicity or race-based discrimination, a meta-analysis of studies using the Implicit Association Test[40] concluded that implicit bias is less an integral trait of individuals than one triggered by context, suggesting that "situational conditions can powerfully sway even the relationship between implicit bias and spontaneous behaviors" (p. 184). A reason for this effect of context is found in a meta-analysis examining the Implicit Attitude Test and intergroup behavior in both field and laboratory studies.[41] It found that implicit cognitions, despite their label, are subject to conscious introspection, introspection that can be promoted by the situation.

These findings from psychological studies complement the finding from Kalev and colleagues' investigations of actual employment outcomes in organizations, discussed directly above. They indicate that particular situational conditions, including accountability, mitigate the operation of bias in managers' decisions.

> Conditions that hold managers responsible for their personnel decisions produce greater employment improvements for underrepresented groups than do educational efforts aimed at attitude change.

As is captured by the merit and accountability practices element in our Framework, the contextual condition of accountability matters, producing changes in behavior (such as seeking more information on the particular individual's qualifications) that result in less biased decisions.

> In sum, research evidence indicates that organizations can more readily control bias through creating conditions of accountability that motivate responsible behavior than through efforts aimed directly at changing attitudes.

In the next chapter, we consider combining attitude-change training with behavior-change initiatives in order to strongly signal organizational rules and norms for inclusion. However, behavior-change approaches remain primary.

The question of intent

How do some organizational programs produce inclusion for diverse members without diversity-focused?

Relatively slight attention has been given to the impacts on diversity and inclusion of organizational programs that are not explicitly and formally focused on promoting diversity. We identify here two types of such programs, one with research evidence supporting its impacts on inclusion and another backed by its widespread managerial experience of task success. Not surprisingly, given the importance that we place on mixing diverse members frequently and with equal status in interdependent collaborations, both programs involve teams that bring together a diverse set of individuals from different work units in an organization. The programs feature strong support from organizational leaders who emphasize the importance of their performance outcomes.

Cross-job collaboration

Projects to increase coordination across jobs and organizational functions are not thought of as diversity-related efforts. However, workplaces are frequently segregated in terms of membership in particular occupations or functions, with members of different gender, race and ethnicity being crowded into particular jobs. A common example is women in clerical roles supporting men in higher-level jobs, or people of color being more common in support functions that do not carry good prospects of promotion to executive positions.

> Bringing different job groups together in a team charged with improving their coordination has the effect of mixing members of underrepresented groups with others in a collaborative effort to improve performance. This collaborative mixing benefits those members' job outcomes.

The Evidence. Further analyses in the research by Alexandra Kalev[42] found that improved odds of White and Black women and Black men moving into managerial positions resulted from self-directed work teams and cross-job training, but not from within-function, problem-solving teams, or within-job training. The difference between cross-function and within-function programs and training indicate that the upward mobility impacts of the cross-functional efforts are due to relational processes that restructure interaction from segregated to collaborative relations across gender, race and ethnicity.

Kalev notes that self-directed teams typically are concerned with coordinating across different jobs, bringing members of underrepresented groups into the teams. She attributes the effects of these teams and of cross-job training to increased networking, eroding of stereotypes and group boundaries, and higher assessments of the capabilities of the program's members from underrepresented groups. Ultimately, these processes lead to improved chances for job transfers and promotions. We would add that, since they are not labeled as diversity initiatives, these cross-functional programs are unlikely to trigger stereotyping through competitive threat, as discussed in the preceding chapter, such as White men perceiving that women or people of color are being favored in a diversity initiative. To the contrary, the cross-job programs are promoted as improving performance in a way that benefits all members of the work units.

> Self-directed teams engaging in cross-job training leads to increased networking and eroding of stereotypes and higher assessments of the capabilities of the program's members from underrepresented groups. This ultimately results in improved chances for job transfers and promotions. These initiatives, because they are not labeled as diversity efforts, are unlikely to trigger stereotyping through competitive threat.

A practical example: Inclusion from agile teams for software development

The finding that inclusion benefits from cross-job teams but not from within-function teams suggests to us that team processes developed in various industries for the purpose of increased performance (rather than increased diversity) can produce inclusion in diverse workgroups. One striking example is agile teams in software development,[43] in which particular practices are followed to rapidly produce software that meets customer requirements. These practices have been developed, refined, and spread within the practitioner community of project managers over more than two decades.[44] This process of knowledge generation and dissemination, termed "Type 2,"[45] contrasts with "Type 1" knowledge generation that occurs in academic settings through formal inquiry, testing and publication, the type of knowledge generation that underlies most of the material presented in this book. An advantage of Type 2 over Type 1 knowledge generation lies in the practicality of the knowledge. Review articles such as that by Dikert and colleagues[46] focus not only on the nature of agile methods and their effectiveness but also on the managerial challenges of implementation and how to overcome them.

In practitioner-oriented engineering literature, agile teams have been reported to be ten times more effective than traditional methods of software development.[47] The essence of agile team methodology is rapid flexibility in the software development process achieved through high-frequency communication between the customer and team and among the team members coming from various jobs and functions. Work is focused on short-term sprints of several weeks, with daily meetings of members within a sprint and iterative meetings at the end of each sprint. Across and within iterations, product requirements change based on experience. The high levels of interaction relate to inclusion, with the engineering literature noting agile being a *social process*[48] and occasionally referring to inclusiveness as a valuable part of the process.[49]

This process of high-frequency, task-focused interaction has been found to lead to inclusion in terms of cross-cultural diversity: Agile principles applied in globally distributed teams, wherein work is passed across teams in different countries for around-the-clock development, help create trust across different cultures.[50]

> *The Evidence.* This performance-enhancing social integration across cultures can be attributed to particular social practices reported in a systematic review[51] as those most frequently associated with successful global agile software development: Standup meetings, sprint iterations, continuous integration, sprint planning, retrospective meetings, and pair programming. Such practices have been directly linked to enhanced communication within agile teams, with one qualitative study of co-located agile teams identifying the efficacy of particular practices that parallel the preceding list:[52]
>
> 1. co-located office space, enabling rapid access among members;
> 2. daily standup meetings for high-frequency communication during and after meetings;
> 3. iteration planning meetings with the customer, held once during each design iteration and often preceded by a grooming (pre-meeting) session for the software developers;

4. pair programming, with two members developing code together, a particular benefit for new team members to gain know-how;

5. sprint retrospective meetings within the team to identify and solve problems and to specify lessons learned;

6. sprint reviews with the customer to discuss the results of the last iteration, focusing on major issues that hindered progress.

Note that these agile practices map well to the practices for inclusive interactions in our Framework. All contribute to a continual emphasis on shared purpose, a frequent mixing of members, and interdependent collaboration. More subtly, the daily and periodic planning meetings allow for constructive conflict handling, and the pair programming helps to provide equal status and self-efficacy among members, including the acquisition of know-how by new members. Yet more subtly, the sprint retrospectives and reviews, while less frequent, contribute over time to member comfort since the lessons learned enable the development of improved communication processes. As stated in The Agile Manifesto,[53] the document that initially defined agile methods, "At regular intervals, the team reflects on how to become more effective, then tunes and adjusts its behavior accordingly." In effect, daily and periodic problem-solving, reflection, and process correction address tensions and discomforts constructively. Taken together, the social practices found to be effective for direct interactions in agile teams cover our Framework's specification of six practices for inclusive interactions.

Agile teams have not been instituted with the intent of producing inclusion for social justice. Social integration in global teams is not sought on the basis of improving equity but of enabling team performance by developing trust. In agile teams, producing inclusion in the form of frequent interactions, strong communication and mutual reliance is a means to an end, the end being team performance.

Agile practices match with our Framework's practices for inclusive interactions because both sets of practices are aimed at sustaining productive, learning, meaningful interactions across all team members.

The nature of inclusion implemented for performance reasons with agile teams matches inclusion as specified in the categorization-elaboration model—that is, inclusion that produces performance from diversity through elaborating information needed for effective decision-making. With the exception of fair employment practices, inclusion in agile teams also matches Lisa Nishii's[54] specification (as discussed in this book's Introduction) for a climate of inclusion for diversity: integration of differences, and inclusion in decision-making. When organizational programs such as agile teams specify practices for performance that amount to inclusive practices, they can establish a climate for inclusion from diversity.

> Simply put, inclusive practices are inclusive practices, whether the motivation for their implementation is performance or equity or both.

For agile team practices to produce inclusion for equity as well as performance, the team must be composed of diverse members. If the agile team is co-located, this means representational diversity must be present within the single geographic unit, across the roles (e.g., marketers, code developers) in the team. Global agile teams are inherently diverse culturally. With their several national teams collaborating across great distances, additional practices such as using multiple modes of communication are beneficial.[55] As noted above, agile practices in global teams have been found to develop trust and social integration across national cultures, suggesting that practices that create high-frequency, task-focused interactions produce performance and inclusion benefits.

> Within agile teams, whether the intent is equity-focused or performance-focused, the type of interactions can be expected to generate and sustain inclusion across members of diverse teams benefiting members from underrepresented groups or different cultures.

The managerial prospects for informed, creative actions

Particular beliefs among various managers drive their decisions regarding whether and how to address diversity in their organizations. The evidence-based discussions in this chapter shed light on the validity of some of those beliefs. With regard to diversity's effects on performance, a variety of beliefs exists among managers and researchers: "Diversity improves performance" or "Diversity improves performance on creative tasks" or "Homogeneous groups have higher trust and perform better." The empirical literature supports all these differing beliefs, with systematic reviews pointing to the importance of organizational and workgroup conditions that favor one or the other of the competing positive and negative effects of diversity on performance. We conclude that whether the positive effects dominate the negative depends on the particular social practices found in workgroups and teams. Do the practices promote frequent, positive diversity interactions? Do they make conflict constructive? Do they elicit and incorporate varying perspectives, producing more information that leads to better decisions?

> When practices promote frequent, positive diversity interactions over extended time periods, members are more likely to be willing and able to overcome stereotyping and interaction discomfort. The result is inclusive and productive workgroups where social practices and trust make conflict constructive and all voices valued.

Another set of beliefs concerns how organizations should pursue diversity and equity goals. As judged by what organizations commonly do, the belief is "Inclusion and equity for underrepresented groups is best achieved through formal, diversity-focused initiatives." Again, the answer is, "Yes, Maybe, and No. It all depends." Evidence tells us that the answer is "Yes" for creating responsibility and account-ability among managers in order to overcome implicit bias in personnel decisions. The answer is "Maybe" for support groups and networks. They are effective for some underrepresented groups and not others. The answer is "No" in terms of some currently common approaches, such as awareness training, that evidence indicates to be ineffective. The answer is also "No" in the sense that some organiza-tional programs without any diversity intent produce strong positive effects for the inclusion of underrepresented groups. In particular, evidence indicates that cross-job team and training programs, created with performance intent rather than diver-sity intent, produce benefits for underrepresented groups that exceed the benefits of diversity-intended initiatives. Especially where occupational segregation exists, as is widespread on the basis of gender, race and ethnicity, creating cross-job teams can produce gains in performance and equity.

Knowledge generated in laboratory and in-the-field research and by leaders in project management leads to a promising opportunity: That there is a largely untapped way for many organizations to overcome social forces of exclusion in order to achieve performance, diversity, and equity. That way lies in managers pursuing programs for cross-functional, multidisciplinary, and semi-autonomous teams having diversity in their membership. The close matching of agile team social practices, developed by practitioners to improve performance, with our Framework's practices for inclusive interactions, developed on the basis of aca-demic research, provides cross-validation across two types of knowledge generation. The performance benefits of inclusive interaction practices, then, are supported from two sources of knowledge: practical experience with agile teams, and research findings on situational conditions for success from diversity. Managers can be opti-mistic about their ability to structure practices for inclusive interactions in a var-iety of settings, since many managers and organizations have already done so by adopting cross-job teams and training and by extending agile teams from software development to other types of projects.[56] Since self-directed cross-job teams and agile teams are particular examples of the broader category of semi-autonomous teams, the potential for managerial application of inclusive practices exists in a wide variety of settings. For instance, one of the cases discussed in Chapter 3 illustrates the feasibility of semi-autonomous teams in a health care setting. Social practices intended to boost performance through the inclusion of all members in diverse semi-autonomous teams can be expected to produce equity benefits as well.

Strategic options for diversity

We have identified three strategic options for utilizing diversity in organizations. The first is occupational segregation, forming workgroups that are relatively homogeneous internally but differing across workgroups, as in women in nursing and men in engineering. This option fails to allocate people according to their talents. The second option is to utilize heterogeneous workgroups that assimilate the diverse members into a dominant workgroup culture, a culture preexisting prior to the entry of diverse members. The categorization-elaboration model tells us that such assimilation will reduce information elaboration and workgroup performance. We will discuss these two options further in Chapter 8 in terms of their likelihood of producing valuable outcomes from diversity. However, the findings presented in this chapter clearly point to the superiority of the third option—utilizing inclusive workgroups and teams where work-relevant differences are invited and tensions are dealt with constructively to make better decisions.

> Performance and equity are enhanced by inclusive workgroups where work-relevant differences and tensions are dealt with constructively to make better decisions.

The leadership challenge with this option is to boost information elaboration while avoiding categorization phenomena that cause fault lines between subgroups within the workgroup. One demonstrated way to do this is by creating self-directed, agile teams that are diverse and charged with a performance goal, operating with principles and norms that are inclusive. The challenge involves leaders creating and sustaining appropriate workgroup norms through the practices for inclusive interaction specified in this book's Framework. The leadership challenge is also to foster individualized adjustment by all newcomers to a workgroup, to maintain performance-related differences. In the following chapter, we consider how newcomers can be encultured into inclusive workgroup norms while avoiding assimilation and retaining a readiness to offer their individual, differing talents.

Organizational leaders should be both critical and optimistic. Informed by evidence, they can critically examine the investments for performance and equity that they are currently making and consider additional possibilities for their intelligent, creative, persistent actions. We return to this issue in Chapter 9 with illustrative examples of effective managerial strategies that achieve inclusive practices.

Notes

1 Bertrand, M., & Duflo, E. (2016). *Field experiments on discrimination*. National Bureau of Economic Research (NBER) Working Paper 22014, p. 7. http://www.nber.org/papers/w22014.

2 Spencer, S. J., Logel, C., & Davies, P. G. (2016). Stereotype threat. *Annual Review of Psychology, 67*(1), 415–437.

3 van Knippenberg, D., De Dreu, C. K., & Homan, A. C. (2004). Work group diversity and group performance: An integrative model and research agenda. *Journal of Applied Psychology, 89*(6), 1008–1022.

4 Ibid; van Knippenberg, D., & Schippers, M. C. (2007). Work group diversity. *Annual Review of Psychology*, *58*(1), 515–541.

5 Ibid.

6 Stahl, G. K., Maznevski, M. L., Voigt, A., & Jonsen, K. (2010). Unraveling the effects of cultural diversity in teams: A meta-analysis of research on multicultural work groups. *Journal of International Business Studies*, *41*(4), 690–709; van Knippenberg, D., & Mell, J. N. (2016). Past, present, and potential future of team diversity research: From compositional diversity to emergent diversity. *Organizational Behavior and Human Decision Processes*, *136*, 135–145.

7 van Dijk, H., van Engen, M. L., & van Knippenberg, D. (2012). Defying conventional wisdom: A meta-analytical examination of the differences between demographic and job-related diversity relationships with performance. *Organizational Behavior and Human Decision Processes*, *119*(1), 38–53 (p. 49).

8 Joshi, A., & Roh, H. (2009). The role of context in work team diversity research: A meta-analytic review. *Academy of Management Journal*, *52*(3), 599–627.

9 Stahl et al. (2010). "Unraveling the effects of cultural diversity in teams."

10 van Knippenberg & Schippers (2007). "Work group diversity."

11 van Knippenberg & Mell (2016). "Past, present, and potential future of team diversity research."

12 Guillaume, Y. R. F., Dawson, J. F., Otaye-Ebede, L., Woods, S. A., & West, M. A. (2017). Harnessing demographic differences in organizations: What moderates the effects of workplace diversity? *Journal of Organizational Behavior*, *38*(2), 276–303.

13 Roh, H., Chun, K., Ryou, Y., & Son, J. (2019). Opening the black box: A meta-analytic examination of the effects of top management team diversity on emergent team processes and multilevel contextual influence. *Group & Organization Management*, *44*(1), 112–164.

14 Ibid.

15 Ibid, p. 150.

16 Guillaume et al. (2017). "Harnessing demographic differences in organizations."

17 Ibid.

18 Joshi, A., & Roh, H. (2009). The role of context in work team diversity research: A meta-analytic review. *Academy of Management Journal*, *52*(3), 599–627. (p. 622).

19 van Knippenberg et al. (2004). "Work group diversity and group performance."

20 Guillaume et al. (2017). "Harnessing demographic differences in organizations."

21 van Knippenberg et al. (2004). "Work group diversity and group performance."

22 Buse, K., Bernstein, R. S., & Bilimoria, D. (2016). The influence of board diversity, board diversity policies and practices, and board inclusion behaviors on nonprofit governance practices. *Journal of Business Ethics*, *133*(1), 179–191; Fredette, C., Bradshaw, P., & Krause, H. (2016). From diversity to inclusion: A multimethod study of diverse governing groups. *Nonprofit and Voluntary Sector Quarterly*, *45*(1_suppl), 28S–51S.

23 Cornforth, C., & Brown, W. A. (2014). *Nonprofit governance: Innovative perspectives and approaches*. Routledge.

24 Brown, L. D. (1983). *Managing conflict at organizational interfaces*. Addison-Wesley.

25 Bernstein, R. S., & Salipante, P. (2017). Intercultural comfort through social practices: Exploring conditions for cultural learning. *Frontiers in Education*, Vol. 2, Article 31. doi:10.3389/feduc.2017.00031. http://journal.frontiersin.org/article/10.3389/feduc.2017.00031/full?&utm_source=Email_to_authors_&utm_medium=Email&utm_content=T1_11.5e1_author&utm_campaign=Email_publication&field=&journalName=Frontiers_in_Education&id=272155.

26 Goncalo, Chatman, Duguid, & Kennedy (2014), cited in Guillaume et al. (2017), p. 289.

27 Mor Barak, M. E., Lizano, E. L., Kim, A., Duan, L., Rhee, M -K , Hsiao, H.-Y., & Brimhall, K. C. (2016). The promise of diversity management for climate of inclusion: A state-of-the-art review and meta-analysis. *Human Service Organizations: Management, Leadership & Governance, 40*(4), 305–333.

28 Ibid, p. 322.

29 Allport, G. W. (1954). *The nature of prejudice.* Addison-Wesley.

30 Guillaume et al. (2017). "Harnessing demographic differences in organizations."

31 Brown (1983). *Managing conflict at organizational interfaces.*

32 Guillaume et al. (2017). "Harnessing demographic differences in organizations," p. 294.

33 Festinger, L. (1957). *A theory of cognitive dissonance.* Stanford University Press.

34 Kalev, A., Dobbin, F., & Kelly, E. (2006). Best practices or best guesses? Assessing the efficacy of corporate affirmative action and diversity policies. *American Sociological Review, 71*(4), 589–617; Dobbin, F., Schrage, D., & Kalev, A. (2015). Rage against the iron cage: The varied effects of bureaucratic personnel reforms on diversity. *American Sociological Review, 80*(5), 1014–1044.

35 Paluck, E. L., Green, S. A., & Green, D. P. (2019). The contact hypothesis re-evaluated. *Behavioural Public Policy, 3*(2), 129–158.

36 Stangor, C. (2009). The study of stereotyping, prejudice, and discrimination within social psychology: A quick history of theory and research. In T. D. Nelson (Ed.), *Handbook of prejudice, stereotyping, and discrimination* (pp. 1–12). Psychology Press.

37 Kalev et al. (2006). "Best practices or best guesses?"; Dobbin et al. (2015). "Rage against the iron cage."

38 Dobbin, F., & Kalev, A. (2016). Why diversity programs fail. *Harvard Business Review, July-August,* 1–8.

39 Spencer, S. J., Logel, C., & Davies, P. G. (2016). Stereotype threat. *Annual Review of Psychology, 67*(1), 415–437.

40 Oswald, F. L., Mitchell, G., Blanton, H., Jaccard, J., & Tetlock, P. E. (2013). Predicting ethnic and racial discrimination: A meta-analysis of IAT criterion studies. *Journal of Personality and Social Psychology, 105*(2), 171–192.

41 Kurdi, B., Seitchik, A. E., Axt, J. R., Carroll, T. J., Karapetyan, A., Kaushik, N., Tomezsko, D., Greenwald, A. G., & Banaji, M. R. (2018). Relationship between the Implicit Association Test and intergroup behavior: A meta-analysis. *American Psychologist, 74*(5), 569–586.

42 Kalev, A. (2009). Cracking the glass cages? Restructuring and ascriptive inequality at work. *American Journal of Sociology 114*(6), 1591–1643.

43 Dybå, T., & Dingsøyr, T. (2008). Empirical studies of agile software development: A systematic review. *Information and Software Technology, 50*(9), 833–859.

44 Hummel, M. (2014, January 6-9). State-of-the-art: A systematic literature review on agile information systems development (pp. 4712–4721). Paper presented at the 2014 47th Hawaii International Conference on System Sciences.

45 Gibbons, M., Limoges, C., Nowotny, H., Schwartzman, S., Scott, P., & Trow, M. (1994). *The new production of knowledge: The dynamics of science and research in contemporary societies.* Sage.

46 Dikert, K., Paasivaara, M., & Lassenius, C. (2016). Challenges and success factors for large-scale agile transformations: A systematic literature review. *Journal of Systems and Software, 119,* 87–108.

47 Paasivaara & Lassenius (2006), cited in Shrivastava, S. V., & Date, H. (2010). Distributed agile software development: A review. *Journal of Computer Science and Engineering, 1*(1), 10–16.

48 Inayat, I., Salim, S. S., Marczak, S., Daneva, M., & Shamshirband, S. (2015). A systematic literature review on agile requirements engineering practices and challenges. *Computers in Human Behavior, 51*, 915–929.

49 Dikert et al. (2016). "Challenges and success factors for large-scale agile transformations."

50 Paasivaara, Durasiewicz, & Lassenius (2009), cited in Shrivastava & Date (2010). "Distributed agile software development."

51 Jalali, S., & Wohlin, C. (2012). Global software engineering and agile practices: a systematic review. *Journal of Software: Evolution and Process, 24*(6), 643–659.

52 Hummel, M., Rosenkranz, C., & Holten, R. (2015). The role of social agile practices for direct and indirect communication in information systems development teams. *Communications of the Association for Information Systems, 36*(15), 273–300.

53 Beck, K., Beedle, M., van Bennekum, A., Cockburn, A., Cunningham, W., Fowler, M., Grenning, J., Highsmith, J., Hunt, A., Jeffries, R., Kern, J., Marick, B., Martin, R. C., Mellor, S., Schwaber, K., Sutherland, J., & Thomas, D. (2001). *Manifesto for agile software development.* http://agilemanifesto.org.

54 Nishii, L. H. (2013). The benefits of climate for inclusion for gender-diverse groups. *Academy of Management Journal, 56*(6), 1754–1774.

55 Hossain, E., Babar, M. A., & Paik, H. (2009). *Using scrum in global software development: A systematic literature review* (pp. 175–184). Paper presented at the 2009 Fourth IEEE International Conference on Global Software Engineering.

56 Conforto, E. C., Salum, F., Amaral, D. C., da Silva, S. L., & de Almeida, L. F. M. (2014). Can agile project management be adopted by industries other than software development? *Project Management Journal, 45*(3), 21–34.

6

STRUCTURED INTERACTION PRACTICES FOR ADAPTIVE BEHAVIORAL LEARNING

Systematic reviews of research-based evidence discussed in the two previous chapters repeatedly emphasize the importance of workplace conditions and procedures in activating or countering exclusionary forces that inhibit performance and equity. Here, keeping in mind those forces and programs that counteract them, such as accountability and cross-job collaboration, we discuss how individuals and groups adapt to diversity by learning how to work effectively, inclusively together as they engage in inclusive interaction practices. Those inclusive interaction practices and processes for adaptive behavioral learning, labeled *adaptive learning*, as illustrated in Figure 6.1, are the centerpiece of our Framework.

> The chapter melds sociological ideas that emphasize the impact of social conditions with psychological ideas that emphasize an individual's cognitions.

Melding sociological and psychological ideas enables us to understand why and how individuals behave, think, and perform in diverse workgroups. With the goal of presenting knowledge that managers can act on, we proceed through a series of questions focused on workgroup members' cognitive and behavioral learning:

Question: What diversity experiences lead individuals to performance-enhancing adaptive learning over time?
Answer: *Cognitive adaptation* **occurs by individuals working through the discomfort of inconsistency between stereotypes of others and their actual experiences with them.**

DOI: 10.4324/9780367822484-10

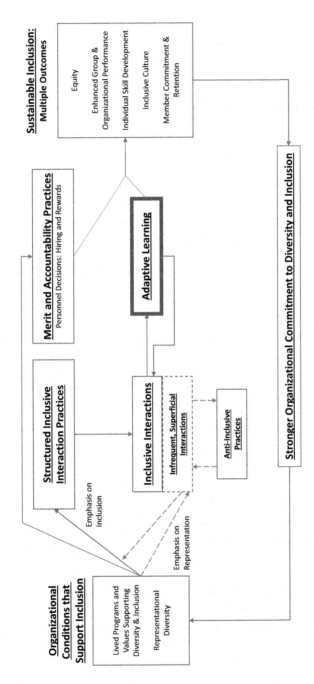

FIGURE 6.1 The Framework for Inclusive Interactions: Adaptive Learning

Q: **What conditions surrounding diversity interactions lead to adaptive behavior and attitude change?**
A: *Intergroup contact theory* **specifies particular conditions of contact that reduce prejudice between groups.**

Q: **What do collective adaptation and inclusive practices look like?**
A: *Practices,* **habitual routines that members engage in together, shape emotions, understandings, and behavioral skills.**

Q: **How do workgroup members become carriers of practices that sustain the inclusion of performance-enhancing individual differences?**
A: *Personal-identity socialization* **enables newcomers to fit in authentically and play to their strengths.**

Q: **What level of adaptive learning enables high performance and equity to be sustained through inclusion?**
A: *Intergroup friendships* **produce adaptive learning through self-disclosure.**

Tying together the insights resulting from these questions leads to questions regarding managerial action: What does research-based evidence suggest that organizations do to aid adaptive learning in diverse workgroups, and why have so few diversity initiatives incorporated that knowledge? From considering the evidence bearing on these questions, we reach two practical conclusions for organizations and their diverse members: that the adaptive learning that matters most in organizations is primarily behavioral, and that this learning is best initiated and sustained through practices that keep members of diverse workgroups interacting over lengthy periods of time in a properly comfortable and productive way.

Cognitive adaptation by individuals

What diversity experiences lead individuals to performance-enhancing adaptive learning over time?

This section discusses adaptive learning that raises individuals' performance and capabilities. First, we consider adaptations by members of groups who are coping with being stereotyped and stigmatized, then adaptations by individuals initially holding negative stereotypes of others. Research evidence has revealed processes that enable individuals to reduce prejudices and stereotypes, and their detrimental effects. A theme common to adaptations by both sets of individuals is that discomfort is raised by diversity interactions and needs to be worked through in order for more comfortable and productive interactions to become frequent.

Initiatives to facilitate psychological and behavioral adaptation

If managers are to attain sustained performance and equity from diversity, stigmatizing must be addressed. As noted in Chapter 4, implicit bias is widespread. When it is triggered into action, the resulting stereotype threat for women and those from underrepresented groups harms their performance by creating anxieties and reduced feelings of self-efficacy. However, remedies for countering stereotype threat have been identified.

> *The evidence.* Spencer, Logel, and Davies'[1] review of psychological research concludes that particular remedies that enable individuals to cope with being stereotyped have good research support. With regard to actions that organizations can take, the review's findings emphasize the importance of leaders creating identity-safe environments for stereotyped group members through such actions as:
>
> - facilitating positive contact with majority group members,
> - providing role models of successful members of underrepresented groups, and
> - creating single-identity (such as all-women) workgroups or teams.
>
> The review also identifies actions that can be taken by those from underrepresented groups themselves to cope with the current reality of being stereotyped and stigmatized. In effect, the stereotype threat can be high but not triggered if the individual reconstrues the situation. To avoid triggering, research indicates the value of believing that the stereotype is illegitimate and of engaging in self-affirmation activities or mindfulness training.

The review recommends that the research findings from laboratory experimental studies should be taken into organizations to be implemented and evaluated, just as is done with medical research being tested in clinical trials.

Knowledge gained in psychology experimental studies is ready for managers to implement in field trials in their organizations.

We note that, to some degree, that has been done by some organizational programs that aid those who are stigmatized in reconstruing their situation. The value of programs that provide single-gender support (networking) groups for White women and mentoring for Black women that was identified in Chapter 5 can be explained by those support groups and mentors affirming the individuals' efficacy and advising them how to mitigate or work around being stigmatized.

Regarding the recommendation for single-identity workgroups, consider the experience of one of our interviewees, described in Box 6.1.

BOX 6.1: A CASE OF SINGLE-IDENTITY TEAMS BY GENDER

Julia, a data analyst and writer in a technical field, noted dynamics that led to dominantly single-gender teams in the organizations in which she had worked. In one, she was a member of a unit of approximately forty people that produced and published research reports. Working virtually in teams of five to eight members scattered across the United States, each team engaged for nine months or more in a series of related projects, headed by a project leader. Teams met as a whole once or twice a week, with some individuals meeting daily, as needed. Julia remarked that, while there was much diversity in terms of ethnicity and age, the project teams were typically either dominantly female or dominantly male. Primarily, this occurred during team formation, with much discretion both on the part of the project leader choosing team members and the unit's members choosing which team to join. Occasionally, a man would join a dominantly female team but not remain long-term. She said, "Leaders with billable work tended to select insular teams that could get the work done in relative harmony." She also noted that the women managing the high-profile projects have reputations for being "pushy" and "intimidating" at work but friendly in more casual settings.

In this case, several gender-based dynamics appear to be operating, including stereotyping of the women leaders and self-segregating by team members. The gender effects seem to follow a rule of avoiding discomfort and reducing tensions. In those ways, and consistent with the evidence presented above, the single-gender teams are offering identity-safe environments. In so doing, they enable sustained diversity, with less need for dissatisfaction to lead to quitting. However, they are weaker on sustained inclusion. While single-identity teams may decrease anxieties and increase members' self-efficacy, thereby improving their performance, such teams may also reduce the diversity in perspectives that produce information elaboration and yet stronger workgroup decision-making, as covered in the preceding chapter. We see single-identity teams as a second-best solution that may sometimes be useful in the short-term as members of underrepresented groups prove themselves, but there should then be progress over time to units having a fuller culture of inclusion that supports diverse teams.

From interaction discomfort to comfort: Cognitive and behavioral adaptation by individuals holding stereotypes

Discomfort and anxieties in diversity interactions, triggered for members of underrepresented groups by being stigmatized, can also occur for individuals who hold the stereotypes that stigmatize others. The discomfort occurs when they encounter individuals who do not fit the stereotype. This discomfort can be functional in producing cognitive adaptation on their part. Applying the theory of cognitive dissonance,[2] we would expect that when individuals holding a negative stereotype repeatedly engage in positive interaction behavior with differing others that counter the stereotype, they will experience dissonance and adapt over time by reducing the stereotyped attitude.

> Cognitive dissonance theory holds that an inconsistency among an individuals' various attitudes, or between attitudes and behavior, causes a discomforting dissonance that the individual strives to correct.

Evidence from psychological studies confirms this expectation and provides insights into how the process occurs. Richard Crisp and Rhiannon Turner[3] drew together empirical studies and social psychological theories on acculturation, cognitive development, categorization, stereotype threat, and creativity. Their integrative review sought to understand when and how individuals adapt to culturally different others by changing their preconceptions. The resulting model emphasizes the individual's progression through four stages of cross-cultural adaptation and the social conditions that sustain progression through the stages:

Categorization → Cognitive Processing → Adaptation → Generalization

> Discomfort occurs when we experience stereotype inconsistency where people we encounter do not fit our existing stereotypes or images of them—an inconsistency between our prejudgment of a group's members and our actual experience with them.

We can describe this adaptation process in personal terms. According to the model, our adaptation in terms of emotions and interaction skills starts with *stereotype inconsistency*. We experience an inconsistency between our prejudged categorization of a group's members and our actual experience with them. That inconsistency produces psychological discomfort for us. Consistent with the idea that stereotypes are resistant to evidence that they are faulty (Chapter 4), we may choose to deal with the discomfort by avoiding members of the group in the future or seeing them as exceptions to the rule. We thereby avoid future psychological discomfort and hold on to our stereotype. According to Crisp and Turner's review, only if social conditions encourage us are we willing and able to work through the discomfort.

> Adaptation occurs only in conditions that make individuals willing and able to repeatedly interact with differing others.

By continuing to interact repeatedly with particular differing others, we progress through the more taxing process of cognitive processing, adaptation, and generalizing to the broader groups that we are stereotyping. That is, if we are to achieve adaptive learning that reduces discomfort and increases our interaction skills, our social situation should involve three factors—motivation, ability, and repetition. Facilitating conditions can include (1) being interdependent with different others and accountable for interacting with them, which creates motivations to be more accurate in assessing others and (2) pursuing shared goals, which encourages individuals to expand their in-group boundaries to include those different others.[4] Both processes break down stereotypes and, so, contribute to adaptive learning.

> *The evidence.* Research by this book's authors and others identifies that when interactions with differing others are infrequent and superficial, interaction discomfort is prevalent, particularly in the presence of norms of political correctness.[5] In contrast, when individual comfort is achieved, it results in an ability to accommodate oneself and produce appropriate behavioral responses with people different from ourselves.[6] Crisp and Turner's review finds that cross-cultural adaptation, when achieved, enhances various cognitive skills, including creativity and attention to alternative or minority viewpoints.

Cross-cultural adaptation enhances individuals' attention to alternative viewpoints, so it contributes to a workgroup's ability to achieve information elaboration. Less cognitive effort is required when with differing others, encouraging more and more productive interaction.

> Adaptation reduces the distraction of having to continually monitor oneself in diversity interactions, enabling more focus on the task.

The most important point concerning an individual's adaptation is that it requires conditions that exert some force toward repeatedly engaging with dissimilar others. Otherwise, as noted, the individual can diminish the discomfort of stereotype inconsistency simply by lack of engagement, by self-segregating. Without some forcing of repeated, productive interaction, as through task interdependence within a workgroup, members will find it easiest to resolve the discomfort by avoiding the discomforting interactions. With conditions that do provide a force for positive engagement over time, cross-cultural stress can be overcome to produce reductions in discomfort and gains in judgment.

Conditions that provide a force toward repeated, positive engagement lead to adaptation.

Particular organizational practices can reduce discomfort while an individual works through the processing and adaptation stages. For example, norms of political correctness in workgroups can be beneficial rather than detrimental in this process. As noted in the preceding chapter, such norms have been shown to reduce psychological uncertainty about acceptable behavior and raise the performance of newly formed diverse workgroups.[7]

Norms of appropriate interaction raise the performance of newly formed diverse workgroups.

In an organization, the conditions affecting motivation and repetition, and thereby adaptation, reside in the workgroup. But what are the particular workgroup conditions that foster an ability and willingness to engage repeatedly and positively? We turn to sociology, with its emphasis on social structures, for insights and evidence.

Intergroup contact theory

> What conditions surrounding diversity interactions lead to adaptive behavior and attitude change?

The major sociological theory on diversity, intergroup contact theory,[8] has been available since the 1950s. Its basic proposition—that prejudice between groups is reduced when the groups contact each other under certain specified conditions—has been supported repeatedly by empirical research investigations,[9] and its specification of conditions provides direct guidance for organizational action. Yet, surprisingly, the practical knowledge gained from this stream of research is little known nor applied in organizational efforts to improve diversity and inclusion.

The knowledge from research on intergroup contact undergirds the central element of our Framework, inclusive interaction practices. Over the years in our own research studies, findings kept emerging that fit with this theory. Hence, there is a tight relationship between our use of the term "interaction" and the theory's term, "contact."

> The Framework for Inclusive Interactions reconceptualizes contact theory's "conditions," a static concept, to "practices," a dynamic concept better suited to understanding how managers can produce change over time.

In our Framework, we have reconceptualized contact theory's "conditions," a static concept, to "practices," a dynamic concept pointing to contact's effects as emerging over time. The concept of practices is also better suited to the goal of managers producing change in diversity and inclusion in organizations. However, in the following discussion we retain the use of the term "conditions," to be true to the terminology used by authors in the contact theory literature.

Consistent with knowledge of the exclusionary forces discussed in Chapter 4 and the negative performance impacts of categorization noted in Chapter 5, contact theory does not suggest that intergroup contact alone results in prejudice reduction. The essence of the theory[10] is that four social conditions bear on whether intergroup contact leads to prejudice reduction or not. As stated by Thomas Pettigrew and Linda Tropp,[11] in their massive review of research testing the theory, the theory's conditions for reducing prejudice are:

- Equal status among members
- Pursuit of common goals
- Intergroup cooperation
- Support from authorities, law, or customs.

These conditions are proposed to produce personal, intimate contact. They correspond directly with central elements in our Framework, with support from authorities being a valuable condition for achieving inclusion and practices of equal status, shared goals, and interdependent collaboration being a means to that end. The evidence is clear that prolonged contact under the proper conditions leads to adaptive learning in terms of behavior and attitudes.

> *The evidence.* Drawing on over 700 independent samples in over 500 studies, Pettigrew and Tropp's meta-analysis found that
>
>> Intergroup contact typically reduces intergroup prejudice..., the more rigorous studies yield larger mean effects, ... these contact effects typically generalize to the entire outgroup, and they emerge across a broad range of outgroup targets and contact settings.[12]
>
> In a subsequent report, Pettigrew et al.[13] state that these effects occur across nations, genders, and age groups and are due to the intergroup contact reducing anxieties and increasing empathy. In a meta-analysis of studies on friendships, Davies and colleagues[14] similarly confirm contact theory: "there

are sufficient experimental and longitudinal studies to be confident in a causal relationship whereby cross-group friendship improves attitudes".[15] And the review by Hewstone and Swart[16] identifies reductions in implicit bias and reduced anxieties and threat responses to out-group members. The most recent review, by Paluck, Green, and Green,[17] focused on experiments that tested the effects of contact. These experimental studies confirmed that contact reduces prejudice.

Research evidence is clear that structured intergroup contact reduces prejudice.

These repeated findings on contact reducing prejudice and generalizing to the broader out-group present strong support for the developmental process of categorization → processing → adaptation → generalization in Crisp and Turner's cognitive adaptation model, indicating the potency of prolonged, personal, positive cross-group interaction. Combining the findings on contact with those on stereotype content discussed in Chapter 4, we conclude that such interaction can break down prejudiced categorizations on the two dominant dimensions of stereotypes: warmth, whether the other is seen as friend or foe; and competence, whether the other is seen as able or unable.

We noted above that Crisp and Turner's review found that cross-cultural adaptation leads to skills such as creativity. This is confirmed by contact studies showing that prolonged contact has benefits in personal development other than prejudice reduction.

Adaptive learning from prolonged diversity contact benefits personal development in skills of creativity, leadership, and critical thinking.

The evidence. In a series of studies on college campuses, investigators have found that diversity interactions—contacts across a variety of members of differing racial and ethnic groups—lead to personal growth in skills such as leadership and critical thinking[18] However, this development depends on the nature of the interactions. If the interactions are of minimal or moderate frequency, the developmental effects are minimal. Only when the diversity interactions are positive and of high frequency does adaptive learning, in the form of attitude change and skill development, occur.[19]

As a consequence of their findings on students' skill development, researchers Bowman and Park recommend that "universities should consider settings that promote continuous, casual, and meaningful cross-racial interaction, such as diverse roommate pairings, racially diverse classes, and diversity in co-curricular activities."[20] That is, adaptations in the form of skill development can be fostered by organizational leaders structuring situations that create positive and frequent diversity interactions, with a mixture of formal and informal contact. Their examples, and ones we present in this book based on our interviews, make clear that structuring such situations is highly feasible for leaders.

> Adaptative learning in the form of skill development can be fostered by structuring situations that create positive and frequent diversity interactions, with a mixture of formal and informal contact.

Are contact theory's conditions necessary for prejudice reduction?

Whether the four conditions specified in contact theory were present or not, studies of contact still tended to show reductions in prejudices. Similarly, without specifying conditions, Bowman's research on college students found that a high frequency of positive diversity interactions with a variety of diverse individuals over the course of years in college leads to adaptation in terms of personal growth. It appears that however prolonged personal contact happens, it is likely to produce adaptation.

> Evidence indicates that the key to adaptation is repeated, positive contact. The organizational challenge is to keep people in contact when the default forces of exclusion, such as self-segregation, interaction discomfort, stereotyping and stigmatizing, and implicit bias, would have them distance themselves.

Familiarity breeds liking, so keeping individuals in contact leads to more positive attitudes.[21] On the other hand, the reviews of research on cognitive adaptation and on contact theory both note that anxieties and discomfort must be quelled if prejudice reduction is to occur. The organizational challenge is to keep people in contact when the default forces of exclusion, such as self-segregation, interaction discomfort, stereotyping and stigmatizing, and implicit bias, would have them distance themselves. Consequently, shaping organizational conditions can make the difference in whether contact is superficial and infrequent or positive and frequent, sufficiently meaningful and prolonged to gradually generate familiarity and reduce discomfort.

> *The evidence.* Members of student teams collaborating and getting together frequently to perform tasks led over time to more positive relationships between diversity and social integration in workgroups and, in turn, to higher workgroup performance.[22] Pettigrew and Tropp's review found that structured

programs for intergroup contact produced greater reductions in prejudice. Overall, they found that the strongest effects of contact on prejudice reduction were in studies that best matched the set of contact theory's four conditions. The findings from their review led Pettigrew and Tropp to conclude,

> consistent with Allport's original contentions, we believe that optimal conditions for contact are best conceptualized as functioning together to facilitate positive intergroup outcomes rather than as entirely separate factors.[23]

Field studies performed in the 1970s[24] led to the same conclusion that the conditions work best in combination.

Optimal conditions for contact to result in prejudice reduction should be understood as functioning together, not separately.

Particular conditions working in combination implies synergy. Seeing the conditions specified in contact theory as independent and additive rather than synergistic may be faulty, given the findings regarding affirmative action plans discussed in Chapter 4. Such plans represent a degree of support from the top authorities of an organization, one of contact theory's specified conditions, yet they were found to lead to stereotyping and stigmatizing. This form of support from authority became a negative rather than a positive, one with sufficient strength to counter other attitude-change efforts, such as diversity training, that were being made. Without a strong presence of other facilitating conditions, such as a structured program that embeds multiple conditions, the default forces of exclusion can dominate.

Consistent with the research on contact studies and on cross-job collaborations (Chapter 5), in our Framework we do not see the specified practices as separate and additive factors but as a set of complementary elements. The various elements interact to overcome exclusion by reducing personal interaction discomfort and prejudice and increasing adaptive learning.

In particular instances, choosing to institute some of the conditions for adaptive contact and not others can be counterproductive. We recommend the inclusive interaction practices as a set of complementary elements, structured by management or by workgroup members themselves.

That conditions of contact matter is illustrated by a landmark study, presented in Box 6.2, of in-group vs. out-group conflict.

BOX 6.2: A CASE OF PREJUDICE IN A SUMMER CAMP[25]

At a summer boys camp, researchers generated tensions between two groupings of campers. When the 24 campers, all 12-year-old White Protestants, arrived in the camp, they bunked in one large room, allowing time for friendships to form naturally. After a few days, the campers were randomly split into two groups that then competed in games with valuable prizes. In-group/out-group animosities developed between the two groups as they competed for these scarce resources, and friendships realigned to within group. The researchers then created conditions that reduced the animosities. The conditions were a supposed threat to the camp as a whole and the creation of team tasks requiring interdependence among the campers to respond to the threat.

This case, not involving diversity, points to the condition of intergroup competition as one cause of conflict and to interdependence around an important shared purpose as a condition that reduces tensions.

Interdependence around a shared purpose reduces intergroup tensions.

All four of the conditions specified in intergroup contact theory were met and reduced the cross-group prejudices: common goals, cooperation, equal status among members, and support from (camp) leaders.

Behavioral and attitudinal adaptation from prolonged, even vicarious contact

By whatever conditions it is achieved, prolonged contact appears to be key to reducing prejudice. Adaptive learning is a developmental process requiring time. As noted in the preceding chapter, Paluck and Green's[26] review of approaches intended to reduce prejudice found that instructional efforts designed to change attitudes lacked evidence of effectiveness. Most instructional efforts fail to provide effective contact on two counts: There is no meaningful intergroup contact and no engagement prolonged over time, since these efforts are typically singular or periodic. Options exist for better, meaningful contact. It can be either direct, or surprisingly, indirect, as Paluck and colleagues found in field experiments on prejudice reduction. They report that the best quality studies are on cooperative learning in the classroom.

> *The evidence.* Cooperative learning involves students teaching and learning from one another. Meta-analytic reviews[27] of these experiments find positive

behavioral effects of this cooperative student interaction on peer relationships and helpfulness across students of differing race, ethnicity, and ability.

Cooperative learning, with differing individuals teaching and learning from one another, produces improvements in helpful behavior.

Field experiments involving school children reading about another culture or race over a multi-week period also indicate prejudice reduction, especially when the reading enables vicarious experiences of cross-group friendship. They viewed these reading experiences as an extension of contact theory from actual to *vicarious contact*.

The review by Hewstone and Swart[28] reported that prejudice-reducing *indirect contact* occurs in two forms, *imagined contact*, such as these vicarious friendship experiences, and *extended contact*.

Meaningful prolonged contact can be indirect, involving *imagined, vicarious contact* through media, or *extended contact*, observing others having diversity friendships.

Extended contact involves knowing or observing a member of one's in-group having a friendship with a member of an out-group. It produces greater prejudice reduction for those individuals having little experience of direct contact. Findings indicate that the prejudice-reducing effects of extended contact are due to the mediating process of reduced anxieties about intergroup interaction, and that the effects of imagined contact occur due to the development of in-group norms that approve of intergroup contact.

Imagined and observed diversity contact may be most useful for individuals lacking diversity experiences, as a prelude to their having direct contact.

Indirect contact can be of practical value in organizations through members of non-diverse workgroups observing or hearing about positive cases of intergroup contact and friendships in diverse workgroups or task forces. With extended contact producing greater prejudice reduction for individuals who lack the experience of direct contact than for other individuals, that form of contact may be most useful as a prelude to direct contact. (See Box 6.3 for an example of the benefits of extended contact.)

BOX 6.3: AN EXAMPLE OF EXTENDED CONTACT

In a scientific establishment, a cross-functional task force was established to improve coordination between the dominantly White male scientists and the support staff who here are dominantly women of color. After approximately six months, the members of the task force developed sufficient comfort with each other that they were able to function well and begin to achieve their charge. Over the ensuing year that the task force operated, and subsequent to its conclusion, more comfortable and productive interactions among scientists and support staff on the task force could be observed by other scientists and support staff, facilitating the spread of more inclusive practices to the members of the two groups who had not been on the task force. (This case is presented in more detail in Chapter 10, as an illustration of an effective change process that raised inclusion.)

Field studies reported in the economics literature find that contact leads to adaptations in behavior and that economic incentives can play a role in creating positive intergroup interactions. A review by Marianne Bertrand and Esther Duflo[29] of organizational field experiments in economics revealed causal effects: Once behavior takes the form of protracted, direct interactions, broader behavioral and attitudinal learning can occur.

> *The evidence.* For schoolchildren from high-income families holding prejudices against children from low-income families, a field experiment by Rao[30] found that one-time contact—choosing to team up and interact with those children for several hours in a sports competition—could be stimulated by monetary incentives. In another experiment, Rao found that more protracted exposure to low-income students in economically diverse classrooms produced pro-social learning such as attitudes of fairness. Contact also led to behavioral adaptation, with high-income children more willing to have play dates with low-income children, as well as producing more general acts of generosity and attitudes of fairness.

The indication from this type of research and those on indirect contact supports the view that prolonged direct or imagined interactions with particular members of stereotyped groups can favorably affect behavior and attitudes toward members of those groups more generally. Given their consistency with findings from the massive review of contact studies by Pettigrew and Tropp, it is appropriate to generalize the findings from studies involving primarily youth or student samples to adults. From their review of a variety of field experiments, Bertrand and Duflo conclude that there is a causal connection in real-world situations: intergroup contact reduces prejudice.

> Field experiments provide validated knowledge that teamwork and repeated cross-group engagement in a structured situation reduce prejudice.

To sum up, contact that involves repeated, cooperative interactions, as reflected in our Framework's inclusive interaction practices, promise a general reduction of biased attitudes toward out-groups.

A reduction in prejudiced *attitudes* follows from positive contact behavior rather than behavioral change following attitudinal change. The attitudinal adaptation that results from behavioral adaptation implies that effective contact can reduce implicit bias and so lead to improvements in reward decisions and equity for members of underrepresented groups, while reductions in prejudiced *behavior* demonstrated in economic field experiments represent the bottom-line in terms of more effective workgroup functioning and acceptable behavior that mitigates performance disparities due to stigmatizing.

> *Attitudinal adaptation* results from positive contact behavior and implies greater equity due to less stigmatizing and less biased personnel decisions for members of underrepresented groups. *Behavioral adaptation* to diversity—learning how to interact more comfortably and effectively—enables sustained intergroup contact to lead to both higher performance and greater equity.

From that perspective, the conditions and practices that shape intergroup behavior, as found in the Framework's inclusive interaction practices, are primary for achieving those joint ends. And, for those ends to be achieved in a workgroup, the behavioral adaptation must be collective, shared among workgroup members, an issue to which we now turn.

Practice theory

What do workgroup adaptation and inclusive practices look like?

For diversity and inclusion in organizations, we propose that practices are at the heart of the matter. Practices are what members do together, how they behave and engage with their work and with each other. From the findings on contact theory, changing how members behave as they work, what they do together, should be favored over direct attempts to change attitudes. In this section, we find that diversity contact that is adaptive in terms of behavior may not always affect whether individuals report having particular stereotyped attitudes toward an out-group. That is, effective interactions can be sustained even in the presence of some conscious stereotyped beliefs. When contact behavior does affect attitudes, it is a developmental process, as suggested by the cognitive adaptation research discussed above, with attitudinal change following behavioral change.

> Two of our basic premises are that (1) what matters for performance and equity in organizations is what people actually do with each other, their interactions and their decisions and (2) conscious attitudes are not a reliable predictor of behavior.

As Hewstone and Swart[31] put it, "we know that general-level attitudes do not correspond to, and hence typically do not predict, individual-level behaviours" (p. 378). What, then, does explain behavior, in particular, behavior in social settings such as organizations? Practice theory (Box 6.4) offers valuable insights on this question.

BOX 6.4: PRACTICE THEORY

Reckwitz[32] describes the nature of practices by drawing on a body of social theory that is concerned with explaining how order occurs and is sustained in social settings. Members of a society, or of a social group of any type, engage in practices that have evolved in that group. Each practice in a group is a way of doing something,

> is a routinized type of behaviour which consists of several elements, interconnected to one another: forms of bodily activities, forms of mental activities, "things" and their use, a background knowledge in the form of understanding, know-how, states of emotion and motivational knowledge.[33]

Many different, often unique, actions manifest a practice, with each individual member carrying the practice in the ways that they act and understand their actions in the particular social context. That is, cognitions in the specific setting, the ways that things are understood in that setting, are shaped by the practices in the setting. Competent members have a *practical consciousness*[34] of how to behave and think in the setting, an intertwining of the body (behavior) and the mind (understandings) in a habitual, taken-for-granted, somewhat unconscious way.

Practices are distinctive to particular organizations, occupations, and social settings. For example, consider a particular way that members of a medical specialty habitually diagnose their patients, or an engineering group uses design software to produce a prototype, or a diverse workgroup pools their information and experiences to solve a quality control problem, or that check-out clerks in a high-image store chat with customers. The individuals who participate in those habitual practices at their workplaces are likely to behave and think differently in other settings, such as when arguing over politics with friends or when responding to a questionnaire measuring implicit bias.

> A workgroup's members can behave and think differently when in that group than when engaging in practices elsewhere, such as sports competitions or family get-togethers.

The reproduction over time of discrimination or inclusion

Practice theory has been applied specifically to diversity by Maddy Janssens and Chris Steyaert[35] to generate insights into how and why equality or inequality persist in particular organizations. Many of these insights are reflected in our Framework and preceding discussions. Their particular terminology, the jargon of their field, draws on particular metaphors that can bring the dynamics to life. Equality or inequality is seen as arising from a dynamic *entanglement* of a *bundle* of practices over time, such as the six practices of inclusive interactions combining with each other and with accountability practices to influence the overall *practicing of inclusion*—that is, whether and how inclusion is being actively practiced in an organization.

> The inclusive practices are seen as proceeding from the *recursive* interplay over time of actions with structures, producing a particular social order in an organization.

Consider as an example the practices for formal and informal networking in a particular organization and locale. Who meets with whom, to do what, and with what consequences? What are the informal social structures, such as cliques, that determine the influence and visibility of particular groups? Do men from various job levels in a work unit get together to attend and engage in sports that women do not? Are Black managers assigned to key operational decision task forces that provide a path to advancement or to community service activities that do not? Depending on the specific nature of the practices, the social order that they produce can be one that involves discrimination and inequality or inclusion and equity.

Practice theory emphasizes that social structures in the organization—such as hierarchies, organization into functional units, governance entities, and incentive systems—influence members' actions, and those actions, in turn, influence the social structures. We see this later in this chapter in the case of a Finnish multinational company. There, particular structures—a decentralized structure combined with a common set of technical terms provided by the company—encouraged engineers from different cultures to work out effective ways of interacting with each other. Most importantly, those ways, those actions feed back over time to influence the structures, such as maintaining the common lexicon and decisions being made locally through effective cross-cultural interactions. The result is that practices *reproduce* a particular social order over time.

Inclusive practices *reproduce* a particular social order, a particular organizational culture, over time.

Changes in practices intended to foster inclusion can be countered by lack of change in other social practices that reproduce prejudice.

An explanation for halted progress on diversity is that changes made only in some biased practices are countered by lack of change in other biased practices, particularly ones that are taken-for-granted and unexamined.

In the next chapter we will see how the implementing of fair employment practices helped to mitigate bias in some personnel decisions, such as performance appraisal ratings, but not in the most important ones, the final reward decisions. Reproduction of discrimination is explained, then, by the Swiss cheese metaphor (see Box 2.2 in Chapter 2). One slice of the cheese covers some problems, but holes in the cheese enable the liquid of discrimination to continue to flow through the system.

However, the interplay of actions with structures also creates opportunities for organizational change, by individuals changing their actions or the organization changing its structures, with consequent evolution (or *emergence*) of practices. Put another way, practices are always in flux to some degree, with consequences for diversity, inclusion, equity, and performance. In that sense, when inclusion is achieved, its practicing by members is a *continuing accomplishment*, requiring periodic attention lest the inclusive practices be eroded by anti-inclusive, biased practices.

When inclusion is achieved through changes in structures and actions, its practicing by members is a *continuing accomplishment*, requiring periodic attention lest the inclusive practices be eroded by anti-inclusive, biased practices.

For instance, in Chapter 9, we will see that the continuing accomplishment of inclusion, the sustaining of inclusion, can be aided by a tool (a structure) as simple as employee badges carrying the organization's mission and values statements, a tool used in the practice of members holding each other accountable for anti-inclusive behavior.

To sustain diversity in organizations, the primacy of behavior over attitudes

Interpersonal interactions and relationships are central to practices, with members learning the practices from each other and, as we discuss below, contributing to how the practices change by bringing their individual differences into their practicing with each other.

> Practices are highly relational, in terms of the ways that members interact with and treat each other and the ways that changes emerge in the practices themselves.

Individual members invest themselves bodily and emotionally in the practices of their workgroup, affecting each other and contributing to the evolution of its practices. However, since individuals follow different practices in their various social settings—organization, family, friendship circles—the idea of fixed attitudes and beliefs that transcend settings is called into question. Understandings that apply in one situation can be influenced and changed as the individual experiences different understandings associated with practices in another situation. An example related to the discussion above is stereotype inconsistency, experiencing interactions with another that challenge one's stereotype.

> Stereotypes that were developed and transmitted in demographically homogeneous social groups outside the organization can be challenged by experiences shaped by inclusive practices in a diverse workgroup.

A parallel example would be individuals stating stereotyped attitudes in one setting while engaging inclusively in ways that violate those stereotyped attitudes in another setting. A study of vicarious contact illustrates how such inclusive behavior can occur even when individuals report stereotyped beliefs.

The study. Among hundreds of Rwandan citizens, the practice of listening to a radio soap opera that dealt with people struggling with prejudice and violence produced changes in perceptions of social norms and in empathy and actual behavior, including intermarriage, a rather inclusive behavior, even while not changing listeners' personal beliefs.[36]

This case suggests the priority of social norms over beliefs in determining direct interaction behavior. The role of norms mirrors practice theory: practices and their associated understandings in one context can differ from those in another. Individuals can continue to report prejudiced beliefs about an out-group while inclusive behavior with out-group members contrary to those beliefs occurs in particular settings. For organizations, the applicable issue is what happens within the organization. Do the organization's practices mitigate biases being triggered into behavior, such as managers' decisions on rewards? Do the ways of carrying out missions and tasks involve behaviors and understandings that are free of stereotyping and stigmatizing one's fellow organizational members, or not?

> For organizations, the bottom-line issue is not whether its members carry implicit biases in some settings, as appears to be ubiquitous. The issue is whether or not the organization's practices mitigate those biases being triggered into behavior in the organization, such as self-segregation or inequitable reward decisions.

Organizational conditions stimulate performance-enhancing inclusive practices

Particular inclusive practices carried by organizational members produce and reproduce the developmental process of adaptive learning at a collective level, overcoming discomfort and preventing fault lines and tensions that otherwise produce categorization. Consider findings from a study in a Finnish multinational corporation. Here, rich description and analysis from a qualitative study inform us on how inclusive practices evolve as a result of particular organization-wide conditions in the form of values and tools.

> *The evidence: Analysis of linguistic code-switching practices.* Ahmad and Barner-Rasmussen[37] investigated the effect of "code-switching"—in meetings involving members of different nationalities, some members switching to their mother tongue rather than continuing in the organization's main language. Prior research has found that this behavior produces negative effects, with members who do not know the other language feeling a threat of being excluded, leading to tensions and distancing that reduce knowledge-sharing. In the Finnish multinational, the opposite was discovered. Code-switching was felt by members of the various nationalities to contribute to their ability to better understand and share knowledge. The researchers discovered this positive effect was due to particular practices, norms and routines that prevented members of one subgroup from interpreting bad intent on the part of code-switching individuals, such as telling all members what had been said in the other language.

> Performance is aided by norms and routine practices that prevent members of one subgroup from interpreting bad intent on the part of another subgroup.

Three specific norms addressed the subgroup differences—here, linguistic differences—that otherwise would have created tensions: developing and relying on a shared technical vocabulary; the value of enhancing inclusion in knowledge-sharing interactions; and facilitating for each other the depth of the knowledge being discussed.

In our Framework, the particular organizational conditions on the left side of the model are more likely to influence whether inclusive or anti-inclusive practices are present in the organization. In the Finnish multinational organization, the researchers attributed the production and reproduction of inclusive code-switching practices to several broader conditions in the organization. Those conditions can be seen as social structures and included: (1) the firm's positive valuing of multiculturalism; (2) the firm providing a company common language specifying particular words to be used in technical discussions; (3) members being concerned about their team's reputation for performance, and seeing the benefit for team performance of inclusion in knowledge-sharing; and (4) the firm being decentralized, such that power issues between functional and geographically dispersed subgroups were minimized, reducing the development of cross-subgroup fault lines. This case illustrates how organizations can create organization-wide conditions that support inclusive practices both in terms of values—here, multiculturalism—and in terms of tools that support inclusion—in this multinational case, the company common language.

> An organization can support inclusion by creating particular organization-wide conditions in the form of values and tools used by all members in everyday task interactions.

This study highlights practices at two levels: specific practices followed in the workgroup or team to address particular diversity challenges, such as linguistic, and broader organizational-level practices, such as decentralization and multi-culturalism, that supported the specific workgroup-level practices. And the study provides insight into adaptive learning by workgroup members. Over time, individuals learned the effectiveness of code-switching for ends that they valued, namely improved knowledge-sharing and team performance.

> Individuals learned the value of inclusive interaction practices for ends that they all valued.

Through the routine behavior of telling others the task-related, workgroup-benefiting reasons that they were code-switching, they sent positive relational signals,[38] signals that built and maintained trust.

This example tells us that, in diverse workgroups, specific inclusive practices are important in helping individuals favorably interpret others' actions, avoiding interpretations that stem from and sustain negative stereotypes or misattributions of intent.

> Favorable, respectful interpretation of others' actions and intent, stimulated by inclusive interaction practices, is the everyday, ongoing essence and indicator of adaptive learning.

The study also shows how inclusive practices and adaptive learning can feed on each other, with the practices facilitating adaptive learning about how to behave effectively, about "know-how." That adaptive learning incorporates relatively unconscious understandings about why the practices are important and should be carried forward, and about the fact that members of other subgroups can be trusted.

Individual enculturation into organizations

> How do workgroup members become carriers of practices that sustain inclusion of performance-enhancing individual differences?

It is one thing to specify useful practices that members follow, as in the code-switching study. For managers striving to institute those practices, it is equally important to specify how workgroup members come to follow those practices or how those practices evolve to fit changes in workgroup tasks and membership. For that, we turn to the literature on organizational socialization, how individuals are socialized into an organization's ways of doing and thinking. We note two issues regarding socialization, one involving too little socialization and one reflecting too much, or improper, socialization. Too little socialization would mean inadequate enculturation and carrying of the inclusive practices by a workgroup's members, too little sharing of effective practices. For example, if some workgroup members use code-switching without the associated practices that quell anxieties, others become upset, inhibiting further use of that effective communication tool and creating in-group/out-group fault lines. On the other side of the coin, too much socialization would mean members being pressured to conform in narrow ways, becoming so similar to each other that differences would be submerged, harming the psychological well-being of members from underrepresented groups and the performance of the workgroup as a whole due to a lack of information elaboration. For agile teams in a multinational organization, for instance, that would mean individuals from other than the home country being forced to suppress their differing perspectives and styles. Accordingly, we would like to know whether socialization practices can enable members of underrepresented groups to both fit in and to express their authentic selves and talents in their work. Put in terms of the categorization-elaboration model discussed in the preceding chapter, the relevant question is: Will social integration impede the information elaboration that contributes to group performance?

An important qualification must be noted about our treatment of these issues in comparison to the other issues examined in this book's chapters. Since the research that we draw upon here has not explicitly examined the effects of diversity, we are being more speculative by assuming that the findings generalize to diverse workgroups. However, we address issues of socialization to make managers aware of the need to monitor the nature of inclusion in their workgroups.

> Managers can monitor the state of inclusion by assessing whether members from underrepresented groups fit in, are enculturated but not assimilated, and continue to contribute by bringing their differences to bear on the workgroup's functioning.

The research findings on socialization are provocative. They fit well with concepts of inclusion and are especially informative regarding how to avoid assimilation.

Enculturation processes

Consider first the issue of achieving enough socialization so that individuals become carriers of organizational practices. Research on organizational socialization has investigated newcomers moving into an organization or workgroup and learning the ways of that group. The research has produced strong evidence of the effectiveness of formal procedures for socializing newcomers.

> *The evidence.* Organizational practices for socialization that involve off-the-job training, clear stages of progression in learning task requirements, and being guided by insiders[39] are found by a meta-analytic review by Bauer et al.[40] to lead to important adjustment processes for newcomers.

> Formal practices for socialization, including off-the-job training and guidance from insiders, improves performance and retention for newcomers.

> In turn, the processes lead to beneficial outcomes, including higher job performance and lower turnover. The adjustment process involves role clarity (understanding task priorities), self-efficacy (gaining confidence in the role), and social acceptance (feeling liked and trusted).

The adjustment processes of role clarity, self-efficacy, and social acceptance represent elements required for inclusion in a workgroup. These findings support the view that inclusion matters since these three aspects of inclusion are found to improve performance—in this case, of newcomers.

> The three adjustment processes for newcomers—understanding task priorities, gaining confidence, and feeling liked and trusted by coworkers—are integral to inclusion, and this inclusion raises performance.

We speculate that these findings on newcomers' socialization being facilitated by off-job training, time-staged learning, and insider guidance can be generalized to existing members of a workgroup. These members could be resocialized into a more inclusive set of practices by their managers and by members of already inclusive workgroups. Overall, the research on organizational socialization tells us that formal socialization practices on the part of an organization can make more likely a workgroup's members becoming carriers of inclusive practices.

Avoiding narrow conformity while gaining individual and collective adaptation

We see the findings on socialization as raising the cautionary issue identified above: Might effective socialization be accompanied by strong pressures for conformity, such that differences in perspectives needed for information elaboration are subdued? Put another way, will effective socialization of new members about tasks and how to interact be taken too far, with newcomers pressured to remain narrowly within the dominant groups' ways of thinking and doing? Newcomers need to be socialized such that they learn the social and technical routines but are able to add their own knowledge and technical and social skills.

> Effectively socializing newcomers means that, once inclusive interaction practices are embedded in a workgroup, they can be maintained as new members join.

One reason to believe such problems may be less serious in the case of diverse workgroups is that very diversity itself. The meta-analysis by Bauer and colleagues reported above was based on a sample that was 86 percent White. From the literature reviewed at the beginning of this chapter on the adaptation of members from underrepresented groups, we know that their socialization is likely to be more problematic, that they often must engage in self-monitoring to reduce being stereotyped and stigmatized. The study of code-switching in an inclusive environment provides an illustration of relational practices that enable an individual's competence and helpfulness to be evident.

> Socialization processes for new members are less likely to lead to reduced information elaboration in inclusive, diverse workgroups than in workgroups that lack diversity.

Socialization that maintains and leverages useful individual differences involves recognizing that enculturation is a two-sided coin:[41] One side is the individual fitting into the workgroup culture, but the other side is the newcomer changing the group culture. The culture is not a fixed, unitary thing shared identically by all members, but rather one that is interpreted by various members, including newcomers, who interact to shape each other's behavior and interpretations and, thereby, the culture.[42] (Box 6.5 illustrates how informal interactions enhance acculturation for new workgroup members.)

> The entry of newcomers is an opportunity to evolve the workgroup culture.

This flexibility and shaping are true to a greater or lesser degree in different workgroups and organizations, either discouraging or encouraging a too-narrow conformity.

BOX 6.5: SOCIALIZATION ALLOWING DIFFERENCES IN A ROLE

A model of role acquisition by Thornton and Nardi[43] distinguishes early stages in which the newcomer is greatly influenced by the existing culture to later stages of enculturation when the once-newcomer is becoming an insider and can personalize the role in a way that influences others. Through interactions with existing workgroup members, newcomers first make *social adjustments* by learning the role's formal prescriptions for behavior, attitudes, and technical performance. Then, through *informal interactions,* they learn the "mays" (vs. the "musts") of the role. The breadth of views within the group concerning the "mays" eventually gives new members freedom to personalize the role.

To the degree that they are allowed to personalize their role, as noted in Box 6.5, they achieve a psychological adjustment to their individual needs. They then express the role in their own style, achieving adaptation through the fusing of self and role and leading to some degree of change in the workgroup's culture.

Personal-identity socialization

There exists a particular practice of newcomer socialization that aids adaptation being two-way. In this practice, newcomers personalize their roles and achieve psychological adjustment by playing to their distinctive identities and strengths. This practice also has promise for helping to resocialize existing workgroup members toward greater inclusion. The practice is termed *personal-identity socialization*, since it asks individuals to specify personal interests and strengths that they can bring into their role as they fit into the workgroup.

> *The evidence.* Performing a field experiment in a call center in India, Cable, Gino, and Staats[44] found that personal-identity socialization, in comparison to a more traditional socialization process focused on organizational identity, produced as high customer satisfaction while it reduced employee turnover.

Being asked to identify personal interests and strengths that fit the work role leads to stronger engagement and job satisfaction.

> A follow-up laboratory experiment involving short-term employment at a U.S. university found that these positive performance and retention effects were explained by improved work engagement and job satisfaction attitudes that resulted from individuals having greater levels of authentic self-expression.

Personalized socialization fits with the latter two of the three elements of inclusion for diverse members that Nishii[45] specifies for social justice, as discussed in the Introduction chapter—namely, integration of differences and inclusion in decision-making—meaning that this form of socialization serves both equity and performance ends. The third element of inclusion—fair employment practices that help to eliminate bias—is also favored by personal-identity socialization since it legitimizes for existing workgroup members the expression of differences by newcomers.

There is a valuable mutuality between personalized socialization and the inclusive interaction practices in our Framework: Personal-identity socialization supports inclusive interaction practices that leverage differences, and those ongoing inclusive interaction practices support a personalized process of newcomer enculturation.

> Instituting the practice of personal-identity socialization with both newcomers and existing workgroup members can encourage the expression and inclusion of performance-valuable differences.

Consequently, instituting personalized socialization processes is one way to stimulate the workgroup to adopt the inclusive practices specified in our Framework. These processes could be used periodically with all workgroup members to encourage the expression and inclusion of performance-valuable differences.

With diversity, socialization can be done in a manner that aids organizational adaptation. Encouraging the expression of differing perspectives and knowledge within the normative structure of the workgroup produces information elaboration in the short run. And, in the longer run, the presence of valued differences leads to the evolution of the workgroup's practices and a learning organization[46] that innovates and adapts more agilely to changes in the organization's labor pool, markets, and stakeholder pressures.

> Socialization into norms that encourage the inclusion of differences can aid organizational adaptation to external changes.

Managers can draw on the above evidence and concepts to design appropriate socialization and re-socialization processes that enable organizational members from a variety of backgrounds to fit in yet draw out their best selves and achieve high performance. Managers can be guided by two ideas: members from underrepresented groups can both be enculturated into and modify an existing organizational culture, and they can play to their strengths and express their perspectives when socialized with a personal-identity focus.

> Managers can design formal (re-)socialization practices that favor inclusion and information elaboration, resulting in multiple payoffs.

The payoffs to be anticipated are: a gradual evolution of the workgroup culture to fit the characteristics of a workforce population changing in various ways; strong newcomer performance and retention; high workgroup performance through continued information elaboration; and agile organizational adaptation to various external changes.

Behavioral engagement

What level of adaptive learning enables high performance and equity to be sustained through inclusion?

The evidence on code-switching, formal socialization, and personal-identity social-ization provides us with a sense of what inclusion looks like in terms of everyday practices. It is characterized by comfortable but authentic diversity interactions that increase personal skills, group performance and organizational learning. Inclusion of that type can be understood as requiring a high level of adaptive learning, including prejudice reduction, in order to produce the skills such as creativity that Crisp and Turner's review identifies for cognitive adaptation. Similarly, inclusion at a high level fits with Bowman's findings that high-quality, high-frequency diversity interactions lead to the development of skills such as leadership. But what actu-ally happens in prolonged intergroup contact for that level of adaptation to be sustained? Research on intergroup friendships offers us insights into this question. Cross-group friendships represent a high level of diversity interactions and require the development of interaction skills to sustain them.

> Cross-group friendships represent a high level of diversity interactions and require the development of interaction skills to sustain them.

Examining friendships can provide better insights into the development of a high level of inclusion, going beyond adaptive behavior that simply accords with organizational norms of civility and respect. In particular, friendships point to the important role of personal, informal communication.

> *The evidence.* A meta-analytic review of cross-group friendships by Kristin Davies and colleagues[47] identifies three important features of friendships that produce the highest levels of adaptation in attitudes through behav-ioral engagement: time spent together, self-disclosure, and the development of positive emotional ties. They state:
>
> > Attitudes are most likely to improve when cross-group friendships involve behavioral engagement[48]
>
> Research on global virtual teams has found the value of personal, informal communication being combined with task communication to produce trust.[49] Our research[50] identifies a dynamic, recursive process involving friendly informal interactions—namely, a virtuous cycle among norms for comfortable interaction, disclosure of experiences and perspectives, and increased time spent together.

The three important processes of friendships noted directly above counter the anti-inclusive forces discussed in Chapter 4, helping to explain the connection between inclusive interaction practices and adaptive learning in our Framework. Time spent together is promoted by practices for frequent mixing, as depicted in Figure 6.2,

Individual Inclusive Interaction Practices

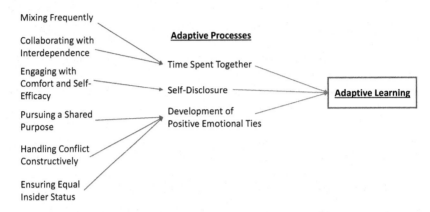

FIGURE 6.2 Inclusive Interaction Practices and Processes for Adaptive Learning

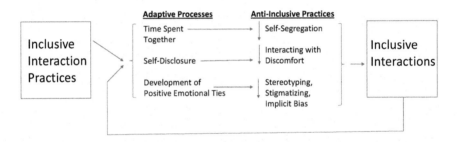

FIGURE 6.3 Adaptive Processes Countering Exclusion

and is the opposite of self-segregating, reducing that anti-inclusive practice, as depicted in Figure 6.3. Self-disclosure is promoted by the practice of engaging with comfort and is the opposite of interaction discomfort. And the development of positive emotional ties is promoted by the practice of equal status and the opposite of stereotyping and stigmatizing. As shown in Figure 6.3, the adaptive processes stimulated by inclusive interaction practices diminish anti-inclusive practices and increase inclusive interactions. Over time, a virtuous cycle occurs with adaptive processes facilitating inclusive interactions and those interactions feeding back to stimulate the adaptive processes.

> Self-disclosure and time interacting with each other lead to the largest prejudice reduction and to skills for interacting meaningfully.

Intergroup friendship development parallels the developmental sequence of processing stereotype inconsistencies, adaptation, and generalization that Crisp and

Turner specify for cognitive adaptation: Time spent together and self-disclosure generate stereotype inconsistency and emotional ties help to cement adaptative learning

Although close friendships are not required for inclusion in diverse workgroups, the three adaptive processes of intergroup friendships provide useful indicators of the adaptive process that workgroup members go through. Managers can use these indicators to judge whether adaptive learning is occurring or not.

> Useful indicators of adaptive intergroup learning among workgroup members are time spent together and meaningful conversations that are sometimes personal.

If adaptive learning is happening across subgroups in their workgroup, a manager would observe members spending time together, having meaningful conversations that are occasionally personal and informal (as occurred by providing a shared lunchroom for the medical research unit in Chapter 3), and exhibiting some caring for each other.

Managerial application of knowledge on adaptive learning

What does research-based evidence suggest that organizations do?
Why have so few diversity initiatives incorporated that knowledge?

Adaptive learning for inclusion brings together the goals of organizational performance and equity. The categorization–elaboration model discussed in Chapter 5 specifies conditions for avoiding prejudice-based stigmatizing and for achieving high performance—namely, social integration that brings the reduction of individual anxieties and the collective development of trust. When combined with fairly implemented personnel practices, the prescriptions of the model correspond to the characteristics of inclusion noted earlier: integration of differences through expectations and norms around openness and diverse members' perspectives challenging the status quo and influencing decisions.[51]

> Social integration comes from prolonged positive intergroup contact, from reduced anxieties and behavioral comfort, behavioral and cognitive adaptation, skill development by group members, and from personalized socialization, as depicted in Figure 6.4.

These processes for adaptive learning are best produced and sustained by organizational conditions and norms that reside in members' everyday contact—their

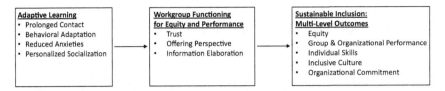

FIGURE 6.4 Adaptive Learning and Workgroup Functioning

practices for equal status, intergroup cooperation, pursuit of common goals, and support from leaders. The resulting social integration enables inclusion of differences in a workgroup or team such that all members influence decision-making through information elaboration, offering their differing perspectives and engaging cooperatively and interdependently. In sum, research-based evidence informs us that inclusion for performance, equity, and sustained diversity rests on these social and psychological realities of adaptive behavioral learning, learning that is produced and evolved by organizational members in their everyday practices.

It is ironic that so many past and contemporary organizational approaches to diversity appear to ignore important psychological and social realities and the lack of evidence of the approaches' efficacy, while diversity approaches that research does indicate to have efficacy—creating organizational conditions and practices for prolonged, positive, adaptive, skill-building interactions—are only rarely advocated or used for diversity purposes. One explanation is that institutional realities, such as those involving legal compliance, lead to the continuation of commonly used approaches, an explanation discussed in this book's final chapter. A second explanation, discussed in the next chapter, is that the adoption of some fair employment practices has created complacency due to a misguided belief that organizations have achieved a meritocracy. A third explanation is that achieving the conditions that create adaptive contact is difficult.[52] However, that concern about difficulty, expressed several decades ago, is contradicted by the more contemporary success of non-diversity organizational programs exhibiting inclusion described in Chapter 5—cross-training and self-directed teams that produce cross-job collaboration—and by routine practices for positive intergroup contact in some organizations, such as code-switching in the example described here. These programs and practices create inclusive interactions over prolonged time periods. The success of these programs and practices, and parallel efforts such as agile teams in international software development, confirms the managerial feasibility of introducing new conditions, of implementing inclusive practices that produce group performance and equity gains through adaptive learning among all members. Producing gains from diversity, then, rests not only on accountability, as we have noted previously, but also on managerial commitment to fostering inclusive practices through performance-oriented programs that extend over prolonged periods of time to produce adaptive learning.

Notes

1 Spencer, S. J., Logel, C., & Davies, P. G. (2016). Stereotype threat. *Annual Review of Psychology, 67*(1), 415–437.

2 Festinger, L. (1957). *A theory of cognitive dissonance.* Stanford University Press.

3 Crisp, R. J., & Turner, R. N. (2011). Cognitive adaptation to the experience of social and cultural diversity. *Psychological Bulletin, 137*(2), 242–266.

4 Fiske, S. T. (2005). Social cognition and the normality of prejudgment. In J. F. Dovidio, P. Glick, & L. A. Rudman (Eds.), *On the nature of prejudice: Fifty years after Allport* (pp. 36–53). Blackwell.

5 Bernstein, R. S., & Salipante, P. (2017). Intercultural comfort through social practices: Exploring conditions for cultural learning. *Frontiers in Education*, Vol. 2, Article 31. doi:10.3389/feduc.2017.00031. http://journal.frontiersin.org/article/10.3389/feduc.2017.00031/full?&utm_source=Email_to_authors_&utm_medium=Email&utm_content=T1_11.5e1_author&utm_campaign=Email_publication&field=&journalName=Frontiers_in_Education&id=272155.; Ely, R. J., Meyerson, D. E., & Davidson, M. N. (2006). Rethinking political correctness. *Harvard Business Review, 84*(9), 78–87.

6 Noble, G. (2005). The discomfort of strangers: Racism, incivility and ontological security in a relaxed and comfortable nation. *Journal of Intercultural Studies, 26*(1-2), 107–120.

7 Goncalo, J. A., Chatman, J. A., Duguid, M. M., & Kennedy, J. A. (2015). Creativity from constraint? How the political correctness norm influences creativity in mixed-sex work groups. *Administrative Science Quarterly, 60*(1), 1–30.

8 Allport, G. W. (1954). *The nature of prejudice.* Addison-Wesley; Williams, R. M. (1947). *The reduction of intergroup tensions.* Social Science Research Council.

9 Hewstone, M., & Swart, H. (2011). Fifty-odd years of inter-group contact: From hypothesis to integrated theory. *British Journal of Social Psychology, 50*(3), 374–386.

10 As specified by Williams (1947) and Allport (1954).

11 Pettigrew, T. F., & Tropp, L. R. (2006). A meta-analytic test of intergroup contact theory. *Journal of Personality and Social Psychology, 90*(5), 751–783.

12 Ibid, p. 751.

13 Pettigrew, T. F., Tropp, L. R., Wagner, U., & Christ, O. (2011). Recent advances in intergroup contact theory. *International Journal of Intercultural Relations, 35*(3), 271–280.

14 Davies, K., Tropp, L. R., Aron, A., Pettigrew, T. F., & Wright, S. C. (2011). Cross-group friendships and intergroup attitudes: A meta-analytic review. *Personality and Social Psychology Review, 15*(4), 332–351.

15 Ibid, p. 332.

16 Hewstone & Swart (2011). "Fifty-odd years of inter-group contact."

17 Paluck, E. L., Green, S. A., & Green, D. P. (2019). The contact hypothesis re-evaluated. *Behavioural Public Policy, 3*(2), 129–158. This review reported effects that were smaller than in other reviews, and smaller for cross-ethnic contacts than other contacts. Overall, the experimental studies confirmed that contact reduces prejudice. They noted that the experimental studies had not examined prejudice reduction in people older than 25. However, as noted in Chapter 5, Alexandra Kalev's (2009) study found that cross-job collaborations, a form of prolonged contact, produced improvements in minorities and women advancing to managerial positions. These advancements undoubtedly involve individuals older than 25 years and suggest that contact in cross-job collaborations reduces prejudice among older individuals.

18 Bowman, N. A. (2013). The conditional effects of interracial interactions on college student outcomes. *Journal of College Student Development, 54*(3), 322–328; Bowman, N. A., & Park, J. J. (2015). Not all diversity interactions are created equal: Cross-racial interaction,

close interracial friendship, and college student outcomes. *Research in Higher Education,* *56*(6), 601–621; Pascarella, E. T., Martin, G. L., Hanson, J. M., Trolian, T. L., Gillig, B., & Blaich, C. (2014). Effects of diversity experiences on critical thinking skills over 4 years of college. *Journal of College Student Development, 55*(1), 86–92.

19 Bowman, N. A. (2013). How much diversity is enough? The curvilinear relationship between college diversity interactions and first-year student outcomes. *Research in Higher Education, 54*(8), 874–894.

20 Bowman & Park (2015). "Not all diversity interactions are created equal," p. 617.

21 Zajonc (1968) cited in Pettigrew and Tropp (2006).

22 Harrison, D. A., Price, K. H., Gavin, J. H., & Florey, A. T. (2002). Time, teams, and task performance: Changing effects of surface- and deep-level diversity on group functioning. *Academy of Management Journal, 45*(5), 1029–1045.

23 Pettigrew & Tropp, p. 766.

24 Cook (1971, 1978), cited in Paluck, E. L., & Green, D. P. (2009). Prejudice reduction: What works? A review and assessment of research and practice. *Annual Review of Psychology*, 60(1), 339–367.

25 Sherif, M., & Sherif, C. W. (1953). *Groups in harmony and tension; an integration of studies of intergroup relations.* Harper & Brothers.

26 Paluck, E. L., & Green, D. P. (2009). Prejudice reduction: What works? A review and assessment of research and practice. *Annual Review of Psychology, 60*(1), 339–367.

27 Johnson and Johnson (1989) and Roseth et al. (2008), cited in Paluck et al. (2019).

28 Hewstone & Swart (2011). "Fifty-odd years of inter-group contact."

29 Bertrand, M., & Duflo, E. (2016). *Field experiments on discrimination.* National Bureau of Economic Research (NBER) Working Paper 22014. http://www.nber.org/papers/w22014.

30 Rao, G. (2019). Familiarity does not breed contempt: Generosity, discrimination, and diversity in Delhi schools. *American Economic Review, 109*(3), 774–809.

31 Hewstone and Swart (2011) draw on the work of Fishbein and Ajzen (1975).

32 Reckwitz, A. (2002). Toward a theory of social practices: A development in culturalist theorizing. *European Journal of Social Theory, 5*(2), 243–263.

33 Ibid, p. 249.

34 Giddens, A. (1984). *The constitution of society: Outline of the theory of structuration.* University of California Press.

35 Janssens, M., & Steyaert, C. (2019). A practice-based theory of diversity: Respecifying (in) equality in organizations. *Academy of Management Review, 44*(3), 518–537.

36 Paluck and Green (2008), cited in Paluck and Green (2009).

37 Ahmad, F., & Barner-Rasmussen, W. (2019). False foe? When and how code switching practices can support knowledge sharing in multinational corporations. *Journal of International Management, 25*(3), 1–18.

38 Lindenberg (1997) and Wittek (1999), cited in Ahmad & Barner-Rasmussen (2019).

39 Jones, G. R. (1986). Socialization tactics, self-efficacy, and newcomers' adjustments to organizations. *Academy of Management Journal, 29*(2), 262–279; Van Maanen, J., & Schein, E. (1979). Towards a theory of organizational socialization. In B. Staw (Ed.), *Research in organizational behavior* (Vol. 1, pp. 209–264). JAI Press.

40 Bauer, T. N., Bodner, T., Erdogan, B., Truxillo, D. M., & Tucker, J. S. (2007). Newcomer adjustment during organizational socialization: A meta-analytic review of antecedents, outcomes, and methods. *Journal of Applied Psychology, 92*(3), 707–721.

41 Collins, D. (2009). The socialization process for new professionals. In A. Tull, J. B. Hirt, & S. A. Saunders (Eds.), *Becoming socialized in student affairs administration: A guide for new professionals and their supervisors* (pp. 3–27). Stylus Publishing.

42 Tierney, W. G. (1997). Organizational socialization in higher education. *The Journal of Higher Education, 68*(1), 1–16.

43 Thornton, R., & Nardi, P. M. (1975). The dynamics of role acquisition. *American Journal of Sociology, 80*(4), 870–885.

44 Cable, D. M., Gino, F., & Staats, B. R. (2013). Breaking them in or eliciting their best? Reframing socialization around newcomers' authentic self-expression. *Administrative Science Quarterly, 58*(1), 1–36.

45 Nishii, L. H. (2013). The benefits of climate for inclusion for gender-diverse groups. *Academy of Management Journal, 56*(6), 1754–1774.

46 Tierney (1997). "Organizational socialization in higher education."

47 Davies et al. (2011). "Cross-group friendships and intergroup attitudes."

48 Ibid, p. 332.

49 Jarvenpaa, S. L., & Leidner, D. E. (1999). Communication and trust in global virtual teams. *Organization Science, 10*(6), 791–815.

50 Bernstein & Salipante (2017). "Intercultural comfort through social practices."

51 Nishii (2013). "The benefits of climate for inclusion for gender-diverse groups."

52 Hewstone (1996), cited in Stangor, C. (2009). The study of stereotyping, prejudice, and discrimination within social psychology: A quick history of theory and research. In T. D. Nelson (Ed.), *Handbook of prejudice, stereotyping, and discrimination* (pp. 1–12). Psychology Press.

7

MERIT, ACCOUNTABILITY, AND TRANSPARENCY PRACTICES TO ADDRESS EQUITY AND PERFORMANCE

This book views the achieving of equity and performance from diversity as requiring a systems view. As depicted in our overall Framework (Figure 7.1), numerous practices and processes affect whether diversity leads to equity and performance. Attending to some practices that affect diversity and inclusion and not attending to others—specifically, the anti-inclusive practices of self-segregating, interacting with discomfort, stereotyping and stigmatizing, and acting on implicit bias—is an inadequate strategy that explains the slow and, for some groups, halted progress toward reducing disparities. For example, recall from the Introduction chapter that job outcomes for Black men are no better now than in the middle of the last century, and that the progress of women in many STEM careers has plateaued and regressed. Keeping on only as we have been is unwise. The Swiss cheese metaphor (see Box 2.2) helps us understand that holes left in an organization's employment systems enable implicit bias and the various anti-inclusive practices to continue to operate in today's workplace.

> Viewing an organization's employment system as a whole points to the gaps that enable bias and other anti-inclusive practices to continue to operate and perpetuate inequities and reduced performance.

In this chapter, we examine the role of *merit and accountability practices* in identifying and closing those holes. To continue the metaphor, several slices of accountability practices should overlay the slices of inclusive interaction practices.

> Proper accountability practices combine with practices for inclusive interactions to close the various discriminatory gaps in an employment system.

DOI: 10.4324/9780367822484-11

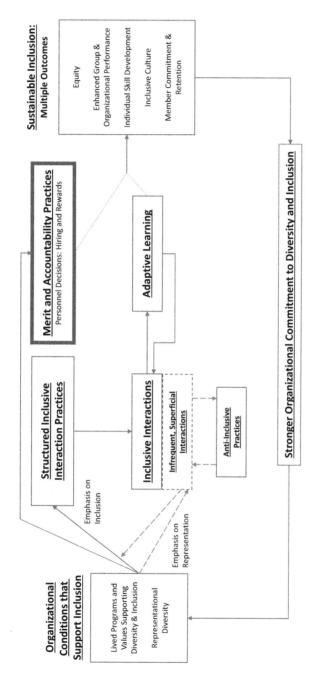

FIGURE 7.1 The Framework for Inclusive Interactions: Merit and Accountability Practices

If they are to be successful in doing so, we will see that accountability practices are in need of some reform.

Why do organizations need both inclusive interaction practices and merit and accountability practices?

Accountability practices for monitoring representational diversity have been in place in many U.S. organizations for decades. Yet, we still see the continuation of disparities and discrimination whether these organizations are in business fields such as engineering, nonprofit fields such as education and health care, or governmental fields such as policing. As we have found from evidence reviewed in this book, a fundamental problem is that changing the representation numbers does not address the continuing presence of stereotyping and implicit bias. Consequently, that bias is expressed as discriminatory behavior through various holes in the employment system, perpetuating disparities. For instance, we will see below one such hole, discovered by research only recently: contemporary merit and accountability systems fail to control bias in reward decisions. An equally or even more fundamental problem is that our practices for accountability do not change individuals' "hearts and minds," their emotions and attitudes toward members of underrepresented groups. Managers and other employees can see accountability as pressures from above or from outside the organization that attempt to force compliance. Our life experiences, as well as research on the impacts of Affirmative Action Plans (Chapter 5), tell us that individuals naturally resist such forces[1] and persist with biased beliefs. In contrast, workgroup conditions in which members have positive, frequent contact with each other (Chapter 6), engaging in inclusive interactions, can change hearts and minds by reducing prejudice.

> Since individuals' attitudes are not likely to change from attempts to force compliance, practices for accountability should be combined with practices for inclusive interactions that do change hearts and minds.

By changing attitudes and emotions in this adaptive way over time, inclusive interaction practices go to the source of discrimination—bias and stigmatizing. In that way, inclusive practices are a necessary complement to practices for accountability. Only by adding the practices for inclusive interactions can we hope to address discrimination at its source—prejudice—and progress to sustained equity and performance from diversity.

What about the reverse? Would inclusive interaction practices be enough to achieve equity and performance from diversity, without accountability practices? Our interviews suggest not, pointing to the importance of practices that hold individuals accountable for behavior toward members of underrepresented groups as well as for inclusive behavior among all members. The process for embedding inclusive interaction practices, such as those involving interacting with comfort and equal status, requires that individuals not be stigmatized by others' behaviors, such as microaggressions. Accordingly, the final section of this chapter discusses practices for holding members accountable for appropriate behavior.

> To control stigmatizing, accountability should include practices that hold members accountable for proper interaction behavior.

Consider another reason that accountability practices are required. As with all goals that are important to an organization, monitoring is required in order to judge progress and to identify problems and opportunities. Like any challenging organizational process—say, satisfying customers or reducing production costs—inclusion is a "continuing accomplishment" (Chapter 6) that requires ongoing monitoring and attention. Particularly while practices for inclusive interaction are being introduced and adaptive learning is underway, accountability practices can identify rates of progress in inclusive behavior and in the outcomes (discussed in the following chapter) that should result from inclusion.

> Accountability practices assess rates of progress in inclusion and identify problems that require diagnosis and improvement.

Monitoring can reveal whether inclusion is happening and paying off and whether a meritocracy that rewards contributions is actually operating. In a particular organization, is inclusion working for some groups, such as White women, but not for others, or for men of color but not women? Monitoring can trigger the examination and diagnosis of problems so that inclusion, equity, and performance can be pursued successfully.

Fortunately, various types of practices for merit and accountability are quite common and have been pursued by organizations for several decades. Later in this chapter, we review research that describes and analyzes the successful introduction in a large service organization of a comprehensive system for accountability. We know that accountability practices are feasible, relatively easy to introduce and operate with available staff and data, but they are also in need of improvement.

> Accountability practices are feasible and common in some fields, but they are also in need of improvement.

Accountability, transparency, and merit in the allocation of rewards

Given the widespread nature of implicit bias that causes flawed personnel decisions, accountability is essential. The massive study by Alexandra Kalev and associates (discussed in Chapter 5) found that equity, as measured by the odds of women and minorities moving into managerial positions, was most strongly predicted by an organization's procedures for encouraging fair decisions and holding managers responsible for them, in contrast to diversity training initiatives that failed to improve equity across these groups. A second body of evidence comes from Spencer and colleagues' review of experimental studies and meta-analyses.[2] The review found that biased personnel decisions are reduced by holding individuals accountable and reminding them of equity norms (as also discussed in Chapter 5).

The organizational stakes are significant not only for equity but also for performance. The two are tightly intertwined. Failure to achieve merit in the allocation of rewards and sanctions means that individuals will perceive inequities that lead them to be demotivated and to withdraw psychologically or physically.[3] Demotivation hampers performance in both the short and the long term. When we assess that our rewards are not commensurate with our efforts, as judged in comparison with others' rewards and efforts, the most straightforward way to remedy the imbalance is to lower our efforts to be commensurate with the rewards.

Inequities in rewards harm performance by reducing motivation, increasing turnover, and decreasing incentives to invest in skill development.

The demotivation may also extend to our decisions about whether to invest in gaining skills and knowledge (our *human capital*) useful to the organization. We are not motivated to become more skilled and make greater contributions if we will not be recognized and rewarded for those contributions. A final way that we can remedy the inequity is by withdrawing entirely from the workplace, increasing our absenteeism, or quitting the organization. In Chapter 4, we saw that stereotype threat and stigmatizing lead to anxieties and lower performance for members of underrepresented groups. Reward inequities are an additional force leading to dissatisfaction and lower performance.

The problem of achieving equity in rewards is substantial. Inequities persist despite decades of attention by organizations, courts, and regulatory bodies. Research has focused heavily on disparities between women and men.

The evidence. Drawing on nearly 30 years of studies, Aparna Joshi and colleagues'[4] meta-analyses find dramatic discrepancies in rewards while identifying particular conditions that heighten or reduce these discrepancies:

We found that the sex differences in rewards ($d=.56$) (including salary, bonuses, and promotions) were 14 times larger than sex differences in performance evaluations ($d=.04$), and that differences in performance evaluations did not explain reward differences between men and women. The percentage of men in an occupation and the complexity of jobs performed by employees enhanced the male–female gap in performance and rewards. In highly prestigious occupations, women performed equally, but were rewarded significantly lower than men. Only a higher representation of female executives at the industry level enabled women to reverse the gender gap in rewards and performance evaluations.[5]

A meta-analysis of over 150 studies by Jeremy Mackey and colleagues[6] revealed that females demonstrated higher job performance than males, whether measured by overall performance, task performance, organizational citizenship behavior, or objective measures, and whether women were highly represented or not in their organization.

> Inequities in rewards vary with job design and social networks.

Combining the findings of these two reviews suggests that women perform as well or better than men, in general, but then do not receive commensurate rewards. The problem may be less one of bias in formal performance evaluations than in subsequent reward decisions. Whatever the actual performance evaluations, there are major flaws when they are translated into rewards. The meta-analysis by Joshi and associates found only small gender differences in evaluations yet large disparities in rewards.

> Inequities are due less to bias in evaluations than to bias in final pay and promotion decisions.

Their findings indicate that other aspects of jobs and women's representation matter in terms of rewards received. On the side of reducing inequities, they attribute equity in industries where women executives are well represented to likely networking effects, with women having social ties with female executives in other firms. These ties provide knowledge of alternative jobs that aids women when they negotiate wages or change jobs. On the opposite side—higher inequities—they note[7] that in complex jobs involving "high involvement" performance-management systems, interactions among peers influence reward allocations through peer evaluations. Due to the exclusionary forces discussed in Chapter 4, with implicit bias and stereotyping being ubiquitous, those interactions can be unsatisfactory and lead to lower peer evaluations and rewards.

Achieving accountability for reward decisions

How can greater equity in rewards be achieved? Where there is accountability and equity in performance evaluations, the findings noted above tell us that the major challenge is overcoming subjectivity in translating those performance evaluations into rewards (see Box 7.1). Evidence indicates where this challenge is the greatest.

> *The evidence.* In their review of lab experimental studies, Spencer and colleagues[8] found that the challenge is greater in high complexity than in low complexity jobs. One study found less pay inequality when employees had a female manager, but only among employees in the lowest-level jobs.[9] Joshi and colleagues found that, across the large number of studies they reviewed, high prestige jobs had higher gender discrepancies between appraisals and rewards. That is, for the same evaluation, a woman was rewarded less well than a man. They note:

> > In these high prestige settings, performance criteria tend to be objective (e.g., billable hours or research productivity), yet reward allocation decision-making is highly subjective, opaque, and adversarial, and often involved high stakes (many such settings having 'up or out' promotion norms).[10]

BOX 7.1: LACK OF ACCOUNTABILITY FOR REWARD ALLOCATION

An example of the failure of accountability for reward allocations is evident at a university located in the Northwest United States. Annual evaluations of faculty follow clearly articulated protocols that require faculty to submit evidence of teaching and research success during the prior year. Subsequently, the faculty meet with their dean or associate deans for a review and goal-setting session. Why then was there, within the same rank, a cluster of female faculty over 40 years old, with stellar teaching and research records at the bottom of the pay scale? At this particular institution, transparency allows for all salaries to be made public. In this situation, the process of evaluation is fairly applied to all, but then the administrators have leeway in setting final salaries. Additionally, the administrators were able to determine who would be put forth for "equity compression" or salary adjustments. This appears to be an example of "managerial discretion"[11] infused with biases, that due to a lack of accountability, went unchecked. The result was detrimental to the women, but also had a potential negative impact on the university because these women felt undervalued and looked elsewhere for employment.

Bias is greater in some stages of the decision-making process than others. A study of the performance evaluations received by individuals hired through employee referrals—individuals who then have a social networking advantage in the organization—illustrates in detail this operation of bias at some stages of the reward process and not others.

> *The evidence.* Analyzing data on sales employees' productivity in a large global firm, Uri Shwed and Alexandra Kalev[12] compared employees' "average performance score" to the "final" performance score that determined their bonuses and other career outcomes. They state:

> > The average performance score is calculated based on a formal written questionnaire, which infuses standardization and accountability to the process, and these seem to do the job of preventing bias. The final stage, where we do find evidence for network bias, is explicitly based on managerial discretion. Top management allows managerial discretion at this stage to correct the formalized evaluation process that failed to create the required distinction between high and low performers.[13]

Providing standard procedures and accountability for performance evaluations but not for final pay decisions leads to inequities due to decision-makers' bias.

The need to create distinctions in appraisals in order to differentiate rewards provided a logic to top management for allowing managerial discretion over final reward decisions, but that discretion produced bias. Shwed and Kalev propose accountability and transparency as a needed remedy to assure organizational performance and individual equity:

> If employers are to guard against unwanted bias, they should supplement discretion with a review, searching for systematic patterns indicative of bias. ... Network favoritism hampers organizations' efficiency and can also create a sense of injustice and unfairness among workers even when a highly formalized, meritocratic system of rewards is in place.[14]

To counter inefficiencies and perceptions of injustice, effective accountability practices should involve searching for systematic patterns that indicate favoritism.

Evidence supports such proposals for accountability. Corroborating Spencer's findings from laboratory experimental studies, two large sample field studies examining effects over time (see Box 4.1 in Chapter 4 for a discussion of the higher confidence we can have in such studies) find important results for transparency and accountability practices.

> *The evidence.* Analyses by Frank Dobbin, Daniel Schrage, and Alexandra Kalev[15] extended their prior research[16] on diversity practices in over 800 workplaces in the United States over a time span of 30 years. The study examined transparency in two forms related to an organization's internal labor market: posting of job openings to all organizational members, and job ladders that specify paths for upward mobility from low-level jobs. Both increased the odds for women and people of color to move into managerial positions.

Advancement for women and people of color was enhanced by transparency in job postings and job ladders, and by monitoring by an external governmental body or an internal diversity manager.

> More dramatically, accountability in the form of monitoring by a diversity officer in the organization or by an external federal (governmental) contract compliance process strengthened the positive effects of effective diversity practices (such as extended recruiting) and nulled many of the negative effects of ineffective diversity practices (such as job tests and grievance procedures). Monitoring by an internal diversity manager was especially effective.

Transparency and accountability involve the production and availability of information and the consequences of that information for individuals. Note the importance of transparency regarding job openings and career ladders within the organization. If only in-group members know of these opportunities, inclusion has failed. Regarding the beneficial effect of monitoring, the researchers attribute much of this effect not to the actual overturning of particular managerial personnel decisions but, instead, to creating *evaluation apprehension* among managers that causes them to check their biases as they make personnel decisions.

Researchers attribute the positive effects of monitoring to its creating *evaluation apprehension* among managers.

The second field study, by Emilio Castilla,[17] examined the effect of introducing new accountability practices in a single organization.

> *The evidence.* Castilla[18] studied the introduction of accountability and transparency practices in a large, multinational service organization. (See Box 7.2.) Doing so reduced or eliminated the discrepancy between evaluations and rewards in the organization, not only for women but also for ethnic minorities and non-U.S.-born employees. Among over 9,000 employees, analyses had established the existence of such discrepancies over the course of seven years, with the analyses controlling for job, work unit, and supervisor.[19] In the following year practices for accountability and transparency were introduced by the organization, and in the next five years the discrepancies for these same groups were halved in magnitude and fell below levels of statistical significance.

Introducing accountability and transparency practices reduced discrepancies between performance evaluations and rewards for members of underrepresented groups over the following five years.

This study indicates that even a complex organization can introduce accountability and transparency practices and expect to reduce inequities in short order. Together, the two studies noted above provide compelling real-world evidence that accountability and transparency practices can counter discrimination that otherwise occurs in reward decisions, indicating that accountability and transparency practices are fundamental to equity in organizations.

BOX 7.2: ACTIONS FOR ACCOUNTABILITY AND TRANSPARENCY

As reported in the study by Emilio Castilla,[20] leaders of a large service-sector company with many thousands of employees took the following merit, accountability, and transparency actions in response to his analyses of company data showing bias in reward decisions:

- Appointed a small *performance-reward committee* of an executive and HR staff members to monitor and report on the fairness of pay decisions made by senior managers, providing *outcome accountability*.
- The committee formalized the process of assigning rewards based on employee performance evaluations, providing *process accountability*.

- All senior managers were informed and trained on how to use the merit-based process, providing *process transparency*.
- Each year all senior managers and high-level managers obtain aggregated information about pay decisions in their units, broken down by gender, race and foreign nationality, providing *outcome transparency*.
- The performance-reward committee was provided with the authority, resources, and support from division heads to modify reward decisions and procedures in order to guide the system over time.

These actions substantially reduced disparities in the years following their implementation.

Belief that practices are meritocratic enables biased decisions

A theme with important consequences for achieving inclusion in organizations emerges from the evidence discussed above—in the meta-analytic reviews, in lab experimental studies, in Dobbin and colleagues' analyses of changes over three decades, and in the study of an accountability intervention in a large organization. The theme is that currently espoused performance-management systems that claim to be meritocratic do not eliminate inequities. That theme is extended in laboratory studies by Castilla and Stephen Benard.[21]

> *The evidence.* Castilla and Benard find from their laboratory experiments that, "when an organization is explicitly presented as meritocratic [as compared to when it is not], individuals in managerial positions favor a male employee over an equally qualified female employee."[22]

Current fair employment practices leave gaps that allow inequities to continue. They fail to achieve meritocracy but support beliefs that they do.

This ironic finding indicates not only that attempts to assure meritocracy in evaluations fail to counter bias in final reward decisions, but that the belief in a meritocratic organization can increase inequities further. Meritocratic elements in the reward system, paradoxically, provide cover for the continuation of inequities.

A belief that an organization has a meritocratic system leads individuals to make more inequitable decisions.

Organizations and pay systems portrayed as meritocratic provide managers with a legitimized, unchecked discretion to allocate rewards for bonuses and promotions. This phenomenon provides one explanation for the persistence and even growth over time of disparities in career outcomes for underrepresented groups, despite organizational reforms.[23]

> Formalized performance evaluation procedures reduce bias, but they also provide unwarranted legitimacy to overall reward allocation systems that enable bias in the final stage of reward decisions.

Managerial discretion, in the form of unchecked behavior and decision-making, opens the door to self-segregation and stereotyping effects that create inequities, while the legitimacy provided by beliefs that the organization is meritocratic counters the challenging of that discretion. Accountability practices address these phenomena by checking legitimacy and countering subjectivity, holding managers responsible for the ways that they make reward decisions, while transparency practices in the form of monitoring reports make clear where and when disparities occur. Without monitoring and discussion of disparities, managers can easily rationalize continuation of the status quo based on stereotyped beliefs about low competence and warmth in members of underrepresented groups.

According to Castilla,[24] effective accountability practices examine both managerial processes and equity outcomes, and they have three dimensions: responsibility and transparency regarding the routines and criteria used to allocate rewards; responsibility and transparency regarding the final reward decisions and results being fair and visible; and the actors and audiences that are being held accountable and are making processes and outcomes visible. We would add that procedures that reflect these dimensions of accountability and transparency should be applied not only to rewards for current organizational members but also to hiring new members, since these decisions have been shown by audit studies to be subject to bias as well (Chapter 4). They should also apply to career development opportunities that underlie advancement.

> Accountability and transparency practices are needed not only to check bias in performance evaluations but also in the final decisions on compensation, career development opportunities, promotions, and new hires.

Training and mentoring opportunities have been found to favor White men.[25] Dobbin and colleagues' analyses showed that enhanced recruitment to management training programs led to meaningful movement of White women and Asian men into managerial positions, but not so for members of other underrepresented groups. The implication is that there has been a continuing failure of outcome accountability for these career development efforts.

Accountability for inclusive behavior

While accountability and transparency have been studied with regard to the allocation of rewards, we are unaware of similar research reviews on accountability for individual organizational members, managers, and all others, to follow inclusive practices, to display inclusive behavior. By analogy to the studies on the allocation of rewards, we propose that accountability and transparency concerning inclusive behavior are similarly essential to sustain equity and performance. We found this to be an important theme in the interviews conducted for this book.

Chapters 4 and 5 make clear the stakes for conflictual behavior in diverse workgroups. Stereotyping and stigmatizing produce stereotype threat for members of underrepresented groups, reducing their performance and creating tensions that impede information elaboration and the performance of diverse workgroups. Routine practices that hold members accountable for their interpersonal behavior in diversity interactions are necessary and valuable in reducing these threats to workgroup performance and individual equity.

> Our interviews indicate that it is important to have practices that hold individuals accountable for displaying inclusive behavior.

These "holding-accountable" practices can be seen as connecting the practice of engaging with comfort and self-efficacy (Practice 5 in our Framework) with the accountability and transparency practices for rewards. Unless interpersonal behavior is respectful and warm in diversity interactions, whether in normal task collaborations or when task-productive disagreements are being processed, it will be difficult to sustain the social integration needed for high workgroup performance.

In our interviews, examples showed that managers had learned this lesson. In the medical research unit discussed in Chapter 3, from the time that the new unit was established and continuing over time in the unit's normal meetings, the director stressed the need for warm relationships within and across the unit's two teams. In an international financial services company, women who successfully led high-performing business units experienced tensions with men leading functional units. In the face of these tensions, performance remained high for a time. However, over time and with a subsequent change in higher management, the high-performing women leaders left the organization. In engineering firms, with cases that we discuss in Chapter 9, our interviewees reported a strong focus of higher management on respectful, inclusive behavior within the organization as a whole, with the top leaders of these firms having learned over time that open conflict due to interpersonal tensions disrupted the performance of their workgroups.

As one of our interviewees put it, the leaders acted on "the knowledge they have as to where behaviors have gone wrong." In consequence, the organizations promulgated values and tools that held people accountable for behaving respectfully, which members termed "professional behavior." The indicator of an organization's success was not only that managers were holding their workgroup members accountable but, more so, that peers were holding their co-workers accountable.

Strategies for accountability and inclusion

The evidence from research and organizational practice is clear: To better achieve meritocracy, comprehensive accountability and transparency practices are necessary.

> Achieving meritocracy requires more comprehensive practices for accountability and transparency.

These practices have beneficial impacts, and they are feasible. In developing and assessing the adequacy of practices for merit-based personnel management, leaders can be guided by Castilla's three dimensions, which we enlarge here to encompass interpersonal behavior:

1. Instituting responsibility and transparency regarding the *procedures and criteria* used to make reward decisions—including hiring, compensation, development, and promotions—and to assess that interpersonal behavior is inclusive;
2. Instituting responsibility and transparency to assure that these *decisions are fair and visible and that behavior is inclusive*;
3. *Identifying the actors and audiences* that are being held accountable and those that are responsible for making processes and outcomes visible.

An important caution emerges from the discussion above: Efforts toward fair, meritocratic employment practices typically miss important stages of reward decisions, and they neglect inappropriate interpersonal behavior. Fair employment practices instituted by organizations are only partial, yet they provide organizational members with mistaken beliefs of meritocracy that, paradoxically, enable them to engage in biased decision-making. And they leave interpersonal behavior untouched. To remedy these flaws in well-intended systems, an appropriate strategy for managers and leaders is to identify and address *all* the points at which bias can enter into behavior and decisions.

> Since efforts toward fair, meritocratic employment practices typically leave important gaps uncovered, leaders should identify the several points at which bias is entering into behavior and decisions, then provide accountability and transparency practices that address each.

These points of bias activation involve not only reward decisions on compensation, development opportunities and promotions but also, as we saw in Chapter 4, self-segregation, stereotyping, and stigmatizing. These latter points require policies and practices that address interpersonal behavior, holding members accountable for inclusive behavior toward their fellow organizational members, whatever those members' backgrounds and functions.

Returning to the "hearts and minds" issue discussed earlier, a final caution: the broad behavioral problems that emerge from bias—self-segregation, stereotyping, and stigmatizing—cannot be expected to disappear or be effectively handled solely through accountability and transparency practices. Those practices can control the activation of bias into decisions and behavior, but they should not be expected to reduce the bias itself. For that purpose, inclusive interaction practices are also needed. Those interaction practices, emphasized in our Framework, operate on a daily, routine basis to shape behavior and, over time, reduce behavioral problems at the source by reducing prejudice. The reverse is to be expected as well: inclusive interaction practices will operate more effectively, for both performance and equity, when combined with practices for accountability and transparency. A combination of practices for inclusive interactions and for accountability increases the likelihood that the talents of underrepresented group members will be properly utilized and fairly rewarded in a sustained fashion. In the next chapter, we discuss the outcomes that can be expected from this combination of practices.

Notes

1 Dobbin, F., & Kalev, A. (2016). Why diversity programs fail. *Harvard Business Review, July–August*, 1–8; Dobbin, F., Schrage, D., & Kalev, A. (2015). Rage against the iron cage: The varied effects of bureaucratic personnel reforms on diversity. *American Sociological Review, 80*(5), 1014–1044.
2 Spencer, S. J., Logel, C., & Davies, P. G. (2016). Stereotype threat. *Annual Review of Psychology, 67*(1), 415–437.
3 Mowday, R. T. (1991). Equity theory predictions of behavior in organizations. In R. M. Steers & L. W. Porter (Eds.), *Motivation and work behavior* (pp. 111–131). McGraw-Hill; Sweeney, P. D. (1990). Distributive justice and pay satisfaction: A field test of an equity theory prediction. *Journal of Business and Psychology, 4*(3), 329–341.
4 Joshi, A., Son, J., & Roh, H. (2015). When can women close the gap? A meta-analytic test of sex differences in performance and rewards. *Academy of Management Journal, 58*(5), 1516–1545.
5 Ibid, p. 1516.

6 Mackey, J. D., Roth, P. L., Van Iddekinge, C. H., & McFarland, L. A. (2019). A meta-analysis of gender proportionality effects on job performance. *Group & Organization Management*, *44*(3), 578–610,

7 Joshi et al. (2015), citing Capelli (1999).

8 Spencer et al. (2016). "Stereotype threat."

9 Abraham, M. (2017). Pay formalization revisited: Considering the effects of manager gender and discretion on closing the gender wage gap. *Academy of Management Journal*, *60*(1), 29–54.

10 Joshi et al. (2015), p. 1533.

11 Shwed, U., & Kalev, A. (2014). Are referrals more productive or more likeable? Social networks and the evaluation of merit. *American Behavioral Scientist*, *58*(2), 288–308.

12 Ibid.

13 Ibid, p. 304.

14 Ibid, pp. 304–305.

15 Dobbin, F., Schrage, D., & Kalev, A. (2015). Rage against the iron cage: The varied effects of bureaucratic personnel reforms on diversity. *American Sociological Review*, *80*(5), 1014–1044.

16 Kalev, A., Dobbin, F., & Kelly, E. (2006). Best practices or best guesses? Assessing the efficacy of corporate affirmative action and diversity policies. *American Sociological Review*, *71*(4), 589–617.

17 Castilla, E. J. (2015). Accounting for the gap: A firm study manipulating organizational accountability and transparency in pay decisions. *Organization Science*, *26*(2), 311–333.

18 Ibid.

19 Castilla, E. J. (2008). Gender, race, and meritocracy in organizational careers. *American Journal of Sociology*, *113*(6), 1479–1526; Castilla, E. J. (2011). Bringing managers back in: Managerial influences on workplace inequality. *American Sociological Review*, *76*(5), 667–694.; Castilla, E. J. (2012). Gender, race, and the new (merit-based) employment relationship. *Industrial Relations: A Journal of Economy and Society*, *51*(s1), 528–562.

20 Castilla (2015). "Accounting for the gap."

21 Castilla, E. J., & Benard, S. (2010). The paradox of meritocracy in organizations. *Administrative Science Quarterly*, *55*(4), 543–676.

22 Ibid, p. 543.

23 Amis, J. M., Mair, J., & Munir, K. A. (2020). The organizational reproduction of inequality. *Academy of Management Annals*, *14*(1), 195–230; Castilla, E. J. (2012). Gender, race, and the new (merit-based) employment relationship. *Industrial Relations: A Journal of Economy and Society*, *51*(s1), 528–562.

24 Castilla (2015). "Accounting for the gap."

25 Bertrand, M., & Duflo, E. (2017). Field experiments on discrimination. In A. V. Banerjee & E. Duflo (Eds.), *Handbook of economic field experiments* (Vol. 1, pp. 309–393). North-Holland.

8

SUSTAINABLE INCLUSION

Multiple outcomes for individuals, workgroups, and organizations

To be sustainable, inclusion must confer continuing benefits to individuals and their organizations, with the benefits being felt across the members of the organization. With mutual benefits, the relationship between the organization and its members can be maintained, fulfilling the expectations of an acceptable employment (or volunteering) contract.[1] Most fundamentally, sustainable inclusion represents a continuing achievement, a process that enables its workforce and the organization to prosper through adapting to each other and the organization's stakeholders, including the clients that the organization serves.

> Sustainable inclusion is a process of continuing achievement such that an organization and its workforce prosper through adapting to each other.

From the perspective of this book, and as specified in its Framework, depicted in Figure 8.1, this continuing achievement comes down to a combination of practices that overcome anti-inclusive practices and promote adaptive learning, equity, and commitment for the organization's members. For the organization, the result is stronger performance, an organizational culture that sustains inclusive interactions among its members, and a valuing of diversity and inclusion, as seen in the box titled, *Sustainable Inclusion: Multiple Outcomes*, on the right side of the Framework. In this chapter, we bring together evidence first to outline the challenges that must be understood if we are to succeed with diversity and inclusion, and then to consider how these challenges can be addressed to achieve beneficial outcomes for organizations and their members from all backgrounds.

DOI: 10.4324/9780367822484-12

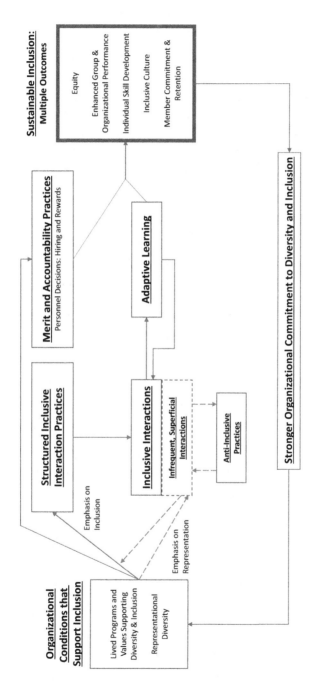

FIGURE 8.1 The Framework for Inclusive Interactions: Sustainable Inclusion

Processes that sustain disparities

To be pragmatic in efforts to achieve sustainable benefits from diversity, we should not shy from vexing questions about the challenges:

- Why have so many organizations found it difficult to achieve beneficial outcomes of equity and performance from diversity?
- Why have large employment inequities persisted over time?
- What role do common organizational processes play in the *reproduction* of these inequities in particular organizations and in the larger society?

If we understand how the reproduction of inequities occurs in organizations, we have the capabilities to interrupt it by organizing human talent more wisely.

For decades, despite significant efforts, many organizations and their larger societies have borne opportunity costs in how they allocate and use the talents of their workforces. That is, we are leaving money on the table, money for organizations and for individuals, by misallocating our human resources. Evidence tells us that in the United States, half a century after the passage of equal employment opportunity legislation, these costs persist. For instance, as noted in this book's Introduction, the portions of the male–female and Black–White wage gaps that are not explained by rational economic factors such as education and occupation have been growing, not shrinking, for three decades. Furthermore, estimates based on evidence from a large body of research indicate that gender inequities in hiring in a single year lead to one million more male than female hires among equally qualified candidates.

> Organizations and societies are bearing opportunity costs—that is, leaving money on the table—by their practices for developing and using the talents of their workforces.

The disparities for some minorities are yet worse than for women, with the employment status of Black men no better in the twenty-first century than in the middle of the last century, prior to civil rights legislation. We have underestimated the challenges and not given sufficient thought to what works and what does not.

In the Preface, we identified a dysfunctional relationship between academics—both researchers and educators—and managers as one contributor to the reproduction of inequities and lost performance. For example, we educators taught the importance of fair employment practices and training, relying on theory rather than empirical evidence to propose, rather simplistically, that these would ensure equitable and effective use of human talent. Meanwhile, researchers in particular academic disciplines were producing valuable findings but failing to connect them to those of researchers in other disciplines or to managerial practice.

> The communities of managers, educators, policymakers, and consultants have persisted with insufficiently effective practices. Why?

Another contributor to the reproduction of disparities has been organizational reliance on particular diversity practices, such as types of mandatory awareness training and a limited set of fair employment practices, that are legitimized by the judicial system, advocacy organizations, and consultants. In their limited totality, these practices have fallen short, but we continue to rely on them. Why?

Common rationalizations vs. embedded practices in a vicious cycle

The underlying cause of inadequate efforts and the most powerful contributor to the reproduction of inequities and lost performance may be *complacency* rooted in beliefs that societal change was on the right track. With a general feeling among dominant group members and organizational and institutional leaders that our advanced societies were doing what was necessary, progress could be seen as slow but steady, not as plateaued or regressing.

> Complacency about current diversity and inclusion efforts being sufficient provided a rationalization for slow progress.

And rationalizations for the slow progress were plentiful: Over the period of a few generations, members of underrepresented groups would gradually be advanced into higher and higher positions in organizations, so patience was required. And, with meritocratic systems in education and employment, if a particular group remained underrepresented, it must be because its members did not perform well enough or were not suited to higher-level positions. Further, since occupational segregation persisted, it must be that members of some groups preferred to be in particular occupations—such as home care rather than engineering, or human resource management rather than line management—and in job levels—such as clerical rather than managerial—that pay less rather than in higher-status, higher-paying ones.

In contrast to these rationalizing explanations, evidence accumulated over the past several decades and reviewed in the preceding chapters tells us that inequities and lost performance continued to be reproduced by everyday practices in organizations and labor markets. Even as many organizations pursued representational diversity with particular diversity efforts, anti-inclusive practices and discrimination in personnel decisions continued to exist. Meritocratic practices did not reach into managers' final personnel decisions, and accountability for those decisions was lacking. Consequently, subtle discrimination in the form of managers' hiring and advancement decisions based on implicit (largely subconscious) bias produced inequitable effects as strong or stronger than overt discrimination.

> Being satisfied with current efforts fails to recognize the effects of more subtle discrimination in the form of implicit, largely subconscious bias that results in anti-inclusive behavior and inequitable decisions.

Diverse organizational members were adversely affected not only by such biased decisions but also from being stereotyped and stigmatized, from being the recipients of others' biased behavior. This stereotype threat and its associated aggressions led to lowered self-confidence and lower evaluations of performance by themselves and by others. The ubiquitous phenomenon of self-segregation, of people preferring to associate with similar others with whom they feel most comfortable, further hampered diverse individuals' contributions by excluding them from key processes and decision-making.

> Reproduction of inequities and misallocation of human capital over the decades can be understood as a vicious cycle.

Evidence, then, leads to a more realistic view of the reproduction of inequities and misallocation of human capital over the decades, reproduction that can be understood as a vicious cycle:

1. Members of underrepresented groups are crowded into lower-status jobs, and that low status leads others to stereotype and stigmatize them as having low competence.
2. Laws and organizational practices designed to remedy low status are interpreted by some organizational members as favoring others, creating competitive emotions that lead to stereotyping and stigmatizing diverse individuals as low in warmth and ability to work with others.
3. Stereotypes act in a self-fulfilling fashion. Stereotyping, stigmatizing, and implicit bias lead to inequitably low performance evaluations and to emotional burdens and reduced performance of diverse members. These processes sustain a stereotype of low competence and low capability for advancement. Stereotyping leads many organizational members to experience discomfort when interacting with diverse individuals, inhibiting the frequency and quality of interactions. That discomfort and distancing sustains a stereotype of low warmth and dampens the opportunities for diverse individuals to contribute, further "confirming" the stereotype of low competence or low suitability for higher-status positions.
4. Implicit bias in managers' personnel decisions produces reward inequities that demotivate individuals. More directly, the biased decisions result in less hiring, developing, and promoting of members of underrepresented groups into

higher-level positions, reproducing the low status of (1) above and the need for continuing the diversity practices of (2), completing the vicious cycle.

At the heart of the vicious cycle is the stereotyping and stigmatizing of groups due to their low job status, with that stigmatizing leading to lower performance and discriminatory personnel decisions that effectively maintain the groups' low job status.

---

5. In the broader economy, the continuing reproduction of inequities in employment produced by the above processes in organizations creates disincentives for members of underrepresented groups to make personal investments in education and job-related skill development. And the low wealth resulting from low economic status impedes their ability to make such investments. These two factors further sustain low occupational status and the corresponding stereotype of low competence.

Reproduction of inequities and unsustainable diversity

When up against the forces that reproduce stereotypes and inequities over time, efforts to achieve representational diversity can fall short. Consider what diversity looks like when some degree of representation has been achieved but inclusion has not. Individuals, workgroups, and the organization as a whole experience the consequences of an ongoing state of suboptimal and sometimes conflictual diversity. Due to the vicious cycle described above, this state involves persistent inequities in the treatment of members of underrepresented groups and the rewards, formal and psychological, that they receive. Lawsuits and public relations problems may occur. More importantly, and at a more hidden level, inequities and performance costs result from several interrelated causes. Stigmatizing results in raised anxieties and lowered performance among those from underrepresented groups.[2] They tend to be segregated into lower-status jobs and cut off from skill development and upward mobility opportunities,[3] resulting not only in inequities but also in opportunity costs as talent is misallocated. The most talented individuals are the most likely to leave, as they have the best prospects in the labor market, and talented recruits are less likely to join the organization. Due to a lack of social integration, the performance of workgroups is limited by an artificial ceiling caused by tensions that are not handled constructively, inhibiting teamwork and the inclusion of members' expertise.[4]

One view is that the costs of poorly managed diversity are born only by members of underrepresented groups. An understanding of opportunity costs disputes this view. While the performance-based opportunity costs for the organization may be hidden, they are still consequential. And, due to tensions, majority-group members may be experiencing dissatisfaction and communicate to their peers and prospective members that the organization is not a good one to work for. As a consequence of these effects within and outside the organization, it will be at a competitive disadvantage compared to organizations that have figured out how to do diversity well.

> When workgroup tensions create employee dissatisfaction, the organization will be at a competitive disadvantage compared to those that have figured out how to do diversity well.

When nearly all organizations were handling diversity equally poorly, a state of "collusive competition" existed[5] that avoided competitive disadvantage for any one organization. As more organizations figure out inclusion and gain competitive advantage, the competitive environment is shifting.

Figuring it out involves leveraging diversity in a sustainable, inclusive way that is characterized by multiple benefits.

> *First, equity for all individuals*, not only those from underrepresented groups, as individuals are fairly rewarded for their contributions. This equity motivates all members to perform well,[6] and equity helps the organization establish a strong reputation in its labor market and, due to favorable public relations, in its product markets.
>
> *Second, higher workgroup performance* that results from a personalized form of social integration that enables all members to express their best selves and contribute their expertise continually.
>
> *Third, a creative level of tension* in workgroups that energizes and motivates individuals and produces higher performance.[7]
>
> *Fourth*, for the organization, *an adaptation to markets* with diverse populations due to organizational members understanding those markets.[8]
>
> *Fifth*, for the organization, *an effective allocation of human capital* that maximizes individual contributions to the organization and enhances organizational adaptation to its environment through ongoing organizational learning.[9]

These five benefits are dynamic, progressing over time. As such, and as with all successful organizational endeavors, continuing to produce them requires ongoing attention and evaluation, an understanding of the organization's distinctive strengths, and an unwillingness to rely only on short-term fixes.

Outcomes from three strategic options for diversity

In Chapter 5, we briefly considered three organizational approaches to managing diversity. By consciously making a choice, leaders can see these approaches as representing strategic options, pursued consciously as labor market strategies, rather than as more implicit and unconscious choices. The discussions in the preceding three chapters provide clear guidance on the relative social and economic outcomes expected from the various options. We do not consider here a non-diversity option, termed "statistical discrimination" in the economics literature.[10] That option uses broad generalizations and stereotypes concerning the labor productivity of particular identity groups in order to decide whether anyone from one of those groups will be recruited for hire or considered for advancement. However, that approach, with the supposed advantage of avoiding costs of search, is clearly illegal. And, technology has reduced the costs of search, making that option even less defendable in efficiency terms.

The first option for the use of diversity is one of occupational and job segregation, forming workgroups that are relatively homogeneous internally but differing across workgroups. The organization's workforce reflects the composition of the broader external labor force, with women and minorities crowded into particular occupations with lower status and underrepresented in higher-status occupations and hierarchical levels. The classic example is men in engineering and women in nursing or clerical occupations. And, even in those occupations, as in nursing, women are underrepresented in higher-level administrative positions.

> Crowding members of underrepresented groups into particular, typically lower status, jobs fails to leverage talent.

The drawbacks of this common option are several. Organizational members are occupationally segregated, with arbitrary allocation to jobs that ignore individual talents relevant to potential organizational contribution. This represents a misallocation of human assets, of lost opportunities for higher performance. The findings on cross-job collaborations (Chapter 5) tell us that there are both performance and equity advantages to opening up opportunities for talent trapped in particular workgroups to become visible and mobile within the organization. In addition, the findings from research investigating the categorization–elaboration model (Chapter 5) tell us that there is too little information elaboration in homogeneous workgroups, too little tension for the most effective decision-making and performance. And the identity-based differences across workgroups create coordination difficulties, reducing efficiency and calling for the creation of cross-functional teams.

The second option for organizations is to utilize heterogeneous workgroups that assimilate the diverse members into a narrow conformity with the dominant workgroup culture, a culture typically preexisting prior to the unit becoming diverse. This option opens up possibilities for diverse members to find jobs more suited to their talents, benefiting them in terms of formal rewards and, to some degree, the workgroup in terms of enhanced performance.

> Opening opportunities to higher-status jobs in diverse workgroups utilizes talent more effectively, but expecting narrow conformity with the existing culture lowers satisfaction and contribution to better decision-making.

However, due to the need to bow to the existing workgroup culture, diverse members need to suppress some aspects of their talents, creating a lack of psychological adjustment that, as discussed in the preceding chapter, will lead to lower self-confidence and performance and to categorization by majority-group members as less competent. And the categorization-elaboration model again tells us that such assimilation will lead to lower information elaboration and workgroup performance.

The evidence discussed in the three preceding chapters clearly points to the third option—utilizing inclusive workgroups and teams where work-relevant differences are invited and tensions are dealt with constructively to make better decisions—as the best strategic alternative, as the option that represents sustainable inclusion with benefits for the organization and its members. The leadership challenge with this option is to boost information elaboration while avoiding categorization phenomena—stereotyping and stigmatizing—that cause fault lines between subgroups within the workgroup.

> The challenge for leaders is to create and sustain appropriate workgroup norms utilizing the structured inclusive interaction practices while fostering individualized adjustment by all newcomers to a workgroup.

Achieving equity, or not

In this and the following sections, we outline the various sustained outcomes that our Framework specifies as following from the inclusive interactions characterized by adaptive learning. For each of the outcomes depicted in Figure 8.1, we consider its basis in the evidence emerging from the bodies of research reviewed in the preceding chapters.

The main barrier to achieving equity is stereotyping and stigmatizing. Building on the discussion earlier in this chapter about the reproduction of inequities over time, Figure 8.2 depicts the various ways in which stereotyping and stigmatizing produce and perpetuate inequities in organizations. Note that there are several sub-cycles of self-fulfilling prophecies within a larger vicious cycle. As discussed in Chapter 4, hiring inequities—members of underrepresented groups with equal qualifications being passed over in favor of dominant group members—result from implicit bias that reflects a negative stereotype of low competence being attached to groups having low economic status. For those who are organizational members, the exclusionary forces of stereotyping and stigmatizing cause raised anxieties, reduced personal performance, and lowered self-evaluations due to being stigmatized as low in competence. Since the stereotyping and stigmatizing produces self-fulfilling prophecies, it can appear well-founded.

> Inequities in the present fuel inequities in the future through self-fulfilling prophecies produced by stereotyping and stigmatizing.

Members of groups crowded into lower-status jobs are stereotyped as of low competence and those among them who are in higher-status jobs are seen as tokens with whom one is in competition, resulting in a stereotype of being difficult to work with. Those stereotypes lead to superficial and uncomfortable relationships among peers, and biased decisions by managers lead stereotyped members to receive fewer development and promotion opportunities. Their failure to be advanced confirms in some minds the stereotypes. This vicious cycle and its self-fulfilling prophecies operate at any organizational level, since those members of underrepresented groups who do advance to a higher level are seen as tokens and as competitive threats to the organization's dominant identity group. Those views sustain stereotyping and stigmatizing at that higher level. In effect, stigmatizing leads to discounting and reducing the contributions and rewards of members of underrepresented groups at all organizational levels.

Stereotyping and stigmatizing produce yet additional self-fulfilling prophecies that are not depicted in Figure 8.2. Biased decisions of hiring and rewarding result in inequitably lower pay for members of underrepresented groups. Perceptions of inequities in rewards then demotivate these members and lower their efforts and, consequently, their performance. The lower pay also has a wealth effect. With less

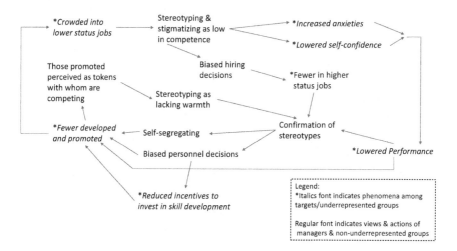

FIGURE 8.2 Inequities: Self-fulfilling Prophecies of Stereotyping and Stigmatizing

wealth, individuals are less able to invest in education and other developmental activities, resulting in lower skills. The lower performance and skills that result from biased reward decisions serve to confirm stereotypes of lower competence.

Example 8.1: Institutional challenges that persist

According to data collected, analyzed, and reported by the *New York Times*,[11] in 2020–2021, the percentage of Black economists in the Federal Reserve Bank (an important entity of the U.S. federal government) was 1.3 percent, against 3–4 percent of Ph.D. graduates in economics each year and 13 percent of the U.S. population being Black. In its Washington, DC headquarters, only two of the 417 economists, half of 1 percent, were Black. Consider these statistics in light of the following history contained in the report:

> Fed jobs should be open "to all competent Americans," Henry Gonzalez, a Democratic congressman from Texas, once told the Fed chair at the time, Alan Greenspan. Mr. Greenspan assured lawmakers the Fed was working toward diversity. That was 1993.
>
> As this organization pursued representational diversity over the years, what went wrong? The report examined the experience of one young recent Black recruit, J. Monroe Gamble, a research assistant at the Fed. Following his college graduation, the Fed did not hire him for a research position despite recommendations from prominent academic economists. In contrast, he was selected by Harvard University as a research scholar, and the following year he was hired at the Fed's San Francisco branch. However, he felt out of place at the branch and struggled to find meaningful work. He began asking around and learned that he was the first Black person ever to hold a research assistant job [at that branch]. Within months, he was looking to leave. At a lunch with him, the recently promoted president of the branch, Mary C. Daly, encouraged him to remain and offered her help. Eventually, Mr. Monroe became her research assistant and his situation improved. However, he found that the bank's current research assistants helped to hire the next set of assistants and suspected that a desire to hire people similar to themselves disadvantaged Black candidates. Since the Fed is a gatekeeper to success in economics, as illustrated by Mr. Monroe now moving into a predoctoral program at New York University, lack of representation and inclusion of Blacks in these research positions hurts equity not only at the Fed but more broadly in U.S. society.

As does another analysis by the *New York Times*[12]—of disparities in Black representation at the top levels of the U.S. military, despite its being the first major U.S. institution to be desegregated shortly after World War II—this case illustrates a number of problems depicted in Figure 8.2. These problems represent the institutionalizing of inequities. First, the prevailing lack of Black Ph.D. economists feeds stereotypes of low competence for such positions, leading to bias in recruitment and selection decisions. The involvement of current position-holders in hiring future recruits enables homophily (self-segregation forces) to play a further role in biasing selection decisions. For those Blacks who are hired, through unimpeachable credentials such as selection by Harvard University and recommendations from famous individuals, the challenge then becomes inclusion. As we know from Chapter 4, prevailing stereotypes lead to stigmatizing, hampering inclusion. For Mr. Monroe, the lack of inclusion caused anxieties that led him to plan to leave his position prematurely, which would have contributed to the persistence of low representation at the Federal Reserve Bank and in society, confirming in some minds the stereotype of low competence. Encouraged by the intervention of the regional bank's leader, Mr. Monroe persisted and succeeded. However, this intervention represents the personal actions of a leader who had experienced similar problems in her career. It did not represent institutionalized practices for inclusion and accountability that can be expected to continue once she is no longer the leader, nor practices that are embedded in other branches of the organization.

Evidence points to two ways of overcoming the barrier of stigmatizing, both of which will be necessary in many situations. The first way, discussed in Chapter 7, involves practices that promote accountability for inclusive behavior and merit in the allocation of rewards, including compensation, developmental opportunities, and promotions, plus organizational members following inclusive interaction practices that produce adaptive learning. The second way involves enhanced recruitment, development, and cross-functional collaboration programs, as we now consider in more detail.

Equity from recruiting and cross-job contact

Achieving equity involves opening opportunities for initial hiring and for subsequent development and advancement. As noted in Chapter 5, Alexandra Kalev and associates'[13] study of promotion advertisements for women and minorities provides strong evidence on the value of these initiatives, finding that over a multiyear time span, organizational programs for enhanced recruiting pay off in terms of equity. This is in sharp contrast with educational (training) efforts that actually produced null or negative effects for underrepresented group members holding managerial positions. The follow-on study by Kalev[14] found positive effects on equity for cross-job training and self-directed teams, together indicating that efforts that bring people from different functions together in collaborative endeavors produce equity benefits.

> Achieving equity is aided by adopting enhanced recruitment efforts and programs for cross-job collaboration.

The underlying causes of the improvement in equity were argued to be increased visibility for talented members of underrepresented groups. And, as noted in Chapter 6, findings on intergroup contact and cognitive adaptation provide an additional explanation: the prolonged intergroup contact inherent in these ongoing cross-functional activities leads otherwise prejudiced individuals to recognize inconsistencies between their stereotypes and the performance of the diverse members with whom they interact, leading to reductions in prejudiced behavior toward those individuals and, more generally, toward the identity groups to which those individuals belong.

Achieving performance, or not

Diversity carries the potential for stronger performance, but research evidence makes clear that diversity in terms of representation alone is not enough to reliably produce improved performance (Chapter 5). As noted above and detailed in the preceding chapters, for organizations and workgroups with a diverse membership, the evidence points to three problematic social processes.

> For organizations and workgroups with a diverse membership, three problematic social processes must be overcome: (1) implicit bias, (2) categorization of subgroup members, and (3) stereotyping and stigmatizing.

One process is as described for equity problems: the unconscious application of implicit bias (Chapters 4 and 7) that results in discriminatory, flawed pay, hiring, development, and advancement decisions on the part of the organization and decisions to leave on the part of talented individuals. These decisions harm performance as well as equity, since less-qualified individuals are advanced to more consequential jobs, and commitment to the organization is eroded among the more qualified individuals that are passed over. A second and related process affecting performance is categorization (stereotyping) of subgroup members, creating fault lines and divergence within the workgroup, as noted by findings on the categorization-elaboration model (Chapter 5). The resulting tensions hamper the performance of the workgroup as a whole. The third process is stereotyping and stigmatizing of subgroup members, creating anxieties, lowered self-evaluations and lowered measured performance, as noted in Figure 8.2 . This process also lowers group performance. The negative results from these processes are not theoretical but actual, as they have been found in multiple systematic reviews of large numbers of studies.

> Strong performance outcomes from diversity, even stronger than from homogeneous workgroups, requires convergence among workgroup members while embracing beneficial differences.

To produce strong performance outcomes from diversity, stronger than from homogeneous workgroups, the challenge is to raise convergence among workgroup members while not submerging valuable differences. The convergence is in the form of social integration that reduces anxieties, increases comfort in interactions, and elaborates (broadens) the perspectives and information shared in the workgroup to inform better decisions. Many situational factors are found to influence the social forces of convergence and divergence, supporting the importance at the workgroup level of the practices specified in our Framework. As presented in Chapter 6, social integration for working together effectively rests on these practices and associated practices of socialization (especially personal-identity socialization that identifies each individual's distinctive task-relevant interests and capabilities). The practices produce adaptive learning—reducing prejudiced behavior and attitudes—and higher satisfaction that enables workgroup members to benefit from each other's efforts and expertise.

> Inclusive interactions, personal-identity socialization, and equitable rewards enable workgroup members to benefit from each other's expertise and efforts.

There is strong evidence from controlled experiments, including those in organizational settings, of this adaptive learning occurring through prolonged, positive diversity interactions and even through vicarious, imagined contact. Creating adaptive learning through practices that foster prolonged, positive intergroup contact is a practical path for managers to raise performance.

Achieving skills, or not

> Skill development that results from cross-group engagement is another area where all organizational members, regardless of their identity groups, benefit.

Encountering individuals different from oneself can create cognitive discomfort in the form of inconsistencies with one's stereotypes of the groups that those individuals represent in one's mind. If the discomfort is simply avoided by staying away from such individuals in the future, then an opportunity for skill development has been lost. Similarly, distancing between diverse members occurs when job segregation exists.

However, in such cases, cross-job training across functional areas can enable members to acquire additional skills, as well as producing the equity benefits noted above.

> If the initial discomfort experienced during intergroup contact is overcome and interactions are frequent, cognitive development in the form of adaptive learning occurs, along with skills for critical thinking and leadership.

Whatever the reason for intergroup contact, if the initial discomfort is overcome by the familiarity that results from continued interaction, then cognitive development in the form of adaptive learning occurs.[15] From the research on intergroup contact theory, we know that the prejudice reduction and familiarity from repeated, positive contact generalizes beyond the specific individuals contacted to the groups that they represent. It is natural that some of these cognitive changes are accompanied by behavioral skills for interacting with dissimilar others. However, some broader, related skills develop as well. These skills take the form of critical thinking and leadership. These skills do not result from superficial and moderate frequency contact but, rather, from high-frequency and positive diversity interactions, as found most prominently in intergroup friendship formation (Chapter 6). Many workgroups provide the conditions enabling high-frequency intergroup interactions. *Hence, the managerial challenge for developing members' skills is to make these interactions positive rather than anxiety-producing.*

Achieving an inclusive culture and its benefits, or not

Diversity alone can lead to fault lines between subgroups that, regardless of any beneficial performance and equity effects, can lead to member dissatisfaction and intentions to leave. In contrast, changes that address the challenges of diversity and turn differences into assets through reducing anxieties for members of underrepresented groups are often changes that respond to all employees' needs and concerns. Diversity often brings those needs and concerns of all members to a more visible level for managers to see and respond to. This point was made to one of us by a White male director of human resources. When constructive changes stimulated by experiences with diversity are embedded in ongoing inclusive practices that are experienced by all workgroup individuals, the organizational culture has been enhanced for all types of members. The organization is then a more attractive and motivating one for members. Consider evidence that was not covered in the preceding chapters:

> *The evidence.* Research on inclusion as an umbrella concept remains sparse. However, a sufficient number of studies have been performed in social service organizations to permit a meta-analysis.[16] The review reported that research on employees of the U.S. government[17] found negative views of job

satisfaction or workgroup performance in the presence of diversity, but not when the employees perceived that diversity was managed effectively. In the review's meta analyses, organizational members' perceptions of a climate of inclusion were found to be related to a variety of beneficial outcomes such as commitment to the organization and to a lesser incidence of detrimental outcomes such as turnover.

> An inclusive climate plays a role in transforming workgroup diversity into organizational commitment and team creativity.

Similarly, a study of more than 50 engineering work teams in two multinational companies[18] found that the greater the climate for inclusion in a team, the more that the team's cultural diversity led to information exchange and information elaboration that raised team and employee creativity.

The limited research to date indicates that inclusion as a broad concept has an impact on organizational members' attitudes and performance. In our Framework, inclusion has been decomposed into parts—namely, workgroup and organizational practices—that are more concrete and have been more directly studied, providing evidence of their effectiveness. One specific example is *personalized socialization* (Chapter 6), where the desire to benefit from diversity can lead an organization to adopt onboarding procedures that encourage new members to express their interests and talents in their new work role. This approach to onboarding benefits all new members, increasing their intention to remain with the organization and to express their expertise in ways that benefit the workgroup.

The idea of inclusion can be expanded beyond its meaning for diversity, as can be seen in stated principles for organizational initiatives such as cross-functional collaborations, international agile teams for software development, and semi-autonomous teams in manufacturing and health care (Chapter 5).

> Inclusion initiatives are pursued on the basis of organizational effectiveness.

These initiatives are pursued on the basis of organizational effectiveness. As such, inclusion can be considered to be a strategically chosen general value in an organization. Sustaining it in the form of inclusive interaction behavior is then a desired outcome. Whether labeled as *inclusion* or with some other term, such as fellowship, the value is designed to shape effective, mission-driven behavior on the part of organizational members.

> Inclusion is designed to shape effective, mission-driven behavior on the part of organizational members.

An example is the language code-switching behavior by members of a multinational corporation (Chapter 6), where performance-enhancing behavior was underpinned by a norm of inclusion that produced effective knowledge sharing among members of different nationalities.

When inclusion as a general value is promulgated on the basis of organizational effectiveness, it aids in counteracting backlash that can result from perceptions of favoritism toward one identity group or another in the organization.

> Inclusion as a general value embedded in programs that are pursued for higher performance avoids backlash effects that are common for programs framed as diversity initiatives.

However, even with a general value of inclusion, unconscious, implicit bias can operate and undermine inclusive engagement in particular interactions. The undermining can be countered in part by merit and accountability practices that sustain equitable personnel decisions, but to prevent stereotyping, more is necessary as well. This was particularly well-illustrated in one of our interviews.

Example: Norms that overcome implicit bias

John stressed that his high-tech organization strongly and repeatedly upheld values of respectful interactions across all members at all levels of the organization. Despite these values, he had once made assumptions about some international members lacking task-relevant expertise based on their lack of skill in speaking English, which was not their mother tongue. He learned otherwise from experience that proved him wrong, experience that was gained due to continuing interactions guided by the organization's norm of inclusion.

For a general value of inclusion that transcends diversity to be sustained in a way that applies to diverse members, leaders can support the value's application to all members, so that the effects of implicit bias and stereotyping erode with members' experience over time.

> Leaders can emphasize inclusion as a performance-relevant value to be applied to all members, enabling members' to have diversity experiences over time that lead to prejudice reduction.

Since this valuing of inclusion is fundamentally upheld by norms of inclusive engagement, it supports the achieving of each of the outcomes discussed above: equity, performance, skill development, and enhanced organizational culture. And, the reverse, as specified by the feedback loop from the sustainable inclusion outcomes to the supportive organizational conditions in the Framework (Figure 8.1): The beneficial outcomes that represent sustainable inclusion confirm to leaders that the organization should continue to uphold the basic values and programs for diversity and inclusion that give rise to those outcomes.

> Achieving the benefits of inclusion confirms to organizational leaders that they should continue the values and practices that support diversity and inclusion.

Achieving commitment, retention, and sustained inclusion: The role of leaders

Sustainable inclusion involves retaining diverse organizational members, especially those from underrepresented groups. Retention, an indicator of member engagement and commitment, has not been addressed substantially in diversity-specific research covered in the preceding chapters. However, we know from broader employee research that inequities in rewards are related to reduced commitment and higher turnover (Chapter 7). We will see below that the small number of studies that have addressed turnover and workplace diversity indicate the power of inclusion, and a larger number of studies indicate the broader problem of higher turnover among members of underrepresented groups, whether in high or low-level jobs. With costs of turnover acknowledged to be many and high[19] and representational diversity at risk, retention of members from underrepresented groups, and indeed all members, is a bottom-line issue. Since diversity in the presence of anti-inclusive practices can be expected to produce conflict (Chapter 5), the resulting anxieties have the further potential to increase turnover. Bias in the allocation of opportunities and rewards (Chapter 7) has the same potential. A meta-analysis of studies on turnover[20] supports the role of these factors, with age diversity and lack of internal mobility being associated with higher turnover among employees in general. The study also found that turnover was associated with detrimental performance outcomes, including higher counterproductivity and error rates among employees, and lower customer satisfaction, production efficiency, and sales efficiency.

Several important studies more directly investigated the effects of workplace diversity on turnover.

> *The evidence.* A study of over 5,000 managers in a U.S. retail organization[21] found that pro-diversity work climate perceptions were associated with a higher commitment to the organization. A higher commitment was, in turn,

strongly related to lower intentions to quit. These connections held for White men as well as women, and for Hispanics and Blacks, with the findings being strongest for Blacks.

A well-controlled study of turnover among employees in low wage jobs in over 800 workplaces, also in a U.S. retail service organization, concludes:

> All of the minority groups, Blacks, Hispanics, and Asians, were more likely to quit whiter workplaces. In this sense, our results suggest that diversity is difficult to sustain"[22] and "the problem for managers is that each new hire raises isolation (being in the numerical minority) for some groups at the same time that it decreases isolation for others. Managers can benefit by helping employees thrive in a world of racial diversity—a prescription that is easier to state than to implement.[23]

The second study indicates that the default situation for managers is one in which issues of similarity and self-segregation play out through workgroup members' decisions to remain or leave. Although the effects of diversity on turnover are modest, they can accumulate over time and erode attempts to increase representational diversity.

Representational diversity is difficult to sustain, since members of underrepresented groups are more likely to quit when anti-inclusive forces are not countered.

Data at the societal level paint a similar picture.

> *The evidence.* Bureau of Labor Statistics data show retention rates for minorities being considerably lower than for Whites, with minorities having 30 percent higher voluntary turnover.[24]
>
> Ethnicity and race are not the only aspect for which sustainable inclusion is at risk. Confirming common views that women were exiting from corporate positions, a statistical analysis published in 2008 found higher turnover rates among women than men among 400,000 professionals and managers in major U.S. firms. The higher rates persisted after controlling for potential explanatory factors. Drawing on their findings on gender and race, the authors stated:
>
> > It would seem that establishments are more successful at recruiting minorities but are less successful at forestalling their early attrition.[25]

The challenge of retaining women in STEM jobs, particularly engineering, is well known. Retention can be a signal of whether inclusion is being achieved or not, with the exit of talent a warning sign of organizational dysfunction.[26]

The evidence. In a study of women who had graduated from engineering departments at 30 U.S. universities, the top three sets of reasons for their leaving engineering jobs and the field were:

1. "poor and/or inequitable compensation, poor working conditions, inflexible and demanding work environment that made work-family balance difficult;
2. unmet achievement needs that reflected a dissatisfaction with effective utilization of their math and science skills; and
3. unmet needs with regard to lack of recognition at work and adequate opportunities for advancement."[27]

These reasons point to dysfunction in terms of organizational practices that under-utilize talent and lack inclusion, leading to the loss of diverse members. Leaders play a pivotal role in these practices, with effects on members' attitudes and retention. A refined understanding of this role is provided by a study of supermarket departments.[28] The study investigated the phenomenon of high demographic (surface-level) diversity leading to high turnover.

> *The evidence.* The study examined the practices of departmental leaders in terms of the quality of personal relationships that they had with their department's various members. Members of each of nearly 350 departments assessed their leader's relationship with them. A high average level of positive relationships with the leader was important in diverse workgroups. It reduced the effect of higher surface-level diversity producing higher departmental turnover.
>
> When there were greater differences in assessments across members— meaning that different members assessed their relationship with the leader as more positive or less positive—departmental turnover was higher. When there were fewer differences in how the followers assessed a leader, turnover in a department was lower. The lowest turnover was in departments where the average assessment of a member's relationship with the leader was high and differences across members was low.

The researchers note that greater differences across members, when they assess their relationship with the department's leader, indicate the presence of in-groups and out-groups. When leaders favor an in-group's members, that reinforces the in-group's negative beliefs about the out-group. In terms of what we know about stereotyping, such leader behavior legitimizes stigmatizing and increases anxieties among members of underrepresented groups. In contrast, when a leader has positive relationships with many group members in a diverse workgroup and low differences in those relationships (indicating less in-group vs. out-group formation), the leader *de-legitimizes* the negative beliefs that some members may have toward other members. In effect, the findings indicate that the more inclusive a leader's relationships with all workgroup members, the lower the turnover.

In diverse workgroups, the more consistently good the leader's relationship is across the various members, the lower the turnover. This effect may be due to such leader behavior de-legitimizing in-group/out-group stereotyping and stigmatizing.

Inclusion and the role of leaders

Our reviews of research-based evidence in the immediately preceding chapters, when integrated into this chapter, point to the various ways in which discrimination and inequities perpetuate themselves in organizations, presenting significant challenges to organizational leaders. The evidence also offers guidance on dealing with the challenges, indicating that sets of practices specified in the Framework lead to the two outcomes of primary importance—equity for individuals and performance for workgroups and organizations. In this chapter, we also see that the practices are associated with sustaining equity and performance through favorable influences on members' organizational commitment, retention, and skill development, and through establishing a culture of inclusion.

However, the Framework of Inclusive Interactions does not specifically depict the role of leaders in structuring inclusive practices. Directly above, we have elaborated on the leadership study by Nishii and Mayer in part because it highlights the role of leaders in instituting and following inclusive practices at the ground level of departments and workgroups. It is leaders at all levels of an organization—whether managers or staff, as we will see in the next chapters—who are in a position to initiate, model, and evolve inclusive practices. The leaders' practices signal to others the behaviors and understandings that are legitimate in the organization. These behaviors and understandings underlie the continual achievement of the beneficial outcomes of sustainable inclusion. In the following two chapters, we present cases and examples that can guide leaders in playing the crucial role of instituting and sustaining effective inclusive practices.

Notes

1 Rousseau, D. M. (1995). *Psychological contracts in organizations: Understanding written and unwritten agreements.* Sage.
2 See the section on stigmatizing's impacts and stereotype threat in Chapter 4.
3 See the section on cross-job collaboration in Chapter 5.
4 See discussion of the categorization-elaboration model in Chapter 5.
5 Hirschman, A. O. (1970). *Exit, voice and loyalty: Responses to decline in firms, organizations and states.* Harvard University Press.

6 Mowday, R. T. (1991). Equity theory predictions of behavior in organizations. In R. M. Steers & L. W. Porter (Eds.), *Motivation and work behavior* (pp. 111–131). McGraw-Hill.

7 See the section on managing tensions in Chapter 5.

8 Thomas, D. A., & Ely, R. (1996). Making differences matter: A new paradigm for managing diversity. *Harvard Business Review, 74*(5), 79–90.

9 See the section on avoiding narrow conformity in Chapter 6; also see Thomas and Ely (1996).

10 Bertrand, M., & Duflo, E. (2017). Field experiments on discrimination. In A. V. Banerjee & E. Duflo (Eds.), *Handbook of economic field experiments* (Vol. 1, pp. 309–393). North-Holland.

11 Smialek, J. (2021, February 2). Why are there so few Black economists at the Fed? *New York Times.* https://www.nytimes.com/2021/02/02/business/economy/federal-reserve-diversity.html

12 Cooper, H. (2020, December 9). "Is Austin on your list?": Biden's Pentagon pick rose despite barriers to diversity. *New York Times.* https://www.nytimes.com/2020/12/09/us/politics/biden-lloyd-austin-defense-secretary.html

13 Kalev, A., Dobbin, F., & Kelly, E. (2006). Best practices or best guesses? Assessing the efficacy of corporate affirmative action and diversity policies. *American Sociological Review, 71*(4), 589–617.

14 Kalev, A. (2009). Cracking the glass cages? Restructuring and ascriptive inequality at work. *American Journal of Sociology 114*(6), 1591–1643.

15 Crisp, R. J., & Turner, R. N. (2011). Cognitive adaptation to the experience of social and cultural diversity. *Psychological Bulletin, 137*(2), 242–266.

16 Mor Barak, M. E., Lizano, E. L., Kim, A., Duan, L., Rhee, M.-K., Hsiao, H.-Y., & Brimhall, K. C. (2016). The promise of diversity management for climate of inclusion: A state-of-the-art review and meta-analysis. *Human Service Organizations: Management, Leadership & Governance, 40*(4), 305–333.

17 Choi, S., & Rainey, H. G. (2010). Managing diversity in U.S. Federal agencies: Effects of diversity and diversity management on employee perceptions of organizational performance. *Public Administration Review, 70*(1), 109–121; Pitts, D. (2009). Diversity management, job satisfaction, and performance: Evidence from U.S. federal agencies. *Public Administration Review, 69*(2), 328–338.

18 Li, C.-R., Lin, C.-J., Tien, Y.-H., & Chen, C.-M. (2017). A multilevel model of team cultural diversity and creativity: The role of climate for inclusion. *The Journal of Creative Behavior, 51*(2), 163–179.

19 See, for instance, Nishii, L. H., & Mayer, D. M. (2009). Do inclusive leaders help to reduce turnover in diverse groups? The moderating role of leader–member exchange in the diversity to turnover relationship. *Journal of Applied Psychology, 94*(6), 1412–1426.

20 Heavey, A. L., Holwerda, J. A., & Hausknecht, J. P. (2013). Causes and consequences of collective turnover: A meta-analytic review. *Journal of Applied Psychology, 98*(3), 412–453.

21 McKay, P. F., Avery, D. R., Tonidandel, S., Morris, M. A., Hernandez, M., & Hebl, M. R. (2007). Racial differences in employee retention: Are diversity climate perceptions the key? *Personnel Psychology, 60*(1), 35–62.

22 Leonard, J. S., & Levine, D. I. (2006). The effect of diversity on turnover: A large case study. *Industrial and Labor Relations Review, 59*(4), 547–572. (p. 565).

23 Ibid, p. 569.

24 McKay et al. (2007). "Racial differences in employee retention."

25 Hom, P. W., Roberson, L., & Ellis, A. D. (2008). Challenging conventional wisdom about who quits: Revelations from corporate America. *Journal of Applied Psychology, 93*(1), 1–34. (p. 25).

26 Hirschman (1970). *Exit, voice and loyalty.*

27 Fouad, N. A., Chang, W.-H., Wan, M., & Singh, R. (2017). Women's reasons for leaving the engineering field. *Frontiers in Psychology, 8*(Article 875), 1–11 (p. 1).

28 Nishii and Mayer (2009). "Do inclusive leaders help to reduce turnover in diverse groups?"

PART II SUMMARY
Guidance for making diversity and inclusion work

At an increasing rate over the last two decades, research published in academic and industry journals has produced knowledge that can guide managers in achieving high performance and equity from diversity and inclusion. That achievement requires understanding where and why some current efforts have come up short and, on the opposite side, how some non-diversity organizational programs have unexpectedly produced that achievement. Drawing on systematic literature reviews that assess knowledge generated in a large number of individual studies, and on several highly-informative large scale studies, we find that research performed in a variety of academic fields and sectors of society provides a high degree of certainty on the following insights.

Inclusive interaction practices are necessary to facilitate positive, meaningful inclusive interactions among workgroup members (Chapter 3):

- Six inclusive interaction practices are presented that foster inclusive interactions to produce equity and high performance:
  1. Pursuing a shared task orientation or mission,
  2. Mixing the members frequently and repeatedly,
  3. Collaborating with member interdependence,
  4. Handling conflict constructively,
  5. Engaging in interpersonal comfort and self-efficacy, and
  6. Ensuring equal insider status for all members.
- Practices 1–4 foster and support Practices 5 and 6, which we consider fundamental to inclusion—all practices achieved in terms of actual behaviors.
- Adoption of any individual practice does not ensure inclusion.
- The implementation of the six practices combined with practices that hold members responsible for their inclusive behavior acts to strengthen frequent, meaningful inclusive interactions while subduing anti-inclusive forces.

DOI: 10.4324/9780367822484-13

Social forces create barriers to inclusion in societies and organizations, producing high costs (Chapter 4):

- Individuals' tendencies to interact with familiar others leads to distancing from dissimilar others, even in integrated settings (self-segregation).
- Individuals experience communication anxieties when they interact with dissimilar others. Proximity often leads to tensions rather than understandings (interaction discomfort).
- Stigmatizing, disgracing members of another group as incompetent and cold, is triggered when organizational initiatives are perceived as strongly favoring that group (stereotype content).
- Stigmatizing reduces the performance of members of underrepresented groups, creating a self-fulfilling prophecy (stereotype threat).
- Implicit bias, negative stereotypes held largely unconsciously, is ubiquitous in society and produces discriminatory effects at least as great as overt discrimination.
- These exclusionary forces reinforce each other. They threaten organizational diversity initiatives and create high costs for organizations and individuals, leading to discriminatory treatment of organizational clients, such as health care patients, and according to estimates based on research findings, half a million flawed hiring decisions per year in the United States on the basis of gender alone.

Social forces of exclusion are not counteracted by some dominant diversity initiatives but are by intentional inclusive interaction practices, accountability and transparency efforts, and by particular non-diversity initiatives that focus on performance improvement (Chapter 5):

- Direct attitude-change initiatives, such as sensitivity training, are largely ineffective and sometimes harmful.
- Behavior-change efforts are more successful. The effects of implicit bias on behavior can be counteracted by making decision-makers accountable for their decisions and by individuals learning and applying validated decision-making practices.
- Whether workgroup diversity leads to higher or lower workgroup performance depends on organizational conditions that influence social integration across members, anxiety reduction, and the inclusion of diverse perspectives that result in the elaboration of information used to make better decisions (categorization-elaboration model).
- There is largely untapped potential in the form of organizational programs that are not diversity-intended but that promote inclusion through cross-functional collaboration. Unlike mandatory attitude training programs, these produce improved job outcomes for women and underrepresented group members.

- Global teams for agile software development, an example of semi-autonomous teams operating on the basis of inclusion and pursued for performance improvement, demonstrate the practicality of achieving performance from diversity through inclusive practices such as a daily "huddle."

Achieving sustained benefits from diversity and inclusion requires prolonged intergroup contact that is fostered by practices that shape workgroup members' behavior (Chapter 6):

- Through interacting with dissimilar others over prolonged periods of time, individuals engage in cognitive, adaptive learning that reduces prejudices and increases their intergroup skills and broader personal development, including leadership skills.
- Particular sets of practices produce greater adaptive learning—equal status among members, pursuit of common goals, intergroup cooperation, and support from authorities (intergroup contact theory).
- Spending time together and engaging in conversations involving self-disclosure leads to higher levels of adaptive learning.
- Adaptive learning at the level of a workgroup means that group members routinely, habitually engage in behavioral practices that involve the inclusion of dissimilar others, as through developing and following rules about when and how to use different languages in a multinational organization (practice theory).
- Formal socialization practices for new members enable enculturation into the workgroup's practices. Personalized socialization enables diverse members to be behaviorally enculturated but not assimilated, expressing their authentic selves to provide diverse perspectives and skills valuable to the group.

Accountability practices can increase the equity of rewards received by underrepresented group members and monitor behavior for inclusive engagement (Chapter 7):

- Accountability counteracts the implicit bias that results in flawed personnel decisions that negatively impact women and members of underrepresented groups.
- The major cause of inequities in rewards for women does not appear to be due to lower performance evaluations but, rather, to the flawed translation of those evaluations into rewards, because implicit bias and stereotyping are ubiquitous.
- Accountability and transparency practices are needed to reduce the subjectivity in translating performance evaluations into rewards.
- Currently, espoused performance-management systems that claim to be meritocratic do not eliminate inequities. Paradoxically, they provide cover for the continuation of inequities.
- Accountability practices check for meritocracy and counter subjectivity by holding managers responsible for how they make reward decisions.

- Transparency practices in the form of reports make clear where and when disparities occur.
- Accountability and transparency practices concerning inclusive behavior are similarly essential to sustain equity and performance.

Achieving sustainable inclusion comes from adaptive learning as a result of experiencing repeated, inclusive interactions and from equitable merit and accountability practices. This results in optimizing of performance benefits for individuals and their organizations (Chapter 8):

- Research- and practice-based evidence demonstrate that the crowding of members of underrepresented groups into lower-status jobs leads to stereotyping and stigmatizing them as less competent. Negative stereotypes represent self-fulfilling prophecies that lead in a number of ways to lower performance and reduced rewards for underrepresented groups.
- Unsustainable diversity results when inclusive practices are not enacted. Talented individuals leave, while performance is limited by tensions that inhibit teamwork and devalue members' expertise.
- Achieving equity requires that the barriers of stigmatizing are addressed and overcome, including through deliberate recruiting strategies and cross-job contact.
- Optimization of performance entails overcoming the effects of implicit bias, stereotyping, and stigmatizing on flawed hiring, development and advancement decisions, and the departure of talented individuals. Strong performance comes from raising the convergence among workgroup members while not submerging valuable differences.
- Skill development and adaptive learning results from encountering individuals different from oneself, experiencing cognitive discomfort that is gradually overcome by familiarity from repeated, positive interactions.
- Establishing an inclusive culture within the organization and its workgroups means managing for repeated inclusive interactions among members.
- Sustainable inclusion enables equity for all individuals, higher workgroup performance, a creative tension that energizes and motivates individuals, organizational adaptation to diverse market environments, and allocation of human capital that maximizes individual contributions through ongoing adaptive learning.

PART III OVERVIEW

Achieving sustainable inclusion: Multilevel outcomes

Many societies and organizations have been experiencing sustained disparities and inequities rather than a sustainable inclusion that is based on the inclusion of all members. In the following section, we draw on our evidence-based framework and additional research-based evidence to specify outcomes resulting from diversity sustained by inclusion. However, given the past history, it is first important to understand the particular nature of the challenges involved. Why have so many organizations found it difficult to achieve beneficial outcomes of equity and performance from diversity? Why have large employment inequities persisted over time? What role do organizational processes play in *reproducing* these inequities in particular organizations and in the larger society? Understanding these questions, and the answers to them provided by research findings presented in the preceding chapters, can lead managers to understand why particular practices are required to curb this reproduction and improve organizational functioning. The practices lead to allocating human capital in ways that produce greater equity and higher workgroup and organizational performance.

Inequities and opportunity costs are large and persistent. In the United States, how can it be that these problems persist half a century after the passage of equal employment opportunity legislation? For instance, as noted in this book's Introduction chapter, the portions of the male–female and Black–White wage gaps that are not explained by rational economic factors such as education have been growing, not shrinking, for three decades. And estimates based on evidence from a large body of research indicate that gender disparities in hiring in a single year lead to one million more men than women hires among equally qualified candidates. The disparities for some underrepresented groups are yet worse than for women, with the employment status of Black men no better in the twenty-first century than in the middle of the last century, prior to civil rights legislation.

DOI: 10.4324/9780367822484-14

In the Preface, we identified a dysfunctional relationship between academics—both researchers and educators—and managers as one contributor to the reproduction of inequities and lost performance. For example, we educators taught the importance of fair employment practices and training, relying on theory rather than empirical evidence to propose, rather simplistically, that these would ensure equitable and effective use of human talent. Meanwhile, researchers in particular academic disciplines were producing valuable findings but failing to connect them to those of researchers in other disciplines or to managerial practice. Another contributor to the reproduction of disparities has been organizational reliance on particular diversity practices, such as types of mandatory awareness training, that are legitimized by the judicial system and providers but that frequently produce backlash effects.

However, the most powerful contributor to the reproduction of inequities and lost performance may be complacency rooted in beliefs that societal change was on the right track. With a general feeling among dominant group members and organizational and institutional leaders that our advanced societies were doing what was necessary, progress could be seen as slow but steady, not as plateaued or regressing. And rationalizations for the slow progress were plentiful: Over the period of a few generations, members of underrepresented groups would gradually be advanced into higher and higher positions in organizations, so patience was required. And, with meritocratic systems in education and employment, if a particular group remained underrepresented, it must be because its members did not perform well enough or were not suited to higher-level positions. And, since occupational segregation persisted, it must be that members of some groups preferred to be in particular occupations—such as home care rather than engineering, or human resource management rather than line management—and in job levels—such as clerical rather than managerial—that pay less rather than in higher-status, higher-paying ones.

In contrast to these rationalizing explanations, evidence accumulated over the past several decades and reviewed in the preceding chapters tells us that inequities and lost performance have continued to be reproduced by everyday practices in organizations and labor markets. Even as many organizations pursued representational diversity with particular diversity efforts, anti-inclusive practices and discrimination in personnel decisions continued to exist. Meritocratic practices did not reach into managers' final personnel decisions, and accountability for those decisions was lacking. Consequently, subtle discrimination in the form of managers' hiring and advancement decisions based on implicit, largely subconscious bias produced inequitable effects as strong or stronger than overt discrimination. Diverse organizational members were adversely affected not only by such biased decisions but also from being stereotyped and stigmatized, from being the recipients of others' biased behavior. This stereotype threat and its associated aggressions led to lowered self-confidence and lower evaluations of performance by themselves and by others. The ubiquitous phenomenon of self-segregation, of people preferring to associate with similar others with whom they feel most comfortable, further hampered diverse individuals' contributions by excluding them from key processes and decision-making.

Evidence, then, leads to a more realistic view of the reproduction of inequities and misallocation of human capital over the decades, reproduction that can be understood as a vicious cycle:

1. As a result of being crowded into lower-status jobs, members of underrepresented groups find that their low status leads others to stereotype and stigmatize them as having low competence.
2. Organizational practices and regulations designed to remedy low status are interpreted by dominant group members as favoring others, creating competitive emotions which stimulate stereotyping and stigmatizing of underrepresented individuals as low in warmth and difficult to work with.
3. The negative stereotype of low competence and low capability leads underrepresented group members to feel stigmatized, thus lowering their performance. The bias of low warmth and low competence inhibits the frequency and quality of interactions with diverse individuals, dampening opportunities for those individuals to contribute.
4. Managers' personnel decisions, when impacted by implicit bias, results in less hiring, developing, and promoting of individuals from underrepresented groups into more advanced positions, thereby reproducing the low status of (1) above and the need for continuing the inclusive interaction practices of (2).
5. The continuing reproduction of inequities creates disincentives for those from underrepresented groups to invest in education and job-related development. The low wealth resulting from low economic status impedes their ability to make such investments, further sustaining their low occupational status.

The causes of continuing inequities, then, are multiple and tend to reinforce each other. However, the evidence presented in the preceding chapters indicates that frequent, positive diversity interactions and inclusive practices that facilitate adaptive learning among members and hold managers accountable for their personnel decisions are powerful and interrupt the dynamics that sustain inequities and restricted performance. Organizations and managers that implement and evolve particular practices—for inclusive interactions and for accountability—can reproduce diversity and inclusion rather than sustained dysfunctions. Sustainable inclusion means a workplace in which talents are utilized impartially and effectively, and implicit bias is controlled, particularly with respect to personnel decision-making. With sustainable inclusion, diverse members—such as women in STEM careers—have proper incentives to remain and invest themselves in an organization and occupation that uses their skills and knowledge,

Chapter 9 (Case examples: Practices for inclusive actions and accountability) presents eleven organizational cases. These differing cases illustrate the ways in which particular organizations have pursued inclusion, with varying degrees of success. The more successful cases demonstrate the feasibility of achieving sustainable inclusion through practices for inclusive interaction and accountable behavior. The book concludes with Chapter 10 (Performance through diversity and inclusion: Leveraging organizational practices for equity and results), which presents challenges, opportunities, and options for implementing the structured inclusive interaction practices as a means for achieving sustainable inclusion—optimizing performance, equity, and results.

9
CASE EXAMPLES
Practices for inclusive actions and accountability

This chapter presents case examples of workgroups and organizations that have implemented some or all of the inclusive interaction practices specified in this book's Framework for Inclusive Interactions (Chapter 2). Whereas Chapter 3 presented each practice separately, here, we look organization by organization at the combination of practices used, highlighting the opportunities for instituting the six inclusive interaction practices and holding members accountable for inclusive behavior. The cases are from a variety of organizations and, through comparing and contrasting, they show how inclusion is achieved:

> at different levels of organizations,
> to different degrees,
> and with the six inclusive practices taking different forms.

The range of contexts covered by the cases aids in applying this book's research-based evidence to a particular organization. Since research findings are often general, drawn across many organizations, or sometimes based on a single organization, informed managers and researchers can feel: "The finding on that program or practice won't work in my organization because we are different." Indeed, the reality is that each organization has a distinctive history and current situation, and so can benefit from customizing any new practice. The cases aid such custom design efforts by presenting variations in the forms that inclusion and accountability practices have taken in a number of different organizations. Some of the practices originate at the organizational level, while others are at the workgroup level. In addition to the Framework's practices for inclusion and accountability, the case examples draw on other themes and concepts covered in the preceding chapters, such as cross-functional collaboration, stereotype threat, and justifying inclusive practices on the

DOI: 10.4324/9780367822484-15

basis of performance. Each case is critiqued in order to identify criteria useful in designing diversity efforts.

A key issue facing organizations is whether or not to pursue a bundle of practices at one time. As noted in Chapter 6, research on contact theory indicates at one and the same time that not all of its conditions—practices, in terms of our Framework—are necessary to produce prejudice reduction, but the strongest reductions occur when they are found together. Since achieving inclusion depends on the entanglement of a number of practices, and since organizations can expect anti-inclusive practices to be present, at a minimum in subtle forms, the more complete the bundle of practices favoring inclusion, the better. Organizational experiences with other programs of organizational change, such as quality management through ISO 9000 or rapid software development through agile teams, suggest that a performance-oriented program of practices is best pursued as a whole, as a logically consistent package of practices. The proviso is that all such programs inevitably allow for local variation to fit a particular organization, but with the logic of the whole program guiding that variation.

Certainly, the full set of practices should be pursued over time. Due to factors such as the implementers' span of control in the organization, implementation of all the specified practices at one time might or might not prove difficult. Moving forward with several of the practices can be beneficial in tipping the balance toward inclusion, performance, and equity and, as several of the cases indicate, in identifying challenges that need to be overcome with further implementation. Among the cases, those that achieved the full set of practices indicate that prejudice reduction and adaptive learning follow from repeated meaningful, positive interactions and lead over time to sustainable inclusion and enhanced performance outcomes. (See Box 9.1.)

BOX 9.1: LESSONS LEARNED FROM THE PRESENTED CASES

Overall, the cases lead to several conclusions regarding issues raised in the preceding chapters:

- Inclusion is, most fundamentally, about behavior and decisions shaped by organizational and workgroup practices, with inclusive practices operating within each workgroup or team, and accountability practices operating across the organization.
- For organizational-level change where anti-inclusive practices have been historically dominant, diverse representation is only the first step.
- Tying inclusion to mission performance facilitates and sustains inclusion.
- Once achieved, inclusive practices in workgroups tend to reproduce inclusive behavior among new members.

- Top management support is valuable but not essential to achieving inclusion at the workgroup level.
- Potent opportunities exist for managers to achieve inclusion in their workgroups.
- Organization-wide inclusion is sustained with everyday resources and occasional enforcement that convey a commitment to inclusive engagement and keep individuals accountable for their behavior.

We start with a set of five cases that clarify what inclusion looks like when it is achieved at a high level through effective practices and, in contrast, how some organizations struggle to achieve even a modest level of inclusion. We then analyze three cases of inclusion at the level of workgroups, where success was achieved through practices put in place by the workgroup's managers. A final set of three cases then deals with larger-scale organization-wide inclusion. Within each of these three sets of cases, we contrast greater with lesser success to understand the challenges and the role of practices in producing differing types and degrees of success with inclusion. Within each set, we end with the case that, we believe, best illustrates the achievement possible in a commonly-found type of organization.

Set 1: Achieving inclusion

Al-Anon: Socializing into practices for high inclusion

The nature of inclusion is illustrated well by Al-Anon, a faith-based organization that serves individuals having family or friends suffering from alcoholism. Unlike its partner organization, Alcoholics Anonymous, it is not predicated on members adhering to a belief in God. While many religious organizations lack diversity in representation, Al-Anon is intentional in serving a diverse group of clients or members. It is spiritual in nature but is explicit in welcoming all who show up to its meetings. The case here concerns chapters that are demographically diverse and that exemplify achieving a high degree of inclusion.

"If only the whole world could act this way," said Allison, a long-time member of two Al-Anon groups. Al-Anon is an example of an organization that uses an inclusive socialization process to honor member differences, enable psychological adjustment, and establish group norms. Allison and her fellow group members frequently make the above statement, reflecting their awareness of the high-functioning meetings. "Yes, for sure," Allison said, in regard to whether or not her Al-Anon meetings used the six structured inclusive interaction practices. As a longtime member, Allison highlighted how new members are welcomed and enculturated into the groups in a way that respects differences while encouraging the continuance and evolution of inclusive practices. The Al-Anon group practices include the strongly shared mission, mixing of the group members frequently by sitting facing one another, meeting weekly, rotating leadership of the meetings ensuring everyone has equal status within the group, and conflict handling processes. Everyone who shows up is welcomed and made comfortable. Established norms dictate that at the beginning of each meeting, the Serenity Prayer is read, new members are welcomed, and introductions are made followed by a review of the meeting "rules." The rules state "no cross-talk, no judgment, no double-dipping (speaking again before everyone else has had an opportunity to speak), and no advice, just support." It is expected that everyone will take a turn as team leader in order to foster participation, which is considered key to harmony. Al-Anon is an organization where the use of structured inclusive interaction practices has fostered inclusive socialization processes that facilitate enculturation into the groups, setting up a virtuous cycle that reinforces the inclusive culture of these groups.

Nonprofit boards of directors: Progressing from diversity to inclusion

Historically, many nonprofit boards have been club-like in their functioning, and as with boards of directors in business organizations, they have lacked diversity. As some nonprofit boards have committed to becoming more diverse, they have struggled with achieving inclusive engagement for new diverse members, despite the advantage of congruence with the first inclusive practice specified in our Framework—shared purpose. Nonprofit organizations have an obligation to serve a large variety of stakeholders including clients, employees, and community. Above all else, nonprofits are mission-focused organizations with board members and often the staff, sharing this passion for the mission. To best serve the stakeholders, boards seek to effectively and efficiently accomplish their responsibilities to guide the organization.

As seen in Box 9.2, nonprofit boards need to make strides in representational diversity. Nonprofits that are pursuing diversity "agree that it is important to incorporate diversity and inclusion into the organization's core values"[1] to signal their stakeholders that the board has thought about what diversity means to the organization and why it is important to their mission. Empirical studies have demonstrated that board diversity, in combination with inclusive behaviors and practices, improves board and organizational performance.[2] However, if diversity is perceived only as representation, whether for the organization as a whole or the board, it will not be central to mission-attainment. When the board's practices are inclusive—sharing power, gearing communications toward all, and treating all members equally—members of color report that they do feel included.[3]

BOX 9.2: NONPROFIT LEADERSHIP DIVERSITY

- Boards are 82 percent White, 52 percent male, and tend toward older members with those less than 40 years old representing 17 percent of board composition.

- CEOs are 90 percent White, 72 percent female, and 56 percent are 50–64 years old.
- Board chairs are also 90 percent White, 58 percent male, and 43 percent are 50–64 years old.

Source: BoardSource. (2017). Leading with intent: 2017 national index of non-profit board practices. https://leadingwithintent.org/wp-content/uploads/2017/11/LWI-2017.pdf

The structure and functioning of nonprofit boards create an ideal opportunity for implementing the practices and accountability measures proposed in the Framework for Inclusive Interactions.

The practice of *collaborating with member interdependence* is essential for board function as members are charged with both individual and collective roles and responsibilities. When joining a board, new members typically are made aware of what is expected of them in terms of fundraising, community outreach, meeting preparation, attendance at organizational functions, committee responsibilities, and recruiting new board members. During meetings of the board, the members make strategic decisions, provide oversight, and keep the focus on achieving the mission. Therefore, nonprofit board members need to be trusted to work independently and collectively for the good of the organization. During discussions, particularly in advance of a vote, hearing all voices and perspectives enriches the members' ability to vote wisely and prudently.

Because many nonprofits have missions involving equity for some populations, diversity and inclusion are issues for both internal and external functioning. This is becoming increasingly true for business and governmental units as well. A unique challenge associated with nonprofit organizations and their boards is the significance of understanding broader societal racial issues. Nora, the lawyer and nonprofit diversity, equity, and inclusion consultant, highlighted the need for "understanding White dominant culture and its impact on others, usually people of color because of the type of work nonprofits, in particular social sector organizations, are engaged in, such as educational, health, and housing dispar-ities. These organizations' performance is dependent on an understanding of root causes of the problems they are trying to address in their mission." To successfully address this, Nora sees this as "both mission education, self-education and mix of these with the education occurring at both the organization and self-levels." A commitment to diversity, "needs to be driven from the organizational level and permeate all discussions." This provides an opportunity for individual board members to challenge their pre-existing stereotypes as they strive to achieve the nonprofit's mission. Nora spoke of the need to be "authentic" recognizing that people learn to act differently, or appropriately, in different contexts, and that one's "authentic self" exists at the intersection of their differing identities where they are able to express their talents in a particular situation. To achieve this, "patience or a willingness to listen and learn and really hear about other's experiences" is necessary.

> "What does equity for *all* look like in this organization? Commitment to equity means *not* doing business as usual... By being inclusive, the cost-benefit is beyond money, it is moral and provides the organization with credibility." (Nora)

Nonprofit boards have the opportunity to mix members frequently and repeatedly due to frequent meetings and attendance at organizational activities. With monthly meetings, Nora observes that "the quality of the interactions and discussions are more genuine. Time together allows for quality and depth of the interactions. Over time, deeper conversations emerge where the board members can try to figure out what is the real issue and engage in self-education, as opposed to training to see a shift in the conversations and interactions." Education provides the members with a willingness to use a different lens when examining problems, enabling better outcomes to emerge in keeping with the categorization-elaboration model (Chapter 5). Nora feels successful when a board asks themselves, "What is the work we are committed to doing together and how do we dig a little deeper and push against the status quo?" Referencing a board Nora is currently sitting on, she said, "This enables the board to constantly discuss equity and have frank conversations about where we need to change" and ask, "How do we do the work?" (See Box 9.3 for an example of how to integrate diversity work into board operations.)

BOX 9.3: CHECKING THE BOX—NOT!

"Boards say that they want to be diverse, but often they truly just want to check the box on the board matrix and not do the hard work," said Nora. These boards just want me to "give them tactics or tools and then are good." But "tools are not enough. Inclusion is an on-going, long-term commitment and must be included in all aspects of the board's work." For example, Nora says she commonly hears that things are "binary" meaning that the board will say, "we can do strategic planning or diversity work, or a capital campaign or diversity work." Her response is that diversity, equity, and inclusion should be part of all discussions, and it must be driven at the organizational level."

Given the tremendous fiduciary responsibilities of governing members of nonprofit organizations, *granting equal insider status to all members* allows for everyone to contribute to organizational success. Because of the standard that all members have one equal vote, it would appear that boards operate, by default, with equal standing for all members. However, ensuring equal status means that everyone is able to participate fully in discussions and decisions. Consistent with information elaboration (Chapter 5), it is important to value diverse members for their contributing perspectives and approaches. To increase the experience of board members of color, the majority board members must engage in inclusive behaviors, including discontinuing offensive jokes or comments, ensuring power is shared, making communications accessible to all and ensuring inclusivity is discussed and acted upon.[4] Otherwise, equal insider status and interpersonal comfort will not be achieved.

> "DEI takes work, intentionality, commitment, but it is not rocket science. We can fix this, and we can solve this." (Nora)

Nonprofit boards of directors must adhere to the Duty of Obedience, which obligates the board members to follow all laws, including the by-laws. These governing documents provide the board with guidance on how to conduct votes and, when necessary, to remove board members for a variety of causes. The practice of *handling conflict constructively* is often made easier by having the guidance found in the by-laws. However, in terms of individual interactions, this is often not enough. According to Nora, most importantly, members need to "accept and learn when you have offended others. You must address the elephants in the room. There will be obstacles, challenges, and possibly even barriers," such as those board members who will claim that diversifying the board will have a negative impact on decision-making, fund-raising, board recruiting, and other duties. The boards need to recognize that challenges will come, but they "can be addressed in a deeper way if there is a commitment to equity for all, even if it takes more time and resources."

> "This takes time, you must be in it for the long haul." (Nora)

A challenge for boards is that, in contrast to most organizational workgroups, their members interact relatively infrequently. The practice of *engaging in interpersonal comfort and self-efficacy* often takes time to develop, as new members build trust, overcome the fear and insecurities they may feel, and become acculturated into the norms of the workgroup. Quite a number of a board's regular, periodic meetings may be required, meetings in which strong, positive interactions with diverse others occur in an environment where the members feel respected for their opinions and experience, building interpersonal comfort and self-efficacy. Changing behaviors in order to move from discomfort with their interactions with diverse others to feeling comfortable with all the board members comes only as a result of having "authentic relationships with different others," said Nora.

A board's responsibility for diversity and inclusion requires that it is accountable for its selection of new members. When shared negative stereotypes reside in members' implicit biases, selection decisions can disfavor members of underrepresented groups or lead to the selection of members of these groups who are most similar to existing members rather than those whose talents and resources would best contribute to effective board decisions. As indicated in Box 9.4, and consistent with research indicating the value of making decision-makers more conscious of the basis for their decisions (Chapter 5), formal procedures ensuring proper discussion of selection criteria can aid boards in making valid selection decisions.

BOX 9.4: BOARD RECRUITING

The focus should be on "hiring for skill sets we do not have, which is different than recruiting for how we get along with one another." According to Nora, "management and boards fail at this." She often hears board members (and others doing new board member recruiting) using the word "fit" when evaluating someone, but this is frequently code for someone who does not belong because they are different. Boards often seek members for their diversity, including age, geography, race, ethnicity, skills, knowledge, and experience. To maintain this diversity, boards can conduct a board audit prior to searching for new members. This keeps the board accountable for their commitment to diversity and limits individual biases from influencing recruitment.

To sum up, nonprofit boards often struggle to achieve both representational diversity and inclusion. Many cases will necessitate intentional efforts to move beyond representation to inclusive practices, and then time for those practices to become embedded and produce benefits for the organization's mission attainment.

Girl Scouts of the United States of America (GSUSA): Diversity and occasional inclusion

As a national organization, the Girl Scouts of the United States of America was an early pursuer of diversity, starting in the 1990s as part of a goal to increase its membership. As a pioneering organization seeking to achieve "pluralistic diversity," we focused on it in our own research.[5] GSUSA made significant strides toward representational diversity at the aggregated level of its geographically defined councils, but often lacked ethnic diversity at the more localized level of its troops. We found that the organization's members, both adult volunteers and young girls, routinely and periodically engaged in situations, particularly inter-troop get-togethers, that provided opportunities for inclusion in direct interactions. Some inter-troop activities structured interactions, such as jump-rope competitions, that mixed the troops in ways that provided *equal status to all members*. During the inter-troop activities, the girls, regardless of which troop they belonged to, were of equal standing. The activities and the values they represented were common and comfortable for all the organization's members. When combined with a shared commitment to the *organization's purpose* of youth development, the activities resulted in temporarily activating the common in-group identity of Girl Scouts in addition to their primary social identity group differences. The common identity represented *insider status* for all, insiders committed to the same values and familiar with the developmental activities. Girl Scout staff reported that, during the shared activities, the girls tended to forget their differences and went from "us and them" to "we." Girls with less experience in the organization and with less equal standing failed to achieve that common identity and insider status.

In the terms of our Framework, the girls' diversity interactions produced inclusion in the short term, but the activities were not sufficiently widespread and frequent. The multi-troop gatherings were only occasional, and in many of those meetings, most troops did not engage with other troops unless particular programming practices were followed, and even then, that inclusion was only brief. The insider-status practices for inclusion produced useful developmental experiences, but many more such opportunities could have been structured.

Leadership fellowship: Reproducing high inclusion

Many communities have leadership training programs designed to reinforce the concept of informed and committed civic volunteerism by training a new and continuing source of future leaders. These programs are cohort-based and, in the case of the leadership fellowship, a program of a large nonprofit foundation in the Pacific Northwest. According to its website, this leadership program has a *stated purpose* to engage grassroots leaders interested in expanding their skills, broadening their networks, and exchanging perspectives with other local leaders. This particular leadership program assembles members from underrepresented groups, including persons of color, those from vulnerable backgrounds, or protected classes, such as veterans, and is grounded in a curriculum of self-awareness, community engagement, and social/racial equity. The cohort described here was composed of 13 members that met twice monthly and included meetings with local leaders across the sectors, field trips, retreats, and other formal sessions over 18 months, satisfying the practice of *mixing the members frequently and repeatedly.*

During their initial meetings, the leadership fellowship drafted community agreements that addressed conflict management, respect, what group behaviors will or will not be tolerated, and a voting process. These agreements laid the groundwork for how the fellowship will interact and maintain respect and integrity. For this particular cohort, one of the agreements stated that "all voices will be heard," which enables *equal insider status for all members*. The process of creating the agreements enabled the members to *collaborate together,* build trust and ultimately, address *conflicts,* as they arose, *constructively.*

"It took longer than I thought it would, several months for the group to over-come fear and become open with one another," said Phillip, the cohort member we interviewed. As Nora noted for nonprofit boards, Phillip said that authenti-city was an issue. He attributed "the fear and discomfort of speaking authentically [as] the biggest issue inhibiting interactions and growth." Phillip attributed this to the overwhelming fear of being 100 percent honest. For himself, he said, it took about six months to feel enough trust and comfort to speak about difficult subjects, including race, with others in the group because he was afraid of saying the wrong thing. The repetitions of interactions enabled Phillip to engage in what he referred to as "authentic personal time," where he was able to talk about things other than race and create individual bonds within the group. The leadership fellowship structured "bonding moments" and weekend retreats to foster "authentic personal time" where members could talk outside the structured meetings. These informal interactions allowed for members to learn to value the others in the group for their unique traits and to build the comfort needed to overcome the initial "fear" and, as Phillip said, "Learning how ignorant you are." Facilitating such interactions were group norms and practices. For example, prior to each meeting, the members take a five-minute silent, meditative walk with a different team member, followed by five minutes of sharing with the walking partner their meditative thoughts. For his personal growth, he often just had to stop talking and listen to others, "listening in order to understand, instead of listening in order to respond." Yet, he knew this was not enough; he had to talk to learn in order to "deeply challenge his existing ideas and search for the truth." This led him to conclude that he "needed to question everything."

> The leadership fellowship demonstrates the value of informal interactions to build comfort and trust.

Phillip repeatedly emphasized how the structure of the fellowship builds trust, without which "it would have taken so much more time to get where we are. People needed to leap off a cliff into a trust pool. Without trust, we may never speak with one another. Trust enables one to endure harm." These statements illus-trate the significance of the practice of *engaging in interpersonal comfort and self-efficacy* for inclusive interactions. Though it took the fellowship about six months to achieve the trust necessary to open up and learn from one another, Phillip felt once there was trust established, he was able to "come with imperfections and be accepted and loved." The fellowship is an example of a group that comprehended the power of behavior coming before adaptive emotional learning. The initial for-mation of the community agreements created behavioral expectations. However, it was only after the six months of being together that trust was built and a sense of comfort achieved so that the interactions changed from superficial to inclusive, "when we became comfortable enough to call something out, we knew the person wanted to learn and change." Adaptive learning followed. In this example, the leadership fellowship had a strong shared purpose or mission, met frequently and repeatedly, created the community agreements to ensure that all members were granted equal status and to determine how they would navigate conflict, and finally, came to value one another for each member's uniqueness as trust was built and the members exhibited interpersonal comfort and self-efficacy. The result of group norms and inclusive practices was adaptive learning and sustainable inclusion.

This example is not unique to this particular cohort as each new cohort works from the outset to create the community agreements and mature together as a group. The potential disadvantage to the cohort model—a model that parallels the creation of a new task force in an organization—is that there are no existing members, as in Al-Anon, to help with acculturation to the group norms and behaviors. Nevertheless, like Al-Anon, a high level of inclusion was achieved. The values and practices embedded in the leadership fellowship organization as a whole reproduced inclusion at this high level for each new cohort. Chapter 10 presents a detailed case on a newly formed task force achieving inclusion in an organization that lacked the pre-existing organizational practices found in the leadership fellowship.

Coed service fraternity: Reducing prejudice through inclusive practices

The increased representational diversity on higher-education campuses, combined with institutional policies that have focused on formal educational activities such as diversity and awareness training and multiculturalism classes, has not produced widespread inclusive interactions.[6] This likely reinforced the competitive perspective of some majority group members, resulting in limited or even negative interactions. Additionally, students who joined homogeneous ethnic/cultural social groups and co-curricular organizations were found to have lower proportions of diversity in their friendship networks.[7] Empirical research indicates that, despite the increased opportunity for cross-cultural contact[8] that comes with representational diversity, actual cross-cultural interactions on campus are typically superficial.[9] Countering the superficiality of typical campus interactions, and consistent with intergroup contact theory, some extra-curricular activities provide an opportunity for cross-group friendships, which are a particularly significant contributor to positive contact and prejudice reduction (Chapter 6). While many campus associations are ethnically and gender homogeneous, including most Greek societies, various types of co-curricular college associations, ones created for purposes unrelated to surface-level similarity, present favorable conditions for close heterogeneous association.

The coed service fraternity was promoted not for its diversity but as a mission-based organization. By pursuing its goals of fellowship, leadership, and community service, it had developed practices that fit those in our Framework and saw performance benefits and individual skill development. Its practices resulted in inclusive interactions among the members, regardless of their backgrounds. First introduced in Chapter 3, the service fraternity is a national organization with thousands of student members performing community service in chapters on hundreds of U.S. campuses. We studied the service fraternity on two campuses in different regions of the United States.[10] The fraternity's *shared purpose* is to develop leadership, promote fellowship, and provide service. This shared purpose attracts a diverse membership who desire to engage in community service. Each week students are encouraged to attend an organizational meeting, a community service activity, and a fellowship or social event. Participating in the organizational activities alongside a variety of members provided multiple opportunities to *mix with one another frequently and repeatedly*. The emphasis on fellowship was perpetuated by inclusive interaction practices that over time encouraged self-disclosure while performing service or socializing together.

For purposes of mission attainment, rather than diversity, the service fraternity had established norms and traditions that contributed to developing a welcoming environment for diverse individuals and assisted members in getting to know one another. The socialization activities included the requirement for each new member to interview all existing members. Students reported these programmatic norms reduced interaction anxieties and supported the organization's fellowship ethic while fostering interpersonal comfort. Members signed up for their service activities using means that produced continually differing groupings from one week to the next, contributing to the members *mixing*. *Collaborating* at service activities and weekly organizational meetings sustained Crisp and Turner's[11] adaptive cognitive processing conditions of individuals being motivated and able to interact repeatedly. This fraternity, whose stated goals did not include diversity nor intercultural learning, found members reporting positive, inclusive interactions there, which they contrasted with their superficial diversity interactions outside of the fraternity. In fact, the organization's national director was surprised to learn that the individual chapters were fostering meaningful diversity interactions and intercultural relationships.

The practice of *ensuring equal insider status to all members* of the service fraternity was supported through another element of the organization's mission, leadership development. Leadership positions rotated every term, with no member running for a leadership position twice until all members had the opportunity to be leaders. As a result, no one group became dominant and cliques were actively discouraged. According to the students, the welcoming climate and the frequent, repeated interactions led to interpersonal comfort with diverse others. Taken together, the fraternity's inclusive interaction practices produced a shared mission and a common in-group identity in addition to members' other identities. Members reported changed interethnic attitudes, enhanced skill development, and a comfortable environment for expressing divergent opinions.

Adaptive learning was expressed by a White male student in personal terms: *"There are a couple of instances where because of people's backgrounds I thought they were going to be like sort of ignorant. And then I, in turn, was actually the ignorant one."*

> This organization met all the practices for inclusive interaction, producing meaningful interpersonal relationships, and changing prejudiced attitudes.

Lessons from Set 1

The five cases in this set all concern voluntary organizations where individuals may join for limited periods. They can readily cease their voluntary engagement when uncomfortable or dissatisfied with their experiences. Thus, there is an incentive for the organizations to create welcoming, satisfying cultures through inclusive practices oriented around their missions. Several of the cases show that inclusion can be established and sustained over long periods, with new members and even entirely new cohorts being socialized into inclusive practices. The more successful cases—Al-Anon, leadership fellowship, and service fraternity—demonstrate the value of the entire bundle of six practices. They also demonstrate that the exact nature of a practice can differ according to organizational mission, values, and context. For instance, mixing members frequently and repeatedly was achieved through the virtually random assignment of members to work on service projects in the service fraternity and could have been achieved through more frequent and properly structured activities in the inter-troop meetings of the Girl Scouts. Managers can design the best options for achieving the Framework's six practices in ways that fit the characteristics of their particular organizations.

Voluntary organizations have the advantage that many of their members join due to a shared commitment to a particular mission. In Al-Anon, leadership fellowship, and service fraternity, inclusive practices flowed from the mission and its associated values, such as fellowship and mutual personal development. In such cases, there appeared to be little need for practices of accountability. Tying inclusion to mission and values was sufficient to facilitate and reproduce inclusion over time. Inclusion occurred organically, as a natural part of the processes for attaining the mission.

Set 2: Creating inclusion in workgroups

In organizations where individuals typically join more for employment and less for mission than in voluntary organizations, how is inclusion achieved? In this set of cases, we concentrate on workgroups and the practices that managers establish in them. A large body of evidence (Chapter 5) and common experience tell us that diversity in workgroups and teams produces differences and tensions that can lead to dysfunction or improved performance, depending on the practices followed in the workgroup. As a consequence, the practices fostered by workgroup managers can make or break successful outcomes from diversity.

International joint ventures: Coping with differences

In Chapter 1, Box 1.2, we presented a comparison of three American and Japanese international joint ventures,[12] which demonstrated that having opportunities for mixing members with differing identities is insufficient to benefit from diversity, but that additional, inclusive interaction practices can make a dramatic difference in achieving success.

Recall that all three joint ventures—JVA, JVB, and JVC—started with the advantage of the first two structured inclusive interaction practices (pursuing a shared task orientation or mission and mixing members frequently and repeatedly). JVA and JVB, unlike JVC, experienced significant cross-cultural tensions that enhanced American engineers' and technicians' stereotypes of their Japanese counterparts as sometimes untrustworthy and less competent. As a result, knowledge sharing was impeded, negatively impacting decision-making and learning.

In JVC, the American personnel did not report the same level of tension, noting that such stereotyping did not accurately characterize their Japanese counterparts. What differentiated JVC from JVA and JVB was the enactment of two particular practices—conflict-handling and collaboration—that fostered productive and learning experiences. These inclusive interaction practices reduced tensions that impeded learning, keeping the focus on manufacturing performance instead of the personal character of the other cultural group members. The two key practices were:

1. a daily morning meeting to address outstanding issues and set agendas, and
2. "running a trial" as a procedure in order to resolve differences in proposals for addressing production problems. This frequently resulted in creating a prototype of multiple suggested production solutions to see which is best.

As a result of the inclusive interactions at JVC the employees engaged in adaptive learning and the anti-inclusive practice of stereotyping was reduced, as compared to JVA and JVB. As a result JVC members behaved appropriately in their diverse workplace. The focus on effective interaction practices and accountable behavior resulted in higher achievement of JVC's learning goal. When cultural collisions occurred at JVC, these were viewed as opportunities for social and technical learning. The result was higher workgroup performance that benefitted all members and the company.

Banking: Inclusion sustained by managers' everyday practices

"This is good, especially since organizations often have diversity and inclusion programs that are totally not effective." This is how Rachel, a Black woman working as a banking executive with a major U.S. bank, responded to our introduction of the Framework for Inclusive Interactions. "The model makes sense because of the focus on behaviors—that's definitely different" than the traditional emphasis on training. Rachel, who during her long career has worked in both very homogeneous and very diverse workgroups, noted that she had experienced diverse groups as "more effective," with the key to the diverse workgroup success being "relationship building."

Rachel, in reflecting on the six inclusive interaction practices, specified the strategies she has implemented in her own workgroup, comprised of 15 members. In her promotion of equal status, she makes team members take turns leading their weekly meetings—including reaching out to other members, developing an agenda, and facilitating the meeting. We observed similar sharing of meeting leadership regarding the service fraternity and Al-Anon, demonstrating that some specific practices work well in both business and nonprofit settings. (See other examples of commonalities in the list of specific practices in Box 9.5.) Additionally, like others we have presented, this workgroup participates in a daily 15-minute "standup call." Rachel said that "collaboration with member interdependence is key" in terms of giving team members the autonomy and tools to get things done but making sure they know that they can come to her if there is a problem. The member's autonomy and insider status is possible because she is "transparent with the team, making sure they know what I'm hearing from higher-level executives, and keeping them aware of things that may be coming." Even with respect to handling conflict, she asks team members (or those involved in the conflict) to come to her prepared with some options for resolving the conflict, often prompting them by asking, "have you thought about some other ways to think about this?" "Collaboration among the workgroup members," said Rachel, "fosters an environment where you have the tools that you need by empowering the team members with autonomy and decision-making." She also has a practice in the first five to eight minutes of weekly meetings of asking each team member, "Tell me something good! And it can't be work-related." Rachel said that this increases their familiarity with each other. As a result of this, team members have discovered shared interests and that they have more in common than they thought, mentioning, for example, two members who discovered a love of gardening. In addition, when new team members come on board, they have to present one slide to the team called "All About Me" to help team members know them better.

BOX 9.5: PRACTICES FOR FREQUENT, POSITIVE INTERACTIONS

Practices explicitly noted in the cases are grouped into the six categories specified in the Framework for Inclusive Interactions. In some cases, placement into a category is arbitrary, since one specific practice can serve the purposes of several categories. The essence of an inclusive interaction practice is one that promotes frequent, positive diversity interactions.

Abbreviations for Cases:

Al-A: Al-Anon	NPB: nonprofit boards
GSUSA: Girl Scouts of the USA	LF: leadership fellowship
SF: service fraternity	IJV: international joint venture
B: banking	HC: health care
MB: military base	CE: civil engineering
HT: high tech	

An asterisk (*) indicates a less useful version of the practice, as discussed in this chapter.

1. Pursuing a shared task orientation or mission
Voluntary joining due to passion for the mission (Al-A, NPB, GSUSA, LF, SF)
Opening meetings with goals, values, and rules statements (Al-A, HC)
Emphasizing competition with other teams, internal and external (HT)

2. Mixing the members frequently and repeatedly
Formal meetings, the more frequent, the better for inclusion
    Daily: "morning meeting" (IJV); "standup call" (B); "huddle" (HC)
    Weekly (Al-A, SF)
    *Monthly or less (NPB)
Sitting facing one another at meetings (Al-A)
Inter-troop/cross-unit activities (GSUSA *only occasional)
All-member retreats (LF, B)
Informal social bonding activities
    Walk with different person at each meeting (LF)
    Community service activities together (SF, weekly; B, quarterly)
    Shared physical spaces (HC)
    Off-site social get-togethers (HT)

3. Collaborating with member interdependence
Providing support but not advice (Al-A)
Decision-making by votes after group deliberations (NPB)
Competition among teams created by mixing different troops (GSUSA)

Collaborating on service projects (SF)

Self-managing by the unit (Al-A, SF, LF, B, HC)

Empowering members and sharing manager's tasks with members (B)

Role differentiation with reliance on each other's expertise (HC, CE; HT)

4. Handling conflict constructively

Group generates own rules and procedures for managing tensions, such as prototyping tests (IJV) and no cross-talking, no judging (Al-A)

Emphasizing norms of positive personal relationships (LF, SF, HC, HT)

At morning meeting deciding which routine procedures to use to address previous day's issues (IJV)

"Bitching" session at quarterly retreat (B)

Taking the time needed to include different voices (NPB, B)

Calling out/addressing when one has offended another (NPB, HT)

Managers taking responsibility and using tools (employee badges) to prevent cross-generation and cross-cultural issues from impeding team performance (HT)

5. Exhibiting interpersonal comfort and self-efficacy

Socialization to welcome newcomers who are made comfortable (LF), as by each newcomer interviewing each existing member (SF) or internships prior to hiring (HT)

Reviewing rules for behavior at each meeting (Al-A)

Showing respect for others' perspectives (NPB)

Developing authentic relationships (NPB, LF, SF)

Identifying non-work interests shared with another member (B)

Engaging in activities/routines common to all organizational members (GSUSA, IJB)

Allowing time (months) to develop trust within new teams (LF, CE)

Informal, personalized mentoring for self-confidence (CE).

6. Ensuring equal insider status for all members

Rotating leadership in formal positions (Al-A, SF) or in meetings (B)

Group deliberations with all voices heard (NPB) as through behavioral rules of no "double-dipping" before all others have had a chance to speak (Al-A)

Transparent communications accessible by all members (NPB), as through sharing information with all in daily meetings (B, HC, IJV)

Enculturation with pride in a common ingroup identity (GSUSA; SF; HC)

Discouraging cliques (SF)

*Achieving equal status by having to prove one's competence (CE)

7. Accountability practices for inclusive behavior

Discontinuing offensive comments or jokes (NPB)

Being mentored to change managerial style (B)

Leaders making reward decisions that respect perspectives of underrepresented group members (B)

Creating behavior accountability tools, such as values statements on employee badges (HT)

Team members calling each other out for inappropriate behavior (HT)

Spurring informal interactions with a shared purpose, Rachel has the team come together quarterly, even bringing in those who work out of town or the country, to take a day away from the office where they volunteer with a nonprofit in the morning, have lunch together, and then some more "structured activities" in the afternoon, explaining that this was a euphemism for getting everyone into a room for "bitching sessions." Work with the nonprofit might be going to a senior citizen's home and passing out gifts to patients or working with a food pantry to prepare "friendship trays" for people in need. According to Rachel, this has "helped gel friendships." (Box 9.6 provides an example of how Rachel was held accountable for her behavior.)

BOX 9.6: BEING HELD ACCOUNTABLE FOR BEHAVIOR

Rachel is originally from the Northeast, and when she joined her current bank, located in a Southern city, she found that her "no-nonsense, get-it-done kind of attitude rubbed people the wrong way." Rachel, "oblivious" to this reaction of her coworkers, was fortunate that her supervisor told her that this approach did not fit the bank's culture, providing her with an opportunity to learn, adapt, and change her behavior.

Accountability extends to reward decisions as well as behavior. Based on her several decades in the banking sector, Rachel stressed the importance of "buy-in" from the organization, leadership, workgroup members, and stakeholders with respect to our six inclusive interaction practices. She felt this is particularly important because "non-diverse individuals do not understand the motives of diverse individuals," which can raise tensions and detract from performance. Providing an example of this, Rachel shared:

> When you offer someone to take a lower status position, even if salary is the same how this might not be a problem with White women, but to a person

of color who has fought so hard for status, this is a big insult. When the company was reorganizing after an acquisition, the executives were given the option to continue in their current roles, with same title, pay [and responsibility, presumably], or to become an "individual contributor" which means not retaining the title, but still having the same pay. As a Black woman who has worked hard to get to the point of being a senior executive [in a field that is significantly underrepresented in terms of Black women] there is no way I would give up my title.

Rachel's team was able to perform at their highest levels during the winter of 2020 and the outbreak of COVID-19. According to Rachel, "the team was working 80-90 hours a week, and everyone was on board with this." Amazingly, "this was not problematic because of the strength of the team culture." Box 9.7 details strategies Rachel uses to promote diversity and inclusion in the workgroups she manages.

BOX 9.7: RACHEL 'S EXPECTATIONS FOR FOSTERING DIVERSITY AND INCLUSION

a. "There's no 'I' in team; we all work together."
b. Everyone has a clear understanding of what makes them tick. This allows Rachel and other team members to acknowledge and take advantage of their strengths. For example: "one team member loves doing research tasks and detailed stuff, so if I get something that requires that, I'll give it to that team member and another member is good at summarizing, so I might ask that person to be a 'second set of eyes' on a memo that is going to higher-level executives." This, "makes the relationships more relational."
c. Empowering her team members as much as possible to be successful.
d. She is a "participative exec" who has an informal "open door policy." Everyone is required to share their cell phone numbers.
e. "Total transparency has created this team culture."

Health Care: Structuring an organizational unit for inclusion

Returning to the medical research unit, first introduced in Chapter 3, the unit's director, with an eye on improving performance outcomes, was able to embed institutionalized behaviors and traditions into much of the day-to-day operations when he initially established the unit and its workgroups from the ground up 16 years ago. Since then, the unit has evolved and grown in ways such that members interact and have become sufficiently comfortable in the expected normative behaviors that they largely reproduce themselves when new members are added. These behaviors and norms are reinforced by the unit director and the "chiefs" (subgroup leaders) in more subtle ways, such as with daily huddles for each team and mission quizzes at the start of meetings. Support for the mission may be embedded in multiple layers of leadership as emphasized by Gary, the director of the research unit, who did not micro-manage the semi-autonomous teams but rather, relied on the chiefs to model expected behaviors. But, in this case, the benefit of starting from a particular point in time enabled the process of structuring interactions according to particular practices and norms to be in itself developmental. Once the practices are embedded, adaptive learning can occur far more quickly, with new members rapidly become acculturated to them. This case demonstrates how norms of behavior become part of the organizational culture, which, in turn, facilitates the enculturation of new members.

Lessons from Set 2

In the three cases in this set, inclusion revolved around work unit performance. Even though business organizations typically lack the high degree of personal commitment to mission often found in voluntary organizations and in health care, the managers in the international joint venture and banking cases introduced and embedded inclusive practices with the goal of achieving the workgroup's purpose. In keeping with the categorization-elaboration model (Chapter 5), these practices transformed differences and potential tensions into task effectiveness. The practices drew diverse members together around the daily interdependent pursuit of group performance. As did several of the cases in Set 1, the Banking case illustrates that members can be drawn together more tightly by managers structuring periodic social moments and activities. These create familiarity and perceptions of similarity based on sharing personal histories and identifying common interests.

Set 3: Organization-wide inclusion

In the cases of Set 2, individual managers used their discretion to establish inclusive practices within their workgroups. For broader change, inclusion requires leadership efforts to shape the practices of managers and other organizational members across the organization and at all levels.

Military base: Embedding inclusive behavior

The case of the military base, first introduced in Chapter 3, highlighted the changes that occurred after the change in leadership at the installation with many thousands of employees. The new Commanding Officer (CO) implemented a new strategic plan which emphasized to all managers and employees the organization's guiding values and principles. In creating the new strategic plan, the CO relied heavily on the workforce for input and buy-in. In addition to this plan, which highlights, among other things, excellence, teamwork, and integrity, the CO "leads and lives [these values] daily, [through actions that are] infectious and inspiring," said Richard, the supervisor trainer in Human Resources. The CO's behavior, combined with her emphatically stressing that the military base "needs to shake things up" and "stop using old ineffective methods," has put everyone on notice that things are changing in order to create a "safe [working] environment for all." In addition, the CO has established a new internal office, reporting directly to her, to investigate all unfair work practices and also established a hotline for reporting problems. These actions are indicative of her no-nonsense approach and desire for accountability with respect to unacceptable behaviors. This case exemplifies how top leadership can influence organizational behaviors and set the tone for what is acceptable and what is not.

Civil engineering firm: Equal status from performance interdependence

In Chapter 3 we introduced you to Amy, a White female civil engineer with more than 30 years of experience. She is amazed that after all these years, the top leadership is "virtually all White men" who form a strong clique with an outside-of-work common interest in football. Among the remaining employees, diversity may be measured by gender (about 25 percent female), race ("Whites are not necessarily the majority"), religion, international origin, and age. The firm is well-known for its work on multi-year projects. Throughout the decade or more of working on these projects, many teams were formed and reformed, with each team task-oriented to a smaller aspect of the project for about a year. Because each team operates independently, this acts to inhibit the opportunity for interactions across the teams. Amy feels such mixing interactions would "help achieve better outcomes and for getting to know one another." In the teams, gaining equal insider status is a challenge. The "new person must prove themselves technically," demonstrating that they are competent in terms of completing their work. In the teams, "it takes about six months or more to get to know everyone and work well with them." Amy feels that there is a great benefit to "really get to know the people well and get to a point where there is a comfort level within the team." Amy expressed that in each team, there is an "overall goal for everyone to learn and enhance the team culture." However, the reality is that "individuals are different and have different goals for achievement and advancement." For example, she has seen members' interactions restrained by "millennial attitudes" coming into conflict with the more seasoned engineers and conflicts that have arisen due to cultural differences given the international diversity within the teams. According to Amy, it is often difficult in these cross-cultural situations to know whether one is dealing with cross-cultural or within-culture (personality) differences.

> "In engineering, a great team means that the majority of the time, the groups work well. When they do not, it was almost always due to an incompetent leader and not related to diversity issues." (Amy)

Ensuring equal insider status in decision-making is an inclusive interaction practice whose nuances are well-illustrated by Amy's firm. "In a sense, we are almost military in that the director makes final decisions." But, she continued, the director "gets input equally from teams," though the input gathered is weighted by "perceived knowledge… or job site experience, etc., with more experience weighing more heavily in decision-making. Within a workgroup, status and influence in decision-making are based on who has the skills for what you need. Qualifications for what needs to be done "becomes the most important consideration." In interacting with diverse others, "it still depends on qualifications and knowing that you may depend on whoever it is to follow through on assignments, be reliable and dependable, and have demonstrated that over time." Continuing on, Amy said that the "expectation of having the knowledge and skills" creates a reliance on others and drives collaboration and interdependence among the team members. This firm's actions are not inconsistent with equal insider status once the power of the ultimate decision-maker is accounted for. What matters is equal, insider status based on members' expertise and relevance to a decision rather than on gender, ethnicity, race, age, or other surface differences.

Amy, consistent with the evidence on stereotype threat (Chapter 4), found that, personally, it took her time to build self-confidence in her ability to do the work and make the right decisions. She credits strong mentoring, arranged by the firm, and the ability to be freer to interact and ask questions with this one person, as opposed to the workgroup. In turn, Amy helps new, younger employees, especially the women, giving them feedback in a nice way and boosting their self-confidence. In addition, Amy credits the firm-sponsored social activities, including parties and picnics, as helping her become comfortable with others and boosting inclusive interactions.

> "People are impacted by political correctness. So, for example, a man won't comment on how someone is dressed. There is a fear of saying the wrong thing. People get written up and reprimanded, even if the person may not have been intentional." (Amy)

While inclusive practices, including equal insider status, are found at the team level, it remains unclear to what degree there is inclusion at the higher organizational levels. As mentioned in Chapter 3, Amy was used as a token woman when the firm was seeking contracts. Being used as "window dressing" demeans her knowledge and skills as an engineer. Furthermore, the high emphasis on within function teams rather than cross-functional collaboration may, as discussed in Chapter 5, be less likely to improve equity outcomes. If, as Amy has expressed, inclusion is skills and knowledge-based, then special efforts will be necessary, as discussed directly below for another engineering firm, to counter bias regarding competence. Otherwise, non-majority members are more likely to be discounted, at least initially, due to commonly prevailing negative stereotypes. Amy's experiences, her own and that of other women, regarding lack of self-efficacy are consistent with research showing that being stigmatized leads to reduced assessments by others and by oneself (Chapter 4).

This case indicates that, within interdependent teams, inclusion based on individuals' contributions to team performance can be attained, but that members of underrepresented groups are likely to face inequitable initial hurdles to establish their expertise. The case also indicates the value that can be ascribed to effective personal mentoring in some instances. However, recall from Chapter 5 that, in general, formal programs for within-group networking benefit some underrepresented groups, principally White women, and not others.

High-tech: Holding each other accountable for inclusive engagement

Experiences in the two preceding cases suggest the advantage in organizations with entrenched anti-inclusive cultures of support from top leadership, support that was strengthened in the military case by the appointment of a woman to the highest position at the base. This action sent a signal that inclusion is to be a lived value in the organization. A case involving high-pressure workgroups in high-tech companies provided many positive examples of the lived organizational values of inclusion, values tied to team performance through tools for inclusion that appeared to be missing in the two cases above.

Interviewee John, a Black decades-long veteran of high-tech who has worked with four well-known companies, told us that our Framework for Inclusive Interactions "looks like the successful workplaces I have been in." In his current firm, the workgroups are very culturally, age, and gender diverse where "everyone looks and sounds different. If you do not have an accent, then you feel like an outsider!" The 60-member team operates across distance with a large contingent in Eastern Europe. Women make up about 10 percent of the team and the cultures and ethnicities represented include African Americans, Hispanics, Chinese, Filipinos, Indonesians, Koreans, Pakistanis, and White Americans. The ages range from post-college to 65 years. The younger team members almost always had held internships with the company so that when they later were hired into a team, they understood the expectation of "behaving professionally. It is amazing how members work together. It is amazing."

"The driver is the shared mission of achieving market share," which means that the diversity of the team "doesn't stop anyone from collaborating." According to John, the organization is top-down with its expectations about norms of inclusive behavior. In high-tech companies, a key support or mandate from top leadership is the explicit expectation of "professionalism," that you must "step over biases you may have brought to the room. Drop it at the door. We need to get work done and be professional." These expectations from authorities are clearly transmitted in ways used throughout the organization to hold team members accountable for inclusive behavior. The corporate values, "in blatant statements," are printed on every employee's badge with the expectation that they will be followed and that it is appropriate and expected to call someone's attention to the values when necessary. In particular, when a workgroup member "belittles an idea or takes a shot at someone, I, or another team member, will say, it sounds like you need to read #5 on the back of your badge—'mutual trust and respect at all levels'. No one is afraid to say anything. You can't do that unless the company pushes that."

The use of the badge to keep the company's core values ever present is an example of an accountability tool, one that members themselves use to hold teammates accountable for inclusive behaviors. This is in stark contrast to John telling us that the word "inclusion" is viewed by team members as a human resource "buzzword" that is frequently ignored. The company values and expectations of professionalism are "drilled into everyone during onboarding" because in the "hardware tech companies, people know that unprofessionalism does get in the way of mission achievement, and we need to have a level of professionalism to overcome issues." In this case, the term professionalism was used to define the expected norms of behavior within the organization and is suggestive of a workplace culture of mutual respect.

New, mostly younger employees at all four of the firms John has worked for in high-tech learn the "professional behavioral expectation during onboarding, but they may not know how to articulate these behaviors or that brand-wise it is being a professional." During this time, the company values are instilled and they learn the "harmonious structure" necessary for acculturating new team members and optimizing performance. In keeping with practice theory's emphasis on what people do routinely (Chapter 6), this learning by younger members demonstrates the primacy of behavioral adaptation, of adaptive learning. There is a complementary "understanding," an attitude in that sense, but not the ability of the newcomers, according to John, to articulate the belief of "professionalism." In high-tech, some of the companies list professionalism as a core value, indicating the prevalence of this behavioral expectation. At his current firm, John also attributes the team's success to the recruiting process where "each manager knows what they are looking for." Acculturation is the result of "part selection and part onboarding." According to John, "engineers are often introverts," which is okay if they have "the skills to know when they need to open up, even if it is uncomfortable for them to communicate." So, the knowledge they gain is framed by the organization as knowing the collaborative behavior needed to be professional, especially when and how to communicate. The knowledge is not framed in terms of diversity but, rather, in terms of performance. The skills team members need are "to execute the communication and collaboration, adding tasks, closing tasks, estimating work times, scheduling, etc."

> "Knowledge is knowing how to be professional and skill is knowing when to execute." (John)

During John's extensive career, he experienced one manager who was not "professional," but instead dictatorial in his dealing with the team. The company sent the manager for leadership courses, but ultimately the manager was sent to Germany. Over the years, John has observed at the organizational level a decreased tolerance with individuals who are sources of complaints by many people, observing that as "diversity increased in upper management, human resources got more forceful where there were complaints. The old boys' network has been eroding and the aggression of the older folks declined." This suggests that human resources are enforcing inclusion around equity, which is an example of the proper use of contact theory's condition of "support from authority."[13]

> Over time, a virtuous cycle for inclusion evolves: Support from authorities for inclusion increases as upper management becomes more diverse.

Within John's company, "they use competition with other teams to drive the work, so we want to have a great team to be more successful than the others." We are being told, "There is work to be done and you are accountable to get the work done." Over the course of a project, within a larger program, you "see other teams progressing and there is peer pressure, so we can't let personal issues get in the way." In addition to the internal competition among the teams, John feels that performance pressure also comes from outside the company because within high-tech "everyone is always watching their competitors who are successful and emulating one another." When there are clashes or biases, "there is eventually a point of reality where you just get on with [the work]." The managers, such as John, use time pressure as a tool to get people to move past interpersonal tensions. Research has indicated that time pressure to make a personnel decision leads to the triggering of implicit biases (Chapter 4), but in this case, time pressure is beneficial, being used to emphasize the need for collaboration and commitment to the mission.

> Accountability for inclusive behavior and performance is tied together: So, do folks have biases? "Yes, especially the older guys. For example, a 65-year-old employee asked one of the women engineers in the group about her marriage plans during COVID-19. Another team member said, 'This is not the old days; you cannot ask that.' So, people do call each other out." Without such interference, anti-inclusive behavior delays and threatens team performance. (John)

In these firms, the top management, who have been around for decades, determine the core values statements. The statements are not ambiguous at all, being based on "their history in their company and the knowledge they have as to where behaviors have gone wrong." The specific statements from John's current company are in Box 9.8. Within these companies, there is no specific diversity or inclusion training. "Truthfully, there is a Catch 22, with the workforce and community so diverse, there is no need for diversity training because if you can't handle it, you will move." John did comment that within the high-tech community and the whole region, there is no dominant majority group, "Everyone knows that they are a bit different from everyone else." Outside of work, he sees the same positive interactions among the extremely diverse high school team John coaches, where the students also exhibit socio-economic diversity, "Just get along." Yet, despite the larger community's generally favorable views toward diversity, the company still emphasizes the blatant communication of the company values, the common drive for market share, and professionalism in order to ensure adaptive learning. "Adaptive learning, love that term, that is what is happening," John said, "over the course of a major program [comprised of many projects]."

John, as a Black American, "had to get used to the accents of those without proper English," acknowledging that he was initially biased in his assumption that "poor English meant they were not well educated." Quickly, he learned that the engineers, especially the Vietnamese and Chinese and Filipinos, etc., are still sharp engineers despite their language differences. "It was just their dialect. I had adaptive learning! There definitely is an adaptive learning curve." Because the workforce and community are both diverse, there is a basic diversity ethic within the region. At his current company, there is some "sensitivity training that teaches how to treat one another in workplace, not so much in team, but in passing and in the cafeteria." This, he found useful with respect to engaging in superficial interactions. But John felt the training was important for teaching the values and need for mutual trust and respect, providing awareness that there is an expected way to act. On a personal level, John said, "There was comfort in knowing that everyone else is not a wizard at these behaviors."

BOX 9.8: THE CORE VALUES ON JOHN'S BADGE

1. Customer focus: We employ a relentless focus on understanding and exceeding customer expectations.
2. Achievement: We believe in challenging goals and a continuous passion for achieving.
3. Accountability: We accept responsibility for our decisions, actions, and results.
4. Teamwork: We believe in people working cohesively toward common goals, which enhance our ability to succeed.

5. Employee value: We believe each employee brings unique value and potential that can be developed to mutually enrich the individual and the organization.
6. Integrity: We act honestly and hold ourselves to the highest ethical standards.

It is striking that the values messages delivered on the employee's badges (Box 9.8) directly connect the inclusive interaction practices of collaboration, insider status, and comfortable, self-efficacious interactions to the shared purpose of team performance. The badges provide a ready means for members to hold themselves and others accountable for following inclusive practices.

With the arrival of COVID-19 in the winter of 2020 and the blaming of China for the pandemic, "Human Resources was proactive sending out a notice about maintaining a sense of inclusion." This was timely and important, given the large number of Asian-Pacific Islander employees and the fact that, "There are those in the company who call all of them Chinese." (John)

Lessons from Set 3

The cases in this set illustrate how progress in inclusion is being attained within workgroups across the organizations. Structuring inclusive practices and finding ways to communicate to members the nature of inclusive behavior and hold them responsible for it produces inclusion that is sustained by managers and coworkers alike. However, work remains to be done to achieve inclusion in many geographical regions where diversity is not as favorably experienced as in the high-tech community. The cases here, across Sets 1 to 3, illustrate that pursuing a full bundle of inclusive practices on the basis of workgroup performance is a path to such achievement. Many organizations that are less values-based than voluntary organizations can take a lesson from John's experience regarding the value of socialization and tools to convey appropriate behavior and hold members accountable for it.

An important organization-wide issue is not addressed by any of the cases in Set 3: the need for accountability practices to counter biased decisions in allocating rewards (Chapter 7), principally for retention and advancement to higher levels. Meeting the practice of equal insider status requires equal access to developmental opportunities and promotions. In engineering firms in general, this problem has been acknowledged for female engineers. Their relative absence in higher-level positions is consistent with statistics in the engineering field, indicating that only about 13 percent of women persist in engineering, up from 11 percent a decade ago.[14] Much research has examined the low retention of women in engineering.

However, it remains unknown whether this is attributable to a failed emphasis on gender inclusion.

Achieving inclusion is practical

This chapter provides cases from a variety of settings revealing how the Framework for Inclusive Interactions may be applied, with the specified inclusive practices taking various forms in different settings. (See Box 9.9 for an audit you may adopt or adapt for your organization to assess its use of the inclusive interaction practices.) The practices succeeded in shaping inclusive behavior, sometimes only for a short period, as in Girl Scouts of the USA, and in more successful cases, long term. Several cases demonstrate that in the absence of organization-wide practices for inclusion, managers can have sufficient discretion to design and institute inclusive interaction practices in workgroups that they oversee, with ongoing acceptance by workgroup members. Once embedded in a workgroup or organization, the inclusive practices reproduced inclusion with new members and even with new cohorts. Strikingly, inclusion in these cases was not pursued on the basis of diversity but of mission attainment, with all individuals being treated, behaviorally, in a manner that invited them to contribute. Representational diversity alone is unlikely to be sufficient to achieve inclusion in this behavioral way. Several of the cases, including the non-profit boards, military base, and high-tech firm, indicate that inclusive behavioral treatment is far from automatic for many dominant group members and that negative stereotypes can be held by any member, requiring persistence with the inclusive practices and optimally support from authorities. That support can include the use of everyday tools that signal behavioral norms and hold individuals accountable for the desired behaviors. Practices of accountability appear to be less necessary in some voluntary organizations, perhaps due to values associated with mission attainment serving to complement the inclusive interaction practices.

BOX 9.9: WORKGROUP AUDIT

We invite you to consider taking an audit of the inclusive interaction practices that currently are utilized in your workgroups by asking the following questions:

1. Are some already part of the norms and behaviors? Are others absent?
2. Try to envision what happens if you are only partially successful at implementing the practices.
   a. Will your workgroup members be able to advance to adaptive learning and inclusive engagement?
   b. Will the interactions be professional?
   c. Will there be more conflict, and will it inhibit performance?
3. How can we best enculturate newcomers to our workgroup and its norms?

Several of the most successful cases—the campus service organization, the leadership fellowship, and the high-tech firm—indicate the importance of time, typically around half a year, for adaptive learning to occur and the role of onboarding (socialization) practices in initiating that learning. As research has revealed about college students who engaged in frequent, positive diversity interactions (Chapter 6), in the most successful cases, investment in the practices led organizational members to experience personal development. Following the practices—routinely, bodily, and emotionally—affected not only their behavior, interpersonal skills, and comfort, but also their understandings of people different from themselves and the advantages of engaging inclusively with them.

Notes

1 BoardSource. (2017). *Leading with intent: 2017 national index of nonprofit board practices.* https://leadingwithintent.org/wp-content/uploads/2017/11/LWI-2017.pdf, p. 16.

2 Buse, K., Bernstein, R. S., & Bilimoria, D. (2016). The influence of board diversity, board diversity policies and practices, and board inclusion behaviors on nonprofit governance practices. *Journal of Business Ethics, 133*(1), 179–191; Fredette, C., Bradshaw, P., & Krause, H. (2016). From diversity to inclusion: A multimethod study of diverse governing groups. *Nonprofit and Voluntary Sector Quarterly, 45*(1_suppl), 28S–51S.

3 Bernstein, R. S., & Bilimoria, D. (2013). Diversity perspectives and minority nonprofit board member inclusion. *Equality, Diversity and Inclusion: An International Journal, 32*(7), 636–653.

4 Ibid.

5 Weisinger, J. Y., & Salipante, P. F. (2005). A grounded theory for building ethnically bridging social capital in voluntary organizations. *Nonprofit and Voluntary Sector Quarterly, 34*(1), 29–55; Weisinger, J.Y., & Salipante, P. F. (2007). An expanded theory of pluralistic interactions in voluntary nonprofit organizations. *Nonprofit Management and Leadership, 18*(2), 157–173.

6 Moss-Racusin, C. A., van der Toorn, J., Dovidio, J. F., Brescoll, V. L., Graham, M. J., & Handelsman, J. (2014). Scientific diversity interventions. *Science, 343*(6171), 615–616.

7 Stearns, E., Buchmann, C., & Bonneau, K. (2009). Interracial friendships in the transition to college: Do birds of a feather flock together once they leave the nest? *Sociology of Education, 82*(2), 173–195.

8 McPherson, M., Smith-Lovin, L., & Cook, J. M. (2001). Birds of a feather: Homophily in social networks. *Annual Review of Sociology, 27*(1), 415–444.

9 Halualani, R. T. (2008). How do multicultural university students define and make sense of intercultural contact? A qualitative study. *International Journal of Intercultural Relations, 32*(1), 1–16.

10 Bernstein, R. S., & Salipante, P. (2015). Comfort versus discomfort in interracial/interethnic interactions: Group practices on campus. *Equality, Diversity and Inclusion: An International Journal, 34*(5), 376–394; Bernstein, R. S., & Salipante, P. (2017). Intercultural comfort through social practices: Exploring conditions for cultural learning. *Frontiers in Education,* Vol. 2, Article 31. doi:10.3389/feduc.2017.00031. http://journal.frontiersin.org/article/10.3389/feduc.2017.00031/full?&utm_source=Email_to_authors_&utm_medium=Email&utm_content=T1_11.5e1_author&utm_campaign=Email_publication&field=&journalName=Frontiers_in_Education&id=272155.

11 Crisp, R. J., & Turner, R. N. (2011). Cognitive adaptation to the experience of social and cultural diversity. *Psychological Bulletin, 137*(2), 242–266.

12 Weisinger, J. Y., & Salipante, P. F. (2000). Cultural knowing as practicing: Extending our conceptions of culture. *Journal of Management Inquiry, 9*(4), 376–390.

13 Allport, G. W. (1954). *The nature of prejudice*. Perseus Books.

14 U.S. Bureau of Labor Statistics. (n.d.). *Labor force statistics from the current population survey* https://www.bls.gov/cps/cpsaat11.htm

10

PERFORMANCE THROUGH DIVERSITY AND INCLUSION

Leveraging organizational practices for equity and results

The purpose of this final chapter is to draw on the preceding chapters to consider how leaders (and researchers, by engaging with leaders) can move organizations toward sustained inclusion that produces enhanced performance and equity from diversity. The chapter calls for leaders to supplement, and in some cases modify, their past efforts, based on the practices and processes specified in this book's Framework for Inclusive Interactions, depicted in Figure 10.1.

Our most fundamental argument in this book, based on the various bodies of research reviewed, is that reliance on currently dominant approaches to diversity and inclusion will continue to prove inadequate. This chapter then discusses the implementing of more promising approaches, following several evidence-based premises:

1. The most realistic, tenable view of the past and current situation is that, for many identity groups and in many quarters of society, *exclusion is institutionalized* in organizations and employment systems. This view contradicts beliefs that our current systems are meritocratic. It calls into question organizational efforts that are not systemic, that do not address the full range of problematic institutionalized practices.
2. The costs of exclusion are social inequities and decrements in the performance of our organizations and economies.
3. Consequently, the task for organizational leaders is to
    a. Control the effects of practices that institutionalize exclusion, practices that are rooted in prejudices, by *institutionalizing practices for accountability*.
    b. Counter the practices of exclusion by reducing prejudices at their source through *institutionalizing inclusive interaction practices*, embedding them in the organization's distinctive culture.

DOI: 10.4324/9780367822484-16

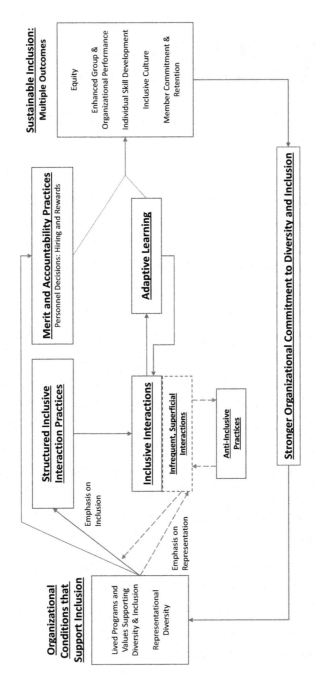

FIGURE 10.1 The Framework for Inclusive Interactions

This chapter focuses on the latter of those two tasks, implementing inclusive interaction practices. Accountability systems have been addressed in some detail in Chapter 7. These systems are familiar, and organizations are generally skilled at collecting and analyzing data to address problems. However, to rely solely on practices of accountability is to fight an uphill battle, since accountability systems do not address the source of the problem, prejudices. Organizations have attempted to reduce prejudices through education and training approaches, but the evidence indicates that such approaches have substantial limitations and, in common forms, can do more harm than good. Meanwhile, the approach to reducing prejudices that research evidence does support as effective—frequent, positive intergroup interactions—is not being recognized as a path to achieving inclusion. For that reason, we focus this concluding chapter on the implementing of practices for inclusive interactions. Through prejudice reduction over time, and through the influence over member behavior that comes from institutionalized practices, leaders can stimulate progress. Whether the practices are espoused for diversity or not, they offer serious prospects for achieving stronger equity for individuals and effectiveness for organizations.

> By simultaneously enhancing performance and equity, sustained inclusion is a means by which leaders can align the interests of two key stakeholder groups: owners and members.

While the chapter draws on research-based evidence, it asks individuals to combine in a creative way the knowledge from that evidence with their own knowledge of their organization and its members. And, consistent with views that leadership can occur at all organizational levels, the chapter is addressed to a wide range of individuals capable of making a difference in their organizations. Members from the bottom to the top, in various formal roles, have opportunities to improve inclusive practices and accountability. The chapter focuses on challenges, opportunities, and options for action, not on a recipe of actions to be plugged in. Presenting an organizational case of action-in-progress and drawing on numerous examples, it offers broad guidance based on a central idea that follows from the preceding chapters: Leaders' focus should be on the bundle of on-the-job social practices in the organization that affect inclusion, some practices being inclusive and some anti-inclusive.

> To achieve sustainable inclusion, organizational leaders' focus should be on the social practices that affect inclusion: Increase inclusive practices and decrease anti-inclusive practices.

Identifying and reducing anti-inclusive practices and increasing inclusive practices is a straightforward way to conceive of useful, feasible action with distinct perform-ance and equity payoffs. The payoffs apply to the organization as a whole and all of its members, including those from underrepresented groups. Box 10.1 highlights the uniqueness of the Framework for Inclusive Interactions.

BOX 10.1: WHAT MAKES OUR APPROACH TO INCLUSION SO UNIQUE?

In the nearly 20 years since the initial studies for this book were conducted, we still find our research approach to vary from so many other researchers. In quantitative studies on diversity, organizational researchers typically ask, "What is the outcome of this or that aspect of diversity (independent vari-able) on the workgroup?" This question is useful for evaluating the effects of widely instituted diversity programs, as we reviewed in Chapter 5. However, it fails to connect with interaction practices that can make or break those programs and that managers and other members experience on an everyday basis—that is, with practices that are truly relevant and forceful "where the rubber meets the road." We, on the other hand, began our studies by exam-ining the outcomes (dependent variables) and investigating what led to them. We asked such questions as "What differentiated between effective and inef-fective cross-cultural knowledge exchange and performance? Where is there effective cross-racial interaction in this particular context? Where do you see the most effective diversity? Where and how is prejudice (and counter-productive friction) reduced?" Then, using qualitative methods and follow-up quantitative studies, the focus was on identifying the factors, procedures, structures, and processes that impacted these outcomes. The factors that we identified in these inductive, then deductive ways guided us to see the value of intergroup contact theory (Chapter 6). Over time, drawing on the large bodies of research-based evidence from several disciplines and fields reviewed in this book, we have reduced the factors, procedures, structures, and processes to the six "practices" presented in our Framework as shaping people's behavior to be inclusive. We believe that this methodology has enabled us to capture the complex dynamics and the operation of many phenomena and variables, fitting the realities that leaders experience as they search for practical, effective actions.

In interpreting our findings and writing this book, we were able to connect research from many fields of study, particularly applying sociological and social psychological concepts, to our findings in order to specify, based on current knowledge, how to shape behavior and change attitudes over time. We have relied on practice theory to argue that what matters for equity and perform-ance is how people behave in response to the social structures they are in. Our focus on structures in the workplace led us to the inclusive practices and to the importance of accountability for behaving inclusively and following specified norms of behavior. As a result, we feel confident that performance as well as diversity logics are necessary for implementing effective interaction practices and reducing backlash and resistance by managers and employees. Interacting with diverse others enables members to recognize—sometimes implicitly, sometimes explicitly—the operation of the anti-inclusive social phenomena of self-segregation, interaction discomfort, stereotyping and stigmatizing, and implicit bias and to control them through interaction and accountability practices, producing inclusive engagement. Finally, because we found the inclusive practices to be ongoing in regular organizations, we know that they are feasible, and this has been further confirmed by our interviewees' examples.

An example of the interplay of inclusive and anti-inclusive practices is identified by research (Chapter 7) concerning promotions. Inclusion is favored by fair employment practices that provide equity in performance evaluations and opportunities for personal development. But the benefits of these practices are then undone by allowing managers to make the final decisions on whom to promote, when they may default to using anti-inclusive practices, such as implicit bias, that fall below their own and the organization's radar. Maddy Janssens and Chris Steyaert[1] offer an example of how subtle this process can be: If the individual being considered for promotion is a White man recommended by his supervisor, the routine practice might be to accept the recommendation and promote. If the individual being considered is a person of color, the routine practice might be to fully debate the pros and cons of that person being selected, identifying negatives that lead to a greater possibility of rejection. In effect, implicit bias comes into play in what otherwise appears to be a useful practice of debate. The challenge for leaders at all levels is to identify such anti-inclusive practices and work to change them (see Box 10.2), and to introduce the inclusive interaction practices identified in this book. The goal is to seize opportunities to move the entire bundle of practices toward inclusion, based on arguments of improved performance and improved equity.

BOX 10.2: IMPLICATIONS FOR INQUIRY BY LEADERS AND RESEARCHERS

1. The anti-inclusive practices that can be expected in organizations by default—self-segregating, interacting uncomfortably with different others and distancing from them, stereotyping and stigmatizing, and making personnel decisions based on implicit bias—are likely to be entangled with a variety of everyday, taken-for-granted work and decision-making practices that members follow. The challenge for both leaders and researchers is to

identify those often-subtle practices, the individual practices, and their roles in bundles of practices that create exclusion rather than inclusion. The method proposed for doing so[2] is ethnography, the long-established method involving participant observation of ongoing social and organizational life.[3] Organizational members, including leaders at all levels, are in a favorable position to observe and systematically analyze ongoing practices. Researchers would do well to partner with organizational leaders in such systematic pursuit of the practice-based underpinnings of discrimination. These methods will also allow direct examination of the various forms that the Framework's six inclusive interaction practices can take in differing workgroups and organizations, how they work as a bundle, and whether additional practices favoring inclusion can be identified.

2. One set of organizational practices not covered in this book but worthy of examining by leaders and researchers is work–life benefits. Since these benefits are available to all members of an organization, they share with performance-oriented programs of practices the avoidance of backlash effects that can occur with diversity-specific efforts. The review by Nishii and colleagues[4] indicates that work–life benefits are received positively by members of underrepresented groups, likely due to the signals the benefits send about concern for members' well-being.

In pursuing opportunities, leaders at all levels can draw on change processes and other ideas presented in this chapter in order to overcome challenges. We start this chapter with an overview of the beneficial outcomes that leaders can expect to achieve as they move from representational diversity to inclusion, then consider how leaders can pursue inclusion through particular processes that produce support, rather than resistance, from other organizational members. This is followed by an example where support was achieved, showing what is possible in a relatively short time when the guiding individuals, all at middle levels of an organization, are sufficiently committed and informed. To further guide leaders, a general set of challenges is then identified, leading to further suggestions of promising, realistic processes for producing high performance and equity by combining diversity with inclusive practices.

Moving our organizations beyond representational diversity to inclusive practices

To achieve the benefits of sustainable inclusion associated with the Framework for Inclusive Interactions, organizations and workgroups are challenged to leverage their representational diversity. Sustainable inclusion includes the multilevel outcomes of equity, workgroup and organizational performance, individual skill building, enhanced valuing of diversity and inclusion, and improved organizational culture that increases members' commitment. Beyond that scope of the workgroup and organization are the outcomes related to social justice in the larger society. Generally, at that societal level, we observe the impact of the social justice principles in the workplace, including (1) equity where the fair distribution of human resources is ensured, (2) access to fair employment, (3) participation primarily with respect to equal status in decision-making, and (4) individual rights for all. Also at the societal level are economic gains in gross national product from the higher performance of individual organizations and more effective utilization of the society's human capital.

How do we get from diversity to organizational effectiveness and to individual equity and social justice from inclusive practices, and what do these practices look like in everyday organizational life? Throughout the book, we presented a myriad of examples to demonstrate various forms that the six inclusive interaction practices can take and their impact on performance and equity. We emphasize three key points. First, that the proposed inclusive interaction practices are not diversity specific. Rather, it is their performance rationale and advantages that make them applicable to all workgroup members, rendering them more feasible, acceptable, and followed by all members while providing benefits for diversity. However, separate and more diversity-specific accountability and transparency efforts should be present at the organizational level, holding members accountable for their actions and decisions through a values-based framework compatible with the performance focus of inclusive interactions. Second, that changes in interaction behavior and skills are primary, with workgroup members becoming followers of the inclusive practices, performing in ways that produce adaptive learning and eventually associated changes in attitudes. In this approach, attitudes follow behavior, with members' understandings being embedded in their speech, bodily behavior, and comfortable emotions when they interact. Because of the distinctive characteristics and context of each organization and workgroup, there is no one specific or correct form for the inclusive interaction practices to take in order to create this behaviorally embedded inclusion. Third, that opportunities for implementation exist at many levels of management, as demonstrated in the examples ranging from lower-level employees at the military base to trustees on governing boards.

Knowledge and know-how are required to implement the inclusive interaction practices, to keep them vibrant and evolving in ways relevant to changes in personnel, tasks, and technology, and to reap the performance and equity benefits. In Chapter 9, we presented various organizations that have implemented many, if not all, of the practices. The implementation strategies must be fluid and developed respecting the individual context, nature, and mission of each organization and workgroup. The interviewees we spoke with, across the spectrum of workgroups, indicated that their organization's values were not necessarily specific to diversity, inclusion, and equity but rather often focused on respect, fellowship, and treating fellow members well, highlighting positive inclusive interactions among workgroup and organizational members for performance reasons. This approach may, according to research we have presented in this book, contribute more to continually achieving the ultimate goal of sustainable inclusion and performance enhancement. A performance emphasis for inclusive interaction practices complements and balances the traditional diversity, inclusion, and equity-focused values initiatives, which alone often create negative backlash from majority group members and fail to accord with the treatment and outcome realities experienced by members of stereotyped groups.

Gaining leader and member support for change

Lisa Nishii, Jasmein Khattab, Meir Shemla, and Rebecca Paluch[5] conducted a substantial integrative literature review and created a multilevel process model to capture when and how diversity practices produce desirable results. Their review of diversity research published since 2000 complements our Framework for Inclusive Interactions in not only espousing diversity practices but, more importantly, enacting them for results. Many organizations are responding to external pressures to improve the effectiveness of diversity initiatives indirectly through institutional pressures in their fields, including external legal and political pressures, or directly through relationships with key business partners and employees. Enacting the diversity practices must be undertaken with authenticity demonstrated by leadership. (See Box 10.3 for examples of how to apply the inclusive interaction practices.) As opposed to superficial motives for external legitimacy, authenticity will enhance internal credibility and increase the likelihood that members attribute the desire to adopt the practices to genuine internal motivation on the part of the organization. As Nishii and colleagues state, "Employees' perceptions of diversity practices are influenced by cues from the organizational environment that reinforce the authenticity of the intended signals communicated by a practice,"[6] signaling to employees the organization's values and expectations.

Joining Frank Dobbin, Daniel Schrage, and Alexandra Kalev,[7] Nishii and colleagues argue that diversity initiatives may fail as a result of internal factors, particularly resistance from managers who do not see the value in and are, therefore, not willing to enact diversity practices and, they add, employees who do not perceive that the organization is authentic in its desire to take diversity and inclusion seriously. "In the absence of strong accountability mechanisms for ensuring desired practice implementation, the symbolic adoption of a meritocratic initiative might not only fail to reduce biases, but could even backfire and exacerbate them."[8] In contrast, they note that research has demonstrated that when employees actually participate in diversity practices, the outcomes are more consistent. Furthermore, as noted above, employees recognize the lack of legitimacy of diversity practices that are espoused and not acted on. Hence the need for accountability structures that create *evaluation apprehension*[9] that motivates managers to implement the practices carefully and reliably. Accountability, additionally, enables leaders and supervisors to determine whether their practices actually elicit the organizationally intended outcomes.

Nishii and her colleagues'[10] conclusions from their research review concur with ours in a number of ways. First, the need for organizations and workgroups to ensure that diversity policies and practices hold managers and leaders accountable for specified outcomes. Second, that diversity-related activities should not be in isolation but, rather, in "bundles." Third, the need to understand why diversity-related activities fail by asking the following questions:

1. Are the espoused initiatives implemented as planned?
2. Do implemented initiatives result in desired behaviors?
3. Do the new employee behaviors produce positive organizational outcomes?

BOX 10.3: INCLUSIVE ENGAGEMENT—CREATIVE APPLICATION OF INCLUSIVE BEHAVIORS

What does it look like when you have inclusive behaviors in a workgroup? Or conversely, what does it look like when you do not have inclusive behaviors? These two commonly asked questions may be used as a barometer of the success a workgroup's members have in becoming followers of the six structured inclusive interaction practices. While workgroup inclusive behaviors will vary from context to context, we list here a set of illustrative behaviors that represent inclusive engagement. Assessing your workgroup's use of behaviors such as these can be used to hold people accountable for their behavior towards others. Additional examples of each of the six practices are presented in Chapter 3. Chapter 9 provides more examples of how workgroups strategically implement the behaviors associated with each of the six practices.

*   *Pursuing a shared mission*:
    Imparting the significance of the task; tapping into members' passion for the mission and success of the organization; fostering the idea that task or mission success is shared by all members.
    Celebrating group successes and sharing knowledge by members recounting to each other problems that they have solved.[11]
*   *Mixing members frequently and repeatedly:*
    Actions designed to reduce cliques and promote interactions with diverse others. For example, use name tags and assigning seats at meetings so that members do not always sit with the same people; rotating assignments to committees and task forces.
    Organizing social activities with workgroup and organizational members.
*   *Collaborating with member interdependence*:
    Start meetings with a slide outlining behavioral "rules" and goals. The rules may include such suggestions as giving your full attention to the

meeting, not interrupting, raising your hand, and leaving space for others to offer their ideas.

- *Handling conflict constructively:*
  Recognize an important point of contention and assign a subgroup of members to address it using a constructive procedure, such as gathering additional information or prototyping two alternative approaches.
- *Exhibiting interpersonal comfort and self-efficacy:*
  "Professional" or "warm" behavior that avoids personal attacks and indifference to reinforce that workgroup members are peers and colleagues.
- *Ensuring equal insider status for all members:*
  Respectful behavior—In some contexts, such as academia, challenging others' ideas to demonstrate they are worthy ones to debate; in some other contexts, building on others' ideas or offering alternatives rather than directly challenging.
  Language justice—Using informed and shared language that is understood by all workgroup members and is not off-putting (see Box 3.4).

The Framework for Inclusive Interactions differs from Nishii et al.'s process model in a number of ways. We rely on practice theory (Chapter 6) to argue that what matters is how people behave in response to the social structures they are in, as opposed to their model's focus on attitudes as driving behavior. Their point that resistant attitudes can undermine diversity efforts is well taken, consistent with the anti-exclusionary practices we have emphasized in Chapter 4, as is their point that managerial and member participation in a change process increases their commitment to it. In addition, we emphasize the implementation of inclusive practices at the behavioral level. The practices are embodied, involving learned skills in speech and body language. The practices are also embedded in the materials and technology associated with workgroup tasks, with members pursuing the inclusive practices due to a shared commitment to mission performance. For both performance and inclusion from diversity, the bottom line is engaging routinely, behaviorally, and materially in an inclusive way, with adaptive learning gradually emerging as individuals become followers of the inclusive practices and cease use of anti-inclusive practices. We illustrate this below with a case that details a change process in an organizational unit where anti-inclusive practices had been firmly embedded for years.

A case of creating opportunities: Guiding groups toward the Framework's Inclusive Practices

A cross-functional task force at a governmental scientific research facility illustrates how inclusive interaction practices can be introduced through a focus on performance, achieving both performance and equity gains. The task force produced inclusive engagement, adaptive learning, and a cultural shift. As suggested by Kalev's[12] research discussed in Chapter 5 and demonstrated in this example, cross-functional teams have been demonstrated to have a greater positive impact on diversity outcomes than many diversity-specific practices. Kalev[13] found that women and those from underrepresented groups do better when engaged in cross-job training and self-directed, cross-functional teams because they are then recognized as peers to White men. *Their talents become visible, leading to career-enhancing transfers and promotions.*

In the research facility, it took three years for operations staff to collect data and convince top management to create a task force to study how to increase performance by reevaluating the embedded administration structure, said Sarah, our interviewee. The workgroup was composed of 12 members, four from each of three functional areas—scientists, administrators, and operations staff. The administrators are support staff and, unlike the scientists and operations people, are contractors and viewed as outsiders to the organization. While pitched as a performance-enhancing task force to determine how administrative support was functioning for the scientists, the focus among the operations staff was to ask, "What is going on here?" The facilitator, Sarah, wanted to improve the culture of the organization that she felt was contributing to high turnover among the organization's employees. Sarah was frustrated both by the existing organizational culture and the difficulty of generating work with employees stuck in their "functional boxes." The boxes reflect job segregation, with minorities and women crowded into lower status functions. This functional lens, she felt, held people back. The impetus for the task force was to eliminate the traditional approach within the organization—that the administration had to listen to the scientists. "We had often just responded to what scientists want. Now the scientists are understanding, listening, and more involved at all levels of the organization."

Members of the task force lived the inclusive interaction practice of pursuing a shared task orientation or mission (Practice 1). The group was charged by top management with developing a number of alternative performance enhancement models by examining how the functional areas could work better together. That purpose was not diversity-focused because it was anticipated that support for the project and its changes would be less than if the effort were promoted on the basis of performance improvement.

> "Proposing the task force as a way to improve performance, as opposed to improving diversity and inclusion, was vital in convincing management to support the project". (Sarah)

The realization was that the organization would not spend resources for a one-year task force on diversity alone. Her felt experience is that people have to be willing to change the workplace culture. Not everyone in management will connect with culture's importance but will with performance and associated procedures. The task force became an accepted means for change to occur.

The task force met bi-weekly with additional subgroup meetings, with structured engagement over time. Behavioral change in the form of positive and productive, inclusive interactions among the members began at about four months and peaked at six months. Sarah, as the organizer and facilitator, would meet with three of the members subsequent to the meetings to debrief and plan for the next meeting. They evaluated what had emerged, assessing the group dynamics and whether there was a need to shift the conversation in order to determine how to move forward. This enabled the task force to engage in deliberate iterative activities, use subgroups for feedback, creatively figure how to voice particularly sensitive issues, and determine what was appropriate for the group to share. As a result, breakthroughs were not preplanned but emerged throughout the year. One of the biggest challenges was the power dynamics that existed among the elite scientists who were predominantly White men and the administrative staff, who were often Black women.

When we first met Sarah, she excitedly told us that her task force aligned with our Framework. Why? Because of the Framework's focus on the inclusive interactions among workgroup members. She felt that within her task force, there was an intentionality about fostering interactions and examining processes. The scientists in her organization acknowledged that there were issues with effectiveness and efficiency but did not initially see how this related to interactions. "Nobody wants to come together to talk about racism" or culture. "By initially focusing the group with a specific mission—looking to perform better across the functional areas—we were able to dig in and examine the actual conditions creating ineffectiveness." Sarah observed that it was the task force's mission that brought the people together, but over time, the mission became less important as they dove into the details of group engagement. During the year of its existence, the task force had the autonomy to determine how to achieve its shared mission. "To do this, we structured the conversations and engaged many guest facilitators to address such issues as culture and conflict in order to ensure generative dialogue, including conversations about racism and sexism to create awareness. You cannot learn this in a classroom." This has to be a lived experience where you feel safe enough to participate and "have good generative dialogue." Thus, education played a key role, not in the form of training for the general workforce but, rather, on a need-to-know basis for the task force's mission, motivating members to gain from the education.

The structured inclusive interaction practice of mixing members frequently and repeatedly (Practice 2) occurred with the bi-weekly meetings and the more frequent subgroup meetings. The team members were intentionally picked as having commitment and willingness to do the work, commitment to the mission and the willingness to join for the year. The 12 members of the workgroup were representative of their functional groups with the scientists being older (40–65 years) and primarily White men; the administrator participants were in their late twenties to mid-thirties and included two Blacks and three women; and the members representing operations ranged in age from mid-twenties to about 40, were White except for one Black member, and three were women.

Mixing members, said Sarah, was predicated on the group creating a sense of community and the practice of exhibiting interpersonal comfort and self-efficacy, Practice 5 of the structured inclusive interaction practices. The path to comfort began with the task force members understanding their roles and perspectives, which came from getting input and feedback from members of the functional areas they represented. Subgroup or one-on-one meetings were often employed as a means to bridge gaps, to handle impending conflicts (Practice 4), when the whole task force got stalled on a topic.

> Having a skilled, trusted individual available can aid and guide workgroup members experiencing tensions over their differences.

In such instances, Sarah would call out the subgroups or members as a means of dealing with specific issues in the group, for example, suggesting that it "would be useful if you and you could talk it out." She wanted to ensure that each member had the space to be heard, for others to hear about the issues, and "for the leadership to agree that these things [discriminatory practices] should not be happening." In this way, she exhibited comfort and self-efficacy (Practice 5) in dealing constructively with differences, modeling behavior that others could follow.

As a result of bringing organizational members' negative experiences to the task force, a major transformation occurred with the scientists becoming advocates— advocating even more than the administrators—as they learned how things worked within the larger organization. This has resulted in the more frequent use of cross-functional groups with scientists more involved in hiring and significantly more partnerships around organizational processes.

How was collaborating with member interdependence, Practice 3, developed in this case? Collaboration with interdependence emerged as the various members were trying to produce something together—their shared mission of reevaluating the embedded administration structure. Independently, the individual members went back to their functional areas to discuss the task force's issues regarding the organizational culture and the models to be proposed to top management. Then, interdependently, they used the feedback, the elaborated information (Chapter 5), in the group's deliberations and decision-making. As the task force involved members of their own functions, a broadening of collaboration occurred. The largest changes were observed in the culture of the administrators' and operations' workspaces, as norms of inclusive interaction developed in the task force were exhibited and spread to the functional areas.

To facilitate collaboration, norms in the task force were established at the outset, including beginning each meeting with the reminder "of how we will treat one another and what we are trying to do" and by asking, "What would it take to make this a safe place?"

Throughout the year, many different approaches were tried, including appreciative inquiry, design thinking, and expressing viewpoints with others responding to foster deeper dialogue. Over time, the group did engage in deeper dialogue, but not without some conflict, as noted above.

Adaptive learning took some time. From the outset, the task force members demonstrated a general lack of awareness, particularly with respect to the power or status differences among the three represented areas. This was particularly evident with the scientists who appeared to have no understanding of the significance of the work done by the others to enable them to be successful. In many instances, administrators would say "yes" to the scientists' requests while feeling "disrespected and ordered around." Sarah provided an example of a scientist requesting a travel order while standing above an administrator's desk—symbolizing their status differences—without so much as asking them about their day. This superiority was compounded by the administrator being aware of the educational, gender, and racial differences between herself and the scientist, leading the administrator to feel that she could not engage in a "normal conversation" with the scientist. For the scientist, it was "just doing business and imparting that they don't have time to engage with you as a human." Within the task force, the members were able to acknowledge that "this disrespect is very real, but not intentional." Discussing such issues enabled the scientists to bring such behaviors into their consciousness and recognize the harm this creates for the administrators.

> "The scientists were able to see that such a small action may not impact their scientific work, but it does impact the work of others, which ultimately impacts the organizational performance". (Sarah)

Furthermore, others in the organization, particularly the top management, were not aware of these dynamics. Bringing such issues into the organizational consciousness was a very important goal for the task force. The administrators and a few scientists understood that there were struggles, but it was only Sarah and the other facilitators who were initially aware that the struggles were the result of cultural challenges within the organization.

Handling conflict constructively (Practice 4) through the practices noted above was predicated on using "personal, reflective mediation." Sarah did note that this was potentially risky with respect to the diversity of age, race, and educational status. She told of a task force member who was particularly frustrated with the discriminatory behaviors she had experienced. This woman put together a written statement and bravely, despite Sarah worrying that the statement was conflictual, presented it to the task force. To Sarah's surprise, the group provided space for the issue and reprioritized their thinking. At times, she tried to control the situation, but in hindsight, she reflects that this was not appropriate, and she wished she had addressed these issues earlier and better. Reflecting on how she facilitated the task force, Sarah felt that allowing the members to engage in some conflict by applying the principles of Deep Democracy[14] was valuable. As noted in Chapter 6, the challenge is to develop a capability within a workgroup for constructively handling, rather than avoiding, a higher level of tensions. Deep Democracy suggests that

> all voices, states of awareness, and frameworks of reality are important. It also suggests that all information carried within these voices, levels of awareness, and frameworks are needed to understand the complete process of a system. Deep Democracy is an attitude that focuses on the awareness of voices that are both central and marginal.

She noted that "within the group, it took at least four months for members to feel comfortable, safe, and be able to voice issues."

The scientists, in particular, "did not want to go to the emotional space." Sarah continued by saying that within the organization, we "pretend that emotions are not part of the workspace. Yet, emotions are the big one, and we should have spent more time on awareness of the fact that these show up. It is important to meet people where they are and validate these feelings so that emotional burdens are shared, and people don't feel so isolated."

Practice 6, ensuring equal status for all task force members, was established at the outset, as part of the expected group norms. As a team, "we spent time at the beginning to drive this home!" Sarah wondered aloud if, "maybe in hindsight, we spent too much time managing conversations at the beginning and actually slowed the process by inhibiting positive disruptions that eventually had to be heard," as noted above with respect to handling conflict. Prior to this task force, the scientists had more power in the system relative to other groups. For example, if the scientists would say, "this is an issue," then leadership had to listen, but the equal status rule within the group "made it more normal to have conversations" across the employee groups. "Being in this group enabled them to be colleagues, which is big given the power difference between the groups." No longer is the attitude "What do you provide for me?"

> "Instead of the old transactional perspective, the cross-functional groups now view one another as "partners" in the success of the organization". (Sarah)

In effect, the total power in the system[15]—power in terms of producing desired treatment and work-task outcomes—has increased for all three functional groups.

The practices of mixing (Practice 2) and exhibiting interpersonal comfort (Practice 5) came together for this task force and the larger organization. According to Sarah, when the task force initially convened, they were very "professional," engaging in the sanctioned interactions. However, as the year progressed, task force members organized social events, which became a key component of the group, culminating with a party, playing games, and eating together.

The organization observed the significance of these informal interactions and subsequently has instituted more social events, including BBQs, game days or hours, and holiday observations. Sarah told us, "this was a direct result of the task force and made people view each other as humans." In addition, though not across the entire organization, there has been an increase in town halls and cross-functional events. "Though it takes effort, and the work is continuing to be done, the task force widened the lens making it more normal to have cross-functional conversations." Returning to the task force itself, all the members have remained engaged with one another.

One point of differentiation from the Framework for Inclusive Interactions was a weakness with respect to initial support from the organization's top leadership. As in many organizations, the lack of leadership attention to inclusion and equity was, not surprisingly, coupled with a lack of accountability and transparency with respect to human resource issues. In governmental units, civil service procedures provide a belief in meritocracy that may, as noted in Chapter 7, lead members, and especially leaders, to believe that accountability is being achieved. With regard to another condition specified in the Framework, representational diversity existed within the whole of the organization, but not within each of the functional areas (scientists, administrators, and operations).

In summary, this cross-functional task force demonstrates how the practices work when an inclusive, collaborative effort is made to structure interactions. This task force created an opportunity for larger change within the organization, demonstrating the feasibility and impact of implementing inclusive interactions at the workgroup and organizational unit levels. Sarah found that the task force members were able to adapt and change their language given that they had a safe space for positive interactions and a skilled facilitator. Throughout the year, members explored role differences and became more self-aware. Of course, "having the right resources really helped us get there faster." Today, two years later, the vestiges of the task force can be observed by the strong individual relationships that remain among the members by more cross-functional partnerships, and that the scientific and operations functional areas are now seen as more of an inclusive community. According to Sarah, this was because these two groups

> hold the most positional power and status within the organization and are, therefore, less aware and conscious of how power and status shows up. Within the scientific community, in particular, it's still largely reflective of the White males among leadership ranks which again adds to the complexity/ intersectionality of privilege.

Sarah observed more "aha's" and insights gained from these groups:

> it's important to create a positive, inclusive working culture, and how they play an integral role to it. For the embedded admin staff, they are physically

located [pre-COVID-19 pandemic] with the scientific staff, and so I think there was a systemic assumption that they didn't want to identify with the labs, but they also weren't a part of the operations—so they often felt isolated and like they didn't belong anywhere.

In addition, one of the administrators has moved to the operations office, from a contractor to a regular employee status, which Sarah considered "a symbol of change." In this case, the work of the task force spun out to a degree to the organizational unit but remained dependent on the relationships forged in the task force. This case highlighted the lack of inclusion in the larger organizational culture and the need for the interaction practices to operate within the contexts of the task force and organizational levels. This leaves open the potential for sustainable inclusion to erode as people leave the organization unless the norms of behavior become embedded.

> The likelihood exists that unless the norms of behavior become embedded, sustainable inclusion will erode as task force members leave the organization.

Taken together, the challenge of scaling up the inclusive experiences of the task force members is indicative of achieving sustainable inclusion being viewed as an end point, not as an ongoing cycle. The cycle evident in this case is indicated on the Framework for Inclusive Interactions by the feedback loop that goes from sustainable inclusion outcomes back to the organizational conditions that support inclusion on the left side of the Framework.

Looking ahead, Sarah raised a few issues of concern.

- How can the work of this task force be scaled beyond this one organizational unit to the entire organization?
- How do we quickly deepen the dialogue and maintain it?
- How can we create sustainable practices and norms when, for instance, people leave the organization?
- How do we embed these norms in the organization?
- How do we deal with high emotions?
- How do we ask for change when folks perceive things are already working?

Asking for this kind of change within an organization when those in higher status positions consider things to be working well is a real challenge. At issue is the impact of the recent social movements, including Me Too and Black Lives Matter, on the workplace. Sarah feels that the need for a "civil workplace" will become an area of focus for leadership as employees are more interested in combating discrimination and structural racism. Sarah anticipates a lot more institutional support but is worried that the organizational response may be ignorant of the fundamental structural challenges.

Who has the opportunity to generate inclusion?

This organizational case illustrates well many of the challenges in overcoming anti-inclusive social forces and task structures in long-established organizations, challenges that those interested in increasing inclusion can anticipate and that are described further below. More importantly, the case makes clear that individuals at various organizational levels have opportunities and capabilities to overcome the challenges and produce benefits for all members. Change that benefits inclusion need not start at the top. The opportunities can be seized by concerned organizational members at operational levels. Here, a meaningful move toward sustainable inclusion came through staff members establishing a performance-oriented, cross-functional task force. In other cases, opportunities could be recognized and pursued initially by several managerial or workgroup members rather than by facilitators, subsequently combining their initiative with the involvement of others—managers, diversity officials, other leaders, human resource management specialists, and skilled facilitators—to guide the process constructively.

Anticipating the challenges

Each of the six structured inclusive interaction practices is eminently feasible. Many organizations already employ some or all of the practices in some contexts but intentionality is needed to ensure that they are collectively adopted and maintained. In the many examples provided in this book, we have demonstrated the feasibility of the practices. However, even when deliberately and carefully enacted, challenges may arise. Interviewees suggested five common challenges. Anticipating these challenges can aid managers in structuring inclusive practices.

Challenge #1: Some organizational leaders see diversity as an end state. We heard from multiple interviewees who felt that their organizations and workgroups focused on diversity as something that is done and finished, rather than on inclusion as an ongoing process, a continuing achievement. Elizabeth, at the museum, discussed this challenge when she related that the dominantly White leadership felt that diversity initiatives were something to be accomplished and done with. There appears to be a common lack of understanding that achieving sustainable inclusion and reaping the performance benefits requires, as do any important organizational goals, ongoing processes that need to be nurtured even as they become normative behaviors within the workgroup. This is illustrated in the Framework for Inclusive Interactions by the feedback loop that goes from sustainable inclusion on the right side of the model back to the organizational conditions that support inclusion on the left side. The feedback loop highlights that the processes specified in the Framework are recursive and ongoing.

Challenge #2: Securing leader and member support at multiple levels. In the scientific research facility example above, facilitators displayed concern for leadership buy-in. Members that pursue inclusive practices benefit from support of their top leadership. As discussed in Chapter 4, that support best takes a form that minimizes backlash or activating the anti-inclusionary practices of self-segregating, feeling discomfort in diversity interactions, stereotyping and stigmatizing, and making decisions based on implicit bias. Accordingly, support may include involving managers in devising and using accountability practices[16] and, most importantly, in terms of our Framework, the use of performance-based rationales. These rationales can be emphasized whenever leaders engage in (1) structuring validated and accountable decision-making practices to overcome implicit bias, (2) enacting organizational values, missions, and aspirations that create a superordinate identity and perceived benefits for all organizational members, and (3) designing and implementing training offerings that emphasize skills (e.g., communication) relevant to all interactions. Additionally, interviewees expressed the importance of modeling the inclusive behaviors by superiors and top leadership. For example, we heard from Richard that with the change in Commanding Officer at the military base, he sees the "CO leading and living the organization's values." She is "infectious and inspiring. Leading us to be life-long learners and continually build relationships and inspire." These actions demonstrated to the supervisors that the leadership truly valued creating inclusive workgroups and an inclusive culture, and they were more motivated to follow suit.

Challenge #3: Preserving commitment to change over the time needed for adaptive learning. Workgroup members who carry stereotyping into the workplace need time and positive interaction experiences to confront their stereotype inconsistencies (Chapter 6) and become willing and able to engage comfortably with diverse others. For others, particularly among those from underrepresented groups who have had negative workgroup experiences where the culture was exclusive and they felt stigmatized, undervalued, unheard, disrespected, or diminished in some way, resulting in a distrust of diversity interactions, sharing their uniqueness and personal experiences will take longer than for those whose prior experiences have been positive. Achieving sustainable inclusion and its benefits takes time and, as mentioned in Challenge #1, is not an end state that is ever completed. For instance, George noted that while he was leading a large organizational unit, lesbian, gay, bisexual, and transgender (LGBT) managers in the unit were producing high performance from their teams. However, there were also high tensions due to biases held by some workgroup members. Our interviewee George noted that when he moved on to another leadership position, these issues had not had sufficient time to be resolved and, with less support from leadership, the high-performing managers left the organization.

To overcome this challenge, workgroup members need to "leave their biases at the door" according to interviewee John and, instead, achieve enough comfort to offer and accept differing perspectives, knowledge, and know-how in their diversity interactions. Research reviewed in Chapter 6 shows that individuals can learn vicariously, and that friendships form among some members when diversity contact is prolonged. These effects can go hand-in-hand to deal with the challenge of time and comfort. Based on studies of intergroup contact, leaders can expect that as some friendships develop across differing individuals, other workgroup members who are less comfortable with diversity interactions will observe those friendships and become more willing to question their stereotypes and overcome their discomfort.

Friendships, then, provide opportunities for more rapid adaptive learning in a workgroup, opportunities that managers can support, as we discuss further below, by structuring tasks so that particular individuals work together and by creating activities for informal social interaction.

Challenge #4: Spreading sustainable inclusion across the organization. "How do we scale up this framework for impact across a large organization?" Sarah asked us this question after observing the success she had with the cross-functional task force at the scientific research facility. "When a workgroup succeeds in creating inclusive interactions and engagement, that is wonderful, but now what?" These questions suggest that organizational size matters. For the small leadership fellowship, non-profit boards of directors, and separate workgroups achieving sustainable inclusion is feasible, but Sarah is correct that spreading the behaviors and skills throughout a large organization is more difficult. In this book, we have focused on incorporating the structured inclusive interaction practices into the workgroup or team level and suggest that this is where you begin. Evidence suggests that as workgroup members are moved and reconfigured, they bring with them the skills they have learned and quickly are enculturated into the new workgroup. This requires the organization's commitment to diversity and inclusion to be long-term, acknowledging the ongoing and recursive nature of the processes in the Framework. The military base, with its many thousands of civilian employees, provides insight into this challenge. With the new Commanding Officer being a woman came a top-down emphasis on inclusivity, with an associated new strategic framework, developed with workforce input and well received by the managers and employees. According to Richard, the managers must "articulate the strategic framework to their team and focus on their small area. If a manager does not buy-in to the strategic framework, then the job is probably not right for you and you should leave." He concluded by stressing that you "don't have to believe, but you must behave and then the managers come around." Richard stressed the valuable impact these changes have made to the base.

Challenge #5: High levels of tensions may need to be diffused. These tensions may be culturally based, the result of a prior negative experience, or the anti-inclusionary forces that inhibit positive interactions. George stated that, in his experience in large international organizations, these tensions came from particular subordinates who had culturally based difficulties in being subordinate to female or LGBT managers, despite those managers guiding their teams to high performance. In hindsight, he said, he should have considered dismissing these subordinates. As captured by the categorization–elaboration model discussed in Chapter 5, tensions due to categorizing (stereotyping) others often impede performance. In the situation described by George, performance was high, but tensions made work life unnecessarily hostile and difficult for underrepresented group members even when they were in superior positions. The challenge of tensions highlights the importance of inclusive interaction Practice 4, handling conflict constructively. The challenge may, at times, be sufficiently severe that top leadership support would involve sanctioning some members, holding them accountable for anti-inclusive behavior.

Intentionally structuring inclusive interaction practices

Intelligent, customized implementation of the inclusive interaction practices, which are the cornerstone of the Framework for Inclusive Interactions, may be approached in multiple ways. However, being aware of the challenges and examples described above, we make two overarching suggestions to guide intentional action:

1. Involve managers and workgroup leaders in fluidly applying knowledge and know-how so that practices fit the particular context, nature and mission of the organization and workgroup.
2. Anticipate anti-inclusive practices and backlash and manage them by generalizing organizational values beyond diversity to focus on performance while engaging in respectful behavior, fellowship, and warmth in interactions among all members.

Opportunities and options for individuals in various roles

Here, we provide some options for action toward inclusion at all organizational levels, applicable in small or large organizations in all sectors and even in informal associations. Top leadership, workgroup managers, human resource and diversity staff specialists and consultants, and workgroup members and volunteers can implement and advocate structured inclusive interaction practices and, where necessary, accountability practices. Changes to practices can be bottom-up, top-down or middle-out. Simply put, all members of an organization should be able to see opportunities for improvements in inclusion, no matter their formal role. Most literature on diversity and inclusion focuses on top management's role, a role that we begin with here, but we also consider that major changes achieved in industries worldwide were initiated and evolved by organizational members and specialists engaged in the core tasks of the organization.

Opportunities for top leadership. When a serious problem of any type persists in an organization for many years, a logical conclusion is that top management lacks commitment, knowledge, or both, to ameliorate the problem. In the case of diversity, it may also be that a top management group is convinced that its employment practices are fair and meritocratic, while research has revealed that is typically not the case (Chapter 7). Thus, there are many opportunities for top management to do more, and more wisely.

> Just as they do for other aspects of mission attainment, leaders should develop, implement, and periodically assess and revise a formal strategy for achieving equity and performance from diversity.

In order to generate buy-in, executives can focus on *managing the process* and allowing managers to have strong roles in decisions on practices for inclusion and accountability, as through involvement in diversity task forces[17] and customizing inclusive practices to fit their particular workgroups.

What does managing the process entail? As noted in our Framework's section on Organizational Conditions that Support Inclusion, support from authorities can be an important contributor to achieving sustainable inclusion. Serious organization-wide initiatives may begin with the top leadership implementing programs and exhibiting behaviors that go beyond representational diversity by promoting and monitoring inclusive practices. The efforts should be manifested in part by accountability, transparency, and fair employment practices. Formal instituting of accountability and transparency practices, including metrics and periodic processes for managerial review of them, counters implicit bias in reward decisions and leads to improvements in pay equity for members of underrepresented groups.[18] Distinctive efforts can also be made to ensure that human resource management staff have an equity focus, and that managers are motivated toward pursuing diversity and inclusion through involving them in diversity task forces.[19] Asking for others' commitment is legitimized by the *integrity* of top management's own commitment. That integrity can be demonstrated by inclusive behaviors and decisions, as discussed in the examples of the military base and the medical research team, where the Commanding Officer and Director, respectively, both embraced the lived values of the organizations. Some organizations are including diversity and inclusion criteria in their incentive pay plans for top executives, indicating to managers at lower levels the serious commitment of their boards and top leaders.

Top management can play a strong role in meeting the second organizational condition in our Framework, representational diversity. Top management may find it challenging to recruit members of underrepresented groups and overcome resistance from current employees, but this top-down commitment is a fundamental first step to achieving sustainable inclusion and can be eased by emphasizing high standards for both performance and equity. To do better than organizations have in the past, top leadership in organizations seeking to improve performance and equity outcomes through inclusive interactions should be willing to *adopt evidence-informed management*. The leadership should respect research-based evidence on anti-inclusive social forces and the practices for effective intergroup contact that overcomes those forces. However, it is equally important to incorporate their own and other organizational members' knowledge. Benchmarking other organizations in their field that have achieved high levels of performance and equity through diversity and inclusion is another source of relevant knowledge. Leaders should think in systems terms, considering dynamics at all organizational levels. Their commitment to achieving sustainable inclusion should be evident in forms that encourage individuals at all levels to produce equity and performance improvements from diversity through their individual actions. For example, within high-tech firms, printing the organization's mission, vision, and values on employee badges reminded employees at all levels how they were expected to behave and became a tool for everyone to utilize when respect or professionalism was lacking.

In conducting the research for this book, we found that a commitment to inclusion often occurs without a direct focus on diversity. This is consistent with our approach to the structured inclusive interaction practices, which may be implemented by emphasizing the performance to be gained through inclusive behavior—such as in the cross-functional task force case presented above— indirectly achieving diversity and equity through inclusive practices. We found broadly defined values that transcend diversity, such as fellowship, warmth, respect, and professionalism. An example of this comes from Gary, the medical research unit director, (Chapter 3) who frequently asks his employees, "Are you being treated nicely?"

When programs focus on performance through inclusive interactions, they indirectly produce the benefit of equity.

Programs focused on performance through inclusive interactions indirectly produce the benefit of equity, as demonstrated by the favorable effects of cross-job training and cross-functional, self-directed teams on underrepresented groups moving into management.[20] Programs not previously conceived of as useful for diversity can carry principles that call for inclusion and individual role definition that make the most of each workgroup member's talents and produce collectively high performance. A prime example is agile teams for software development. Their practices include daily huddles, programming by pairs of team members, and reflective team meetings that address tensions constructively. Such inclusive practices have been effective in international virtual teams, producing performance and trust across individuals from different national cultures. Some of our interviews similarly point to the value of self-directed (sometimes termed semi-autonomous) teams, with these teams having practices similar to agile teams. For instance, the medical research unit presented in Chapter 3 exemplifies semi-autonomous teams encompassing practices of collaboration that emphasize mutual respect and responsibility. According to Gary, its director, the success of the unit as it engages with others in the medical center is driven by the expectation of collaboration: "This is not a competition. We work in teams, with everyone responsible for the success of a study and success of the team."

In managing the process, top management should critically assess their traditional diversity programs, taking into account the findings from research presented in Chapter 5. Diversity training and single identity support groups, in particular, should be examined, seeking evidence within the organization on whether and how they contribute to inclusive engagement behavior in workgroups. We suggest that top leadership, particularly in large organizations, scan the organization to find workgroups where inclusive interactions are occurring organically and seek to leverage these situations to foster inclusion more broadly in other organizational units. Beyond practices thought of as diversity-related lie others that top management should address for their compatibility with inclusion. A major set of such practices are those for the socialization (onboarding) of new members. These should support enculturation, but not assimilation (Chapter 6), becoming normative within workgroups. Socialization practices that enable individuals to become effective group members while retaining their distinctive talents involve personal identity socialization in which new members are challenged to identify personal skills and preferences that can maximize their contributions to the group.

As discussed in Chapter 8, three options exist that can guide top management in moving the organization toward a more effective strategy for benefitting from diversity. In the first option, organizations allow people to separate into different functions that mirror occupational segregation in the larger society, such as women being overrepresented in nursing, teaching, or human resource roles. The organization fails to benefit from diversity in other functional areas. The second option occurs when workgroups include diverse members but with a high degree of assimilation, of conformity to the preexisting workgroup culture, as seen for women in traditionally male fields such as engineering. The narrow conformity dampens the performance benefits of diversity and contributes to loss of talent. The third, more advanced frame involves diverse workgroups functioning with inclusion and enculturation rather than narrow conformity. In this final option, which is the focus of the Framework for Inclusive Interactions, organizations reap the benefits of inclusive interactions and sustainable inclusion. Acting strategically, organizational leaders can move toward the third option by instituting extended recruitment for all functions, setting up cross-functional training and teams, establishing accountability practices, and instituting at the workgroup level the Framework's set of inclusive practices, including personalized socialization that avoids overly narrow assimilation.

> Top leadership should adopt a two-pronged approach: (a) shoring up flawed accountability practices and (b) intentionally pursuing inclusive interactions at the workgroup and team level.

A summary for top leadership. Evidence supports a dual approach: (a) shoring up flawed accountability practices and (b) intentionally pursuing inclusive interactions at the workgroup and team level. Accountability, transparency, and fair employment practices specifically focus on measured diversity and equity outcomes across the organization while, within workgroups, inclusive interaction practices focus on producing inclusive engagement behavior for performance and equity. The accountability practices should be made with greater commitment and greater evaluation of the practices' results, especially in terms of final personnel decisions made by managers, than has been traditional in most organizations in the past. The inclusive interaction practices chosen for particular organizational units should similarly be periodically evaluated in order to evolve and improve them over time.

Some specific options for top leadership. Based on research and examples from various types of organizations, we offer options to stimulate top managers' creativity in pursuing performance and equity from utilizing the talents of underrepresented groups.

- *Involve participants*—managers, staff, unions, other members, key stakeholders such as communities, suppliers, customers—*in setting goals* for performance, inclusion, and equity *and in generating options* for specific practices and establishing metrics. (See Opportunities for Workgroup Managers.)
- *Evolve the organization's dynamic capabilities for sustained inclusion* by
  - encouraging experimentation and assessment of various efforts, in order to advance through informed trial and error;
  - meeting with managers individually or in groups to review examples of practices used in various parts of the organization to sustain performance-enhancing inclusion;
  - engaging teams of managers to review progress via the metrics for underrepresented groups and to share knowledge of more vs. less successful efforts.
- *Seize opportunities for mixing members*, including the creating of cross-functional collaborations and events with informal mixing.
- When diverse teams are established, initialize and periodically reinforce them with *personal appearances* that note the importance of practices and norms for
  - mixing frequently and warmly;
  - collaborating by identifying and using individuals' differing strengths; and
  - frequently and constructively resolving differences and tensions.
- *Emphasize performance improvement* as the motivator of change toward inclusion.
  - Depending on the members and surrounding community, the emphasis may include or exclude explicit reference to benefitting from diversity.
  - Institute open posting of jobs, to reinforce the value of transparency in retaining and utilizing the talents of all members across the organization.
- *Provide resources* to support inclusion, including specialists to mediate tensions and to provide skills training such as
  - communication skills customized to functional areas, such as sales and
  - socialization techniques that promote personal-identity socialization.
- *Promulgate inclusive norms and values* by providing tools such as employee badges stating mission and core values that members use to hold each other accountable for inclusive behavior.
- *Share within your industry* knowledge of performance and equity successes arising from use of practices for inclusion and accountability.

Can others produce greater change than top management? The history of significant change efforts in contemporary organizations suggests that meaningful movement toward sustainable inclusion may be more likely to emerge from the efforts of members in the middle of the organization, those concerned directly with the performance of key tasks, than from efforts of top management. For example, as is discussed further below, histories of the development of the principles for agile teams[21] reveal the seminal role of programmers who were coping directly with the problems of software development. When sustainable inclusion from diversity is seen as a performance opportunity as well as an equity opportunity, greater incentives exist for workgroup managers, workgroup members, and performance-oriented specialists and consultants to initiate, evolve, and diffuse improved practice as they move around within and beyond the organization in their professional capacities.[22]

Opportunities for workgroup managers. Key to structuring inclusion is the workgroup manager who, working from the middle out, uses their span of authority to institute the inclusive practices. The goal for the savvy manager is to create frequent, comfortable, productive interactions among members from majority and underrepresented groups, both within the workgroup and with other work units and managers. Examples of this, primarily from our interviews, include:

- Anxiety reduction through informal interactions, on- or off-job, around mutually enjoyable activities that are structured to avoid self-segregation:
    - In Girl Scouts of the USA cross-troop activities for girls and volunteer leaders in troops with different racial demographics.
    - In the finance firm taking a day together for out of the office activities each quarter.
    - In the medical research unit, deliberately planning parties and other socials for its members.
- Daily huddles as a means of checking in with the workgroup members.
    - Morning huddles in the finance firm, the international joint venture (JVC) and high-tech engineering companies.
    - Afternoon huddles in the medical research unit.
- Including in weekly meetings a mission-related or non-work focus.
    - "Tell us something good that is not work related" is a question Rachel asks of the members of her finance workgroup.
    - In the medical research unit, Gary likes to begin his meetings with "pop quizzes," asking his employees about the unit's mission, goals, and values.
- Looking for opportunities for your workgroup members to engage in developmental activities and become visible to others.
    - Inviting the member to make a presentation at a meeting of managers.
    - Cross-job training or cross-functional teams to develop talent and make it visible to other units.
    - Pairing individuals to program together in software development.
- Rotating leadership roles to provide all members with leadership experience while ensuring equal insider status for all members:
    - Al-Anon and the finance workgroup rotate leadership at weekly meetings
    - The service fraternity did not allow students to take a second leadership role until all members had done one.

- Identifying and utilizing the distinctive talents of each member of the workgroup
  - In the finance firm, assigning special tasks based on a member's skills and passion.
- Mentoring and open job posting
  - Pointing talented members to promotion opportunities elsewhere in the organization.
- Identifying underutilized talent elsewhere in the organization and promoting into your workgroup.
- Striving to utilize the entire set of structured inclusive interaction practices.
  - Being prepared to show workgroup members how to address tensions constructively in order to keep their focus on tasks and the mission.
  - Modeling appropriate, respectful, productive interaction behaviors.
- Being aware of the pervasive nature of implicit bias in order to make more conscious and unbiased one's own personnel decisions involving pay, development, and promotions.
- Reporting to other managers one's successes with particular inclusive practices, in terms of workgroup performance and advancement of members of underrepresented groups who would have been overlooked otherwise.

Managers at the workgroup level may decide to proceed with introducing or adding inclusive practices with or without support from their immediate superior. In situations where the workgroup managers do not have support from higher management, they may feel more comfortable delaying confirmation with supervisors and peers until they are able to demonstrate performance improvement results.

Opportunities for staff. The scientific research facility case, presented above, illustrates well the role that staff specialists—in that case, specialists in organization development—can play at operational levels.

> Where there is representational diversity, seeking performance improvements through cross-functional initiatives brings diversity interactions to a visible and discussable level, opening the door to advances in both equity and performance through inclusive practices.

Similar opportunities can be promoted and seized by diversity and inclusion officials and staff members. To their acknowledged responsibilities for enhancing equity, diversity officials can add a focus on performance-driven improvements from inclusive interaction practices that indirectly improve equity. Through persistent working with unit managers to design and institute inclusive work practices, they can foster inclusion at a deeper, on-the-job level that, over time, results in an inclusive culture in the organization. Diversity and inclusion staff are in a favorable position to marry their involvement in accountability practices that focus on the end result of equity with performance-oriented partnerships with managers that provide the means to that end.

Opportunities for workgroup members. In addition to the senior leadership and workgroup managers, the workgroup members may model inclusive behavior and create change from the bottom-up.

> Workgroup members may create change from the bottom up by modeling inclusive behavior.

Workgroup members may suggest and demonstrate inclusive practices to their superiors on the basis of performance improvement. Workgroup members may have a deeper understanding of the importance of creating relationships and partnerships with members of underrepresented groups based on their experiences in other workgroups that have instituted the practices and achieved sustainable inclusion. These members may desire to introduce these behaviors in order to improve the workgroup culture, identify performance improvement and personal development opportunities, and intentionally or unintentionally create cross-functional collaborations. Examples of behaviors workgroup members may enact are the same as those listed above for managers.

Especially favorable opportunities for various organizations

Creative leaders can seize opportunities that arise, or that can be made to arise, in order to encourage and spread inclusive interaction practices. We offer but two examples here: Newly created workgroups and fostering cross-group friendships.

Newly formed workgroups

As a new workgroup with representational diversity is formed, distinctive opportunities exist to establish norms to reduce anxieties among members, then institute practices for comfortable, close, professional interactions, including informal interactions that encourage self-disclosure. This developmental sequence focuses on intentional implementation of the practices of mixing members frequently and repeatedly, handling conflict constructively, and engaging with equal status. Two examples of newly formed workgroups using the inclusive interaction practices are the medical research unit and the leadership fellowship.

The medical research unit, while it exists within a large health organization, demonstrates how deliberate planning enabled the practices to become embedded and part of the norms of the unit. Recall that Gary, the director, planned the space to include a kitchen with eating space and offices with glass doors to foster mixing members repeatedly (Practice 2). Implementing socializing traditions such as picnics and parties furthered the mixing of members. In forming the teams, the director intentionally established the daily huddle to assign members to the next day's tasks and provide a daily opportunity to confront potential conflicts (Practice 4) that otherwise may have festered. The daily huddle also ensured that the members would be rotating through projects with everyone having an equal opportunity to make decisions and collaborate together (Practice 3). Once established, the inclusive culture of the research unit enabled socialization of newcomers into the existing teams, perpetuating the use of the inclusive interaction practices to achieve sustained inclusion and maintain a high level of performance. In this particular example, the director was able to establish rituals and norms that positively impacted the inclusive culture of the work unit. Below we provide an example of members creating the policies and expectations for their workgroup, a bottom-up, as opposed to top-down approach.

A second example of a newly formed workgroup demonstrates a repeated case of an organization using a bottom-up, as opposed to a top-down approach. Members of a new group of leadership fellows (introduced in Chapter 3) deliberately create policies and establish norms for behavior that enable the group to share power (Practice 3), grant all members insider status (Practice 6), give voice to all members, and handle conflict (Practice 4). The leadership fellowship cohorts work together for 18 months interacting during their regular bimonthly meetings plus additional field trips and retreats. During the initial meetings, members work together to create guidelines for how the group will function together. Phillip, our interviewee, emphasized that the group democratically decided for themselves how they wanted to behave. Policies were established on how decisions would be made, conflict handled, and all members would have a chance to speak at meetings. Additional policies were added as necessary. Despite the relatively deliberate and intense nature of the group, Phillip told us that it took six months for members to become trusting of one another and fully engage. In the remaining 12 months, members experienced adaptive learning and the group flourished.

Fostering diversity friendships

Creating situations that favor the development of cross-group friendships is an example of ongoing intentional action by managers that supports inclusive practices. As noted earlier in this chapter, through direct impact on the individuals who develop friendships and vicarious effects on other workgroup members, friendships can help overcome the challenge of prolonged time needed for adaptive learning. Our own research demonstrated the value of friendships and how they were fostered. In one study, we asked university administrators to recommend where on campus students were engaging with diverse others, and we were told the coed service fraternity. We were surprised to learn that deep friendships with diverse others resulted from participation in that organization. Research in other contexts has reinforced the special value of fostering cross-identity group close friendships. Friendships enable adaptive learning with substantial personal skill development, including leadership skills. As discussed in Chapter 6, the key practice contributing to friendship development is the amount of time spent together. In addition to informal social activities structured by a manager, time together can be increased by practices such as pairing individuals to pursue a task (Practice 1), as in pair programming in agile teams for software development. According to one of the White male student members of the service fraternity, "it is through proximity and similar interests and me getting to know someone better. I can fit into their personality and see what they're like, and I get to know them and then they become friends." An Indian female student stressed the importance of feeling comfortable enough to divulge deeper, more personal information. She shared with us that

> at first, I was like, okay, so we're working together. This is like every other club. You work together. It doesn't necessarily mean anything. But as we were working together, we started opening up about things out of her life and I kind of realized they're—it's not exclusive. Becoming friends and working together on a club are not exclusive. This was highly unexpected. I expected to come into [the service fraternity] like cool people to hang out with but not necessarily find friends.

And finally, a third student, a White man, recognized the personal benefit to himself of cross-cultural friendships, "It makes me feel pretty good that I'm sort of branching out, and I'm meeting so many different people, and that I can be friends with so many people from different walks of life. I guess my growing friendships have been a pretty good personal benefit." These student interactions illustrate that even when people are not expecting to form friendships in a particular setting, such as in a workgroup, it can still quite readily occur. Time together (Practice 2) and shared purpose (Practice 1) increase the likelihood that a diverse pair will achieve enough comfort to have self-disclosing personal conversations, developing an inclusive relationship in which they readily offer their perspectives and share their knowledge and know-how, improving task-related decision-making (Chapter 5).

Friendships are not a necessary outcome of inclusive interaction practices but, rather, an added benefit.

In the workplace, where friendships among workgroup members are not the goal, development of civility toward one another and respecting others as colleagues and coworkers with whom they are willing to self-disclose on task-related ideas, and perhaps occasionally on some personal experiences and information, may suffice. However, Gary, the director of the medical research unit, remarked on the cross-cultural friendships that developed among both the JV and Fellows teams in his unit as a by-product of their inclusive workplace culture. It is worth noting that, in our interviews, reports of friendship level engagement were more prevalent among those that are younger—for example, within the research unit and the college student members of the service fraternity. In addition, members of underrepresented groups who have experienced workgroups in which the culture is not inclusive, said they felt unheard, disrespected, or that their contributions are diminished in some way, have indicated a distrust of diversity interactions, inhibiting friendships. In these circumstances, even as a workgroup becomes more inclusive and there *is* a high level of interaction from working together on a daily basis, there may exist a residual level of distrust such that interactions are comfortable *up to a point,* limiting disclosure of personal experiences. This is indicative of the need for the passage of time and continued interactions following norms of inclusion in order to develop an inclusive culture, where the best outcome would be an elevation of the relationship from colleague to friend.

Managers and leaders have the opportunity to structure opportunities for inclusive interactions such that work colleagues can become friends, even in virtual settings without face-to-face contact. The challenge may be to create informal gatherings in which people do not self-segregate on the basis of surface diversity. We heard from John that some of the high-tech firms would host Friday afternoon bashes for all employees. Instead, we suggest limiting the gatherings to the immediate workgroup. Rachel from the finance company provided an example of her workgroup engaging in quarterly non-workdays where they volunteered on a service project in the morning, ate lunch together, and then spent the afternoon in a "bitching" session. These activities were limited to the workgroup members. And, as noted above, Gary, in designing the workplace for his medical research group, insisted on a lunchroom in the office suite, which is frequently used by the workgroup members. With foresight, managers can positively impact their workgroup members' interactions.

Sectoral variations in inclusive practices

Top leadership, workgroup managers, and workgroup members may learn from examples within their own field and from other fields. We have utilized examples from the nonprofit, business, and governmental sectors to demonstrate various forms that inclusive practices can take. Across the sectors, we observed numerous similarities in practices. The inclusive interactions practices fit in each sector, and the way they are implemented in one sector can be instructive for other sectors. For example, within the nonprofit sector, organizations provide strong opportunities for superordinate identity through shared mission commitment. This strong commitment to purpose can be replicated in the governmental and for-profit sectors with clear task orientation. In the for-profit sector, industrial firms often benchmark others in their fields, a practice easily adopted by other types of organizations. At the military base, the strategic plan embedded inclusive interaction practices such that managers needed to pay attention to these top-down guidelines. Making inclusion central to strategy provides accountability and telegraphs to stakeholders the organizational commitment to sustainable inclusion.

Opportunities to generate and diffuse practical knowledge for inclusion

Scaling up is a challenge evident from the cross-functional team case presented earlier in this chapter. Fortunately, natural processes exist to spread effective approaches. Individuals engaged in many roles can aid in generating and diffusing knowledge about how to achieve inclusion from diversity through routine processes in their organizations, sectors, and professions. The processes, elaborated on in Box 10.4, referred to as Mode 2 knowledge generation processes,[23] stand in contrast to the Mode 1 processes, such as peer review and journal publication, common in academic circles. In Mode 2 processes, individuals interact not only within their organizations but also across organizations by meeting in industry or professional association conferences, posting on blogs, or otherwise communicating with each other personally,[24] and by carrying knowledge with them when they change jobs. Through such processes, leaders at all organizational levels, specialists, and consultants can share their knowledge of successes and failures as they innovate with practices for inclusion and accountability.

BOX 10.4: ADDITIONAL BODIES OF KNOWLEDGE

The main focus of this book and its Framework is not on processes for implementing organizational change. While this chapter offers an extended example and a variety of suggestions for the active pursuit of sustainable inclusion by leaders, much valuable knowledge exists elsewhere. We suggest for the reader's further study two bodies of knowledge on successfully producing organizational change.

1. Knowledge shared in industry journals and professional conferences, such as engineering literature on virtual and agile teams.[25]
2. Academic literature on organization development, such as how to manage members' participation during change.

An instructive example of such knowledge generation processes having a major impact on many organizations across the globe concerns the development of a set of principles for agile teams in software development, principles that have informed teamwork in a variety of settings. Dissatisfied with time lags, inefficiencies, and ineffectiveness common for decades in the information technology field, programmers shared their experiences with new approaches. As described in histories of the agile team movement,[26] a key moment was when a number of leading programmers came together at a resort to share both leisure and work. There they worked out the set of principles that brought high visibility and impact to their movement.

At a time when we are realizing anew the need for our organizations to contribute to social justice and to operate more effectively with diversity, and realizing the limitations of our current approaches, generating knowledge for better practice is both a high priority and feasible. Researchers have been making steady progress in generating conceptual knowledge. The opportunities are now many for individuals on the ground to use their Mode 2 interactions to not only be informed by that knowledge but also to critically assess, apply, and add to it, sharing the knowledge-for-practice[27] that they generate in order to produce widespread practical change.

Concluding thoughts on the process of moving forward

The goal of this book is to provide an evidence-based framework that demonstrates how adopting a set of structured inclusive interaction practices benefits workgroup performance, shapes productive relationships and social equity, and enhances skills and learning among organizational members. Based on our transdisciplinary literature review, our own research, and many interviews with practitioners affiliated with a variety of organizational types, we have created the Framework for Inclusive Interactions for achieving sustainable inclusion. To achieve equity and organizational performance, the Framework captures the importance of using six inclusive interaction practices—pursuing a shared task orientation or mission, mixing the members frequently and repeatedly, collaborating with member interdependence, handling conflict constructively, exhibiting interpersonal comfort and self-efficacy, and ensuring equal insider status to all members—to both mitigate exclusionary forces that inhibit inclusive interactions and foster meaningful, positive, inclusive interactions. When combined with accountability practices that focus on the behavior of members and the personnel decisions of managers, engaging in frequent, positive inclusive interactions creates opportunity for adaptive learning, social integration, and information elaboration. In turn, these lead to sustainable inclusion and its beneficial outcomes.

> Sustainable inclusion is not an end goal but a process that involves the intentional maintenance of the organizational conditions that support the practices for structured inclusive interactions and accountability.

A distinctive approach: Structure practices for inclusive interactions

We noted in the early chapters of this book the minimal positive impact of the traditional diversity programs frequently used by organizations. These diversity programs often result in activating the anti-inclusive social practices—self-segregation, interaction discomfort, stereotyping and stigmatization, and making decisions based on implicit bias—that inhibit inclusive interactions and result in increased tension and performance decline. For decades diversity efforts have focused on developing training programs that attempt to change people's thinking about diverse others, but these programs typically suffer from the fatal flaw of being one-time or occasional add-ons, and concentrating on attitudes rather than behavior and skills for inclusion. Effective alternatives are now known to exist, as demonstrated by research findings and by the many examples in this book, providing mechanisms for fundamental change in how workgroups and teams function. The establishment of an inclusive culture focuses on broader processes that support productive, positive contact across a diversity of individuals. Following norms of inclusion, the resulting interpersonal interactions in a diverse workgroup enable members to experience behavioral change, followed by skill development and learning.

Organizations that lack an effective strategy for sustained inclusion most often find themselves implementing fair employment policies and practices in order to be legally compliant. We now know that this approach is insufficient for an inclusive work culture and equity in personnel reward decisions. The Framework for Inclusive Interactions recognizes three essential elements for inclusion: accountability practices that reduce the operation of bias; onboarding practices and ongoing inclusive interaction practices that incorporate the identities of all members such that their whole selves are integrated into the organization; and every day, habitual inclusive interaction practices for engagement and collaboration that result in all members having an impact on workgroup task decisions. Members at all levels of organizations have opportunities for advancing their organization's performance and equity, benefiting those organizations and their economies and societies. The Framework reflects the critical role that intentionally structured inclusive interaction practices play in creating a culture that achieves and sustains such inclusion.

Current research-based evidence, presented here, is more than sufficient to guide intelligent decisions by organizational leaders and members. They can leverage diversity for performance and equity by combining it with their own situational knowledge and experience in fluid, persistent action. We challenge researchers to engage with organizational leaders to further develop knowledge-for-practice, and we challenge leaders to creatively and wisely implement inclusive practices.

We conclude with the words of Elizabeth, reflecting on her experience at the art museum: "Inclusion and equity are ongoing processes that have to be embedded in the workgroup culture. It is an iterative process." Inclusion is "the right thing to do," and to accomplish it, we must change how people work together.

Notes

1 Janssens, M., & Steyaert, C. (2019). A practice-based theory of diversity: Respecifying (in) equality in organizations. *Academy of Management Review*, *44*(3), 518–537.

2 Ibid.

3 See Van Maanen, J. (1998). *Qualitative studies of organizations*. Sage; Appendix A in Whyte, W. F. (1993). *Street corner society* (4th ed.). University of Chicago Press.

4 Nishii, L. H., Khattab, J., Shemla, M., & Paluch, R. M. (2018). A multi-level process model for understanding diversity practice effectiveness. *Academy of Management Annals*, *12*(1), 37–82. A summary focused on practical application is available at https://ecommons. cornell.edu/xmlui/bitstream/handle/1813/73702/No5_17_ResearchLink_Nishii. pdf?sequence=1

5 Ibid.

6 Ibid, p. 68.

7 Dobbin, F., Schrage, D., & Kalev, A. (2015). Rage against the iron cage: The varied effects of bureaucratic personnel reforms on diversity. *American Sociological Review, 80*(5), 1014–1044.

8 Nishii et al. (2018), p. 65.

9 Dobbin et al. (2015), p. 7.

10 Nishii et al. (2018).

11 Orr, J. E. (1990). Sharing knowledge, celebrating identity: Community memory in a service culture. In D. Middleton & D. Edwards (Eds.), *Inquiries in social construction. Collective remembering* (pp. 169–189). Sage.

12 Kalev, A. (2009). Cracking the glass cages? Restructuring and ascriptive inequality at work. *American Journal of Sociology 114*(6), 1591–1643.

13 Kalev (2009). "Cracking the glass cages?"

14 http://deepdemocracyinstitute.org/

15 Tannenbaum, A. S. (1968). *Control in organizations*. McGraw-Hill.

16 Dobbin, F., & Kalev, A. (2016). Why diversity programs fail. *Harvard Business Review, July–August*, 1–8.

17 Ibid.

18 Castilla, E. J. (2015). Accounting for the gap: A firm study manipulating organizational accountability and transparency in pay decisions. *Organization Science, 26*(2), 311–333.

19 Dobbin and Kalev (2016). "Why diversity programs fail."

20 Kalev, A., Dobbin, F., & Kelly, E. (2006). Best practices or best guesses? Assessing the efficacy of corporate affirmative action and diversity policies. *American Sociological Review, 71*(4), 589–617.

21 Nyce, C. M. (2017, December 8). The winter getaway that turned the software world upside down. *The Atlantic*. https://www.theatlantic.com/technology/archive/2017/12/agile-manifesto-a-history/547715/; Rigby, D. K., Sutherland, J., & Takeuchi, H. (2016). The secret history of agile innovation. *Harvard Business Review*. https://hbr.org/2016/04/the-secret-history-of-agile-innovation

22 Gibbons, M., Limoges, C., Nowotny, H., Schwartzman, S., Scott, P., & Trow, M. (1994). *The new production of knowledge: The dynamics of science and research in contemporary societies*. Sage.

23 Ibid.

24 Orr (1990).

25 See for example, Dikert, K., Paasivaara, M., & Lassenius, C. (2016). Challenges and success factors for large-scale agile transformations: A systematic literature review. *Journal of Systems and Software, 119*, 87–108.

26 Nyce (2017). "The winter getaway that turned the software world upside down"; Rigby et al. (2016). "The secret history of agile innovation."

27 Bouwen, R. (2001). Developing relational practices for knowledge intensive organizational contexts. *Career Development International, 6*(7), 361–369.

PART III SUMMARY

Sustainable inclusion for optimizing performance and equity

Application of the Framework for Inclusive Interactions to workgroup and organizational settings leads to sustainable inclusion—a process that enables the organization and its workforce to prosper through adapting to each other—where equity, enhanced group and organizational performance, individual skill development, inclusive culture, and member commitment and retention are sustained.

Case examples of organizations and workgroups that have implemented the inclusive interaction practices provide insight as to how inclusion is achieved at different levels of organizations, to different degrees, and with the six inclusive interaction practices taking different forms (Chapter 9):

- Presented cases clarify what inclusion looks like when it is achieved at a high level through effective practices, when it is instituted at the level of the workgroup, and when it is dependent on larger-scale organization-wide inclusion.
- Voluntary organizations are in a favorable position to create welcoming, satisfying cultures through which inclusive practices are oriented around their missions in order to retain volunteers and members. The most successful cases utilize the entire bundle of six inclusive interaction practices.
- Success in diverse workgroups is highly dependent on the inclusive practices managers establish. Establishing and embedding inclusive practices focuses primarily on the goal of enhancing performance outcomes.
- Organization-wide inclusion requires leadership efforts to shape the practices of managers and other organizational members across all levels of the organization.
- Accountability practices need to be established to counter bias in hiring, promotion, and compensation.

DOI: 10.4324/9780367822484-17

Managers and leaders should strive to integrate the bundle of structured inclusive interaction practices into their workgroups and organizations to produce inclusion and mitigate the anti-inclusive practices. Enacting the social practices that foster inclusion simultaneously enhances performance and equity. Challenges, opportunities, and options for action are presented (Chapter 10):

- Beyond the scope of the organization or workgroup are benefits at the societal level of social justice principles, including fair distribution of human resources, access to fair employment, equal status in decision-making, individual rights for all, and economic gains.
- Generating inclusion may be initiated at all levels of an organization—top leadership, workgroup managers, staff, and workgroup members. Inclusive interaction practices must be intentionally introduced while anticipating backlash and the force of the anti-inclusive practices.
- Challenges to sustainable inclusion include overriding those who see diversity as an end state, securing leader and member support at multiple levels, commitment to the time necessary for adaptive learning to occur, expanding sustainable inclusion found in workgroups to the organizational level, and creating opportunities for high levels of tension to be diffused.
- Newly formed workgroups with representative diversity offer a great opportunity to establish norms of behaviors that support inclusion.
- Cross-group friendships are a common outcome of well managed inclusive workgroups and speed adaptive learning.
- In a long-established traditional organization, a more inclusive culture is attainable through cross-functional collaboration, intentionality, and persistence, as described in a case involving performance-oriented organization development.
- Listed opportunities demonstrate that organizational members in all roles—top executives and board members, managers, operations specialists, diversity and human resource management staff, and workgroup members—can contribute meaningfully to the achievement of inclusion for performance and equity.

INDEX

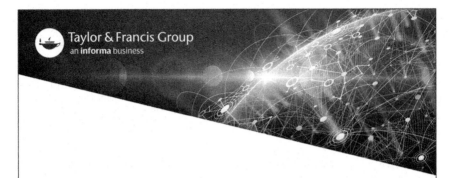

Printed in the United States
by Baker & Taylor Publisher Services